语言、技术与社会

Language,
Technology, and Society

刘小侠 ◎著

北京大学出版社
PEKING UNIVERSITY PRESS

图书在版编目（CIP）数据

语言、技术与社会 / 刘小侠著 . —— 北京：北京大学出版社，2025.8. —— ISBN 978-7-301-36497-0

Ⅰ . H0

中国国家版本馆 CIP 数据核字第 20256NG283 号

书　　　名	语言、技术与社会
	YUYAN、JISHU YU SHEHUI
著作责任者	刘小侠　著
责 任 编 辑	朱房煦
标 准 书 号	ISBN 978-7-301-36497-0
出 版 发 行	北京大学出版社
地　　　址	北京市海淀区成府路205 号　100871
网　　　址	http：//www. pup. cn　　新浪微博：@ 北京大学出版社
电 子 邮 箱	编辑部pupwaiwen@pup.cn　总编室zpup@pup.cn
电　　　话	邮购部010-62752015　发行部010-62750672　编辑部010-62754382
印 刷 者	河北博文科技印务有限公司
经 销 者	新华书店
	787毫米×1092毫米　16开本　21.75印张　560千字
	2025年8月第1版　2025年8月第1次印刷
定　　　价	88.00元

序 言

　　北京大学英语系大学英语教研室刘小侠副教授编写的《语言、技术与社会》是为我国高校非英语专业本科生编写的英语教材，弥补了国内的空缺。

　　从本教材的取名不难看出，本书探索语言、技术与社会三者之间的相互关系，即讨论从"文字"（第二至六章）、机械时代文本处理（第七至九章），到数码时代机器翻译（第十至十二章）、网络语言（第十三章）等各种与语言相关的创新。第一章帮助选修本课程的学生掌握有关语言的基本理论，即语音学、音系学、词汇学、句法学、语义学、语用学。作者把语用学放入本部分的结尾，我认为其用意是提示和帮助学生掌握本课程和教材的重点和应用语境。第二章至第六章都是围绕"文字"展开的。这说明本书不是一般的语言或语言学教材，而是关注文字学，引导学生讨论书写系统——第一项为语言专门设计的技术——与语言之间的关系、读写能力对认知和科学发展的影响等。接下来几章涉及机械时代文本处理的新技术的发展，如第七章的主题是印刷术，印刷术既保证了书面语的稳定性，也推动了语体的多元化；第八章说明打字机的发明引发了个人思维的扩展和不同文体的产生；第九章说明电报技术的应用导致摩尔斯电码的问世并推动了全球各个国家、团体和民众的彼此联系。接下来的三章谈的都是有关翻译和技术的联系。第十章通过语言学、理性主义理论和各种规则系统的讲解介绍机器翻译的诞生；第十一章谈通过语料库的建设和扩展，以及实证论的完善，机器翻译进入完全由数据驱动的水平；第十二章的重点是数码时代机器翻译素养和伦理问题。这些章节说明本教材关注当代学术界的热门话题，如多模态研究和人工智能研究。第十三章介绍当代社交媒体上的语言游戏与自我构建。

　　我曾经在多个场合说过，作为"90后老人"，我虽然是本书作者小侠老师的爷爷辈，但由于年龄老化和体力衰退，已经落后于时代的发展，跟不上学术界的最新成果。学习本教材使我受益匪浅。谨在此向小侠老师表示感谢。也正是这个原因，我将在下面向读者介绍一下我所了解的本教材作者刘小侠。

　　刘小侠在北京大学英语系获得博士学位，导师是现在已经年逾六十的钱军教授。钱军本人在读博期间接受我的引导，专攻功能语言学的布拉格学派，成为国内外享有盛名的布拉格学派研究者，并获得捷克共和国外交部扬·马萨里克铜制纪念奖章。这为小侠老师创造了良好的学习条件，她曾两次（2008—2009年，2016—2017年）去美国伊利诺伊大学香槟分校语言学系访学，研究课题分别为"布拉格学派词序研究"和"《布拉格语言学小组论纲》与布拉格学派结构功能主义"。可见小侠老师没有辜负钱军教授和功能语言学界对她的期望。

小侠老师的科研成果也证实了她的科研能力和水平。除本教材外，她已经出版1部英文专著 *Vilém Mathesius' Thoughts on Word Order: Toward a Linguistic Historiography*（2013, Prague: Bronx），1部译著《英语的成长和结构》（2023/2024, 北京：商务印书馆），发表的论文已有二十余篇。作为主持人，小侠老师完成省部级项目1个，本科重点课程建设项目2个，数字化教材建设项目1个，参与教材编写3部。

值得一提的是小侠老师曾多次获得各种奖励，如北京大学第十届教学大赛二等奖第一名；第七届北京市青年教师基本功大赛二等奖；2010年度北京大学外国语学院优秀教师；北京大学2015年黄廷方/信和青年杰出学者奖；北京大学第四届"新东方青年学者奖"优秀翻译奖；2023年第一批人工智能助推课程建设优秀项目奖。[1]

归纳上面的介绍，我有如下深刻感受。第一，改变了我们对大学英语教学的认识。历史上曾经有一段时间，人们低估了大学英语教学的水平。自从李淑静教授主管北京大学大学英语教学后，情况发生了根本变化。小侠老师开设的英语课程说明了这个新面貌。第二，长期以来，人们认为大学英语教师水平不高，在大学英语教研室工作只能做个教书匠，谈不上科研。事实证明，继大学英语教研室的辜正坤教授和黄必康教授等教师的成就超过部分英语专业的教师后，小侠老师保持了这个优秀传统。第三，从小侠老师开设的课程，我深深感到北京大学其他专业的本科生的英语水平之高在国内高校是少见的。如今这个教材将在全国高校推广，说明我国以英语为代表的外语教学水平普遍提高。

2025年元月
北京大学外国语学院

---

[1] 北京大学教务长办公室《新闻动态》，2023-05-23。

语言问题与思考

（代序）

刘小侠教授的又一部英文著作《语言、技术与社会》（*Language, Technology, and Society*）出版了。祝贺之余，记下在阅读过程中的一点思考以及与同道探讨的问题，聊作序言。

全书十三章，除去概论性质的第一章，主体十二章，其中第二至六章都是关于文字（writing），内容包括文字的起源、古文字的破译等。这部分占比接近主体的二分之一，无论从范围还是篇幅而言，均可谓本书的一个特色，因为即便是在语言专业，除了研究古文字的课程，一般的课程对此很少涉及。作者的理由是，writing is considered the first technology devised for language（1.1）。这部分的内容涉及颇多可以思考的问题，试以英语为例。

一般认为，英语是拼音文字，但其拼读不如法语、德语那样有规律，而且英语重音的位置变化比较复杂。这就是为什么多数法语或德语专业的学生在学习了一年之后，面对一篇未见过的文章，可以正确地读出来，而英语专业的学生难以做到。比如拼读，字母f、ph可以发音相同，/f/：<u>f</u>ive, gra<u>ph</u>eme, <u>ph</u>iloso<u>ph</u>y。字母b在词尾或发音，如club, slab，或不发音，如 bomb, climb。① 字母h在 home, hospital, house, hunt 发音；在heir, honour, honest, hour 不发音；在 herb, herbal 两可，英式英语发音 /hɜ:b/,

---

① 词尾字母 b 不发音的情况，一般是紧邻鼻音 /m/，b 前面的字母构成一个完整的音节（syllable），例如，comb, crumb, dumb, jamb, lam<u>b</u>（比较德语 *Lamm*），limb, numb, plumb, thumb, tomb, womb。不过，不在词尾的 b 也可能不发音，例如 debt, doubt, subtle。

/ˈhɜ:.bəl/，美式英语不发音 /ˈɜ:b/, /ˈɜ:.bəl/。history 似乎也是两可。① Visser 的名著取名 *An Historical Syntax of the English Language*，表明他认为 history 中的字母 h 不发音。英语重音位置的复杂变化也构成朗读难点，比如：ˈfamily, faˈmiliar, familiˈarity, ˈphotograph, phoˈtographer, photoˈgraphic（Jespersen, 1982:22）。

　　一个词表示一个概念，一个词有音义两个方面。比如 horse /hɔ:s/，音义都体现在 horse 之中了。比较甲骨文的"马"字（见2.1.1的图表），它是通过象形来体现意义的。虽然拼音文字（alphabetic writing）与象形文字（pictograms, pictographs）不同，但彼此都面临音义在词中如何体现的问题。比如，汉字有形声字，例如"钱"，"金"是形旁，"戋"是声旁，本义指一种农具。② 值得注意的是，古人认为，声旁"戋"也可以表示意义：

> 　　王圣美治字学，演其义以为右文。古之字书，皆从左文。凡字，其类在左，其义在右。如木类，其左皆从木。所谓右文者，如戋，小也，水之小者曰浅，金之小者曰钱，歹而小者曰残，贝之小者曰贱。如此之类，皆以戋为义也。（[宋] 沈括，《梦溪笔谈》艺文一）③

　　汉字有表意的形旁和表音的声旁，④ 这与英语词不同。英语没有类似于汉语形旁、声旁的构词成分，词的字母组合可以表示读音，但单独的字母一般不表示意义。⑤ 虽然

---

① 大体而言，如果这个词源自古英语（Anglo-Saxon）或日耳曼语族（Germanic），首字母h发音，比如 haft, hag, hail, hair, half, haggle（源自古北欧语（Old Norse））。如果首字母h不发音，多见于外来词，但英语中来自拉丁语和希腊语的词，h 发音和不发音的情形并存。不发音的拉丁语词，比如 honour（拉丁语 *honor* repute), honest（拉丁语 *honestus*), heir (拉丁语 *heres hered*-)。发音的拉丁语词，比如 hospital（拉丁语 *hospes hospitis* host, guest）。不发音的希腊语词，比如 hour（希腊语 *hōra*）。发音的希腊语词，比如 history（希腊语 *historia* inquiry），holism（希腊语 *holos* whole）。与此有一点类似，法语h不发音的词，多源自拉丁语或希腊语；法语h发音的词，多源自中世纪早期法兰克人使用的日耳曼语以及后来的英语，只是这些词今天不再发音，或者只在一些省份的方言中发音（Price, 2008:3—4）。

② https://www.hancibao.com/shuowen/94b1（访问日期：2025-1-1）。

③ https://baike.baidu.com/item/ 王圣美右文说 /7133941#3, https://www.gushiji.org/guwen/2289（访问日期：2025-1-1）。

④ 汉字结构的实际情形比较复杂。据北大中文系董秀芳教授对笔者解释："汉字有象形字、指事字、会意字、形声字、假借字等，其中只有形声字包括表意的形旁和表音的声旁。不过，形声字数量较多，在汉字中占比达90%。形旁和声旁的位置不完全固定，形旁可在左，也可在上或在下等。但形旁在左，声旁在右的数量比较多。很早以来，就有文字学家认为，有些声旁也可以表意，属于'形声包会意'，宋代以后的'右文说'也是认为声旁同时可以表示意义，您引的那段文字就是典型的右文说，'戋'是声旁，但可能也表示'小'的意思。"（董秀芳，私人通信，2025-1-6）

⑤ 习语 from A to Z 可以释义为 from beginning to end，但字母单独使用的这种含义多限于习语或固定搭配，一般不用字母 A 表示 beginning。比如，Notes on how to use this dictionary can be found at the <u>beginning</u> of the book. (https://dictionary.cambridge.org/) 这里的 beginning 就不可以用字母 A 替代。

汉字和英语词表示音义的方式不同，但一般很难解释其音义之间的关系，传统上将之归结为语言符号的任意性。①

　　另一方面，学者们早就注意到语音与语义之间存在某些内在联系。Gabelentz（[1891] 2016：229—236）讨论过"语音象征的感觉"（das lautsymbolische Gefühl）。他的基本思想是，事物及其名称给我们留下相同的印象，但凡有可能，我们的感觉（Gefühl）在词的声音和词的概念内容之间建立起一种联系。词的声音适用于表示象征。比如，gelind /gəˈlɪnd/ 'mild' 似乎声音柔和，hart /hart/ 'hard' 声音强硬，süss /zyːs/ 'sweet' 声音甜美，sauer /ˈzauɐ/ 'sour' 声音没好气，herb /hɛrp/ 'bitter, sour' 声音怨恨。②

　　Jespersen（1933）认为，英语短元音 /i/ 往往表示小的意思：bit, kid, little, slim, slip。③ 这大致是通过元音开口度的大小象征所指对象的大小。虽然有反例big，但/i/的象征价值（symbolic value）确实可以解释一些词，而且语音语义学（phonosemantics）也挖掘出了更多的材料（Magnus, 2001）。此外，也有学者从语音角度分析过为什么说 Mama, Papa（Jakobson, 1960）。

　　我们对文字的关注不限于音义如何体现。比如，英语辅音 /k/ 表现为两种拼写形式，字母k和字母c，试比较：

　　　/k/ kick, kill, kin, kind, kindred, king, kiss

　　　/k/ cap, capital, case, concise, consider, contrite, converse

　　常见的情形是，以字母k开始的词来自古英语，或者是来自日耳曼语族，④比如 kindle, kirk来自古北欧语，kirsch来自德语，kit来自荷兰语，krill来自挪威语 *kril* 'tiny fish'。以字母c开始的词是外来词（拉丁语或法语）。换句话说，辅音/k/的拼写形式可能具有区分词源的功能。⑤

　　说"可能具有区分词源的功能"，是因为有反例。原因在于：

　　其一，源自古英语的词，语音/k/与拼写字母之间不是一对一（one-to-one）而是一对多（one-to-many）的关系，有的词原本就是以字母c开始，比如 colt（young male

---

① 关于语言符号任意性的经典论述，见 de Saussure, 1916。

② Das Wort „gelind" scheint einen gelinden Klang zu haben, „hart" einen harten, „süss" einen süssen, „sauer" und „herb" einen sauren und herben. (Gabelentz, [1891] 2016: 230) 这几个德语词的定义，参见 https://dictionary.cambridge. org/ zhs/ 词典 / 德语 - 英语 /。

③ 对于 Jespersen 这个观点的评论，见 Jakobson and Waugh, 1987; Ullmann, 1959。此外，英语长元音 /iː/ 似乎也可以表示小的意思，试比较 breeze ~ gale。

④ 关于古英语，见 Brook, 1955; Quirk and Wrenn, 1955。关于日耳曼语族，见 Prokosch, 1939。

⑤ 关于英语史、英语与其他语言的关系、英语中的外来词，参见 Bradley, 1904; Luick, 1914—1940; Mossé, 1947; Wyld, 1957; Brook, 1958; Serjeantson, 1961; Baugh and Cable, 1978; Jespersen, 1982; 李赋宁，1991。

horse），come（古英语cuman；比较德语 kommen 'come'）。令人好奇的是，学者们在构建这些词的原始日耳曼语（Proto-Germanic）词源的时候，却是选择字母k。[1] 试比较：colt ~ *kultaz*; cuman 'come'~ *kwem-*。[2]

其二，源自拉丁语的词，有的在进入英语后，首字母c变成了k，比如，拉丁语coquina → 英语kitchen。[3]

其三，源自希腊语以k开始的词，进入英语后没有变化，比如希腊语 kleptēs 'thief' → kleptomania, kruptō 'hide' → krypton。

即便字母k在当代英语词的kn 组合中不再发音，在一定程度上，它依然可以作为一个标识，表示该词来自古英语或日耳曼语族，比如knee, kneel, knife, knight, knit, knock, know。

从拼写形式kn-推测，英语史上存在过辅音丛（consonant clusters）/kn/，以后辅音/k/脱落，/kn/→ /n/，但是记录辅音/k/ 的字母k没有随之消失。英语的亲缘语言德语至今保留 /kn/，可为旁证，比如Kneipe /ˈknaɪpə/ 'bar', Knie /kniː/ 'knee'。

比较英语和德语，源自拉丁语的词进入德语以后，字母c往往变成了字母k，例如Kombination 'combination'（拉丁语*combinationem*），Kooperation 'cooperation'（拉丁语*cooperationem*）。德语似乎是倾向于拼写方面的"同化"，尽管也保留以字母c 开始的外来词，但数量很少，德语词典中c部的词条数量偏少可以说明这一点。

因此，从对比角度看，不妨做一个假设（hypothesis），即英语辅音 /k/ 的两个拼写形式可能与标识词源有关。

回到辅音丛/kn/的问题。假如我们把英语 /kn/→ /n/ 的语音演变归结为省力原则（Zipf's Law, Zipf's Principle of Least Effort），那我们如何解释英语的亲缘语言德语的/kn/没有演变为 /n/?[4] 值得注意的是，英语存在与/kn/→ /n/ 相平行的语音演变 /gn/ → /n/，说它们平行是因为 /k/-/g/ 是一组清浊对立（见下面的讨论），例如，gnash, gnat, gnaw, gneiss（来自德语 Gneis /gnais /）。

与 /kn/→ /n/，/gn/ → /n/ 语音演变类似的还有古英语以/h/ 开始的辅音丛 /hl/，/hr/，/hn/，它们都失去了/h/，同时也失去了字母h，试比较：古英语hlaf→loaf，古英语hring→ring，古英语hnutu → nut。[5]

---

[1] 关于英语词与印欧语的词源关系，见 Watkins, 2011。

[2] https://www.etymonline.com/ (accessed Jan. 1, 2025)。

[3] 词源信息依据 Thompson, 2002。更多信息见 https://www.etymonline.com/ (accessed Jan. 1, 2025)。

[4] 对 Zipf省力原则的看法，见 Martinet, 1949。关于语音演变，参见 Martinet, 1955。

[5] 关于 loaf, ring, nut 的古英语形式，笔者依据 https://www.etymonline.com/ 整理。劳允栋（1983: 96）给出的这三个词的古英语形式与这个网址提供的形式有所不同。

这里还有一个问题，类似于/kn/ 这样的辅音丛，它们在英语词汇系统中的使用程度如何，或者说它们的功能负荷量（functional load）如何？[①] 我们把问题限制在词首辅音丛，发现有如下情形：

/pl/ *please*, /pr/ *proud*

/bl/ *blood*, /br/ *brother*

/tr/ *tree*, /tw/ *twelve*

/dr/ *drive*

/kl/ *clean*, /kr/ *cry*, /kw/ *quick*

/gl/ *glass*, /gr/ *green*

/fl/ *fly*, /fr/ *fry*

*/vl/, */vr/

/sk/ *sky*, /sl/ *sleep*, /sm/ *smile*, /sn/ *snail*, /sp/ *spade*, /st/ *star*, /sw/ *swim*

*/zk/...

根据清浊对立（voiceless consonants, voiced consonants），可以分出如下对立组：/p/- /b/，/t/- /d/，/k/- /g/，/f/- /v/，/s/- /z/（劳允栋，1983：54—55）。对比显示：

第一，在对立组中，清辅音比浊辅音更多地进入辅音丛。/f/- /v/的比例是2:0，/s/-/z/的比例是7:0。

第二，在爆破音对立组，/p/- /b/，/t/- /d/，/k/- /g/，/r/出现频率最高，其次是/l/。

第三，有的辅音丛在英语中不存在，比如/sr/，/vl/，/vr/。法语有/vl/，如vlan 'wham'；/vr/，如vraiment 'really'。因此，在某种程度上，辅音丛也可以作为判断词源、构建语言特征学（linguistic characterology）的一个凭据（Mathesius, 1929, 1931; Vachek, 2016: 65—67）。[②]

如同元音/i/ 具有象征价值，上述辅音丛（至少是其中一部分）也具有这种作用，Bloomfield（[1933] 2002：258—259）称之为词根语素（root-forming morphemes）的象征意义（symbolic connotation），例如：

语素	象征意义	例词
[fl-]	'moving light':	*flash, flare, flame*
[fl-]	'movement in air':	*fly, flap, flit*
[gl-]	'unmoving light':	*glow, glare, gloat*

① 关于功能负荷量，见 Dušková, 2003; Vachek, 2016。

② 关于语言特征学，见 Mathesius, 1928, 2008；刘小侠，2012。

[sl-]	'smoothly wet':	*slime, slush, slop*
[kr-]	'noisy impact':	*crash, crack ,crunch*
[sn-]	'breath-noise':	*sniff, snore, snort*
[sn-]	'creep':	*snake, snail, sneak*

诚如语言学者Hagège (1985/1999：56) 所言，"语言问题千头万绪，但全都能归结到一个问题：音与义如何结合"。

我们今天看到的英语文字，它采用的是拉丁字母。盎格鲁—撒克逊（Anglo-Saxon）属于日耳曼民族，古代日耳曼民族使用如尼字母（the Runic alphabet）。关于如尼字母的简要历史及其在英语里的情况，Fortson 教授解释说：

The runic alphabet was in use by all the early Germanic peoples. It is derived from a variety of the Etruscan alphabet, itself a modification of the Greek alphabet when the Greeks brought the alphabet with them to Italy in the 8th century B.C. The Etruscan alphabet spread both southwards to Rome and environs, where speakers of Latin picked it up, whence the Latin alphabet; it also spread northwards, where it underwent various regional modifications by various peoples speaking various languages in and near the Alps. There were some Germanic speakers in that region, and evidently it was them who picked it up and spread it to their relatives farther north, where it developed into the runic alphabet. The early Germanic peoples were concentrated in northern Europe in the last centuries B.C. and the first centuries A.D., before some of them started to spread southwards and invade parts of the Roman Empire.

Runes were used by the early English-speaking peoples until the Latin alphabet arrived with Christian missionaries from Ireland in the 7th (?) century A.D. I forget which century exactly, but I think it's the 7th. But runes continued to be used to some extent in England after that time. And a couple of them were incorporated into the English version of the Latin alphabet to represent sounds for which there were no Latin letters. All of our manuscript copies of Old English texts, to my knowledge, are written in Latin letters plus the couple of runic letters that were added in. This includes the single surviving manuscript copy of *Beowulf*. Eventually those added runic letters also fell by the wayside. For example, the runic letter called "thorn" (having the shape þ) was used to represent the English "th" sound, for which there was no Latin equivalent. But over time, people came to use the digraph "th" for this sound instead of the runic letter. [①]

起初，祭司用如尼字母刻写祭祀铭文，这与中国的甲骨文有一点近似。不同之处在于，如尼字母多由直线构成。如尼字母被刻写在木头、石头等硬物上，由此推测，采用直线，很可能是为了方便刻写。[②]

今天，在有些场合，我们发现，字母u被v取代，比如在有的建筑物上，刻写的是bvilding。英语字母w的读音是 /ˈdʌb.əl.juː/，意思是double u，似乎u被写作v由来已久。联想到如尼字母多由直线构成，英语字母u写作v，这是否也是为了方便刻写呢？　如是，则是技术影响到文字的一个实例。笔者就此问题与Fortson教授探讨，他的解释富有启示，附在这里供参考：

The answer to your question comes in several parts.

Part 1: Until the 16th century, there was no functional distinction between U and V; they were just different stylistic variants of the same letter, going all the way back to the Romans, who would normally write the letter as V, but in more cursive styles of writing would write the bottom rounded instead of pointy, hence U. For the Romans, the letter represented both the consonant sound [w] and the vowel sound [u], and because the distinction between these was largely subphonemic and predictable based on the position of the letter in the word, there was no need to distinguish these two sounds with two different letters. Basically, V had the vowel pronunciation when between two consonants (e.g. MVRVS = murus 'wall') and the consonantal pronunciation elsewhere, except for a few details that I don't need to go into.

Part 2: Over the course of the development of spoken Latin into the Romance languages, the sound [w] shifted to [v] early on. So now the letter had the pronunciations [v] and [u], and things stayed that way for a good millennium or more. The sound [w] no longer existed in this family of languages.

Part 3: Starting after this time, as a result of the spread of Christianity in Western Europe, some languages were reduced to writing using the Latin alphabet that were not Romance languages and that had the sound [w] in them, especially those in the Germanic branch, such as Old English and Frankish. Since the vowel-sound [u] is very close in nature to the glide [w], the practice arose of using the letter we've been talking about (still

①　Benjamin Fortson, 私人通信，2025-1-3。Fortson，美国密歇根大学（The University of Michigan）古典学、语言学教授，著作包括 *Indo-European Language and Culture: An Introduction*. 2nd ed. Wiley-Blackwell, 2010.

②　如尼字母见 https://www.omniglot.com/writing/runic.htm (accessed Jan. 1, 2025)。

with two shapes, V and U) to write this sound as well. Not infrequently, the letter was written double (so VV or UU) to indicate more clearly that it represented a sound other than [u] or [v]. Different styles of writing this double letter arose too, in particular, the pointy version could be written in such a way that the two V's overlapped a bit.

Part 4: Sound changes in all the languages that we've been talking about are continuing during all this time, of course, and after hundreds of years, [v] and [u] in the Romance languages were no longer predictable, subphonemic variants of one another the way [w] and [u] had been in Latin. And English also had these sounds, plus [w]. It was therefore only a matter of time before people wanted to make sure all three sounds were consistently differentiated in writing. Someone or other decided that pointy V would be used for the sound [v], rounded U would be used for the sound [u], and the doubled version would be used for [w]. V and U together, when they were the same letter, were simply called "ooh" or "yoo", but now a new name "vee" (and similar terms in other languages, like French) was created for the pointy version and the old name remained for the rounded version. As for the doubled one, if people thought of it as being basically two pointy ones, i.e. two V's, they called it "double V" (whence the French term), but if they thought of it as being basically two rounded ones, i.e. two U's, they called it "double U" (whence the English letter-name). (German went a somewhat different path here, but I won't digress on it, though I'll tell you if you want to hear it.) Ultimately the pointy shape won out, but even as late as the end of the 17th century (and perhaps later), both rounded and pointy versions were in use. Typically, VV was the capital form and uu was the lower-case form, but there was a lot of variation that I've seen in older books. And even as late as the 19th century, I have seen girls' and ladies' samplers (pieces of cloth that they would embroider with patterns and letters and numbers to demonstrate their skill in sewing) that only have a V (or a U) and not both letters.

An essentially exactly parallel story to the one above also obtains for the letters I and J, which also were once variant forms of the same letter, and only much later came to have a functional distinction. And here even into the early *20th* century I have seen them still get used as simply stylistic variants of each other....

One does see inscriptions of the style "BVILDING" when people are imitating Roman capital letters, where again V was used for both u and v.[①]

---

① Benjamin Fortson, 私人通信，2024-12-15。

引文略长，否则无法说明问题。可见，BVILDING 未必是技术影响文字的实例。此外，我们也看到，简单问题的背后可能有复杂的历史故事。

从书写的角度看英语，除了印刷体，还有花体（Ornamental Penmanship）。Ornamental Penmanship 是花体的总称，其中的不同类别有不同叫法，比如，round hand script, copperplate script, spencerian script。[①] 在我们的英语教学体系中，据笔者的经历，是要学习花体的，这种花体大致相当于一种连笔字。有些上了年纪的美国人，比如20世纪20年代出生的人，如果手写信件，也往往采用这种花体。

除此之外，还有一种花体，多见于书刊报纸等出版物。这种花体有几种叫法，比如 Gothic，Fraktur，曾经通行于欧洲，1454年出版的古腾堡圣经（the Gutenburg Bible）就是采用这种字体。以后，只有德国继续使用，但最终被Antiqua字体（Antiqua typefaces）替代（参见7.2.2）。[②]

英语的书写还有一个独特的现象：人称代词第一人称单数I总是使用大写形式。笔者读到过一个故事（出处忘了），二战时期，德国煽动仇英，说英语I总是大写，表明英国人以自我为中心。[③] 询问过Fortson，确认有此事：

> I have heard that story, but I have actually never known why "i" is capitalized in English. I just looked it up in the OED, which turns out to be unfortunately (and surprisingly) completely unilluminating on this topic, unless I'm missing something. In the long, long list of historical and variant forms of this pronoun, I see that there are various forms that were capitalized already in Middle English, at least some of the time, but I don't know how significant that is given the vagaries of spelling back then as well

---

[①] https://www.britannica.com/topic/Spencerian-penmanship (accessed Jan. 1, 2025)。

[②] This is called Fraktur, the German term for certain printed varieties of Blackletter or Gothic (which refer to the same thing). It can indeed be difficult to read if one is not used to it, but is useful to know for many German publications up into the early 20th century. It was eventually banned by the Nazis—one of the few things they did that I think most people aren't too unhappy about nowadays. It does still get used for decoration, especially for newspaper mastheads, not just in Germany but elsewhere too (it's very common in the US in that function).
Benjamin Fortson, 私人通信，2024-12-24。参见 A Brief History of Fraktur, https://www.waldenfont.com/Historyof Fraktur.asp (accessed Jan. 1, 2025)。

[③] 德语人称代词第一人称单数 Ich 'I' 只有在句首时首字母大写，在句子的其他位置小写（ich），例如：
Ich bin sehr geneigt, diese Frage mit Nein zu beantworten, soweit meine eigene Person in Betracht kommt; also keine Biographie! Und trotzdem ermutigte ich meinen alten Kameraden Professor Frank, dieses Buch zu schreiben, …
(Albert Einstein. In Frank, Philipp. 1979. *Einstein: sein Leben und seine Zeit*. Mit einem Vorwort von Albert Einstein. Wiesbaden: Friedr. Vieweg & Sohn Braunschweig.)
法语人称代词第一人称单数 Je 'I' 亦然。参见桂裕芳、袁树仁，1983。

as the fact that the use of capitalization in general was not standard like it is today. Poking around on the Internet, apparently (according to some websites) the capitalization has something to do with the fact that this pronoun consists of only a single letter, and "I" is easier to see and read than "i" when standing alone. I also see the claim that capitalizing the pronoun emphasized the importance of the writer, which is a little bit like the anecdote you cited.

I can't say what kind of *volkspsychologische* conclusions one can draw from the capitalization, given that there may be more than one factor involved.

If I find out more, I'll let you know. One website claims that English is the only language in the world where the first person singular pronoun is capitalized in spelling. I don't know if that's true, but I certainly haven't come across other languages that do it. Of course, there are plenty of languages, like Chinese, where the writing system does not have capitalization, so the statement may not be all that meaningful. I believe the distinction between capital and lowercase letters is only found in the Greek, Latin, Cyrillic, and Armenian alphabets. The distinction arose due to developments in handwriting in the Middle Ages in Europe and parts of western Asia.[①]

就英语人称代词系统而言，只有第一人称单数主格是一个字母（比较 I, me, my, mine），第二、第三人称代词的所有形式（主格、宾格、与格、所有格），虽然也都是单音节，但都是不止一个字母。从视觉角度考虑，只有一个字母的 I 比 i 容易识别。

在古英语，人称代词第一人称单数主格形式是 ic，比较德语 ich。到了中古英语，ic 词尾辅音脱落，对应于该辅音的字母 c 消失，ic → i（李赋宁，1991:50）。由此推测，I 的大写很可能是为了增加它的辨识度，便于识别出它是单独使用的，而不是为了强调（英语中由一个字母构成，且可以独立使用的词，大概只有 I）。[②] 英语对于文字的强调手段包括大写、斜体、下划线。强调总是基于与非强调的对立。如果 I 是表示强调（通过大写），那与它对立的非强调形式是什么？强调 I 只能是通过斜体、下划线或者表示强调的句式。

纳粹利用 I 的书写形式煽动仇英，这个例子一方面说明文字与社会生活之间存在密切的关系，另一方面也提示，把文字（或者语言）与文明（或者文化）相联系，在许多情况下，结论可疑（参见 2.1.1 Warburton 对于文字与文明关系的看法）。这里所说的"文明""文化"包括德国语言学经常提及的"民族心理"（Volkspsychologie 'folk

---

① Benjamin Fortson, 私人通信，2025-1-4。

② 参考 https://www.thesaurus.com/e/grammar/whycapitali/ (accessed Jan. 1, 2025)。

psychology'）、"世界观"（Weltanschauung 'world view'）。移民美国的德国学者 Franz Boas，他的美国弟子 Edward Sapir，他们身上或多或少都有德国语言学这方面影响的影子①，甚至 Jespersen 也未能幸免。②

由此想到汉字。今天中国大陆使用简体字，台湾地区使用繁体字。关于简体字的争议一直存在。北大中文系朱德熙教授曾致信裘锡圭教授，就裘先生的《文字学概要》（1988）提出建议，其中提到：

> 这部书是以简化字为"基底"来讲汉字的。这样做会引起许多麻烦。我认为还是以繁体字作基底好。要求读者掌握繁体字并不算过分。③

无独有偶。钱锺书先生不同意《谈艺录》《管锥编》出简体字版。三联书店在2001年12月10日的出版说明中说：

> 为了满足广大读者的需求，继《钱锺书集》繁体字版之后，我们又出版了这套《钱锺书集》简体字版（《谈艺录》《管锥编》因作者不同意排简体字版除外）。④

这两件事情，耐人寻味。或许，在某种意义上，有理由把简体字视为繁体字的一种翻译？在这个翻译过程中，即便达到高度的功能对等（functional equivalence, Nida, 1982, 1993, 1996），繁体字的某些信息仍可能无法传递。⑤ 研究中国文化，需要阅读一些中国文史哲古籍，那么问题来了：是读繁体字版还是简体字版？繁体字的学习如何融入学校的语文教学体系？

---

① 关于德国语言学的信息，见姚小平，1995，2001，2011；Vossler, 1932。.

② Jespersen（1982:25）认为，语言与民族性格之间存在某种联系（a certain connexion between language and national character）。比较德国语言学者 Max Deutschbein（1917）把英语宾格（accusative）的广泛使用归结于英国人看事物观点客观（the objective outlook of the English, Mathesius, 2008: 125）。

③ 该信函收入裘锡圭，2013。

④ 钱锺书，2002，出版说明第 2 页。

⑤ 这是由翻译的性质决定的。意大利人说 "Traduttore, Traditore (Translator, traitor)"，这其实言重了。语言自身的某些特点可以导致翻译困难。Jakobson（1959）讲过一个故事，俄罗斯诗人 Boris Pasternak（1890—1960）有一部诗集，名曰 *Sestra moia — žizn' 'My Sister — Life'*（1922），在俄语里，*žizn'* 'life' 是阴性名词，捷克诗人 Josef Hora（1891—1945）在翻译的时候，几近绝望，因为 *život* 'life' 在捷克语里是阳性名词。美国伊利诺伊大学（UIUC）的 Douglas Kibbee 教授在谈及 *Alice in Wonderland* 英译法的时候，提到了需要考虑的诸多问题：Should Alice address a mouse using the formal or informal forms? How do the French react to the discourse marker "you know"? Back in March I participated in a webinar for the Lewis Carroll Society of North America, discussing the many ways of translating the grammatical mistake in the sentence "Curiouser and curiouser" (the first sentence of Chapter 2 in *Alice in Wonderland*). Douglas Kibbee，私人通信，2025-1-7。

　　这部著作的内容不限于文字（writing），它广博厚重，是一部适合北京大学本科生学习的优秀教材。

钱　军

北京大学英语语言文学系

参考文献

Baugh, Albert C. and Thomas Cable. 1978. *A History of the English Language*. 3rd ed. Englewood Cliffs, N.J.

Bloomfield, Leonard. [1933] 2002. *Language*. Beijing: Foreign Language Teaching and Research Press.

Bradley, Henry. 1904. *The Making of English*. London: Macmillan & Co. Ltd.

Brook, George L. 1955. *An Introduction to Old English*. Manchester: Manchester University Press.

Brook, George L. 1958. *A History of the English Language*. London: Andre Deutsch.

Dušková, Libuše, ed. 2003. *Dictionary of the Prague School of Linguistics*. (The original text published in 1960 by Josef Vachek in collaboration with Josef Dubský; translated from the French, German and Czech original sources by Aleš Klégr, Pavlina Saldová, Markéta Malá, Jan Cermák, Libuše Dušková.) Amsterdam: John Benjamins.

Deutschbein, Max. 1917. *System der neuenglischen Syntax*. Cöthen: Otto Schulze.

Gabelentz, G. von der. [1891] 2016. *Die Sprachwissenschaft: Ihre Aufgaben, Methoden und bisherigen Ergebnisse*. Herausgegeben von Manfred Ringmacher und James McElvenny. Berlin: Language Science Press.

Hagège, Claude. 1985. *L'Homme de paroles: Contribution linguistique aux sciences humaines*. Paris: Fayard. （海然热，1999，《语言人——论语言学对人文科学的贡献》，张祖建译，北京：生活·读书·新知三联书店。）

Jakobson, Roman. 1959. "On Linguistic Aspects of Translation." *Selected Writings* II, 260—266. The Hague: Mouton.

Jakobson, Roman. 1960. "Why 'Mama' and 'Papa'?" *Selected Writings* I, 538—545. The Hague: Mouton.

Jakobson, Roman and Linda Waugh. 1987. *The Sound Shape of Language*. 2nd ed. Berlin: Mouton.

Jespersen, Otto. 1933. "Symbolic Value of the Vowel i." *Selected Writings of Otto Jespersen* II, 557—577. Beijing: World Publishing Corporation.

Jespersen, Otto. 1982. *The Growth and Structure of the English Language*. With a foreword by Randolph Quirk. 10th ed. Chicago: The University of Chicago Press. （奥托·叶斯柏森，2023，《英语的成长和结构》，刘小侠译，北京：商务印书馆。）

Luick, Karl. 1914—1940. *Historische Grammatik der englischen Sprache*. 2 Bände. Leipzig: C. H. Tauchnitz.

Magnus, Margaret. 2001. *What's in a Word? : Studies in Phonosemantics*. Trondheim, Norway: University of Trondheim Dissertation.

Martinet, André. 1949. "Review of George Kingsley Zipf, *Human Behavior and the Principle of Least Effort*, Addison-Wesley Press, Cambridge, Mass., 1949. x + 573 pp." *Word* 5 (3): 280—282.

Martinet, André. 1955. *Économie des changements phonétique*s. Berne: A. Francke.

Mathesius, Vilém. 1928. "On Linguistic Characterology with Illustrations from Modern English." Reprinted in Vachek, Josef, ed. 1964. *A Prague School Reader in Linguistics*, 59—67. Bloomington: Indiana University Press.

Mathesius, Vilém. 1929. "La Structure Phonologique du Lexique du Tchèque Moderne." *Travaux du Cercle Linguistique de Prague* 1: 67—84.

Mathesius, Vilém. 1931. "Zum Problem der Belastungs- und Kombinationsfähigkeit der Phoneme." *Travaux du Cercle Linguistique de Prague* 4: 148—152.

Mathesius, Vilém. 2008. *A Functional Analysis of Present-Day English on a General Linguistic Basis*. Edited by Josef Vachek; translated by Libuše Dušková. Beijing: World Publishing Corporation.

Mossé, Fernand. 1947. *Esquisse d'une Histoire de la Langue Anglaise*. Lyon: IAC.

Nida, Eugene A. 1982. *Translating Meaning*. San Dimas, California: English Language Institute.

Nida, Eugene A. 1993. *Language, Culture, and Translating*. Shanghai: Shanghai Foreign Language Education Press.

Nida, Eugene A. 1996. *The Sociolinguistics of Interlingual Communication*. Bruxelles: Éditions du Hazard.

Price, Glanville. 2008. *A Comprehensive French Grammar*. 6th ed. Oxford: Blackwell.

Prokosch, Eduard. 1939. *A Comparative Germanic Grammar*. Philadelphia: Linguistic Society of America, University of Pennsylvania.

Quirk, Randolph and Charles L. Wrenn. 1955. *An Old English Grammar*. London: Methuen.

de Saussure, Ferdinand. [1916] 1995. *Cours de linguistique générale*. Publié par Charles Bally et Albert Séchehaye; avec la collaboration de Albert Riedlinger; édition critique préparée par Tullio de Mauro; postface de Louis-Jean Calvet. Paris: Payot.

Serjeantson, Mary. 1961. *A History of Foreign Words in English*. London: Routledge and Kegan Paul.

Thompson, Della, ed. 2002. *Pocket Oxford English-Chinese Dictionary*. Beijing: Foreign Language Teaching and Research Press.

Ullmann, Stephen. 1959. *Words and Their Use*. London: Frederick Muller.

Vachek, Joself. 2016. *The Linguistic School of Prague*. Beijing: World Publishing Corporation.

Visser, F. Th. 1963—1973. *An Historical Syntax of the English Language*. 4 vols. Leiden: E. J. Brill.

Vossler, Karl. 1932. *The Spirit of Language in Civilization*. Translated by O. Oeser. London: Kegan Paul,

Trench, Trubner.

Watkins, Calvert. 2011. *The American Heritage Dictionary of Indo-European Roots*. 3rd ed. Boston, MA: Houghton Mifflin Harcourt.

Wyld, Henry. 1957. *A Short History of English*. 3rd ed. London: J. Murray.

桂裕芳、袁树仁编著，1983，《法国文学选读》上册，北京：北京出版社。

劳允栋编著，1983，《英语语音学纲要》，北京：商务印书馆。

李赋宁编著，1991，《英语史》，北京：商务印书馆。

刘小侠，2012，《马泰修斯论特征性与类型学》，载北京大学外国语学院外国语言学及应用语言学研究所编《语言学研究》（第十一辑），北京：高等教育出版社，16—27。

钱锺书，2002，《钱锺书集·写在人生边上，人生边上的边上，石语》，北京：生活·读书·新知三联书店。

裘锡圭，2013，《文字学概要》（修订本），北京：商务印书馆。

姚小平，1995，《洪堡特——人文研究和语言研究》，北京：外语教学与研究出版社。

姚小平，2001，《17—19世纪的德国语言学与中国语言学》，北京：外语教学与研究出版社。

姚小平，2011，《西方语言学史》，北京：外语教学与研究出版社。

前　言

2017年的春天，我在伊利诺伊大学香槟分校的图书馆翻到了一本叫作*Language, Technology, and Society*①的书。作者Richard Sproat将语言技术的历史追溯至书写系统，让我眼前一亮：想给非英语专业本科生开设的和语言学相关的课程有了方向。

语言学，在很多非语言专业学生的想象中，约等于"抽象""枯燥""不实用"。从文字的演化切入，可以打破对语言学的疏离感，具象化、生活化地看到语言学并非悬浮于空，而是深嵌于人类文明进程。从甲骨上的占卜刻痕，到活字印刷的标准化字形，再到键盘上的拼音输入法，所有书写系统都包含对语音的映射，都通过技术手段将语言的声音维度转化为视觉符号。而语言中模糊的语法关系，又被标点符号、空格、分段等排版技术显性化，重塑着我们对语言结构的认知。

从文字开始，我将以语言技术史为线，以语言技术原理为点，以语言技术发展产生的社会影响为面，将语言、技术与社会重要议题关联起来，探索三者之间的相互关系。语言学将转化为一把钥匙，在探讨语言的文本化、机械化、数字化、生态化的过程中，解构"自然vs人工"的认知对立，揭示从古文字破解到编程的逻辑连续性，激活个体语言体验的历史纵深感。

自2018年起，我每年秋季学期开设"语言、技术与社会"课程，疫情期间暂停两年，至今共开过五轮。该课程为北京大学大学英语 C 模块课程，选课学生分为两类：（1）根据入学分级考试成绩编入 C 级，大学英语需修 4 个学分，本课程为其选修的第1 个或第 2 个 C 模块课程；（2）根据入学分级考试成绩编入B级，大学英语需修 6 个学分，已完成 B 级 4 个学分，本课程为其选修的第 1 个 C模块课程。

课程开设之初，语言的"文本化"模块以Sproat著作书写系统相关部分做读本，另外三个模块——语言的"机械化""数字化""生态化"则采用不同著作、文章的节选为读本。很快，我发现有必要写一部自己的教科书，以解决以下问题：一、各读本对术语的定义和用法不同；二、西方中心论的单一历史叙事模式；三、生词密集，句式缠绕，阅读难度大。

---

① Sproat, Richard. 2010. *Language, Technology, and Society*. Oxford: Oxford University Press.

本书的特色在于：一、勾勒了从语言文本化到社交媒体语言生态化的语言技术史链条；二、形成了从中、西两种语境对语言、技术与社会相互关系的系统化阐释；三、以英语作为外语学习的大学生为受众，语言简洁、易懂，可读性强。

在写作过程中，我设定了以下思维目标：一、探讨国内外与语言技术相关的社会问题；二、在国内和国际背景下对问题进行剖析；三、挑战被广泛接受的语言技术假设，从而以思想性带动语言学习，通过描述、阐释、分析和评价语言、技术与社会之间的关系，增强学生的英语综合应用能力，提高综合文化素养，发展学生的跨文化交际能力和批判性思维能力。

全书共十三章，分别对应一学期十五个教学周中十三周的教学内容。课程在第十二章和第十三章之间会安排两次语言技术实践工作坊，内容承上启下：

第一章　什么是语言

第二章　文字的起源

第三章　文字如何表记语言

第四章　语言与文字的互动：埃及圣书字释读

第五章　语言与文字的互动：线性文字B释读

第六章　文字、读写能力与社会

第七章　印刷术、稳定与多变

第八章　打字机、思维与风格

第九章　电报机、摩尔斯码与全球互联

第十章　语言学、理性主义与基于规则的机器翻译

第十一章　语料库、经验主义与数据驱动的机器翻译

第十二章　机器翻译素养与机器翻译伦理

工作坊：生成式人工智能与英文写作

工作坊：网络语言语料分析

第十三章　社交媒体与语言游戏

第一章阐述语言的要素、语言分析的基础方法和理论框架。内容会在后续章节进一步展开。第二章到第六章为第一模块语言的"文本化"，阐释在什么意义上文字是第一项专门为语言设计的技术，演示不同的书写系统如何表记不同的语言，通过古文字释读案例深入考察文字与语言的互动关系，探讨读写能力在不同时期、不同社会的含义，并以中国为例讨论文字改革的形式和社会影响。第七章到第九章为第二模块语言的"机械化"，在历史语境下阐释中西方对印刷术的定义与各自文字性质的关系，分析中西方打字机设计的逻辑依据，其对思维、写作风格以及女性寻求新的职业机会产生的影响，探

究中西方电报的符号学架构及其对通信、新闻、全球互联产生的影响。第十章到第十二章为第三模块语言的"数字化",以机器翻译为例讲述计算机科学如何利用语言学知识用有限的规则生成无限的句子,如何转向数据驱动的统计机器翻译和神经机器翻译,神经机器翻译的底层架构如何成为当代人工智能的核心引擎,人作为文本创造者对机器翻译等人工智能如何做到善用但不滥用。工作坊"生成式人工智能与英文写作""网络语言语料分析"和第十三章为第四模块语言的"生态化",考察语言在硬件载体、平台规则、法律政策等环境下向自组织系统的动态演变,分析弱关系社交媒体内群成员如何通过语言游戏协商、构建身份,保持内群亲密感。

大学生是青年群体中最富主体意识、理性精神和质疑思维的一群人。我很荣幸这门课让他们在评估、比较、分析、探索中体会到了跨学科研究的力量和乐趣。本书第三稿写作过程中,我收到了往届同学的来信[①]:

> I really want to thank you for your LTS class! It was five years ago and I was a math student (and is still now) trying to grind hard, so humanities (not counting math) had been completely out of my sight even though it was the senior year of mine. And there came the class Language, Technology, and Society. Secretly, it ignited something inside me: I had found certain (philosophical, but only later did I know) assumptions of applied math unsatisfactory but never figured out a way to spell out what was in my mind (and that's precisely because I only knew math at that time but the problem is all about meta-mathematics). The reading of LTS somehow ensured me that things would still make sense even if I branched out to other humanity subjects, as long as I tried hard. I started reading some philosophy and sociology in 2020 and eventually went to audit classes on analytical philosophy and aesthetic out of curiosity. I got deeper and deeper into the rabbit hole, picking up anthropology and more philosophy along the way, and the LTS class is really the origin of my liberal arts education. I am really fortunate to get into Stanford and figured out my argument against applied math with more philosophy training here, and that's how I abandoned applied math and carried on pursuing pure/theoretical math now. Looking back, everything seems like coincidence but retrospectively makes so much sense altogether (and also the GPT-3 in 2020).
>
> I also started learning languages here, which again is a very fortunate thing to have the freedom to do. I did two years of Japanese and Russian and will continue doing

---

① Zhihan Li,私人通信,2024-6-18。

second-year Ukrainian next year. The condensed linguistical knowledge I learned from LTS helped so much that I inherently think in word triplets and syntactical structures instead of pure stimulus-response-reinforcement. And language classes are really gateways to interact with other cultures. One of my mid-term goal now is to understand how textbooks convey across cultures/countries/regions.

十五周的阅读和讨论，点燃了一个数学专业学生对哲学、社会学、人类学的兴趣，改变了他学习语言时看待词汇和句法结构的方式，而哲学训练又引导他找到了新的数学研究方向。贡献其中，何其有幸！

我要感谢所有上过这门课的同学，没有他们悉心倾听、热情发问，就没有这本书。我还要感谢我的老师钱军教授，他不仅给第三稿提出了细致的建议，还和我分享了很多关于中国文字学的资料。

欢迎同道、同学对本书多提意见和建议，以便改进不足之处。

刘小侠

2025年2月

于北京大学英语系大学英语教研室

Contents

Chapter I   What Is Language

Study the following expressions containing "language." What do we mean by "language" in each? What distinguishes "human language" from the others? Write down your ideas in a short paragraph.

human language

programming language

animal language

body language

mathematical language

musical language

Despite its seemingly straightforward appearance, the term "language" is anything but transparent. Programming language, animal language, body language, mathematical language, musical language, and human language are all called "language" when language is loosely defined as "a system of symbols for communication."

However, certain fundamental properties set human language apart from the others: 1) it is natural rather than artificial; 2) it is first and foremost vocal, spoken in order to be heard; 3) it is creative, capable of combining the basic units to form an infinite set of well-formed grammatical sentences which are never before produced or heard; 4) it is displaceable, allowing for communicating about things that are not immediately present; 5) it is acquired through social interactions, and is deeply tied to culture; 6) it is imperfect, abound with ambiguity and redundancy. In short, it is what makes us human.

Questions like "Is programming language a language?" "Is animal language a language?" depend on what one means by "language," and answers fall immediately from how that's defined.

1.1   What is language

Anthropocentric in outlook, in this book I define "**language**" strictly as human language. It involves neural activity in the human brain, muscular activity of human organs, and more importantly, social activity which engages individuals interacting with one another (Hu and Jiang, 2002: 2). For the larger hearing community, "language" refers to natural or ordinary language used between humans, typically based on speech.

In light of this definition, **writing** is considered the first technology devised for language, extending its capacities across time and space. Here, **technology** refers not only to new and exciting tools but to all human innovations, including invented technological forms whose use must be expressly taught and learned.

It is worth noticing that many contemporary definitions of language—particularly those influenced by cognitive and computational models (cf. Further reading)—take for granted the existence of writing as a tool for representing language, even though language long predates writing systems. In fact, writing is a relatively recent development in the history of humanity, with evidence of **proto-writing** systems appearing around 5,000 years ago (cf. Chapter II).

However, human language is believed to have existed for at least 50,000 to 100,000 years, if not longer (cf. Nichols, 1998; McBrearty and Brooks, 2000; Lieberman, 2007). During this long pre-writing period, language existed purely as speech. Even today, despite the prominence of literacy, speech remains the primary mode of communication for most people, and it is the default medium through which children acquire their first language.

Yet, once established, writing stands in its own right. Over time, it evolves into an "autonomous system" (Vachek, 1973: 31; 1989: 5) that acquires distinct forms and functions, giving rise to what we call "**written language**." As a reaction to it arises the term "**spoken language**." In other words, writing led to a conceptual division where speech—previously just "language"—was now explicitly called "spoken language" vis-à-vis "written language." The distinction becomes especially pronounced after the mechanical treatment of text, through printing (cf. Chapter VII), typewriting (cf. Chapter VIII), telegraphy (cf. Chapter IX), etc. Therefore, from Chapter VII onward, in some context "language" may refer to "written language."

Today, spoken language and written language function as complementary systems that serve distinct yet interrelated communicative purposes. Digital communication, in particular, has blurred the lines between the two forms, as text-based communication (e.g., emails, instant messaging) often mirrors the informal and interactive nature of spoken language (cf. Chapter XIII). Conversely, audiobooks, podcasts, and videos from expert speakers have allowed spoken language to gain some of the permanence and distribution capabilities traditionally associated with writing.

1.2 Elements of language

Language defined as such can be studied at various levels. They range in depth between the specifics of the sounds we make to form language to the context surrounding speech events. From the most specific to the broadest are phonetics, phonology, morphology, syntax, semantics and pragmatics.

1.2.1 Phonetics

For most people, knowing a language is, first of all, knowing the sounds of that language. A speaker of English knows there are three sounds in the word *top*, the initial sound [t], the second sound [ɔ], and the final sound [p], and is able to recognize the parts in other words.

Though physically the word is just pronounced as one continuous sound, a speaker can analyze the one sound into its individual segments. The ability to identify speech sounds is amazing because no two speakers ever say *top* exactly the same way.

Phonetics studies the sounds of a language. It is concerned with describing the physical aspects of sounds., i.e., how speech sounds are produced, the properties of the sounds, and how the sounds are perceived.

From the perspective of sound being what we pronounce, there are two defining characteristics: place (where it is articulated) and manner (how it is articulated). Figure 1.1 illustrates when producing [s] one lets some air keep flowing out from one's lungs and through one's vocal tract and then out of one's mouth, while pushing the air through a very narrow opening by placing the tip of one's tongue lightly against the ridge behind one's upper teeth.

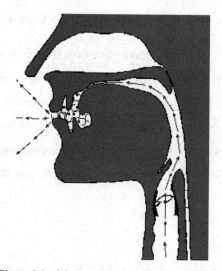

Figure 1.1   Manner and place of articulating [s]
Source: https://wuglife.tumblr.com/post/138067079648/fricatives-are-a-category-of-speech-sound-they
(accessed Aug. 31, 2024)

As an English learner, you must have seen the International Phonetic Alphabet (IPA) consonant chart somewhere before. The horizontal dimension represents the place of articulation, and the vertical dimension, the manner of articulation. Thus, [f], a labiodental fricative, is produced by putting the upper teeth on the lower lip so that the air moving through the mouth generates friction.

THE INTERNATIONAL PHONETIC ALPHABET (revised to 2020)

CONSONANTS (PULMONIC)   ©①© 2020 IPA

	Bilabial	Labiodental	Dental	Alveolar	Postalveolar	Retroflex	Palatal	Velar	Uvular	Pharyngeal	Glottal
Plosive	p b			t d		ʈ ɖ	c ɟ	k ɡ	q ɢ		ʔ
Nasal	m	ɱ		n		ɳ	ɲ	ŋ	N		
Trill	ʙ			r					ʀ		
Tap or Flap		ⱱ		ɾ		ɽ					
Fricative	ɸ β	f v	θ ð	s z	ʃ ʒ	ʂ ʐ	ç ʝ	x ɣ	χ ʁ	ħ ʕ	h ɦ
Lateral fricative				ɬ ɮ							
Approximant		ʋ		ɹ		ɻ	j	ɰ			
Lateral approximant				l		ɭ	ʎ	ʟ			

Symbols to the right in a cell are voiced, to the left are voiceless. Shaded areas denote articulations judged impossible.

Figure 1.2   The IPA pulmonic consonant chart
Source: https://www.internationalphoneticassociation.org/IPAcharts/IPA_chart_orig/IPA_charts_E_img.
html#images/IPA_Kiel_2020_CP.svg (accessed Aug. 31, 2024)

IPA uses alphabetic symbols to represent the sounds. It has developed a set of symbols which aim to describe all human languages including Chinese. The chart below shows IPA and Pinyin (cf. Chapter VI) for four Chinese characters.

IPA	ɕiɛ	tɕʰiou̯	tɕyœ	tɕʰi
Pinyin	Xing	Qiu	Jue	Qi
Example	猩	球	崛	起

Figure 1.3   Comparison of IPA and Pinyin

Mapping sounds to symbols (alphabet), and vice versa, has some very practical uses, for example, Automatic Speech Recognition (ASR) transcribing sound to and text, and Text to Speech Synthesis (TTS) transcribing text to sounds. These are not easy tasks though.

From the perspective of sound being what we hear, sound has three defining characteristics: pitch, loudness, and quality. **Pitch** is how high or low a sound is. It is basically your ears' response to the frequency of a sound, i.e., the number of vibrations or sound waves per second. **Loudness** is the sound energy transferred in a specified direction, i.e., the size of the vibration in air pressure. It is determined by the intensity of sound and sensitivity of ear. **Quality** is the nature of sound. It allows the ear to distinguish sounds which have the same pitch and loudness, due to "the difference in the complexity of the waveform" (Ladefoged, 1996: 27).

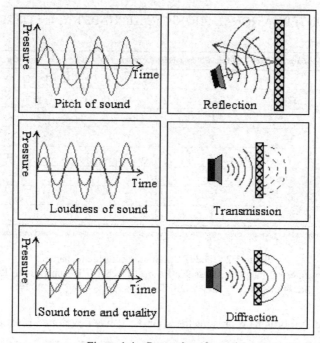

Figure 1.4　Properties of sound

Source: https://www.onosokki.co.jp/English/hp_e/whats_new/SV_rpt/SV_3/sv3.htm (accessed Aug. 31, 2024)

Now let's look at how various kinds of sounds appear on a spectrogram, a graph to represent the frequencies of speech over time. The horizontal axis represents time and is scaled in seconds, while the vertical axis shows frequencies. Darker parts mean higher energy densities, and lighter parts mean lower energy densities.

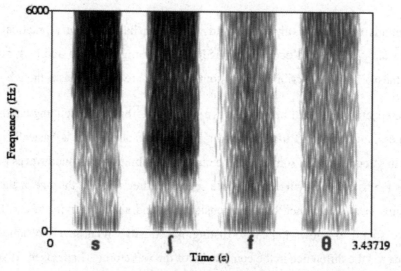

Figure 1.5　Spectrogram of voiceless fricative /f/, /θ/, /s/, /ʃ/

Source: https://home.cc.umanitoba.ca/~krussll/phonetics/acoustic/spectrogram-sounds.html (accessed Aug. 31, 2024)

From left to right, we have

[s] very high energy in the highest frequencies

[ʃ] high energy, but in much lower frequencies

[f] lowest energy with lower frequencies overall

[θ] so similar to [f], but slightly higher energy in the higher frequencies

When using ASR to transcribe sound to text on a cellphone, pitch is much more important for Chinese than English. In non-tonal languages like English, changes in pitch operate mainly above the word level (Zhang, 2018: 1), e.g., asking a question vs. making a statement, to express intonation or emotion. In tonal languages like Chinese, pitch plays a crucial role in determining **tone**—a specific pattern of pitch that remains stable or changes in a particular way over the course of a syllable, which affects the meaning of what is said.

Tone	Pitch pattern	Example
First tone	a high, steady pitch	mā 妈, "mother"
Second tone	a rising pitch, starting mid and rising to high	má 麻, "hemp"
Third tone	a low pitch that dips and then rises	mǎ 马, "horse"
Fourth tone	a sharp falling pitch, from high to low	mà 骂, "scold"
Neutral tone	short and light, with no specific pitch contour	ma 吗, used for asking yes/no questions

Figure 1.6   Pitch pattern description for Standard Chinese four tones, plus a neutral tone

While loudness helps in identifying speech over background noise, modern ASR systems can adjust to varying loudness levels. Even a soft whisper can trigger Siri, the Apple digital assistant. Systems like the one used by Siri are designed to normalize audio inputs to account for varying levels of loudness. Whether one speaks loudly or whisper, the system can adjust the input gain to a level that makes speech intelligible.

Vowel and consonant quality help differentiate between words. In English, the words *bit* and *bet* are distinguished by the subtle variations in vowel quality, which change the meaning entirely. In Chinese, 变老 (biànlǎo, "to grow old") and 电脑 (diànnǎo, "computer") are set apart by the quality of initial consonants, which provides crucial distinctions in meaning.

When two people say the same word at the same pitch and loudness, you can still tell their voices apart due to differences in quality. One might have a more resonant or nasal voice, while the other may have a breathier sound. In ASR, systems generally prioritize quality, and the ranking of pitch varies based on the language and the specific design of the system.

1.2.2　Phonology

Whereas phonetics is concerned with the physical sounds spoken or heard, **phonology** is concerned with the abstract sounds in our minds. It studies the system of mental selection, representation and organization of sounds to signal meanings.

Every time we say a [t] it will be slightly different from the other times we've said it. It might be louder, higher in pitch, or longer in duration, for example. However, in phonology all productions are considered the same sound, as long as it can be distinguished from the other sounds in the system. A speaker of English can feel the difference between [t] in *top* and *stop*. It is aspirated or pronounced with an accompanying forceful expulsion of air in the former, represented by [tʰ] in narrow transcription, but unaspirated in the latter. Despite the difference, what a speaker and a hearer feel themselves to be pronouncing and hearing is still the same unit. The unit is called **phoneme**, the basic unit in phonology.

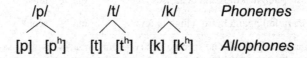

Figure 1.7　English phonemes /p/, /t/, /k/ and their allophones

Phonemes are not physical sounds. They are mental representations of phonological units of a language. Each phoneme has one or more sounds called **allophones** associated with it, which represent the actual sound being produced in various environments. [tʰ] in *top* and [t] in *stop* are the realizations of the phoneme /t/.[①] They are in complementary distribution, viz., they never occur in the same environment. The presence or absence of the property aspiration depends on where /t/ occurs and what precedes it. An English speaker produces [tʰ] at the beginning of a stressed syllable, but [t] if it follows [s]. The replacement of one for the other will not change the meaning of the word. Producing [t] with a little puff of air in *stop* cannot change the word into another. They are "the same but different" (McMahon, 2002: 12).

---

① Phonetic sounds will be written enclosed in square brackets, such as [tʰ], [t], [pʰ], or [p]. Phonemes will be enclosed in slash brackets such as /t/ and /p/.

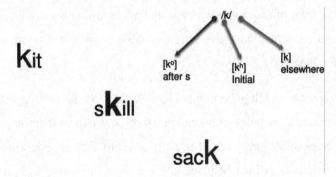

Figure 1.8   Complementary distribution of allophones of /k/

The languages in the world sound so different, because the way languages use speech sounds to form patterns differs from one another. The sound of frying eggs in Chinese is "zizi," in English is "sizzle," in Korean "jigeul," in Estonian "tssss," and in Czech "prsk." Phonology tells us what sounds are in a language, how they do and can combine into words, and explains why certain phonetic features are important to identify a word.

When it comes to natural language processing (NLP), phonology is applied if the text origin is a speech. It deals with the interpretation of speech sounds within and across words. Speech sound might give a big hint about the meaning of a word or a sentence. For example, some Chinese English as a Foreign Language (EFL) learners tend to delete the [l] sound when it is syllable final as in "cool," "fool," "deal," "fall" and "school," viz. the tip of the tongue is not raised to touch the gum ridge behind the teeth.

In addition to deletion, other common phonological processes include: insertion (adding an extra sound, often a vowel, where there isn't one in the target language, e.g., a Japanese EFL learner may pronounce "film" like "filum"), cluster reduction (simplifying a consonant cluster by omitting one or more consonants, e.g., an Arabic EFL learner may pronounce "splash" as "spash"), assimilation (a sound changes to become more like a nearby sound, e.g., a French speaker may pronounce "handbag" as "hambag"), substitution (replacing a sound that doesn't exist in a speaker's native language with a more familiar sound, e.g., an Indian English speaker may pronounce "very very good" as "beli beli good"), stopping (replacing a fricative or affricate with a stop, e.g., an Italian EFL learner may pronounce "think" like "tink"), vowelization (replacing a consonant with a vowel, e.g., a Chinese EFL learner may pronounce "bottle" as "boto"), fronting (replacing a sound made at the back of the mouth with a sound made at the front, e.g., a child may say "tar" instead of "car"), backing (replacing a sound produced in the front of the mouth with a sound made further back, e.g., a child may say "gog" for "dog"), and reduplication (repeating a syllable or part of a word, e.g., a child may say "babanana" for "banana").

ASR systems approach such phonological knowledge through training with diverse data. Some systems incorporate knowledge of phonological rules as part of their language models (Wester, 2003: 69). For example, they might use dictionaries that encode alternate pronunciations and phonetic variations, which help account for known phonological processes in the speech community they're trained on. Advanced models like those based on neural networks (cf. Chapter XI) use context and probabilistic models of speech sounds to handle unpredictable variations (O'Shaughnessy, 2023), improving their ability to recognize speech patterns influenced by phonological processes.

1.2.3 Morphology

A particular string of sounds must be united with a meaning and vice versa in order for the sounds or meaning to be a word in our mental dictionaries. **Morphology** is the study of the forms of words.

The morphological units of language are called **morpheme**s. They are the building blocks which shape the word. Consider a word like "unhappiness."

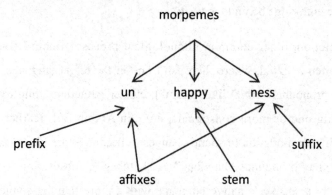

Figure 1.9　Morphological analysis of "unhappiness"

There are three morphemes, each carrying a certain amount of meaning. *un* means "not," while *ness* means "being in a state or condition." *Happy* is a free morpheme because it can stand on its own. When a morpheme appears by itself, it is considered as a stem. In contrast, "un" and "ness" are bound morphemes, because they have to be attached to a free morpheme. An "affix" is a bound morpheme that occurs before or after a stem. To be specific, when it occurs before a stem it is called "prefix," and when it occurs after that it is called "suffix."

Now let's check out the word morphology itself: *morph* is the stem, *logy* the suffix, and the linking element between them *o* is called interfix, which does not contribute a meaning of its own but only functions to create stem-forms that are pronounceable. Phonologically, it belongs to the first constituent of the compound.

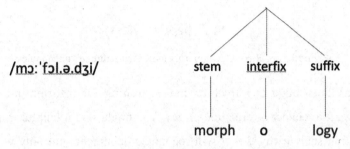

Figure 1.10   Morphological analysis of "morphology"

One thing to note is, like phonemes, morphemes are basic units that are sensed in one's mind rather than spoken or heard. Their actual spoken forms are called **morph**s. Most morphemes are realized by one morph. Some morphemes, however, are realized by more than one morph in relation to their phonological context. For instance, the morpheme of {would} has a set of morphs in different sound contexts. Here we can see, what **allomorph**s to morphemes are what allophones to phonemes. *allo* is a word-forming element from Greek, meaning "other." An allomorph, thus, is a variant form of a morpheme.

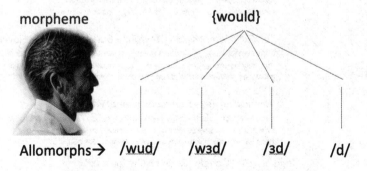

Figure 1.11   Allomorphs of {would}

A word is not a simple sequence of morphemes but has an underlining hierarchical structure. Now let's take another look at the word *unhappiness*. As shown previously, the stem is *happy*, an adjective, to which we added *un-*, an adjective prefix, which is added to adjectives to form new adjective stem *unhappy,* and then we added the noun suffix -*ness*.

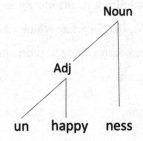

Figure 1.12　Hierarchical morphological structure of "unhappiness"

Morphological knowledge is relevant when searching for information on the internet. Suppose you want to collect information on *tax*. You might find it helpful if the search engine is programmed in such a way that it will recognize documents not only with the word *tax*, but also with the words *taxation*, *taxes*, *taxable*, and *taxability* as relevant. In fact, for many search engines this is not the case. Google takes *taxation* and *taxes* as relevant but *taxable* and *taxability* not.

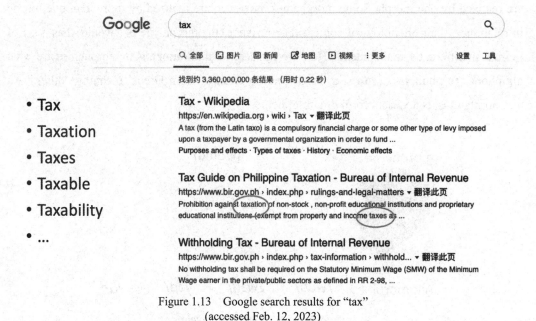

Figure 1.13　Google search results for "tax"
(accessed Feb. 12, 2023)

On the other hand, when searching for information on tax issues, you would not like your search engine to retrieve documents with the words *taxi*, *taxis*, *taxon*, or *taxonomy* that also begin with the letter sequence *tax*.

This example shows that analysis of systematic relations between words is essential for the computational handling of language data. What we need for this purpose is a morphological parser, a computer program that decomposes words into relevant constituents: tax-ation, tax-able, and tax-abil-ity.

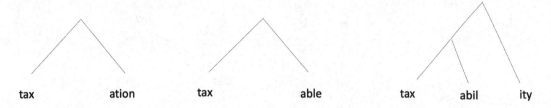

tax   ation   tax   able   tax   abil   ity

Figure 1.14   Morphological parsing of "taxation," "taxable," and "taxability"

1.2.4 Syntax

Syntax studies the way in which words are put together so that they make sense. Syntactic rules determine the order of words and how the words are grouped. Compare the following sentences:

The cat chased the mouse.
The mouse chased the cat.

The two sentences have the same categories and number of words, but different word order, so they have different meanings.

Syntactic category is a set of words or phrases in a language which share a large number of common characteristics. Syntactic categories commonly include: 1) Part of Speech, e.g., Noun, Verb, Adjective, Adverb, Pronoun, Preposition, Determiner (Det)... 2) Phrase Structure e.g., Noun Phrase (NP), Verb Phrase (VP), Adjective Phrase (AdjP), Adverb Phrase (AdvP), Preposition Phrase (PP) ,... 3) Sentence as the core of the structure.

The fact that *the cat chased the mouse* belongs to the syntactic category of Sentence, that *the cat* and *the mouse* are NPs, and that *chased the mouse* is a VP can be illustrated in a tree diagram, which shows that a sentence is both a linear string of words and a hierarchical structure with phrases nested in phrases.

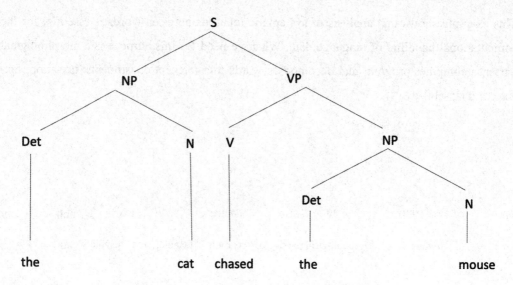

Figure 1.15　Tree diagram for "the cat chased the mouse"

Three aspects of speakers' syntactic knowledge are disclosed in phrase structure trees:

1. the linear order of the words in the sentence
2. the groupings of words into particular syntactic categories
3. the hierarchical structure of the syntactic categories

Phrase structure trees help visually account for sentence ambiguities. Now check out a classic example *old men and women*. It can have two interpretations based on how the words group together. In one reading, the adjective "old" applies to the entire NP "men and women," meaning both the men and women are old.

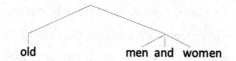

Figure 1.16　Tree diagram for one interpretation of "old men and women"

In another reading, "old men" forms a single NP and the conjunction "and" links the NP "old men" with the NP "women," meaning the men are old, but the women are not necessarily old.

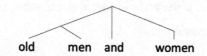

Figure 1.17　Tree diagram for another interpretation of "old men and women"

When we look at other phrase structure tree representations of English, we see certain patterns emerging: In ordinary sentences, the S is always subdivided into NP VP; NPs generally contain Nouns; VPs always contain Verbs (cf. Chapter X). These phrase structure rules form our syntactic knowledge, with which we are able to produce and understand sentences we have never heard before.

The process of syntax analysis and generation is essential to language processing, where it is referred as **parsing**. Google uses SyntaxNet as part of its NLP framework to parse sentences in an effort to understand what role each word plays and how they all come together to create real meaning (Metz, 2016). The system tries to identify what's a noun, what's a verb, what the subject refers to, how it relates to the object, and then using this information, it tries to extract what the sentence is generally about, in a form machines can read and manipulate. Modern NLP algorithms use statistical machine learning to apply these rules to deduce the most likely meaning behind what is said.

1.2.5   Semantics

Semantics is the study of meaning in language. It can be divided into two main areas: the study of meaning of words and meaning of phrases and sentences. The former is called lexical semantics and the latter, phrasal semantics.

Now consider the words:

aunt

maiden

widow

The part of meaning that all three words share is "female." "Female" is a semantic property that helps to define them.

aunt maiden widow	[+ female] [+ human]

They are also distinguished by the semantic property "human," which is also found in words such as *doctor*, *professor*, *bachelor*, *parent*, *baby*, and *child*.

doctor	
professor	
bachelor	[+ human]
parent	
baby	
child	

Our linguistic knowledge about words, their semantic properties, and the relationships among them are illustrated by the Garfield cartoon, which shows that [+small] is a semantic property of *morsel*, but not of *glob*.

Figure 1.18   Garfield, July 11, 1990 comic strips
Source: https://garfield.fandom.com/wiki/Garfield,_July_1990_comic_strips
(accessed May 4, 2024)

Words are related to one another in a variety of ways. These relationships have words to describe them that often end in the bound morpheme -*nym*, e.g., synonym, antonym, hyponym, and metonym.

Synonyms are words that have similar meaning, such as *shut* and *close*. A sign from Traverse City Zoo reads: Please do not *aggravate*, *agitate*, *annoy*, *badger*, *besiege*, *bother*, *discombobulate*, *disturb*, *distract*, *feed*, *grate*, *heckle*, *harass*, *harry*, *irk*, *molest*, *persecute*, *perturb*, *pester*, *plague*, *ruffle*, *tease*, *torment*, *touch*, *unsettle*, *upset*, *vex* or *worry* the animals. By listing numerous words with similar meanings, the sign illustrates the richness of the English language in expressing subtleties of meaning, as each of these words carries slightly different connotations, but all point to the same general behavior the zoo wants to discourage. Such variation in meaning demonstrates that while synonyms are related, they often capture different nuances, making each one unique in its context.

Figure 1.19   Sign of Traverse City Zoo Rules
Source: http://www.someblogsite.com/archives/date/2008/01 (accessed May 4, 2024)

Antonyms are words that are opposite in meaning. They typically share all but one semantic property, viz. the property is present in one and absent in the other. For instance,

A word that is [+heavy] is [-light]
A word that is [+light] is [-heavy]

A **hyponym** is a more specific term that falls under the umbrella of a more general term. For example, red, green yellow, blue, etc., are "color" words, i.e., their lexical representations have the feature [+color] indicating a class they all belong to. The relationship of hyponymy is between the more general term *color* and the more specific instances of it such as *red*.

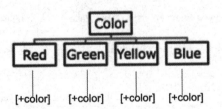

Figure 1.20   Hyponyms have a common semantic property indicating a class they all belong to

A **metonym** is a word or expression used in place of another word or expression which it is closely associated with to convey the same meaning. The connection is typically based on a relationship of proximity, context, or symbolism, e.g., the use of Beijing to refer to the Chinese government, and the White House for the executive branch of the U.S. government. Metonymy expresses meaning in a more indirect but often powerful or poetic way, as illustrated by the following examples,

Beijing calls for resolution of dispute.

The White House canceled the president's planned visit to Denmark.

So far, we have been talking about the meaning relationships and semantic properties on the lexical level. For the most part, however, we communicate in phrases and sentences. The meaning of a phrase or sentence depends on both the meaning of its words and how those words are combined structurally.

In all languages, the verb is central to the meaning and structure of most sentences (Fromkin and Rodman, 1998: 175). In English, the verb determines the number of objects and limits the semantic properties of both its subject and its objects. For example, *find* requires an animate subject and one object. The NP subject of a sentence and the constituents of the VP are semantically related in various way to the verb. The NP *the boy* in *the boy found a story book* is called the agent or doer of the action of finding, and the NP *a story book* is the theme and undergoes the action. Part of the meaning of *find* is that its subject is an agent and its direct object is a theme. In "the boy put the story book in the bag" *the story book* is the theme and *in the bag* is the goal; *the boy* performs the action. The semantic relationship that we have called theme, agent and goal are among the thematic roles of the verb (cf. Chapter X).

Thematic role	Description	Example
Agent	The one who performs an action	Jerry ran.
Theme	The one or thing that undergoes an action	Tom called Jerry.
Goal	The place to which an action is directed	Put the cat on the couch.
Location	The place where an action takes place	It rains in Shanghai.
Experiencer	One who perceives something	Tom heard Jerry playing the piano.
...		

Figure 1.21　Some common thematic roles of the verb

Semantic analysis is significant in NLP. For example, a huge component of Siri's strategy has been categorized under a semantic web (Hogan et al., 2020: 172), which incorporates location, synonyms of a term, current trends, word variations and other natural language elements as part of the search. For instance, when you ask Siri to "find me a sushi restaurant," it parses the NP "sushi restaurant" as the theme of the action "find"; it recognizes "sushi" as a real world concept, potentially including related terms like "food," "dining place," and "Japan."

Search engines know a significant amount about the semantics of natural language, including the meanings and relationships between words. They use smart techniques to detect patterns in search queries, their contexts, and user behavior to establish what a website is about, its relevance to various search queries, and its relative value compared to other websites.

1.2.6 Pragmatics

Compared with semantics, which is concerned with the specific meaning of language, **pragmatics** involves all the social cues that accompany language. It studies the relationships between linguistic forms and the users of those forms.

Pragmatics focuses not on what people say but how they say it and how others interpret their utterances in social contexts. Often, what we say is not literally what we mean. When we ask at the dinner table if someone "can pass the salt" we are not questioning their ability to do so; we are requesting that they do so.

In our daily life, conversation is based on a shared principle of cooperation. This principle is fleshed out in a number of maxims (cf. Chapter XIII).

1. Quantity
Say neither more nor less than the discourse requires

2. Relevance
Be relevant

3. Manner
Be brief and orderly; avoid ambiguity and obscurity

4. Quality
Do not lie; do not make unsupported claims

These maxims, or, more precisely, the violation of these maxims, form the basis for inferences that we draw in conversation. Different ways of violating these maxims give rise to different implications.

1)
A: How is your research going?
B: Sorry, that's confidential.
(Here clearly the maxim of quantity cannot be satisfied; no additional implicature needed.)

2)

C: Where's the Mellower Coffee Shop?

D: Somewhere in the Second Classroom Building.

(To avoid violating the maxim of quality—providing information you know to be untrue—D violates the maxim of quantity—providing less information than was asked for; possible implicature is that D does not know exactly where the coffee shop is.)

Unlike someone who is simply violating a maxim, someone who is **flouting** a maxim expects the listener to notice.

3)

E: Kabul's in Israel, isn't it?

F: Uh-huh, and Boston's in Armenia.

(F is flouting the maxim of quality to tell E Kabul is surely not in Israel.)

The flouting of a maxim is often used for comic effect. The following excerpt from the American Sitcom *Friends* (season 1 episode 1) briefly shows a few of the ways how real-world context influences and interacts with meaning.

4)

Rachel: Guess what?

Ross: You got a job?

Rachel: Are you kidding? I'm trained for nothing! I was laughed at in 12 interviews today.

Chandler: And yet you are surprisingly upbeat.

Rachel: You would be too if you found Joan and David boots on sale... 50% off.

Chandler: Oh, how well you know me...

(Chandler is obviously flouting the maxim of quality.)

...

Monica: Come on you can't live off your parents your whole life.

Rachel: I know that. That's why I was getting married.

Phoebe: Give her a break, it's hard being on your own for the first time.

Rachel: Thank you.

Phoebe: I remember when I first came to this city, I was 14. My mom had killed herself and my stepdad was back in prison. And I got here, and I didn't know anybody. And I ended up living with this albino guy who was cleaning windshields outside Port Authority. And then he killed himself. And then I found aromatherapy. So believe me, I know exactly how you feel.

(Here Phoebe violates the maxims of quantity and relevance, providing irrelevant information and far more information than needed.)

Pragmatics is vital for making interactions more natural with voice assistants, chatbots, and other conversational AI. Xiaodu Smart Speaker, developed by Baidu, is an example of a voice-activated smart speaker that incorporates some elements of social intelligence and pragmatic knowledge. In the following conversation, Xiaodu crafts a response that is both humorous and contextually relevant by using several pragmatic elements.

5)

G: 小度，小度，我的真心值多少钱？

(Xiaodu, Xiaodu, how much does my true heart worth?)

H: 你的心我的心串一串能卖两块五。

(Your heart and my heart strung together can sell for two and a half yuan.)

"你的心我的心串一串"(your heart and my heart strung together) is a lyric from the song *Love* by The Little Tigers, a popular boy band from the late 1980s. This song, with its catchy melody, was a big hit and remains widely recognized in Chinese-speaking communities. By referring to a lyric that resonates with many users, Xiaodu creates a sense of familiarity and connection. Moreover, the playful quality of "能卖两块五" (can sell for two and a half yuan) adds a humorous twist. It suggests that love, while precious, might not be valued in monetary terms, contrasting with the emotional weight typically associated with "true heart." Such layered understanding of language and context is a significant aspect of social intelligence in AI.

Summing-up

When people gather, they talk. Language—fluid, adaptive, and laden with intent—transcends mere words, embodying thought, emotion, and culture. It mirrors humanity itself: rooted in the need to reach one another, yet as complex and layered as the people who wield it.

At its surface, phonetics captures raw sounds, grounding spoken words in physical form, while phonology unveils patterns that give these sounds structure. Morphology, in turn, knits sounds into meaning-bearing units, threading these into the broader tapestry of syntax, where the rules of arrangement shape thought. Semantics deepens this framework, grappling with meaning itself, and finally, pragmatics emerges, demanding a sensitivity to context, intent, and the dance of human interaction. Each level discloses language as both a bridge and a barrier—essential for connection, yet rife with potential for misinterpretation. Effective communication often requires not just a shared language, but also shared context, cultural understanding, and awareness of each other's perspectives.

In language technology, computational difficulty escalates as we progress from phonetics to pragmatics, due to the increasing complexity and contextual dependency. These technologies—from writing to NLP—reshape how we think, interact, and perceive the world around us.

References

Fromkin, Victoria and Robert Rodman. 1998. *An Introduction to Language*. 6th ed. Fort Worth, Philadelphia, San Diego, New York, Orlando, Austin, San Antonio, Toronto, Montreal, London, Sydney & Tokyo: Harcourt Brace College Publishers.

Hogan, Aidan, Pascal Hitzler, Krzysztof Janowicz. 2020. "The Semantic Web: Two Decades On." *Semantic Web* 11, no. l: 169—185.

Hu, Zhuanglin, and Jiang Wangqi. 2002. *Linguistics: An Advanced Course Book*. Beijing: Peking University Press.

Ladefoged, Peter. 1962. *Elements of Acoustic Phonetics*. Chicago: University of Chicago Press.

Lieberman, Philip. 2007. "The Evolution of Human Speech: Its Anatomical and Neural Bases." *Current Anthropology* 48, no. 1: 39—66.

McBrearty, Sally, and Alison S. Brooks. 2000. "The Revolution That Wasn't: A New Interpretation of the Origin of Modern Human Behavior." *Journal of Human Evolution* 39, no. 5: 453—563.

McMahon, April. 2002. *An Introduction to English Phonology*. Edinburgh: Edinburgh University Press.

Metz, Cade. 2016. "Google Has Open Sourced SyntaxNet, Its AI for Understanding Language." *Wired*, May 12, 2016. https://www.wired.com/2016/05/google-open-sourced-syntaxnet-ai-natural-language/. (accessed Feb. 3, 2023)

Nichols, Johanna. 1998. "The Origin and Dispersal of Languages: Linguistic Evidence." In *The Origin and Diversification of Language*, edited by Nina G. Jablonski and Leslie C. Aiello, 127—170. San Francisco, CA: California Academy of Sciences.

O'Shaughnessy, Douglas. 2023. Trends and developments in automatic speech recognition research. *Computer Speech & Language* Vol. 83, Issue C. https://doi.org/10.1016/j.csl.2023.101538

Vachek, Josef. 1973. *Written Language: General Problems and Problems of English*. The Hague: Mouton.

———. 1989. *Written Language Revisited*. Philadelphia: John Benjamins.

Wester, Mirjam. 2003. "Pronunciation Modeling for ASR—Knowledge-based and Data-derived Methods." *Computer Speech & Language* 17, no.1: 69—85.

Zhang, Hang. 2018. *Second Language Acquisition of Mandarin Chinese Tones: Beyond First-Language Transfer*. Leiden & Boston: Brill Rodopi.

Further reading: excerpt from "The Faculty of Language: What Is It, Who Has It, and How Did It Evolve?"

Hauser, Marc, Noam Chomsky, Tecumseh Fitch. 2002. "The Faculty of Language: What Is It, Who Has It, and How Did It Evolve?" *Science* Vol. 298 (22): 1569—1579. Excerpt, 1570—1571.

Chapter II　How Writing Came About

Jumping-in

The term "rebus" comes from the Latin phrase *non verbis, sed rebus*, which means "not by words, but by things." Below is a rebus puzzle, using pictures to represent words which form a sentence when combined. Can you guess what it is?

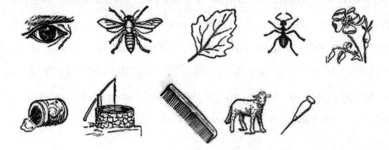

Language is temporally ephemeral and spatially anchored. An artificial device that is created to represent language in a durable and readable form is writing. It expresses languages by "system of more or less permanent marks" (Daniels, 1996: 3), a mode of human communication "parallel to speech and not necessarily subservient to it" (Sampson, 1985: 11). In this sense, writing is the first language-related technology in human history. It enables language to be transmitted across time and space, and allows language to be reconstructed by humans separated by time or space. It permits a society to permanently record its history, literature, science and technology, thereby cognitively as well as sociologically underpinning civilization. The invention of writing therefore is one of the greatest intellectual and cultural achievements.

A stone with inscription dating to the Warring States Period of ancient China (475 BCE—221 BCE) serves as a best example. According to historian, archaeologist, and palaeographer Li Xueqin (Hebei Provincial Institute of Cultural Relics and Archaeology, 2005:16), it reads, "监罟尤臣公乘得守丘，丌臼将曼敢谒后未贤者," which can be translated as "Gongsheng De, who monitors fishing for the king, is guarding the tomb here. Man, his former subordinate, leaves the note to inform gentlemen of the future generations." A romantic floating bottle, the stone carries to us the greetings of our ancestors from 2,300 years ago.

Figure 2.1   Replica of stone with the inscription Jian You Shou Qiu, exhibited in the Hebei Museum
Source: Left: photo taken by the author on Oct. 25, 2023; Right: https://tool.wikichina.com/shufaxinshang/1051.htm
(accessed Aug. 31, 2024)

2.1   How writing originated

How did writing come about? Prior to the 18th century, the creation of writing was the stuff of myths or legends. In a Greek legend, Cadmus, Prince of Phoenicia and founder of the city of Thebes, invented the alphabet and brought it with him to Greece. In Chinese legends, Cang Jie, the four-eyed dragon-god, invented characters in the wilderness. In a Babylonian myth, the Babylonian god Nabu and the Egyptian god Thoth gave humans writing as well as speech. In a Sumerian lore, the goddess Nisaba invented writing and record-keeping. In the Bible, God revealed his will to mankind with the Tables of the Law "written with the finger of God"(KJV, Exodus 31: 18). In these stories, writing systems came into being spontaneously and fully blown. Delightful as they are, the invention of writing in fact comes relatively late in human history, and its development was gradual. As a technology, writing must be taught to each generation of children.

2.1.1   Pictographic theory

In the 18th century, William Warburton (1698—1779), an English writer, literary critic and Bishop of Gloucester, treated the history of writing as a side-issue in a monumental work in nine books on *The Divine Legation of Moses* (1738—1741). In this theological work, Warburton relates the second of the Ten Commandments, i.e., no idolatry, to hieroglyphic writing and thinking. He contends that hieroglyphic writing (see Chapter IV for details) is a specifically Egyptian phenomenon because Egypt is the only civilization that retained the pictorial character of its writing and resisted the usual tendency towards abstraction. He goes on to delineate different stages in the development of idolatry. In the first stage, the figures of animals are just signs which stand for some tutelary gods or deified hero-kings. In the second stage, these figures are worshipped on their own instead of simply being "read" as signs for the various gods. This stage was reached during Moses' time, and that is the reason why the second commandment prohibits the making of images, not the worship of the things themselves.

Based on the traditional idea that an alphabetic script called the Epistolic or Demotic was used alongside with the Hieroglyphic in ancient Egypt, Warburton makes the assumption: the Hieroglyphic was the original and the Demotic was created later; then the Hieroglyphic was reserved for sacred knowledge, and the Demotic was used for communication. He contends that at Moses' time the Demotic was already in use, and Moses chose this script to write down the Law in order to conform to the second commandment.

Thus, Warburton categorizes writing systems as two types: pictorial scripts that represent images or ideas and alphabetic scripts that represent the sounds. He argues that pictorial scripts presuppose a vast amount of knowledge about the nature of those things that are used for signs. New alphabetic scripts lost this epistemological connection with the visible world and turned into purely conventional codes. He describes the process of the development of writing as follows:

> Men soon found out two ways of communicating their thoughts to one another; the first by SOUNDS, and the second by FIGURES: for there being frequent occasion to have their conceptions either perpetuated, or communicated at a distance, the way of figures or characters was next thought upon, after sounds (which were momentary and confined), to make their conceptions lasting and extensive. The first and most natural way of communicating our conceptions by marks or figures, was by tracing out the images of things. To express, for instance, the idea of a man or horse, the informer delineated the form of each of those animals. Thus the first essay towards writing was a mere picture. (Warburton, 1741: 216—217)

Before the invention of the latter type, writing referred to things, not to sounds. Warburton discusses the Mexican Aztec script, Egyptian hieroglyphics and Chinese script as representatives of three stages in the development of writing representing images or ideas. He believes all scripts of this type developed from narrative drawings that became more simplified and abstract over time.

One thing to note is Warburton believes that the development of writing is closely related to the degree of civilization. "Before the invention or introduction of letters, all barbarous nations upon earth made use of hieroglyphics or signs for things, to record their meaning, the more gross, representation, the more subtle and civilized, by analogy and institution." (1738: 44) In other words, progress in civilization shows a gravitation from pictures to letters.

However, attributing the type of writing to the degree of civilization fails to explain why Chinese, one of the oldest writing-systems, is still in use. Oracle bone inscription, i.e., pictographic inscriptions on ox bone or tortoise shell dating from the 14th to the 11th centuries BCE, is the earliest known Chinese writing. Oracle bones were part of pyromantic divination ceremony in which bones inscribed with prophetic markings were burnt over fire until the bones cracked. Prophets interpreted cracks through the inscriptions. During the course of this long history, major changes took place: its overall inventory of characters grew, the shape of the characters evolved and underwent multiple reforms and standardizations, and most recently, the layout structure of Chinese text also altered. The nature of the writing system, however, remained the same. From oracle bone inscription to modern regular script, Chinese writing on the one hand supports the tendency of simplification and abstraction, on the other hand refutes the idea that the form of writing is decided by the level of civilization.

Picture	Oracle Bone Inscription	Small Seal Character	Official Script	Complex Character in Regular Script	Simplified Character in Regular Script
馬(picture)	𢒉	馬	馬	馬	马

Figure 2.2   The evolution of Character 马 (horse) from Oracle Bone Inscriptions to Simplified Chinese

2.1.2 Token theory

Although Warburton's Pictographic Theory failed to offer a perfect explanation of writing systems like Chinese, it had remained the basis for most explanations of the origin of writing for more than 200 years until excavations at the site of the ancient Sumerian city Uruk (1929—1930, 1930—1931) unearthed clay tablets from 4000 BCE, on which many abstract symbols challenged pictographic origin.

The site of Uruk is located in present-day Iraq, on an abandoned channel of the Euphrates River. It covered approximately 250 hectares, and has been called "the first city in world history" by western archaeologists. From the start of excavation at Uruk in the early 1900s, archaeologists found clay tablets with pictographic signs that were recognized as precursors to cuneiform script. The tablets unearthed during the season of 1929 and 1930 were dated to an earlier phase than those of previous

Figure 2.3   Early writing: a proto-cuneiform record of sheep from c. 3400 BCE
This small administrative tablet from Uruk comes from the period of the earliest known examples of writing (c. 3450 BCE—3200 BCE). Impressed into clay, the proto-cuneiform signs on the obverse of this tablet (upper part of photo) indicate seven male sheep, and the tablet likely represents an administrative record.
Uruk IV, c. 3450 BCE—3200 BCE.
Source: Vorderasiatisches Museum, Berlin. Photo courtesy of CDLI.

discoveries. However, these tablets contain some commonly used signs that have arbitrary relationship to their referents, which contradicts the line of thought that writing evolves from the concrete to the abstract. A classic example is that the sign for "sheep" was a circle with a cross inside.

Excavations elsewhere in Mesopotamia steadily produced small clay objects intentionally crafted into many shapes such as cones, spheres, disks, and cylinders, dated to as early as 8000 BCE. These small artifacts are now known as "tokens" as a result of Denise Schmandt-Besserat's work (1992). What were these tokens for?

Figure 2.4   Tokens from Tepe Gawra, present day Iraq, c. 4000 BCE
Source: https://sites.utexas.edu/dsb/tokens/tokens/ (accessed Aug. 31, 2024)

The earliest interpretative study is by Leo Oppenheim (1959), which proved to be key in understanding what the tokens were. The paper concerns a clay bulla, i.e., hollow egg-shaped clay envelope, recovered from the second millennium BCE Nuzi, an ancient city in present-day northern Iraq. It was marked with cuneiform inscriptions on the outside and contained 48 tokens inside. The inscriptions read as follows:

> Stones (referring) to sheep and goats:
> 21 ewes that have given birth
> 6 female lambs
> 8 full grown rams
> 4 male (!) lambs
> 6 she-goats that have given birth
> 1 h[e-goat(!)
> 2] female kids—seal of Ziqarru

As the number of tokens corresponded to the number of animals listed, Oppenheim proposes that the bulla was "a simple device to control the transfer of animals entrusted to illiterate shepherds, to whom the number of pebbles was meant to suggest tangibly the number of sheep and goats in their care"(1959: 123). His proposal was crucial in linking the tokens to counting and administration.

Figure 2.5　HSS 16 149, a clay bulla from Nuzi with an inscription listing the 48 sheep and goats forming the flock entrusted to the shepherd Ziqarru, and which contained 48 stones when found
Source: MacGinnis, et al. 2014

Oppenheim's work sparked subsequent investigations into early administrative systems in Mesopotamia by linking tokens, bullae, seals, and writing. A most prominent leader in this field is Denise Schmant-Besserat (born 1933), who has since the 1970s advanced detailed theories as to the evolution of the use of tokens and their supposed decline with the advent of writing in the third millennium BCE.

Schmant-Besserat (1992, 1996) presents the following hypothesis: the tokens represented various commodities. Before 3250 BCE they were presumably kept in perishable containers; but after this date they were preserved in clay envelopes, each representing a commodity aggregate. This was owed by one person to another or, more often, owed to a temple precinct. At the same time there existed an alternative system using the same tokens. However, these were perforated, stringed, and held together by a sealed button of clay. The debtor was identified with the seal (wrapped around the envelope or impressed on the clay connecting the ends of the strings). This system served as a counting device and an accounting method for control of goods in the pre-historic cultures of the Near East. The envelope was further improved from 3200 BCE. By this time, each token was impressed on the outside of the envelope before it was placed into the receptacle. This enabled identification of the debtor and also a quick identification of the contents without opening the envelope. Once it was realized that markings on the outer surface of an envelope were unnecessary, solid tablets and solid clay balls bearing markings were then used to replace the hollow envelopes filled with tokens. The markings gradually became a system of their own, a system of writing. Based on the above, Schmandt-Beserat concludes that the immediate precursor of cuneiform writing was a system of tokens.

Schmandt-Beserat then summarizes three evolutionary phases of counting: (1) one-to-one correspondence (mainly through tallies, pebbles, and the like); (2) concrete counting (mainly with tokens); and (3) abstract counting (with numerals). The token system reflected an archaic mode of "concrete" counting. She concludes that writing is the outcome of abstract counting which is not, as previously assumed, subservient to writing (cf. Further reading).

Schmandt-Besserat's theory is based on the visual similarities between the elements of the token and writing systems. According to her, the simple, undecorated tokens, which first made their appearance with the beginnings of agriculture in the ninth millennium, developed into the numerical graphs (e.g., those in Figure 2.4). The so-called complex tokens, those that have various markings and incisions and are regarded as a hallmark of the burgeoning urban societies of the fourth millennium, became the logograms of cuneiform (e.g., those in Figure 2.6).

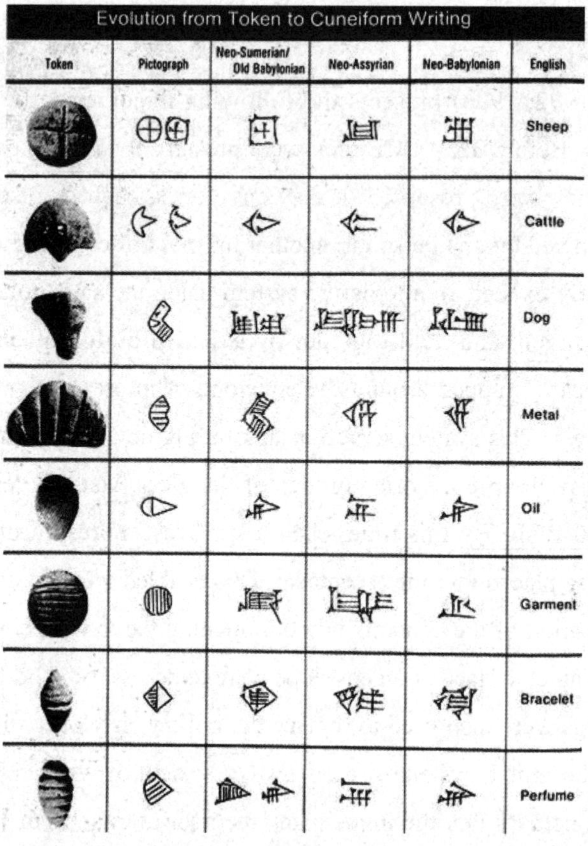

Figure 2.6   Evolution from token to cuneiform writing
Source: https://ancientmesopotamians.com/ancient-mesopotamia-writing-system.html (accessed Aug. 31, 2024)

Although held sway, Schmandt-Besserat's theory is open to criticism. Woods (2015b: 48—49) summarises a few problems that render it controversial: First, it is unlikely that tokens remained a uniform accounting system over such a long period—from the 9th millennium to the end of the 4th millennium, and over such a vast geographic territory—from the Mediterranean to Iran; Second, the lynchpin of the theory—that tokens look like cueiform signs—is subjective, and many identifications are not plausible; Third, the assumption that a symbol present in two distinct systems—in this case the tokens of a prehistoric accounting system and proto-cuneiform—must necessarily have the same value is a methodological pitfall in decipherment, for it is entirely possible that the shared symbol has different values or meanings, in the respective systems.

In short, the origin of writing is a problem of archaelogical evdience as well as theoretical interpretation. The interpretation is largely based on archaelogical data collection and classification. At the same time, new discoveries may overturn or force revisions of theoretical positions. Archaelological research and discoveries are constantly evolving, and ongoing research may shed further light on the intricacies of its early development. In this sense, the origin of cuneiform writing is yet to be fully understood.

2.2   Logogram at the root of invented writing

Under the Pictogrpahic Theory, signs of the pre-cuneiform writing are pictographs of their referents; under the Token Theory, they are pictographs of tokens, i.e., symbolic representations of other symbols. Now let us take the Sumerian word "lugal" (𒈗), which means "king," as an example. In Sumerian, this word is composed of two morphemes:

lu: "man" or "person" 𒇽
gal: "big" or "great" 𒃲

When combined, "lu" and "gal" form the word "lugal," which literally means "big man" or "great person." In the context of ancient Sumerian society, "lugal" referred to a ruler, a king, or a leader, as they were considered the "big men" or "great persons" of the city-states.

Pictographs, in whichever sense, as cuneiform writing evolved and became more complex, started to turn into **logograms**—graphs that represent individual word or, more accurately, morpheme, i.e., the smallest meaningful unit in a language—for scribes to express more abstract concepts and ideas beyond simple pictorial representations. These logographic elements are the crux in committing language to writing.

Over time, the cuneiform script incorporated not only logograms but also **phonograms**— signs that represent syllables or sounds. This combination of logograms and phonograms made cuneiform a more versatile writing system capable of representing a wide range of linguistic elements. As the writing system evolved, logograms and phonograms became more prominent, allowing for a more extensive range of concepts to be expressed in writing.

However, it's important to note that cuneiform writing was highly versatile and flexible, and scribes could use a combination of these sign types within a single text. The mix of signs depended on the intended content of the document. Administrative texts might have a higher proportion of logograms for record-keeping, while literary texts might use more syllabic signs for phonetic representation. Moreover, the distribution of sign types can also vary among different ancient scripts that used cuneiform, such as Sumerian cuneiform, Akkadian cuneiform, Elamite cuneiform, and others. Each script had its own set of signs and usage patterns.

Logogram was at the root of all early full writing systems, i.e., systems widely accepted as inventions without any external influence. The "pristine writing systems," as Woods (2015a: 15) calls them, appeared independently of each other at the dawn of human civilizations. Cuneiform was developed between 3400 BCE and 3300 BCE in Mesopotamia, and shortly afterwards at around 3200 BCE hieroglyph was born in Egypt. Oracle bone inscription emerged by 1300 BCE in late Shang-dynasty China. Olmec-Maya script appeared sometime between 900 BCE and 600 BCE in the cultures of Mesoamerica.

Figure 2.7   Examples of cuneiform script, Egyptian hieroglyph, oracle bone inscription, and maya script
Source:
Left: Summary account of silver for the govenor written in Sumerian Cuneiform on a clay tablet. From Shuruppak or Abu Salabikh, Iraq, circa 2500 BCE. British Museum, London. BM 15826
Left center: Hieroglyphs at Kom ombo temple. https://commons.wikimedia.org/wiki/File:Egypt_Hieroglyphe2.jpg (accessed Aug. 31, 2024)
Right center: Oracle bone recording divinations by Zhēng 争, one of the Bīn 宾 group of diviners from period I, corresponding to the reign of King Wu Ding (late Shang dynasty). https://commons.wikimedia.org/wiki/File:Shang_dynasty_inscribed_scapula.jpg (accessed Aug. 31, 2024)
Right: Maya stucco glyphs diplayed in the museum at Palenque, Mexico. https://commons.wikimedia.org/wiki/File:Palenque_glyphs-edit1.jpg (accessed Aug. 31, 2024)

If we draw a continuum to represent the morphemic structure of these four writing systems, Chinese would be positioned at the higher end as the most morpheme-based. In Classical Chinese, the vast majority of words were composed of single syllables, each carrying specific semantic information. Take the phrase " 天玄地黄 " from the ancient Chinese text *Yijing* (《易经》) as an example:

天 (tiān): "sky"
玄 (xuán): "black"
地 (dì): "earth"
黄 (huáng): "yellow"

Together, the phrase " 天玄地黄 ," meaning "The sky is black and the earth is yellow," encapsulates significant aspects of ancient Chinese worldview, especially the associations between five elements, colors and cardinal directions.

By comparison, modern Standard Chinese has developed into a more polysyllabic language with compound words. For example, the word " 电话 " is a compound consisting of two monosyllabic morphemes:

电 (diàn): "electric" or "electricity"
话 (huà): "speech" or "language"

When combined, " 电 " and " 话 " form the word " 电话 " (diànhuà), meaning "telephone." Now modern Chinese includes many compound words like this, where multiple morphemes come together to form a single word with a specific meaning. They often represent new concepts or phenomena, thereby becoming a flexible way of lexical expansion.

Morphemes have a greater psychological salience for native speakers than the phonemes, or sounds, that constitute morphemes (Sampson, 1985: 36). This is due to the nature of language processing, as native speakers quickly recognize and process entire words as units of meaning. People think in terms of morphemes and syllables, and they are immediately apparent to speakers without the linguistic awareness that allows for the dissection of language into units smaller than the syllable. In contrast, phonemes are often processed more automatically and unconsciously during language production and comprehension. Woods (2015a: 21) points out that to those reared on the alphabet, dividing words into individual sounds smaller than morphemes is not intuitive, but requires a level of linguistic training, which one acquires when one learns how to read and write. Thus, it comes as no surprise that none of the pristine writing systems is alphabetic. Further, morphemes, specifically nouns, can often be represented by motivated, iconic symbols, i.e., by pictures or pictographs, an option that naturally facilitates both the creation and learning of a script. On the other hand, morphemes that do not lend themselves to iconic representation can be expressed by relying upon homonymy and the rebus principle.

2.3 Mechanism in action: the rebus principle

The use of an existing symbol, such as a pictogram, to represent a similar-sounding morpheme unrelated in meaning is referred to in linguistics as the rebus principle. The rebus principle played a significant role in the transition from proto-writing to true writing, allowing for the representation of words or parts of words that may not have a direct pictorial representation. By using the rebus principle, early civilizations could repurpose existing symbols to represent phonetic elements, like sounds or syllables. For example, in English an image of an eye 👁 could be used to represent the sound "I" l👁ke this.

In modern-day texting, however, for this principle to work the symbols involved do not have to be pictograms. For example, "c u l8er" representing "see you later" contain three rebuses: "c" for "see," "u" for "you," and the number "8" for "ate" in "later."

2.3.1 Sumerian cuneiform

By about 2,800 BCE some of the Sumerian glyphs were being used to represent sounds using the rebus principle. For example, the symbol for arrow, pronounced *ti* in Sumerian, was also used to represent the word for life, pronounced *til*, or the word for rib, likewise pronounced *ti* (Powell, 2009: 71—72). Over time, many glyphs could be pronounced the same way while representing different words. To disambiguate the meanings of such glyphs, scribes developed a system of determinatives, which gave one a hint at the category a word belonged to, and of phonetic components, which indicated how to pronounce a word. When the rebus principle was applied to all sounds, the writing system reached a tipping point. In the case of Sumerian cuneiform, which is primarily syllabic, scribes soon discovered that they could combine graphemes (representing single syllables such as [ti]) to form compounds. Through compounding, scribes could express even more complex meanings and relationships, ultimately constructing phrases and clauses. By 2500 BCE, cuneiform system turned into a true writing.

The first example of the rebus principle is believed to be a clay tablet dating back to around 3400 BCE, discovered in the ancient city of Uruk. It recorded the sale of 135,000 measures of barley and was signed "Kushim," the presumed name or title of the person who was in charge of the transaction. Written in a corner (, bottom left of Figure 2.8), "Kushim" combines two symbols that resemble the later known Sumerian syllabic glyphs, thus are believed to translate phonetically as ku and shim. Niessen et al. (1993: 36—46) provide more entries relating to the administrative activities of Kushim, indicating the role of an official responsible for a storage facility containing the basic ingredients for the production of beer. As barley left the granaries of Kushim for processing, the quantities were added up, with each entry quoting the title of the official, thereby locating responsibility for the allocated barley with.

Figure 2.8   The Kushim Clay Tablet (MS 1717, held in the Schøyen Collection in Oslo, Sweden)
Source: https://www.schoyencollection.com/24-smaller-collections/wine-beer/ms-1717-beer-inanna-uruk
(accessed Feb. 3, 2023)

2.3.2   Oracle bone inscriptions

Featuring numerous monosyllabic words, the Old Chinese language had a high amount of homophony or near-homophony, which ensured the potential for extensive rebus. According to Bottéro (2004: 251), 80 percent of the Shang iconic signs represented not just the words conveyed by their iconicity, but also other words unrelated in meaning but similar in sound. A well-known example of the rebus principle in Late Shang oracle bone inscriptions is shown as below.

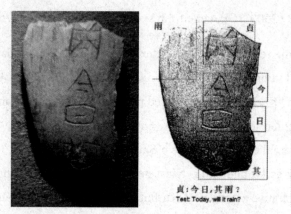

Figure 2.9　Late Shang oracle bone inscriptions 贞今日其雨 (Test: Today, will it rain?)
Source: https://commons.wikimedia.org/wiki/File:OracleSun.jpg (accessed Feb. 21, 2023)

The bone bears ancient character forms of 贞今日其雨 (Test: Today, will it rain?), with 贞今日其 in the vertical sequence on the right and 雨 on the top left. The symbol invented for the word "duspan" 箕 was used for the similar-sounding word "modal particle" 其 . This example shows that the rebus principle was often applied to words with abstract meaning (Shen, 2019).

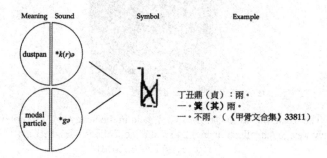

Figure 2.10　An example of rebus principle in oracle bone writing
Source: Shen, 2019

2.4　Mechanism in action: the acrophonic principle

Compared to Sumerian and Old Chinese scripts, where rebus was used exclusively, Egyptian and Mayan scripts used rebus supplemented by the acrophonic principle. Acrophony uses a written sign which originally took the form of a pictorial or logographic symbol of an object to represent the initial sound of that object. For example, in Egyptian the hieroglyph ⌒ *ft* depicting a deadly horned viper is used for the sound *f*. This phonetic value was then extended to represent other words that began with the same sound, even if they had different meanings.

2.4.1   Egyptian hieroglyph

The Egyptian writing system, as mentioned earlier, comprises logograms, semantic determinatives, and phonograms. Phonograms were of three kinds: uniconsonantals (26 signs), biconsonantals (ca. 80 signs) and triconsonantals (ca. 70 signs) (Loprieno & Müller, 2012: 106). As the names indicate, these signs expressed either a single consonant or skeletons of two or three consonants, vowels being omitted. This structure is tied to the morphology of the language, where related words share a common core of consonants, and semantic nuances were marked by vocalic changes, affixes, or both. Take the root consonantal skeleton "k-t-b" as an example:

- Kutub - Scribes (nominative plural)
- Kātib - Writer (singular)
- Kitābah - Writing (noun)
- Kutayyib - Well-written (adjective)

In this example, the consonantal root "k-t-b" relates to the concept of writing. The variations in meaning and grammatical forms are achieved through changes in vowels and affixes. Both vowels and consonants participated in morphological activity, but only consonants were notated in full. This distinction between consonants and vowels arises from the fact that Egyptian consonantal roots hold the core semantic information and, in many cases, the context in which a word was used would provide enough information for readers to infer the appropriate vowels. People who were already familiar with the language and its vocabulary would be able to correctly interpret words based on the consonantal skeleton and the surrounding text.

In contrast, many affixes consisted of only one consonant, and were transcribed with uniconsonantal signs. For example,

- *sš* (scribe, masculine) → *sšt* (fscribe, feminine)
- *šps* (apprentice, masculine) → *špst* - apprentice (feminine)
- *nṯr* (god, masculine) → *nṯrt* (goddess, feminine)
- *ḥr* (high, masculine) → *ḥrt* (high, feminine)
- *wsir* (mighty, masculine) → *wsirt* (mighty, feminine)
- *ḫnt* (small, masculine) → *ḫntt* (small, feminine)

- *jr* (to do) → *jrt* (she does)
- *šn* (to go) → *šnt* (she goes)
- *ḥr* (to see) → *ḥrt* (she sees)

These examples showcase how the "-t" suffix is added to the root words to mark the feminine singular form of nouns, adjectives, and verbs. The need for writing such affixes contributes to the preference for acrophony.

2.4.2 Maya script

Maya is essentially deciphered (with some uncertainties) and represents a logo-syllabary (Valério and Ferrara, 2020). In a logo-syllabary, certain characters (logograms) represent whole words or morphemes, while others (syllabograms) represent syllabic sounds. For example, the glyph ⟨image⟩ represents the word *ut* "eye, face," and the glyph ⟨image⟩ represents the syllable *mo*. More often than not, logograms and syllabograms are combined in a complex way with a great deal of polyvalence, hence most glyphs serve as logograms that can be spelled syllabically.

Many syllabograms were derived acrophonically from the opening syllable of earlier logograms (Houston et al., 2000: 328; Kettunen and Zender, 2019). For example, the syllable *cho* is derived from the word *chol*, "lower jaw," the syllable *mo* is based on the eye of a Guacamaya parrot (*mo'*), and *hu* is derived from the head of an iguana, *huj* in most Maya languages. In the acrophonic process, words lose the final, usually weak consonant and thus the relationship to their original meaning (Grube, 2021).

2.5　Extension and differentiation

Rebus tends to appear as the first choice for phonetisation, as it is direct, intuitive and economical. It uses existing signs (logograms) and expands their values, operating on homophony and syllabic correspondences. Acrophony is the alternative to rebus, as it is indirect and requires some linguistic/phonological awareness. It uses existing signs or leads to the invention of new ones. It truncates morphemes and may be syllabic or segmental (Valério and Ferrara, 2020). By this process, logograms are associated with stable sound values, and thus become elements of an incipient writing system.

After the rebus and acrophonic principles have been widely applied, further development occurs through extension and differentiation. The symbols that were initially used to represent specific words or syllables start to be used for other words with similar sounds. This extension involves broadening the usage of existing symbols to cover a wider vocabulary. This step is crucial for achieving a more comprehensive representation of the spoken language. As the writing system expands to cover a larger vocabulary, the need arises to differentiate between words that may sound similar but have different meanings. This leads to the creation of new symbols or modifications of existing ones to represent distinct sounds or meanings. Differentiation helps improve the precision and clarity of the writing system, making it more suitable for conveying a wide range of information.

In the case of oracle bone inscriptions, for example, by rebus 马/馬(mǎ) "horse" later on was also used to represent the morpheme mā "mother", because mā has a similar sound to mǎ "horse." However, representing two morphemes with the same character eventually became confusing, and the need arose to be able to differentiate the morphemes from each other. Thus, a semantic component 女 "female" was added to 马/馬 to form a new compound character 妈/媽 (mā) "mother." This new character is a semantic-phonetic compound, combining a component that indicates the meaning and a component that provides a clue to its pronunciation. According to Rogers (2005: 45), by the 2nd century CE semantic-phonetic compounds became about four times as large as all the other categories combined. This trend continues. By the 18th century, semantic-phonetic compounds were estimated to constitute about 97% of characters in common use, as noted by Li (2020: 46).

Period	Pictogram %	Abstract pictogram %	Semantic-semantic compound %	Semantic-phonetic compound %	Number of Characters
12th-11th century BCE	23.9	1.7	34.3	28.9	1,155
2nd century CE	3.8	1.3	12.3	81.2	9,475
8th century CE	2.5	0.5	3.1	90.0	24,235

Figure 2.11   Different types of characters as percentage of total inventory over time
Source: Li, 2020: 46 (adapted from Rogers, 2005: 45)

In the case of Sumerian cuneiforms, graphemes (representing single syllables such as [ti]) were combined to form compounds. Through compounding, scribes could express even more complex meanings and relationships, ultimately constructing phrases and clauses.

Summing-up

The pictographic theory posits that writing began with pictograms, which evolved into more complex symbols representing sounds and words. It underscores the gradual abstraction process, where concrete images are used to represent more complex and abstract concepts. The token theory suggests that writing originated from a system of counting and record-keeping using clay tokens, which were used to represent commodities and were eventually impressed onto clay tablets to form the earliest scripts.

While the pictographic and token theories offer different perspectives on the origins of writing, the rebus principle is a common thread committing writing to the representation of language. By using symbols to represent sounds, both theories explain how early writing systems could move beyond simple pictographs or tokens to encode the full range of language. This innovation was critical in the development of writing as a versatile and powerful tool for human communication.

The progression from the rebus and acrophonic principles to extension and differentiation is a natural evolution in the development of a writing system. It reflects the need to adapt the system to effectively represent the complexities of language, encompassing a broader inventory and ensuring clear communication in cases of words with similar sounds. Ultimately, the system moved from forerunners of writing to writing proper, a system of visible marks that could represent language in its entirety. From this system, one is able to recover the spoken words, unambiguously, as demonstrated by the four pristine writing systems which commonly encode both sound and meaning.

References

Bottéro, Françoise. 2004. "Writing on Shell and Bone in Shang China." In *The First Writing: Script Invention as History and Process*, edited by Stephen D. Houston. Cambridge: Cambridge University Press.

Daniels, Peter. 1996. "The Study of Writing Systems." In *The World's Writing Systems*, edited by Peter Daniels and William Bright. Oxford: Oxford University Press.

Grube, Nikolai. 2021. "Writing with Heads: Animated Logographs and Syllabograms in Maya Writing." *Estudios Latinoamericanos* 41: 165—180. https://doi.org/10.36447/Estudios2021.v41.art9.

Houston, Stephen, John Robertson, and David Stuart. 2000. "The Language of Classic Maya Inscriptions." *Current Anthropology* 41(3): 321—356.

Kettunen, Harri, and Marc Zender. 2019. "On the Graphic and Lexical Origins of Maya Syllabograms." In *Tiempo detenido, un tiempo suficiente: Ensayos y narraciones mesoamericanistas en homenaje a Alfonso Lacadena García Gallo*, edited by Harri Kettunen, María Josefa Iglesias Ponce de León, Felix Kupprat, Gaspar Muñoz Cosme, Verónica Amellali Vázquez López, and Cristina Vidal Lorenzo. Wayeb Publication Series, Vol. 1.

Li, Yu. 2020. *The Chinese Writing System in Asia: An Interdisciplinary Perspective*. London and New York: Routledge.

Loprieno, Antonio, and Matthias Müller. 2012. "Ancient Egyptian and Coptic." In *The Afroasiatic Languages*, edited by Zygmunt Frajzyngier and Erin Shay. Cambridge: Cambridge University Press.

MacGinnis, John, et al. 2014. "Artefacts of Cognition: The Use of Clay Tokens in a Neo-Assyrian Provincial Administration." *Cambridge Archaeological Journal* 24(2): 289—306.

Niessen, Hans J., Peter Damerow, and Robert K. Englund. 1993. Translated by Paul Larsen. *Archaic Bookkeeping: Writing and Techniques of Economic Administration in the Ancient Near East*. Chicago and London: The University of Chicago Press.

Oppenheim, Leo. 1959. "On an Operational Device in Mesopotamian Bureaucracy." *Journal of Near Eastern Studies* 18(2): 121—128.

Powell, Barry. 2009. *Writing: Theory and History of the Technology of Civilization*. Malden: Wiley-Blackwell.

Rogers, Henry. 2005. *Writing Systems: A Linguistic Approach*. Malden: Blackwell Publishing.

Sampson, Geoffrey. 1985. *Writing Systems: A Linguistic Introduction*. Redwood City: Stanford University Press.

Schmandt-Besserat, Denise. 1992. *Before Writing: From Counting to Cuneiform*. Austin: University of Texas Press.

Schmandt-Besserat, Denise. 1996. *How Writing Came About*. Austin: University of Texas Press.

Shen, Ruiqing. "The Monosyllabicization of Old Chinese and the Birth of Chinese Writing: A Hypothesis on the Co-evolution of the Chinese Language and Its Writing System." *Journal of Language Relationship* 17(1—2): 44—54.

Valério, Miguel, and Silvia Ferrara. 2020. "Rebus and Acrophony in Invented Writing." *Writing Systems Research* 11(1): 66—93. Published online March 16, 2020. https://doi.org/10.1080/17586801.2020.1724239.

Warburton, William. 1738—1741. *The Divine Legation of Moses*. London: Printed for A. Millar, and J. and R. Tonson.

Woods, Christopher. 2015a. "Introduction—Visible Language: The Earliest Writing Systems." In *Visible Language: Inventions of Writing in the Ancient Middle East and Beyond*, edited by Christopher Woods. Chicago: The Oriental Institute of the University of Chicago.

Woods, Christopher. 2015b. "The Earliest Mesopotamian Writing." In *Visible Language: Inventions of Writing in the Ancient Middle East and Beyond*, edited by Christopher Woods. Chicago: The Oriental Institute of the University of Chicago.

河北省文物研究所，2005，《战国中山国灵寿城——1975～1993年考古发掘报告》，北京：文物出版社。

Further reading: excerpt from *How Writing Came About*

Schmandt-Besserat, Denise. 1996. "Chapter VII Counting and the Emergence of Writing." In *How Writing Came About*, 117—122. Texas: University of Texas Press.

Chapter III　How Writing Represents Language

Jumping-in

Consider the following series of symbols, the beginning of a pictographic story. Do your best to translate them into English. Do these symbols constitute a writing system? Please explain why or why not in a short paragraph.

Figure 3.1　A series of symbols taken from *Book from the Ground: From Point to Point* by Xu Bing (2014)

The series of symbols in the figure above are taken from an avant-garde novel *Book from the Ground: From Point to Point* by Xu Bing (born 1955), an internationally acclaimed artist whose work has been shown and collected by museums and galleries including the National Art Museum of China, the British Museum, the Museum of Contemporary Art Los Angeles, the Museum of Modern Art New York, the Metropolitan Museum of Art, and the Arthur M. Sackler Gallery at the Smithsonian Museum. He is a recipient of a MacArthur "genius" grant and is currently serving as a professor at the Central Academy of Art, Beijing.

Xu Bing presents a graphic novel—one composed entirely of symbols and icons. He spent seven years gathering materials, experimenting, revising, and arranging thousands of pictograms to construct the narrative of *Book from the Ground*, a book intended to be "universally understood" by those thoroughly entangled in modern life.

Innovative exploration as it is, this system may not be equally accessible to all audiences: people across cultures may interpret certain symbols and icons differently. For instance, an icon representing food might be interpreted differently based on regional cuisine, and those showing socializing in a bar might not be easily understood by those strange to Western lifestyle; Some individuals might not be accustomed to deciphering visual narratives and could have difficulty connecting the dots between symbols to form a coherent story. Older individuals may struggle to interpret certain symbols that are more common among younger generations. Similarly, younger individuals might not recognize older or outdated symbols.

3.1 Problems with a "universal" writing system

Xu Bing's endeavor represents one of many attempts over the course of history to develop a universal graphical system, i.e., a symbol system understood by all humans in the world no matter what language they speak. A common example in everyday life is assembly instructions from IKEA.

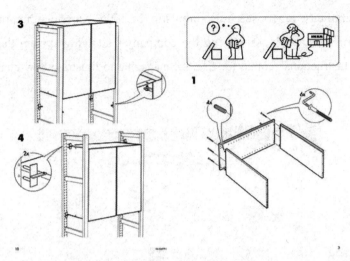

Figure 3.2   An assembly instruction from IKEA
Source: http://justinzhuang.com/posts/wordless-instructions/ (accessed Aug. 24, 2024)

Such attempts are based on the assumption that human brains all share some properties and tend to think along similar lines. Systems of communication that represent ideas and meaning only are labeled **semasiographic**, in contrast to **glottographic**, i.e., those that are bound to language (cf. Sampson, 1985: 29—30).

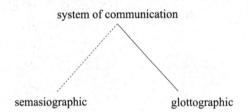

For those familiar with Western urban lifestyle at the point of Xu Bing's creation, the pictographic story may be rendered in speech in various ways without affecting its essential meaning. While semasiographic systems can be particularly useful in conveying basic ideas and facilitating rapid information sharing, they appear inadequate to express precise, abstract or complex concepts that require nuanced explanations. The scope of semasiographic system, be it road signs, mathematical symbols, musical symbols, or emojis, is fairly limited compared to the full range of ideas that humans can conceive and can convey using language.

While Xu Bing's symbols might be repurposed as a travelling aid, we cannot communicate about the difference between "travel," "trip," "journey" and "voyage" in it as we do in English. IKEA graphics-only assembly instructions are far from universally understood. While some appreciate its simplicity, others see it as simplistic. In 2006, American humour writer Mike Sacks was so frustrated with assembling the company's shelving system that he created a satirical "IKEA Instructions" comic for *Esquire* magazine to illustrate how challenging it was without words.

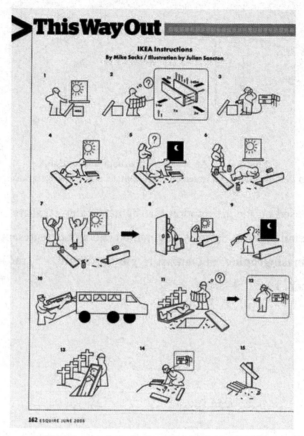

Figure 3.3   This way out IKEA Instructions, designed by Mike Sacks, illustrated by Julian Sancton
Source: https://www.inkoma.com/k/2530/ (accessed Aug. 24, 2024)

Some semasiographs might be intuitive, but others may require learning and memorization due to context specificity or design standard. In other words, symbol systems are necessarily **conventional**. In order for something to be a symbol, there has to be an agreement for what it means and how it is used. When these conventions are absent, the symbols have no definite interpretations. Conventionality is critical and attempts to create symbols that are "universal" in that they do not depend upon prior conventions are generally doomed to fail.

3.2   Glottograhic: logographic vs. phonographic

Writing—real writing that literate societies use to communicate the full range of what can be communicated in language—works because it is tied to language. Writing provides a mechanism for recording ideas that are expressed in language. Writing represents specific utterances of a language in a systematic way, so that proficient readers are able to reliably reproduce what is written and consistently render it back into speech intelligible to the community of speakers of that particular language. Writing, in essence, is "making speech visible" (DeFrancis, 1989: 99). Speech sounds, therefore, are the critical link in connecting language to the written symbols. Thus writing always contains significant amounts of phonological information.

It had been a widespread misconception that Chinese characters are purely **ideograph**s, literally, "writing an idea directly." This misconception was held by many early observers and philosophers, including a few notable figures. Jesuit missionaries in China during the 16th to 18th centuries, such as Matteo Ricci (1552—1610), Nicola Trigault (1577—1628), and Joseph de Prémare (1666—1736), portrayed Chinese characters as ideographs in their writings (cf. Trigault and Ricci, 1615: 25—29; de Prémare, 1831: 303), when introducing Chinese culture to the West. The German philosopher and mathematician Gottfried Wilhelm Leibniz (1646—1716) proposed the "Characteristica Universalis," a universal symbolic system, for which he believed that Chinese characters could serve as a model due to their apparent ideographic nature (Leibniz, 1677, English translation 1995: 234).

"Ideography" in this sense was long thought to be a transitional stage in the development of writing between pictography and logography. It is distinguished from the former by the criterion that it lacks iconic pictorial qualities, and from the latter by the alleged lack of unequivocal linguistic reference (Coulmas, 1999: 224). As introduced in the previous chapter, no full-writing ever worked in this way. However, it is worth noticing that the term "ideographic" is often used in a loose sense to refer to both semasiograms and logograms as they occur in conjunction with signs of other categories in several writing systems such as Egyptian, Sumerian and Mayan.

The figure below illustrates the evolution hypothesis from pictography to ideography and then to logography (Coulmas, 1999: 406). In the first step, A visual sign S designates an object O which is also designated by a word W. No conventional relation exists between S and W; In the second step, in addition to the relations between S and O and between W and O, a relation is perceived between S and W, as yet unstable and secondary. In the third step; the relation between S and O is superseded by that between S and W. S thus becomes a sign which has a word as its primary referent.

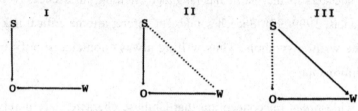

Figure 3.4   Hypothesis of three steps of phonetization
Source: Coulmas, 1999: 406

It is important to note that this is a simplified representation and that the transition between these stages wasn't always linear or distinct. Various aspects of pictography, ideography and logography could have coexisted and interacted in different ways through history. Not all characters necessarily followed the same progression from pictography to logography. Some characters might have retained more pictographic elements, while others became more abstract or phonetic. As noted by Li (2020 : 47) in the following figure, the pictogram for "person" depicts the profile of a standing person in the oracle-bone script, with the shorter stroke representing the arms and the longer one the torso and the legs. The modern character 人 suggests the image of a person standing upright with two equally long legs. It is not exactly the same image, but the picture-like quality, one may argue, is still there. In comparison, other examples in the figure may be less pictorial. Furthermore, different cultures and writing systems followed varying paths of development, and factors such as language changes, cultural influences, and technological advancements played roles in shaping these transitions.

Oracle-bone script	Modern script (traditional)	Modern script (simplified)	Pīnyīn	Meaning
 ⊖	日	日	rì	'sun'
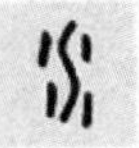 〵〵	水	水	shuǐ	'water'
 人	人	人	rén	'person'
 馬	馬	马	mǎ	'horse'
 女	女	女	nǚ	'female'

Figure 3.5   Examples of pictograms
Source: Li, 2020: 47

Overall, the interplay between visual representation and semantic meaning in Chinese characters contributes to its enduring influence and importance. The character "人" serves as well as an example of how visual elements within characters can convey meaning and maintain semantic continuity over long periods of time. This inherent semantic power is one of the key reasons why the Chinese writing system has stood the test of millennia and continues to be a significant mode of communication and cultural preservation. It allows contemporary readers to access texts from different historical periods because the fundamental meanings conveyed by the characters remain relatively consistent. This is in contrast to alphabetic scripts where words can change significantly over time, making older texts harder to understand without specialized study.

3.3   Phonographic writing systems

Writing which expresses the sounds of speech as opposed to higher-level units, i.e., morphemes and words, is called **phonographic**, literally "sound writing." Such systems focus on representing sound only, but there are different ways of doing this.

3.3.1   Syllabic writing

In a syllabic writing system, a graph represents a syllable. Probably the most famous syllabary is the Japanese *kana* (仮名) system. Japanese is a mixed writing system that uses three different scripts, Chinese characters (漢字, *kanji*) and the two kana systems: Hiragana (平仮名) and Katakana (片仮名). Each kana system consists of 46 symbols, most of which are CV sequences, showing a typical syllable pattern where a consonant sound (C) is followed by a vowel sound (V). Below are examples of two kanas of the same sound:

Hiragana:　か⋯ た⋯か⋯な
Katakana:　カ ⋯ タ⋯ カ ⋯ナ
Sound value: [ka]+[ta]+[ka]+[na]

Very roughly speaking, kanji is used for content words such as nouns, adjectives, and verbs, whereas hiragana is used for native Japanese words and grammatical words (i.e., case markers and other "small" words). Katakana is almost exclusively used today to write foreign words and names.

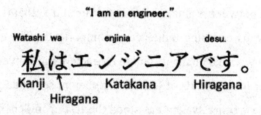

Figure 3.6　An example using three scripts
Source: https://www.mlcjapanese.co.jp/hiragana_katakana.html (accessed Feb. 3, 2023)

The kana system's origins can be traced back to the Heian period (794—1185), when Japan was heavily influenced by Chinese culture and the use of Chinese characters for writing. At that time, Japanese scholars and monks began using Chinese characters to represent Japanese syllables phonetically, creating a kind of "proto-kana" system.

During the Nara period (710—794), a writing system called "man'yōgana"(万葉仮名) emerged. This system involved using selected Chinese characters to represent specific Japanese syllables, but the characters were chosen based on their phonetic values rather than their meanings according to the rebus principle. It was an early form of phonetic representation that eventually led to the development of hiragana and katakana.

Around the 9th century, hiragana script began to evolve from cursive writing of man'yōgana.

For instance, hiragana あ "a" is based on the cursive writing of the kanji 安, and い "i", on 以. Women, in particular, used hiragana to write poems, Japanese style narratives and diaries (cf. Iwasaki, 2013: 25). Of these, *The Tale of Genji* (《源氏物語》), masterpiece of Japanese literature by Murasaki Shikibu (紫式部), played a significant role in establishing the script's literary importance. Over time, hiragana gained broader recognition and acceptance. By the late Heian period, it had been integrated into official documents and everyday communication, coexisting with kanji and katakana.

Figure 3.7　Cursive writing of the kanji 安 and hiragana character あ
Left: Cursive writing of the kanji 安
Right: hiragana character あ and the word あい (ai, i.e., "love") written in hiragana script, calligraphy by 品天龍淚
Source: https://beyond-calligraphy.com/2011/07/12/hiragana-a/ (accessed Feb. 3, 2023)

By comparison, katakana, literally "parts of man'yōgana", was developed from simplifications of certain kanji components. It was primarily used by Buddhist monks as pronunciation aids for ambiguous and difficult to read religious texts. For instance, ア "a" took a part of 阿, and イ "i", 伊. Gradually, katakana also came to be used for other purposes, such as emphasis, onomatopoeia, and scientific terms. The development of the kana systems made the Japanese writing more versatile and accessible, giving way to the representation of native words and sounds that were not easily expressed using kanji alone.

Figure 3.8　Katakana character ア and イ
Upper: Katakana characterア, derived from a fragment of the left part of kanji 阿 in regular script
Lower: Katakana characterイ, derived from the left part of kanji 伊 in regular script
Source: https://www.word-arts.com/blog/2019/09/blog__japanese_katakana_a.php (accessed Feb. 3, 2023)

It would, of course, be possible to write Japanese entirely in kana scripts. However, the existence of a large number of homophones would be issue for efficient reading if that

happens. For example, はし may represent 箸 (chopsticks), 橋 (bridge) or 端 (edge) and き
る may represent 切る (cut) and 着る (wear) in common use. In the following sentence, にわ
represents both 庭 (yard) and 二羽 (two counter for birds), and the fact that Japanese writing
does not use spaces makes reading fast much more challenging.

うちのうらにわにはにわ、にわにはにわとりがある。
うちの裏庭には二羽、庭には二羽鶏が在る。

(In our backyard there are two chickens, and in our front yard there are two.)

Carrying essential meanings, kanji conveys important information to readers immediately. The
combination of kanji and kana provides a way to visually differentiate between grammatical
words and content words, improving text readability and comprehension.

Furthermore, kanji characters often have multiple readings and meanings, and these nuances
are crucial for understanding the layers of meaning in written text. For example, the kanji
character 生 (pronounced as "sei" or "shou" in on'yomi[音読み, Chinese reading] and
"nama" or "ki" in kun'yomi [訓読み, Japanese reading]) is highly versatile and has numerous
readings and meanings when combined with other characters. Here are a few examples to
illustrate its diverse usage: 生徒 (seito): 生—life, literally, "life follower"; 生産 (seisan):
生—produce, "production or manufacturing"; 生まれる (umareru): 生—birth, "to be born";
生の (nama no): 生—raw, fresh, "raw" or "fresh"; 生きる (ikiru): 生—life, "to live"; 生涯
(shougai): 生—life, "lifetime."

To express native concepts and phenomena with greater precision, characters that resemble
kanji were created in Japan. These characters are called *kokuji* (國字). The following list of
kokuji was extracted from the *Kanjidic* dictionary.

kokuji	Reading in kana	Meaning	kokuji	Reading in kana	Meaning
圷	あくつ	Low-lying land	鯑	かずのこ	Yellow fish (herring) eggs (sushi)
遖	あっぱれ	Bravo; admirable	凩	こがらし	Wintry wind
鯏	あさり；うぐい	Short necked clam; dace; chub	鮗	このしろ	Gizzard shad
鈈	ブ	Tin plate	凪	なぎ；な.ぐ	Lull; calm
瓧	デカグラム	Ten grams	鯰	なまず；ネン	Fresh-water catfish

(continued)

kokuji	Reading in kana	Meaning	kokuji	Reading in kana	Meaning
鋲	びょう	Rivet; tack; thumbtack	雫	しずく；ダ	Drop; trickle; dripping
籵	デカメートル	Dekametre	辻	ねた	Wetland; marsh
竕	デカリットル	Decalitre	匂	にお．う；にお．い；にお．わせる	Fragrant; stink; glow; insinuate
癌	がん	Cancer	腺	セン	Gland
蛯	えび；うば	Shrimp	躾	しつ．ける；しつけ	Training
梺	ふむと；ふもと	Base of a mountain	颪	おろし	Wind from mountains
鮠	はえ；はや；カイ；ゲ；ガイ	Dace (carp)	艝	そり	Sled; sleigh
鰰	はたはた	Sandfish	榊	さかき	Sacred Shinto tree
畑	はた；はた；－ばたけ	Farm; field; garden; one's specialty	鱈	たら；セツ	Codfish
働	はたら．く；ドウ	Work	峠	とうげ	Mountain peak; mountain pass; climax; crest
椚	ほくそ	A type of tree	枠	わく	Frame; framework; spindle; spool

Figure 3.9   Examples of kokuji
Source: The Kanjidic (https://users.monash.edu/~jwb/URL=http://nihongo.monash.edu//wwwjdic.html)
(accessed Feb. 3, 2023)

The list may have clued you into the fact that kokuji in general can be classified into several groups—natural species native to Japan, foreign measurement units, tools and craft, to name a few. Compared to kanji characters, kokuji characters remain largely unknown, and thus infrequently used, partially due to increasing usage of katakana writing names of natural species, and partially due to "lack of support by computer systems" (Bossard, 2022). However, some kokuji characters got imported into China. " 鱈 ," " 癌 ," and " 腺 " are such examples.

3.3.2 *Segmental writing*

In a segmental writing system, a **grapheme**, i.e., the smallest meaningful contrastive unit, represents individual sounds, such as consonants and vowels. There are several types of segmental writing systems, each with its own approach to representing these sounds.

3.3.2.1　Abjad: with only (or mostly) consonants

In Hebrew and Arabic scripts, graphs represent only consonants, or mostly consonants with a limited amount of vocalic information. Vowel sounds are either not represented at all or represented using diacritics or optional marks. The following is the Hebrew alphabet. One thing to note is that Hebrew is written from right to left, so *Alef* is the first letter and *Tav* is the last. As you can see, the Hebrew alphabet contains only consonants, no vowels. People who are fluent in the language do not need vowels to read Hebrew.

Figure 3.10　Hebrew alphabet
Source: https://www.jewishvirtuallibrary.org/the-hebrew-alphabet-aleph-bet (accessed Feb. 3, 2023)

It may sound hard for those who do not know Hebrew. The name of a song by American rock band Fall Out Boy may help imagine the situation: "Thnks fr th Mmrs," which is quite readable by a competent English speaker: "Thanks for the Memories."

Now let's try something harder:
t s trth nvrslly cknwldgd, tht sngl mn n pssssn f gd frtn, mst b n wnt f wf.

Did you figure it out? Yes! It is the beginning sentence of the classic novel *Pride and Prejudice* by Jane Austen: "It is a truth universally acknowledged, that a single man in possession of a good fortune, must be in want of a wife."

In the course of time, there arose the concern that knowledge of the correct pronunciation of the Hebrew scriptures might be lost. As early as the 9th century, vowel letters, i.e., letters standing for vowels, were introduced into Hebrew orthography (Morag, 1972: 9—10). These letters are *Alef* (א), *He* (ה), *Vav* (ו)—in ancient Hebrew pronounced as "w," and *Yod* (י), thus known as *matres lectionis* AHWY, literally, "mothers of reading." Here's how they typically function as a vowel:

Grapheme	Hebrew Form	Consonant	Vowel	Constraints on Occurrence as Vowel Designator
A *Alef*	א	?	a, e	Word final only (unless root letter)
H *He*	ה	h	a, e	Word final only
W *Vav*	ו	v (historically, w)	o, u	Word internal and word final
Y *Yod*	י	y	i	Word internal and word final

Figure 3.11   Hebrew AHWY in their dual function as consonant and vowel designators
Source: Joshi and Aaron, eds., 2013: 348

Th AHWY system facilitated consonantal reading, but was not precise and consistent enough. In the 7th and 8th centuries CE (Khan, 1997; Rendburg, 1997), dots and dashes known as *nikud* (dotting, pointing) were added mainly under (and also above and within) the letters to aid pronunciation. The nikud system, noted by Ravid and Haimowitz (2006), is restricted to two contexts: (i) initial reading and writing instruction, and consequently texts for novice readers—children's books and texts for new immigrants; (ii) Biblical and poetical texts, where vocalization ensures precise reading.

Figure 3.12   Hebrew vowel points
Source: https://omniglot.com/writing/hebrew.htm (accessed Feb. 3, 2023)

On the basis of Hebrew alphabet (Fig. 3.10) and Hebrew vowel points (Fig. 3.12), now let's make a guess about the pronunciation of תִיַבְפְלָא.

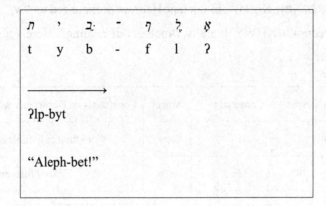

3.3.2.2 Alphabet: with both consonants and vowels

In most segmental writing systems, graphs are intended to represent individual phonemes, including both consonants and vowels. Such systems are traditionally called alphabetic writing systems, and segmental symbols, letters.

The word alphabet comes from the first two letters of the Ancient Greek alphabet: alpha (*A*) and beta (*β*). According to Rogers (2005:153), several facts make it clear that the Greek alphabet was borrowed, perhaps between 1100 BCE and 800 BCE, from Phoenician traders who spoke a language closely related to Hebrew and wrote in the Semitic abjad: First, the ordering of the Greek letters is basically the same as in Semitic; Second, the Greek names of the letters are obviously similar to the Semitic; Third, these names are meaningful and acrophonic in Semitic, but meaningless in Greek; Fourth, the shapes of the letters are similar to those of older Phoenician writing; Fifth, ancient Greek texts refer to the letters as "Phoenician letters."

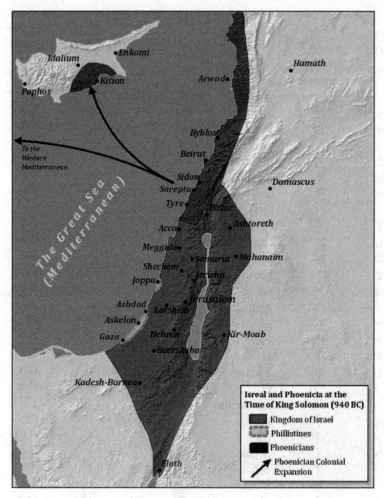

Figure 3.13   Ancient Israel and Phoenicia
Source: http://explorethemed.com/IAIsrael.asp (accessed Aug. 31, 2024)

However, vowels are essential in Greek for preserving the grammatical and lexical information that constitutes the language's structure. To increase accuracy and legibility, the Greeks added distinct symbols for vowels to the system. This step led to a significant change in the nature of the writing system, turning it from an abjad to an alphabet. Rogers (2005:156) shows how the Greek alphabet developed from the Phoenician abjad with the following table.

Phœn. sound	Phœn. shape	Early Greek 8th–7th centuries*	Greek name		Early Greek sound	Modern Greek shape	Numeric value
ʔ		A	ἄλφα	alpha	a, a:	A α	1
b			βῆτα	beta	b	B β	2
g		Λ	γάμμα	gamma	g	Γ γ	3
d		Δ	δέλτα	delta	d	Δ δ	4
h			ἒ ψῑλόν	epsilon	e	E ε	5
w			ϝαῦ	wau digamma	(w)	(ϝ)	6
dz (z)	I	I	ζῆτα	zeta	zd	Z ζ	7
ħ			ἦτα	eta	ɛ:	H η	8
ṭ			θῆτα	theta	tʰ	Θ θ	9
j			ἰῶτα	iota	i, i:	I ι	10
k			κάππα	kappa	k	K κ	20
l			λάμβδα	lambda	l	Λ λ	30
m			μῦ	mu	m	M μ	40
n			νῦ	nu	n	N ν	50
ts (s)			ξῖ	xi	ks	Ξ ξ	60
ʕ	O	O	ὂ μῑκρόν	omikron	o	O o	70
p			πῖ	pi	p	Π π	80
ts (ṣ)		M	σάν, σάμπι	san, sampi	(z)	(ϡ)	900
q			κόππα	koppa, qoppa		(ϙ)	90
r			ῥῶ	rho	r	P ρ	100
s (ʃ)	W		σίγμα	sigma	s	Σ σ ς	200
t		T	ταῦ	tau	t	T τ	300
		Y	ὒ ψῑλόν	upsilon	u, u:	Y υ	400
		Φ	φῖ	phi	pʰ	Φ φ	500
		X	χῖ	chi	kʰ	X χ	600
			ψῖ	psi	ps	Ψ ψ	700
			ὢ μέγα	omega	ɔ:	Ω ω	800

Figure 3.14   The development of the Greek alphabet from the Phoenician abjad
Source: Rogers, 2005: 156
* = 8th century BCE—7th century BCE

In both ancient and modern Greek, there is fairly stable and consistent letter-to-sound correspondence, making the pronunciation largely predictable. Therefore, we can reasonably make out the pronunciation of *Αλφά βητος* quite accurately.

A	λ	φ	ά	β	η	τ	ο	ς
a	l	pʰ	a	b	e	t	o	s

"Alphabetos!"

In principle, alphabetic writing promises a simple one-to-one grapheme to phoneme correspondence, making automatic conversion from writing to language possible. In reality, nothing can be as simple as it should. Varying degrees of complexity come into the corresponding relationship. If we think of alphabetic writing systems arranged along a continuum, then systems such as Finnish, Greek, Italian as well as Spanish would be near one end called "transparency," systems such as German and French might be near the middle, and systems such as Danish and English would be close to the other end called "opaqueness."

Transparency --|-------------------------------------- Opaqueness

Finnish Greek Italian Spanish   German   French   Danish English

The closer to the "transparency" end, the higher a tendency grows for one-to-one correspondence. For example, in Finnish each letter stands for one sound and each sound is always represented by the same letter, except the velar nasal [ŋ], which does not have an allotted letter. The spelling of a word is almost transparent, revealed directly through its pronunciation. Conversely, the closer to the "opaqueness" end, the higher a tendency shows for complexity and ambiguity. Anyone who has learned to write in English is more than aware that spelling words is challenging. Our ears hear [i:]; our eyes will likely see *i* or *e*, but might also see *ee* as in "keep," *ea* as in "leaf," *ie* as in "shield," *ei* as in "receive," and *ey* as in "key." Our eyes see *ough*, but our ears may hear [ɔ:] as in "thought," [oʊ] as in "though," [ə] as in "thorough," [u:] as in "through," [ʌf] as in "rough," [ɔf] as in "cough," [ʌp] in "hiccough," [aʊ] as in "plough," and [ɒk] as in "lough." The high degree of inconsistency can be attributed to a combination of historical, linguistic, and cultural factors that we will discuss in Chapter VII.

While most alphabets in use today employ the Roman script, it is important to mention other scripts that are used for alphabets, including Cyrillic, on the one hand, adopted for writing several Slavic languages such as Russian, Ukrainian, Bulgarian, and Serbian, and Georgian, Armenian, and Korean (cf. Further reading) on the other, which are more specific to given alphabets.

3.3.2.3   Abugida: with vowels indicated

An abugida is a type of writing system that falls between the categories of abjads and alphabets. In an abugida, consonant-vowel sequences are written as symbols in which all vowels are indicated, normally written as diacritics. Abugida contrasts with an alphabet, in which vowels have equal status to consonants, and with an abjad, in which vowel marking is absent, partial, or optional. It also contrasts with a syllabary, in which the symbols have no internal structures and cannot be further segmented into consonants and vowels.

The most famous example of abugida is probably the Indian Devanagari, the script used for writing several Indian languages, including Hindi, Sanskrit, Marathi, and Nepali. It is the most widely used script in India. In Devanagari, consonants are represented, and the inherent vowel sound is usually "a." Other vowel sounds are indicated using diacritics or additional marks attached to the consonant characters. This system allows for efficient writing of syllables by combining consonants and vowels in a consistent way. The graphemes with sound values are listed in the following table.

a	ā		i	ī		u	ū
अ	आ		इ	ई		उ	ऊ
ṛ	ṝ		ḷ	ḹ			
ऋ	ॠ		ऌ	ॡ			
e	ai		o	au			
ए	ऐ		ओ	औ			
ṁ	ḥ						
अं	अः						
k	kh	g	gh	ṅ			
क	ख	ग	घ	ङ			
c	ch	j	jh	ñ			
च	छ	ज	झ	ञ			
ṭ	ṭh	ḍ	ḍh	ṇ			
ट	ठ	ड	ढ	ण			
t	th	d	dh	n			
त	थ	द	ध	न			
p	ph	b	bh	m			
प	फ	ब	भ	म			
y	r	l	v				
य	र	ल	व				
ś	ṣ	s	h	ḻ			
श	ष	स	ह	ळ			

Figure 3.15　The basic symbols of Devanagari
Source: Rogers, 2005: 215

Vowel graphemes have two allographs, i.e., variations or alternate form: one free, and the other bound. At the beginning of an orthographic unit, the free allograph is used; otherwise, the bound allograph is used, i.e., the vowel is written as a diacritic on the preceding consonant. The following table shows the free and bound allographs and the bound allograph with the consonant क [k], forming a complex symbol.

Free	Bound	Bound with <k>	Free	Bound	Bound with <k>
a अ	—	ka क	ā आ	ा	kā का
i इ	ि	ki कि	ī ई	ी	kī की
u उ	ु	ku कु	ū ऊ	ू	kū कू
r̥ ऋ	ृ	kr̥ कृ	r̥̄ ॠ	ॄ	kr̥̄ कॄ
l̥ ऌ	ॢ	kl̥ कॢ	l̥̄ ॡ	ॣ	kl̥̄ कॣ
e ए	े	ke के	ai ऐ	ै	kai कै
o ओ	ो	ko को	au औ	ौ	kau कौ

Figure 3.16   The vowel symbols of Devanagari
Source: Rogers, 2005: 216

Comparing with the previous table, you may notice that the symbol for "k" and "ka" are the same: क. "ka" is without any added vowel diacritics. The absence of vowel diacritic indicates the short [a]: क /k/(=[ka]), viz., the consonant comes in packaged with a vowel [a] at the end. Unless combined with another vowel (e.g., क [ka] +ओ [o] = को [ko]), the default form of the consonant is going to be the consonant sound + [a]. To indicate the absence of a following short [a], a short subscript diagonal line could be added below the symbol to form क्.

In other words, the basic grapheme is a consonant packaged with vowel [a]. If necessary one can clearly break it down into a segment that represents vowel and a segment that represents consonant. Otherwise, this basic grapheme will be foundation for combination with other vowels. The following figure shows क with vowel diacritics.

क का कि की कु कू कृ कॄ के कै को कौ

Figure 3.17 क with vowel diacritics
Source: https://upload.wikimedia.org/wikipedia/commons/2/26/Devanagari_matras.png (retrieved Sept. 18, 2023).

The following table shows द, व, न, ग, र with vowel diacritics preceding the consonant. Then we can figure out how to pronounce दे व ना ग री.

Da	Dā	Di	Dī	Du	Dū	Dr	Dr̄	Dl	Dl̄	De	Dai	Do	Dau	D
द	दा	दि	दी	दु	दू	दृ	दॄ	दॢ	दॣ	दे	दै	दो	दौ	द्

Va	Vā	Vi	Vī	Vu	Vū	Vr	Vr̄	Vl	Vl̄	Ve	Vai	Vo	Vau	V
व	वा	वि	वी	वु	वू	वृ	वॄ	वॢ	वॣ	वे	वै	वो	वौ	व्

Na	Nā	Ni	Nī	Nu	Nū	Nr	Nr̄	Nl	Nl̄	Ne	Nai	No	Nau	N
न	ना	नि	नी	नु	नू	नृ	नॄ	नॢ	नॣ	ने	नै	नो	नौ	न्

Ga	Gā	Gi	Gī	Gu	Gū	Gr	Gr̄	Gl	Gl̄	Ge	Gai	Go	Gau	G
ग	गा	गि	गी	गु	गू	गृ	गॄ	गॢ	गॣ	गे	गै	गो	गौ	ग्

Ra	Rā	Ri	Rī	Ru	Rū	Rr	Rr̄	Rl	Rl̄	Re	Rai	Ro	Rau	R
र	रा	रि	री	रु	रू	रृ	रॄ	रॢ	रॣ	रे	रै	रो	रौ	र्

दे	व	ना	ग	री
[da+e]	[va]	[na+a]	[ga]	[ra+i]

"devanagari"

Figure 3.18 द, व, न, ग, र with vowel diacritics preceding the consonant

Now, can you make out the pronunciation of the Devanagari word अल्फ़ाबेट by referring to Figure 3.15 and Figure 3.16?

अल्फ़ाबेट

al-fā-beṭ

"alphabet"

Did you get it right? Here's the breakdown of the characters:

- अ (a): represents the vowel sound /a/.
- लृ (l): represents the consonant sound /l/.
- फ़ (f): represents the foreign sound /f/, with the dot added below फ (the aspirated /p/).
- ा (ā): represents the vowel sound /a:/ that is bound with फ़.
- ब (b): represents the consonant sound /b/.
- ॆ (e): indicates the vowel sound /e/ follows the consonant ब.
- ट (t): represents the consonant sound /t/.

So, when combined, the characters, spelling out अ (a) + ल (l) + फ़ (f) + ा (ā) + ब (b) + ॆ (e) + ट (ṭ), are the Devanagari representation of the word "alphabet."

Summing-up

Compelling as the idea of a "universal" graphical system is, the diversity of human language, culture, and historical development makes its creation a mission impossible. The systems seemingly universal—be it traffic signs, mathematical symbols, numeral systems or music notation—are always limited in conveying complex ideas or nuanced meanings, and more often than not, require education because symbols, by their very nature, are conventional. Their meanings are agreed upon by users through social and cultural conventions rather than being inherently understood.

Devised to capture the full range of ideas that humans can convey using language, all writing systems—despite wide differences in outer form—carry significant amount of phonological information in that language is, first and foremost, vocal. Logographic systems like Chinese, Egyptian, Mayan or Sumerian incorporate sound on the level of morpheme or word that represents a large amount of semantic information as well. In contrast, phonographic systems such as Japanese, Hebrew, Greek and Devanagari focus on representing sound only, either at the level of syllables (syllabary) or individual sounds (abjad, alphabet, abugida), and do not inherently carry semantic information.

Both types of systems reflect different approaches to encoding language. When it comes to these writing systems, there is no "better" or "worse"—each is most effective when tailored to accurately capture and convey the unique characteristics of the languages they represent. Understanding and respecting the diversity of writing systems ushers in the vast tapestry of human language and culture.

References

Bossard, Antoine. 2022. "Ontological and Quantitative Analyses of the Kokuji Characters of the Japanese Writing System." *Journal of Chinese Writing Systems* 5(2): 115—124. https://doi.org/10.1177/251385022110509.

Coulmas, Florian. 1999. *The Blackwell Encyclopedia of Writing Systems*. Malden, MA: Blackwell Publishing.

DeFrancis, John. 1989. *Visible Speech: The Diverse Oneness of Writing Systems*. Honolulu: University of Hawaii Press.

de Prémanre, Joseph Henri. 1831. *Notitia Lingua Sinicae*. Malacca: Cura Academiae Anglo-sinensis.

Iwasaki, Shoichi. 2013. *Japanese*. Amsterdam/Philadelphia: John Benjamins Publishing Company.

Joshi, R. Malatesha, and P. G. Aaron, eds. 2013. *Handbook of Orthography and Literacy*. London and New York: Routledge.

Khan, Geoffrey. 1997. "Tiberian Hebrew Phonology." In *Phonologies of Asia and Africa*, edited by A. S. Kaye and P. T. Daniels, 85—102. Winona Lake, IN: Eisenbrauns.

Leibniz, Gottfried Wilhelm. 1677. "Preface to the General Science." Revision of Rutherford's translation in Jolley 1995: 234. In *The Cambridge Companion to Leibniz*, edited by Nicholas Jolley, 234. Cambridge: Cambridge University Press.

Li, Yu. 2020. *The Chinese Writing System in Asia: An Interdisciplinary Perspective. London:* Routledge.

Morag, Shelomo. 1972. *The Vocalization Systems of Arabic, Hebrew, and Aramaic*. The Hague: Mouton & Co.

Ravid, Dorit, and Sarit Haimowitz. 2006. "The Vowel Path: Learning about Vowel Representation in Written Hebrew." *Written Language and Literacy* 9(1): 67—93.

Rendburg, Gary A. 1997. "Ancient Hebrew Phonology." In *Phonologies of Asia and Africa*, edited by A. S. Kaye and P. T. Daniels, 65—83. Winona Lake, IN: Eisenbrauns.

Rogers, Henry. 2005. *Writing Systems: A Linguistic Approach*. Malden, MA: Blackwell Publishing.

Sampson, Geoffrey. 1985. *Writing Systems: A Linguistic Introduction*. Redwood City: Stanford University Press.

Trigault, Nicolas, and Matteo Ricci. 1615. *De Christiana expeditione apud Sinas Suscepta ab Societate Jesu*. Lyon: Horatij Cardon.

Xu, Bing. 2014. *Book from the Ground: From Point to Point*. Cambridge, MA: MIT Press.

Further reading: excerpt from *Language, Technology, and Society*

Sproat, Richard. 2010. "Chapter III How Writing Represents Languages." In *Language, Technology, and Society*, 65—72. Cambridge: Cambridge University Press.

Chapter IV   Interaction between Language and Writing: Decipherment of Egyptian Hieroglyph

Jumping-in

Acrophony is the mechanism underlying the development of an alphabet in Egyptian hieroglyphs. Below is sometimes referred to as the hieroglyphic alphabet.

SYMBOL	TRANSL.	NAME
(vulture)	ȝ	aleph ("ALL–if")
(reed–leaf); also \\ (dual strokes)	j	j or i or yod ("yode")
(double reed–leaf)	y	y
(arm)	ᶜ	ayin ("EYE–in")
(quail–chick); also ε (curl of rope)	w	w
(foot)	b	b
(stool)	p	p
(horned viper)	f	f
(owl); also ⟺ (unknown object)	m	m
(water); also (red crown)	n	n
(mouth)	r	r
(enclosure)	h	h
(rope)	ḥ	dotted h
(unknown object); also ⬤	ḫ	third h
(belly and udder)	ẖ	fourth h
(doorbolt)	z	z or first s
(bolt of cloth)	s	s or second s
(pool)	š	shin
(hill)	q	q or dotted k
(basket) (also ⌣)	k	k
(jar–stand); also (bag)	g	g
(bread–loaf)	t	t
(hobble)	ṯ	second t
(hand)	d	d
(cobra)	ḏ	second d

Figure 4.1   Hieroglyphic alphabet
Source: Allen, 2010: 14

Now try your best to decipher the following inscription by referring to the alphabet. Ignore the symbols not included in the alphabet.

The decipherment of Egyptian hieroglyphs, particularly the monumental achievement of deciphering the Rosetta Stone, provides tangible evidence that writing systems are intimately linked to language. The process of its decipherment highlights how writing can accurately represent linguistic elements such as phonemes, syllables, morphemes, and syntax. This achievement bolsters the argument that writing is a medium for encoding and preserving language, enabling communication across time and space.

Hieroglyphs were in use in ancient Egypt from around 3200 BCE until the fourth century CE (Allen, 2012: 15), with variations and developments over the millennia. The script had different forms and styles during different periods, including roughly the Early Dynastic, Old Kingdom, Middle Kingdom, New Kingdom, and Late Period hieroglyphs. The hieroglyphs we are going to talk about belong to the Ptolemaic Period following the Late Period, the last flowering of the native Egyptian rulers. It began when Ptolemy, a former general of the Macedonian Greek Alexander the Great, proclaimed himself pharaoh of Egypt in 305 BCE, and ended with the death of Cleopatra VII and the Roman conquest in 30 BCE. The Ptolemaic Period was marked by intense interaction and blending of the Greek and Egyptian cultures, with Greek used for official documents while Egyptian scripts used for religious, literary, and scientific texts.

As stated in Chapter II, Egyptian Hieroglyphic is historically considered one of the four pristine writing systems, where logograms were at the root. In the fully developed system, individual signs fall into three types based on their functions which are not graphically distinguished: logograms, phonograms, and ideograms. Hence, the same sign can be used as a logogram, or a phonogram, or an ideogram, depending on the context. Logograms are most used for concrete nouns or verbs signifying perceptible actions or movements. Phonograms stand for the sounds, either a homophonous word in accordance with the rebus principle, or a phoneme as a result of the acrophonic principle. In the latter case, they are sometimes referred to as the hieroglyphic alphabet, as shown in Jumping-in above, and can be combined to spell out words phonetically. In comparison, ideograms are mute signs that added an ideographic or classificatory element to a word to clarify its meaning or context.

For example, the mouth-sign ⬭ may serve as a logogram when used to write the word for mouth, which is pronounced "re", and the house-sign ⌑ may serve as a logogram, which is possibly pronounced "per" or "par"—it is based on two consonant p and r combined, but the original vowel omitted is not known with certainty, as Egyptian hieroglyphic writing was an abjad, denoting only the consonantal value of a word (cf. § 3.3.2). Now, here is another word which makes use of the same sound combination p and r:

In this word, ⌐┐ is no longer being used as a logogram, but rather a phonogram to indicate the sound combination pr, and the same is true for ⌒, which reads r but has nothing to do with "mouth" here, being used to complement the reading of ⌐┐ pr. The walking legs ⋀ are used as an ideogram to give us some idea that the word has something to do with motion (cf. Collier and Manley, 2003: 2). Altogether, the word means "go out", transliterated as pr, possibly pronounced "per" by Egyptologists for modern convenience.

Hieroglyph	⌐┐	⌒	⋀
Logographic value	N/A	N/A	N/A
Phonetic value	*pr*	*r*	N/A
Notes			"legs walking" is an ideogram for motion

Figure 4.2   The use of hieroglyphs ⌐┐, ⌒, and ⋀ in the word ("pr", go out)

4.1   Rosetta Stone: pattern of fusion

The above knowledge about Egyptian hieroglyphs had been lost for over thirteen hundred years by the time the Rosetta Stone was discovered.

The Rosetta Stone is a fragment of a granite stela inscribed with three texts. It was discovered in 1799 near the town of El-Rashid (Europeanized as "Rosetta") in the Nile Delta by a French officer during the Napoleonic campaign in Egypt. The first text (14 lines) is written in Hieroglyphic, the second (32 lines) in Demotic, a derivative of hieroglyphic script, and the third (53 lines) in Greek. A reconstruction of the original stela, based on other copies of the Memphis Decree and the Canopus Decree, indicates that more than half of the text is lost from the hieroglyphic section, originally estimated 29 lines (cf. The British Museum Blog).

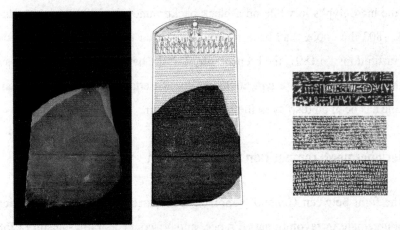

Figure 4.3   The Rosetta Stone and a reconstruction of the original stela (based on other copies of the Memphis Decree and the Canopus Decree, Drawn by C. Thorne and R. Parkinson)
Source: https://blog.britishmuseum.org/everything-you-ever-wanted-to-know-about-the-rosetta-stone/ (accessed Aug. 31, 2024)

The Rosetta Stone records a decree issued at Memphis on March, 27, 196 BCE by a council of priests granting a royal cult to Ptolemy V (reign 204 BCE—181 BCE) in return for his favors to them, including exemption from taxation (cf. Budge, 1905: 199—211). Ptolemy V's reign was marked by revolts and infightings (Fischer-Bovet, 2015), and some tensions had centered around the temples, which were strongholds of Egyptian language and culture. From the nature of the stela—a priestly decree of the Ptolemaic period for display—came the need to inscribe the decree in three scripts: Hieroglyphic, for gods and priests and the traditional audience of Egyptian monuments; Demotic, for the Egyptian-speaking literate populace; and Greek for the administration. Its decipherment thus involves comparing the two incomplete and unknown ancient scripts to the known Greek writing system. The decipherment not only aroused curiosity for cultural secrets of a long-dead society but also intensified competition between France and England.

By the early 19th century, France and England were locked in a heated cultural and military rivalry. In 1798, French political and military leader Napoleon Bonaparte (1769—1821) landed with 35,000 soldiers in Egypt and started a three-year Egyptian campaign, aiming to disrupt British trade routes to India and establish French domination in the exotic east. The invading force was accompanied by a body of mathematicians, scientists, artists, writers and inventors (cf. Strathern, 2009: 12—16). In 1799 when the Rosetta Stone was excavated, the expedition's senior orientalist identified the middle section as Demotic, an Egyptian script known from classical authors, and realized that the stone could act as a printing block. He produced reverse image with the hieroglyphs in white on a black background. By 1800 the copies had reached Paris and by 1803 the copies had been widely distributed throughout Europe to universities and learned institutions. In 1801, the French army lost the battle of Alexandria and surrendered everything they had acquired in Egypt, including the Rosetta Stone, to the British army. Since 1802, the stone has been on display in the British Museum.

4.2   The decipherment: competition and cooperation

Parallel to the fight between General Napoleon Bonaparte, representing republican reform and rising bourgeoisie in revolutionary France, and Viscount Horatio Nelson (1758—1805), representing traditional royalism and privileged elite in Great Britain, is a race between Jean-François Champollion (1790—1832), a French philologist and orientalist with heavy Napoleonic sympathies, and Thomas Young (1773—1829), a respected British scientist and polymath. The decipherment became emblematic for national pride.

Champollion and Young had very different backgrounds. Born in a poor family, Champollion was mostly a self-taught orientalist. Endowed with remarkable prodigious linguistic capacity, at the age of 16 he had mastered Coptic—a late form of the ancient Egyptian language, in addition to Ancient Greek, Latin, Hebrew, Arabic, Syriac, Chaldean, Sanskrit and Persian (cf. Adkins and Adkins, 2000: 50), and read a paper on Coptic before the Grenoble Academy, proposing that Coptic was the same language spoken by the ancient Egyptians (*Encyclopaedia Britannica*, s.v. "Jean-François Champollion"). Obsessed with Egyptian language and culture, he was convinced that hieroglyphs expressed words that could be spoken. In contrast, Young received a well-rounded education in physics, mathematics and medicine at Edinburgh University, Göttingen University and then Cambridge University. Described as "the last man who knew everything" (Robinson, 2007), Young made groundbreaking contributions to various fields, particularly known for works on wave theory of light, interference of light, Young's Modulus, color vision, and accommodation (the eye's ability to focus on objects at different distances) in ophthalmology. He believed in an empirical, rational, mathematical approach to decipherment. In 1814, he began to decipher the Rosetta Stone. A practicing physician, he took deciphering the stone as an intellectual diversion, not a professional goal.

Historical narratives have often been colored by rivalry and aggravated nationalistic sympathies between Champollion and Young (e.g., Robinson, 2007; 2012; Adkins and Adkins,

2000; Parkinson, 1999; 2005). While there might have been differences and disagreements between the two protagonists due to the nature of their work and the time in which they lived, it's important to recognize that they were both pivotal in the decipherment process. They built upon each other's work, and their combined insights contributed to the successful decipherment of Egyptian hieroglyphs.

It is also worth mentioning that many scholars laid the foundation for the breakthroughs made by Champollion and Young. One such scholar is Antoine-Isaac Silvestre de Sacy (1758—1838), a prominent French orientalist and linguist, who achieved the first breakthrough with the Demotic script (Sacy, 1802), identifying personal names including that of Ptolemy, although he was incorrect in his analysis of the individual signs. Another is Johan David Åkerblad (1763—1819), a Swedish diplomat and orientalist, a student of Sacy who took on his work and identified many proper names within the Demotic text (Åkerblad, 1802), but he mistakenly believed the Demotic to be entirely alphabetic.

4.3   Methodology of the decipherment

Despite disputes over their respective contributions, the way Young and Champollion dialogued and cooperated in difficult circumstances serves as a good example for how decipherment frequently proceeds when critical data, in this case—bilingual texts, are available.

4.3.1   Distribution analysis for patterns

Bilingual texts allow one to do **distribution analysis**, which, in various fields such as statistics, business and marketing as well as linguistics, refers to the examination and study of the distribution of data points or values within a dataset. The goal is often to understand how data is spread out, the patterns it exhibits, and the characteristics of the distribution. Distribution analysis helps in making inferences, drawing conclusions, and making data-driven decisions. In the case of hieroglyphic decipherment, it is to search for patterns that repeat across the different scripts. By doing so, Young realized immediately that mathematical and geometrical principles could be applied to the alignment problem: if the word for king appears multiple times, you expect it to appear a similar number of times in the other script, and in roughly the same position; any hieroglyph or symbol combination that appears a similar number of times as any Greek word becomes a possible candidate for translation.

The hieroglyphic text contains six cartouches, i.e., oval loops enclosing a group of hieroglyphs. Three are identical and the other three began the same way but had several hieroglyphs added on at the end. Young observed that they correspond to the Greek name Πτολεμαῖος (Ptolemaios). Using the cartouche as a basis, Young reasoned that the Greek name "Ptolemaios" had to be spelled out phonetically in the Native Egyptian. The hieroglyphs in it would have the sound of the Greek letters, and all together they would represent the Greek form of the name Ptolemy. He posited that in the shorter version individual hieroglyphs represented the sounds of the name, and in the longer ones a title of some kind was added. However, he argued that only foreign names such as Ptolemy were written "alphabetically," and other words such as the epithets in the cartouche were written symbolically.

Figure 4.4   Details of the Rosetta Stone showing the name Ptolemy in hieroglyphics (top, written right to left), Demotic (middle) and as the Greek word Ptolemaios (bottom)
Source: Meggs and Purvis, 2016: 12

written right to left

written left to right

Figure 4.5   A longer cartouche featuring the name Ptolemy on the Rosetta Stone
Source: https://www.britishmuseum.org/collection/image/385347001 (accessed Aug. 31, 2024)

Then he broke down the hieroglyphs in the shorter version, working out which symbols had been used phonetically to spell out each letter of "Ptolemy." Note that in Egyptian "w" and "y" are weak consonants (cf. Griffith, 1898: 11—12), holding double status "consonant/vowel," viz. they are semi-vocalic phonemes, as today "y" does in most uses of the Latin script. For instance, "y" is a consonant in "mayor," but a vowel in "merry." In orthography, Egyptian consonantal "y" could serve for Greek "e" or "i," and "w" for Greek "o" or "ou."

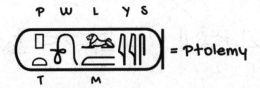

Figure 4.6   Cartouche featuring the name Ptolemy transliterated

4.3.2   Held-out data for verification

Yet, a single transliterated name is not enough to make real progress. Even with the stone, there was not enough data to solve the puzzle completely.

Someone needed to go on the hunt for more data, data that were not used in the initial process but were set aside for validation and testing of the decipherment hypothesis. In this case, it's William John Bankes (1786—1855), an English explorer and traveler, who identified the cartouche enclosing Cleopatra on the granite obelisk that he had excavated at Philae in 1815. The obelisk contains an inscription in two texts: a hieroglyphic text and a Greek text, by Egyptian priests of a petition to and response from Ptolemy VIII, Queens Cleopatra II and Cleopatra III. In the Greek portion the royal names, Ptolemy and Cleopatra, are mentioned, and on the shaft of the obelisk there are cartouches filled with hieroglyphs, assumed to be the Egyptian equivalents of these names. This allowed a vital process in decipherment: verification.

Figure 4.7   Cartouche featuring the name Cleopatra

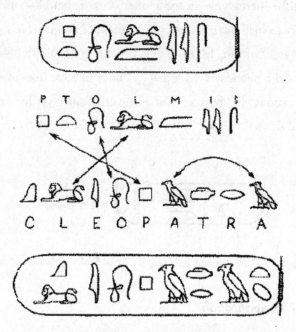

Figure 4.8   Cross-referencing of hieroglyphs on cartouches featuring the names of Ptolemy and Cleopatra

By 1816, Young had identified "Ptolemy" and the probable characters for *p*, *t*, *l*, *m*, *i*, s. This decipherment mostly worked with the obelisk. But the Cleopatra cartouche appeared to contain a different character for *t*, as well as a redundant *t*, and sometimes additional symbols beyond that. In 1819, he listed a 218-word hieroglyphical vocabulary in a supplement on "Egypt" for the *Encyclopedia Britannica*, and proposed phonetic values for 13 of them as "a specimen of the mode of expressing sounds in some particular cases" (1819: 35) , 6 of which he got right.

However, Young was still missing a huge piece: he didn't know the language of Egyptian. He believed that only foreign names were written phonetically this way, and the cartouches offered no insight into the Egyptian language itself. Both the longer Ptolemy cartouche and the Cleopatra cartouche contained additional symbols which seemed to have the wrong phonetic values or that he couldn't assign phonetic values to.

Figure 4.9   Ptolemy cartouche and the Cleopatra cartouche with additional symbols

4.3.3   The underlying language to stand on

Young's mathematical and analytical approach provided crucial initial insights into the structure and potential phonetic values of hieroglyphs, particularly in the cartouches containing royal names. However, as Young was not specialized in ancient languages and lacked a comprehensive understanding of the Egyptian language, he reached a stalemate. The relay was then passed to Champollion, who had an in-depth understanding of the relationships between languages.

Champollion believed that the Demotic had evolved from the Hieroglyphic and they represented the same language. If hieroglyphs were the ancestor to the Demotic, maybe the language was an ancestor to some modern Egyptian language: Coptic, a language still in use, primarily as a liturgical language by Egypt's indigenous Christian community. Champollion then compared symbols in the Coptic with the Demotic:

demotic:						
Coptic:						
pronounced	sh	f	h	j	g	ti

Figure 4.10   Comparison of Demotic and Coptic symbols
Source: Davies, 1990: 98

The overlap of modern Coptic with the Demotic led Champollion to suspect that Egyptian hieroglyphs could be spoken as Coptic or something similar. One should not downplay the methodological difficulty involved. Representing the final stage of the ancient Egyptian language, the Coptic departed significantly from the Hieroglyphic and the Demotic in that it was alphabetic. Therefore, the actual phonetic realities underlying the abstract reconstruction was more elusive. "The traditional pronunciation and transliteration of many Egyptian phonemes rest upon hardly anything more than scholarly conventions, and even for the relatively well-known Coptic, in which Egyptian sounds are rendered in a Greek-based alphabet," commented by Loprieno (1995: 28), "it is difficult to assess reliable phonetic values for some of the Greek signs and the Demotic graphemes that were added to the Greek alphabetic set."

Furthermore, through meticulous analysis of various writing systems, Champollion grasped the relationship between the number of symbols and the type of script. He identified 486 words in the Greek text and 1419 symbols in the hieroglyphic text. This discrepancy ruled out the possibility that one hieroglyph could represent one meaning or word or sound. Given that the hieroglyphic text is only a portion of the original, the total number of symbols would be substantially larger, which amplifies the discrepancy. Therefore, Champollion realized that there had to be a grouping of signs to convey a single meaning—in other words, the presence of phonetic elements. Again, he needed held-out data to test this hypothesis.

In 1822, Champollion received copies of inscriptions from The Temple of Abu Simbel sent by a travelling friend from southern Egypt, who had been at the site with Bankes' party. These include the following cartouche:

Figure 4.11 Cartouche featuring Ramses' name

When he saw the new cartouche, he took a shot to read it in Coptic. By then, he could read the final two signs 𓋴𓋴 as *ss*, and his knowledge of Coptic suggested that the sunshaped sign might represent the word for sun, in Coptic pronounced as "*re*" ; hence the name 𓇳𓄟𓋴𓋴 could be read as "*Re?ses*," instantly suggesting the famous pharaoh Ramses, as known in English, familiar from the accounts of the Greek historian Manetho dating to the third century BCE, who referred to several pharaohs of ancient Egypt with variations of the name as *Ramesses*. Champollion's reading of the cartouche was substantially correct, although he believed that each phonetic sign represented one consonant (taking 𓄟 as *m*), whereas some signs were subsequently recognized to represent more than one (𓄟 actually being *ms*) (cf. Parkinson, 1999: 35).

Another sheet from his friend bore a similar group of signs in a cartouche 𓅝𓄟𓋴, but, instead of the sun-disk, it contained an ibis which classical sources described as the animal of the god Thoth. By comparison with the cartouche of Ramses, this cartouche could be read Thot-M-S Thotmes, another name preserved by the Greek historians as Thutmosis, proving the method was correct. From these names Champollion was convinced that the script was predominantly phonetic, but also included logograms. More importantly, it was used to write native names from the pharaonic period, and so could have been used to write the Egyptian language in the same manner.

These Abu Simbel sketches sparked the Eureka moment! On 14 September 1822, Champollion excitedly visited his brother. Waving his notes in the air, he gasped, "Je tiens l'affaire, vois!" (Look, I've got it!) before collapsing in a dead faint (Adkins and Adkins, 2000: 181). The notes formed the basis of a historic letter in which Champollion outlined his findings on the translation of the hieroglyphs in royal names (cf. Figure 4.12). Champollion's reading of this letter on 27 September 1822 at Institut de France in front of members of Académie des Inscriptions et Belles-Lettres, including Sacy and Young, is considered the moment of decipherment. The letter was later elaborated into his classic work *Précis du Système Hiéroglyphique des Anciens Egyptiens* (Overview of the Hieroglyphic System of the Ancient Egyptians), published in Paris in March 1824.

The conclusion was that the hieroglyphic text was a mixture of phonograms, logograms, and ideograms that indicate the meaning but do not have phonetic values. Champollion called the last ones "determinatives." Determinatives were added at the end of words to help clarify the meaning of words and provide a context for the overall sentence structure.

In the case of cartouches containing the name of a ruler like Ptolemy, it was common to include determinatives that symbolized aspects associated with kingship, divine attributes, or the ruler's qualities. In the longer cartouche of Ptolemy's name, the determinative ♀, a cross surmounted by a loop, signifies "life," and ⤶, "love." In the cartouche of Cleopatra's name, the ellipse or egg symbol at bottom right is a determinative that indicates the word is related to birth, creation, or being born, while the additional "t" at top right functions as a grammatical marker indicating the feminine gender (cf. Figure 4.13).

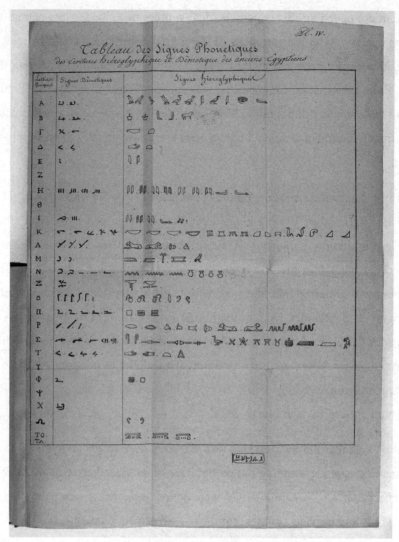

Figure 4.12　Table of phonetic hieroglyphs
Source: Champollion, 1822

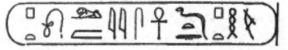

P T O　LM　Y S (life) DT PTH (beloved)

C　L　E　O　P　A　T　R　A

KL　E　O　P　A　PT A　T (goddess Isis)

Figure 4.13　Ptolemy cartouche and the Cleopatra cartouche with additional symbols explained

When comparing hieroglyphs with the Demotic, it can be generally said that hieroglyphs have a higher percentage of logograms and ideograms, while the Demotic is more phonetic in nature. This difference reflects the evolution of the writing system over time and its adaptation to the changing linguistic and cultural landscape of ancient Egypt over time.

4.3.4   Interaction between language and writing

The decipherment of ancient Egyptian hieroglyphs involved a mutual and beneficial interaction between the knowledge of the Coptic language and the understanding of the Demotic and Hieroglyphic scripts. Coptic, a descendant of the ancient Egyptian language, served as a bridge between the modern era and the ancient past. Champollion realized that Coptic retained many linguistic features from its ancient ancestor. Studying Coptic provided insights into the phonetic values and grammar of the ancient Egyptian language.

With the decipherment of hieroglyphs, a script not shown on the Rosetta stone—the Hieratic—was also unlocked. Used from around the third millennium BCE, the Hieratic was an intermediate stage between hieroglyphics and the Demotic. It was a cursive form of hieroglyphics used for everyday administrative and religious texts. This style was intended for writing in a more rapid and linear fashion, with ink on surfaces such as pottery and, especially, papyrus. In around 700 BCE, it gave rise to the Demotic, a simplified, more abstract script used for a wide range of texts, including administrative, legal, and literary documents. The Hieratic received its name from the Greek *hieratikos*, i.e., "priestly," at a time when everyday secular documents were written in the Demotic, from Greek *dēmotikos*, i.e., "for the people."

As you might have figured out in Jumping-in, Egyptian hieroglyphs can be written in multiple directions: right to left, left to right, or top to bottom. The direction in which hieroglyphs are to be read can be determined by the orientation of the symbols, particularly the human and animal figures—they always face the beginning of the line, so if the figures face left, you read from left to right, and if they face right, you read from right to left. When written in columns, the figures face the start of the column, indicating the direction to read downwards. In contrast, both the Hieratic and Demotic are typically written from right to left.

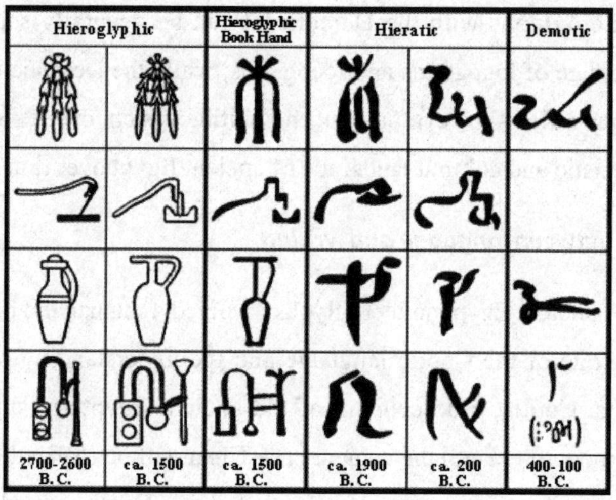

Hieroglyphic		Hieroglyphic Book Hand	Hieratic		Demotic
2700-2600 B.C.	ca. 1500 B.C.	ca. 1500 B.C.	ca. 1900 B.C.	ca. 200 B.C.	400-100 B.C.

Figure 4.14 Egyptian hieroglyphs, hieratic script, and demotic script
Source: https://www.civilization.ca/cmc/exhibitions/civil/egypt/egcw02e.shtml (accessed Aug. 31, 2024)

Why did Egyptian scribes feel the need to create Demotic? Steve Vinson, Professor of Egyptology at Indiana University, explains on the website of American Research Center in Egypt:

> One possible explanation for Demotic's split from Hieroglyphic and Hieratic is that, by 650 BCE, the language that Egyptians actually spoke was almost intolerably different from Middle Egyptian and even noticeably different from Late Egyptian. By this period, scribes may have more and more associated Hieratic with obsolete linguistic forms, and it may have seemed to them silly or counterproductive to write everyday documents in a language centuries out of date. When younger, more adventurous scribes wrote in their own vernacular, they may have felt increasingly free to ignore many of the rules and conventions of Hieratic writing, just as they also ignored the old grammatical rules and vocabulary restrictions of Middle Egyptian and Late Egyptian.

Demotic represented the Egyptian language between Late Egyptian and Coptic. Sharing basically the same phonetic inventory from earlier times, Demotic Egyptian saw a further simplification of the grammatical structure and an increase of loan words. The shift from Hieratic to Demotic script was driven by a combination of linguistic evolution and social transformation. It allowed scribes to align more closely with the linguistic realities and societal dynamics of their time, facilitating a more practical and emotionally resonant means of written communication.

As the Hieroglyphic was decoded, the language itself—often referred to as Middle Egyptian, used primarily from around 2000 BCE to 1350 BCE and continuingly used on as a literary language into the 4th century—began to unfold its syntax and grammar. For example, hieroglyphs representing a verb were consistently placed before those representing a subject and an object, suggesting a verb-subject-object (VSO) word order, which is common in many Semitic languages. Certain symbols or endings were attached to verb hieroglyphs, indicating past, present, or future tense, as well as other grammatical features such as negation or passive voice. The arrangement and combination of hieroglyphs provided clues about a sentence structure embodying a balance between the roles of nouns and verbs.

The decipherment not only provided access to the language but also unlocked the vast treasure trove of knowledge contained in ancient Egyptian texts. This included religious texts, historical accounts, administrative documents, and more. The newfound ability to read hieroglyphs significantly expanded our understanding of ancient Egyptian civilization, culture, and history.

The interaction between language and writing in the decipherment process illustrates how the written word can preserve and transmit knowledge across generations. It also highlights how different branches of linguistic study, from ancient languages to modern ones, can converge to unveil insights into humanity's past.

4.4   Number of symbols and type of script

Recognizing the relationship between symbol count and script type guided Champollion in hypothesizing the nature of the hieroglyphic writing system. Generally, a script containing 20 to 30 symbols is most likely a phonetic alphabet. Lower than 20 might indicate a consonantal abjad; a count between 30 to 90 likely indicates a syllabary; higher than 90 probably indicates a logographic system.

While there might not be a strict mathematical logic between the number of symbols and the type of script, there is a logic of practicality and effectiveness in designing writing systems to match the linguistic characteristics of the languages they represent. Phonetic alphabets are designed to represent individual sounds or phonemes of a language. The focus is on accurately capturing the speech sounds, and the symbols are often designed to correspond to individual consonants and vowels. Since many languages have a relatively small number of distinct phonemes, a phonetic alphabet requires a limited set of symbols. 20 to 30 symbols are usually sufficient to cover the basic phonetic inventory of most languages. Abjads omit vowel sounds, which reduces the overall number of symbols needed to no more than 20. Syllabaries are scripts where each symbol represents a syllable, usually consisting of a consonant and a vowel. Compared to distinct phonemes, many languages have a larger number of potential syllables, requiring a greater number of symbols. A count between 30 to 90 symbols accommodates a range of syllables in various languages.

For logographic scripts, the focus shifts from representing individual sounds or syllables to capturing the meaning of entire words. Representing whole words, morphemes, or concepts with individual symbols, logographic scripts require a much larger number of symbols to cover the diversity of meanings and concepts in a language, with estimates ranging from several hundreds to thousands. The number can vary significantly due to factors like the script's complexity, its intended use, and the linguistic features of the language it represents. For example, the number of distinct cuneiform signs is estimated ranging from around 600 to over 1,000 individual signs, including logograms, syllabic signs, and determinatives. The number of distinct hieroglyphic symbols in ancient Egyptian script varies depending on the time period and the specific corpus of texts being considered. There are thousands of hieroglyphs, but the number used in any given text or inscription would be smaller, often ranging from 700 to 2,000 distinct symbols. The oracle bone script used in ancient China during the Shang Dynasty features approximately 5000 distinct characters, but so far only around 2000 have been decoded. The exact number of distinct Mayan glyphs is debated, but estimates range from around 800 to over 1,000.

Summing-up

Deciphering an unknown script involves making educated guesses about the phonetic values of individual symbols and the rules governing their arrangement. Initially, a decipherer might work with a limited set of inscriptions to establish initial hypotheses. However, to ensure that these hypotheses are robust and accurate, they need to be tested against a wider range of texts. In this iterative process, decipherers gain more insights and refine their understanding of the script to revise their hypotheses.

The decipherment of the Egyptian hieroglyphs required both a polymath and a specialist to crack the code. Young's versatility provided some key initial insights between 1814 and 1819, and Champollion's focus allowed him to perceive system behind the signs in 1822. What finally enabled Champollion to do what neither Young nor any others were able to accomplish was to apply his mastery of Coptic to the problem. "His knowledge of Coptic enabled him to deduce the phonetic values of many syllabic signs, and to assign correct readings to many pictorial characters, the meanings of which were made known to him by the Greek text on the Stone." (Budge, 1905:4) While Young identified parts of an alphabet, "Champollion unlocked an entire language" (Parkingson, 1999: 40). As "decipherment has to stand or fall as a whole" (Daniels, 1996), recognition for this great feat is generally—and properly—given to the French linguist and archaeologist Champollion, who is widely regarded as the founder of Egyptology.

References

Adkins, Lesley and Roy Adkins. 2000. *The Keys of Egypt: The Obsession to Decipher Egyptian Hieroglyphs.* New York: Harper Collins Publishers.

Allen, James P. 2010. *Middle Egyptian: An Introduction to the Language and Culture of Hieroglyphs.* 2nd Edition. Cambridge: Cambridge University Press

Allen, Kathy. 2012. *Ancient Egyptian Hieroglyphs.* North Mankato: Capstone Press.

Åkerblad, Johan David. 1802. *Lettre sur l'inscription Égyptienne de Rosette: adressée au citoyen Silvestre de Sacy, Professeur de langue arabe à l'École spéciale des langues orientales vivantes, etc.; Réponse du citoyen Silvestre de Sacy.* Paris: L'imprimerie de la République.

Budge, E. A. Wallis. 1905. *The Nile, Notes for Travellers in Egypt*, 9th Edition, London: Thos. Cook and Son.

Collier, Mark and Bill Manley. 2003. *How to Read Egyptian: A Step-by-Step Guide to Teach Yourself.* Revised Edition. Berkeley, Los Angeles & London: University of California Press.

Champollion, Jean-François. 1822. *Lettre à M. Dacier relative à l'alphabet des hiéroglyphes phonétiques.* Paris: Firmin-Didot.

Daniels, Peter. 1996. "The Study of Writing Systems." In *The World's Writing Systems*, edited by Peter Daniels and William Bright. Oxford: Oxford University Press.

Davies, William Vivian. 1990. "Egyptian Hieroglyphs." In *Reading the Past: Ancient Writing from Cuneiform to the Alphabet*, edited by John Thomas Hooker, 75—136. London: British Museum Press.

Encyclopaedia Britannica. "Jean-François Champollion." Last revised and updated by Teagan Wolter. https://www.britannica.com/biography/Jean-Francois-Champollion (accessed May 11, 2024)

Fischer-Bovet, Christelle. 2015. Social Unrest and Ethnic Coexistence in Ptolemaic Egypt and The Seleucid Empire. *Past & Present* No. 229: 3045.

Griffith, Francis Llewellyn. 1898. *A Collection of Hieroglyphs: A contribution to the History of Egyptian Writing.* London: Gilbert &Rivington Ltd.

Loprieno, Antonio. 1995. *Ancient Egyptian: A Linguistic Introduction.* Cambridge: Cambridge University Press.

Meggs, Phillip B. and Alston W. Purvis. 2016. *History of Graphic Design.* 6th ed. Hoboken, NJ: Wiley.

Parkinson, Richard. 1999. *Cracking Codes: The Rosetta Stone and Decipherment.* Berkeley: University of California Press.

Parkinson, Richard. 2005. *British Museum Objects in Focus: The Rosetta Stone.* London: British Museum Press.

Pope, Maurice. 1999. *The Story of Decipherment, from Egyptian Hieroglyphs to Maya Script, Revised Edition.* Thames & Hudson.

Robinson, Andrew. 2007. *The Last Man Who Knew Everything: Thomas Young.* Oxford: Oneworld Publications.

Robinson Andrew. 2012. *Cracking the Egyptian code: the revolutionary life of Jean-François Champollion.* Oxford: Oxford University Press.

Silvestre de Sacy, Antoine-Isaac. 1802. *Lettre au citoyen Chaptal au sujet de l'inscription égyptienne du monument trouvé à Rosette.* Paris: Imprimerie de la République.

Strathern, Paul. 2009. *Napoleon in Egypt.* Reprint edition. New York: Bantam.

Vinson, Steve. "Demotic: The History, Development and Techniques of Ancient Egypt's Popular Script."

https://arce.org/resource/demotic-history-development-and-techniques-ancient-egypts-popular-script/ (accessed June 3, 2024)

Young, Thomas. 1819. "Egypt." In *Supplement to the Encyclopaedia Britannica*, Vol. IV, Part I, 1—60. Edinburgh: Archibald Constable and Company.

Young, Thomas. 1823. *An Account of Some Recent Discoveries in Hieroglyphical Literature and Egyptian Antiquities.* London: John Murray.

Further reading: excerpt from *Cracking Codes: The Rosetta Stone and Decipherment*

Parkinson, Richard. 1999. "Chapter 4 The Future: Further Codes to Crack." In *Cracking Codes: The Rosetta Stone and Decipherment*, 178—183. Oakland: University of California Press.

Chapter V   Interaction between Language and Writing: Decipherment of Linear B

Jumping-in

Tick the box that concerns decipherment and explain why in a short paragraph.

		Language	
		Known	Unknown
Script	Known		
	Unknown		

Deciphering an unknown script is often compared to cracking a secret code, as seen in the book title *Cracking Codes: The Rosetta Stone and Decipherment*, where the previous further reading is excerpted from. Yet, they are different in nature. Cryptanalysis is reading of messages which are intentionally disguised—they are designed to baffle the investigator. Decipherment is reading of messages that were meant to be read—they are puzzling just by accident.

In a secret code, a message is encrypted by making it appear random. In an unknown script, the original patterns of language are present. The case that concerns true decipherment is thus an unknown script and a known—sometimes, partially or subsequently known—language. As a result, decipherment involves additional complexities related to linguistics, culture, and historical context, making it a uniquely challenging endeavor.

Despite the difference in nature, decipherment does employ the methods used in cryptanalysis: pattern recognition, frequency analysis, iterative process, etc. The encoded texts are indexed and compared to discover underlying patterns and regularities—in cryptanalysis, these patterns are exploited to break codes, while in decipherment, they're sought after to understand the linguistic or symbolic meanings within the script and to provide clues about the script's structure; The occurrences of individual characters or groups of characters are counted—in cryptanalysis, these frequencies are compared to those expected in the plaintext, while in decipherment, they can help identify potential linguistic features, such as vowels or common syllables; Iterative processes are conducted so that researchers can refine their hypotheses, test them against held-out data, and adjust their strategies accordingly.

Such methods were at play in the decipherment of the Rosetta Stone and that of Linear B. However, the decipherment of the latter is often considered more akin to cryptanalysis than the former, because in the case of Linear B no bilingual can be used as crib.

5.1   Linear B

In 1900, British archaeologist Sir Arthur Evans (1851—1941) began his excavations at Knossos, the ancient city of Knossos in the Mediterranean island of Crete. He uncovered evidence of a hitherto unknown Bronze Age civilization, which he named "Minoan" after the legendary King Minos. According to him, the Minoans founded the first literate and urbanized culture in Europe. Emerging from the indigenous Cretan culture, they began to build spectacular palaces around 2000 BCE. They traded with the Near East and especially with Egypt, and created fine and beautiful works of art in stone, clay and fresco. Evans excavated numerous artefacts, among which were about 3000 tablets bearing a form of ancient script, which he later called Linear Script B. Evans (1909: 18) elucidated that the use of Linear B was preceded by two earlier types found in Crete—one also presenting linear characters, he called "Linear A," the other, still earlier, of conventionalized pictorial aspect, recalling Egyptian hieroglyphics, he called "Cretan hieroglyph."

Figure 5.1   Examples of Cretan hieroglyph, Linear A, and Linear B
Upper left: Green jasper seal with convoluted back, engraved with a design of three signs in the Cretan Hieroglyphic script
Source: https://www.britishmuseum.org/collection/image/1060643001 (accessed Sept. 5, 2024)
Upper right: A clay tablet from Zakros, Crete inscribed with Linear A script
Source: https://www.worldhistory.org/image/17693/clay-tablet-with-linear-a-script/ (accessed Sept. 5, 2024)
Bottom: Clay tablet (PY Ub 1318) inscribed with Linear B script, from the Mycenaean palace of Pylos
Source: https://en.wikipedia.org/wiki/Linear_B#/media/File:NAMA_Linear_B_tablet_of_Pylos.jpg (accessed Sept. 5, 2024)

In 1939, American archaeologist Carl Blegen (1887—1971) unearthed some 600 tablets with script identical to Evans' Linear B when working on the site of Pylos, one of the most important human centers of the Mycenaean civilization. These tablets, known as the "Pylos Tablets," held a potential to reveal the extent of interactions and connections between the Mycenaean civilization and the Minoan civilization.

Figure 5.2   The Mycenaean and Minoan civilizations
Source: https://dinromerohistory.wordpress.com/2020/06/27/the-mycenaean-civilization/ (accessed Sept. 5, 2024)

Linear B texts consist of groups of signs. The length of the groups varies from two to eight signs. A count of these signs shows that they number about ninety, which indicates the script's syllabic nature. Each sign would therefore represent a syllable consisting of either a pure vowel (e.g. a, e) or a consonant + vowel (e.g. ma, ne).

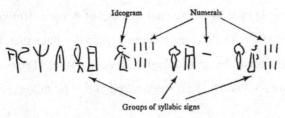

Figure 5.3   Pylos tablet Aa62 showing composition of the text
Source: Chadwick, 1970: 44

Accompanying these in many cases are other signs which stand alone, followed by a numeral; many of these are recognizable ideograms (Chadwick, 1970: 43). Thus, in many cases it was possible to deduce the general subject-matter of the tablets on the basis of ideograms before a single syllable could be read. The following are some obvious ideograms. It was clear that these tablets were not literary texts but administrative records: lists of workers, inventories of pottery and animals, catalogues of weapons and so forth. Thus, a single word followed by the symbol ⚹, clearly a person, was likely to be a person's name or title.

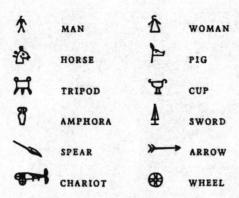

Figure 5.4   Some obvious ideograms
Source: Chadwick, 1970: 45

The numerals were quite straightforward: they are based on the decimal system, but there is no notation for zero, and figures up to 9 are represented by repeating the sign the appropriate number of times, much as in Roman numerals. Vertical strokes denote digits, horizontal strokes tens, circles hundreds, circles with rays thousands, and circles with rays and a central bar tens of thousands (Chadwick, 1970: 44). Thus 12,345 is written:

The above points had been worked out by Evans fairly early, but the decipherment was hindered by the fact that he died in 1941 without having published very many of the Linear B texts. These texts were planned as the second volume of *Scripta Minoa*, the first volume of which had come out in 1909. The second volume was finally published in 1952—11 years after Evans' death, by his friend, the archaeologist Sir John Myres (1869—1954), the retired Professor of Ancient History at Oxford, who was himself at that point very old.

5.2   The decipherment of Linear B

For more than fifty years, the mysterious ancient script fascinated both reputable scholars and talented amateurs. Various attempts had been made, but nearly every attempt prior to the early 1940s went into oblivion.

5.2.1   Alice Kober: building the grid

The turning point was made by Alice Kober (1906—1950), an American classist who mastered a host of languages, ancient and modern. Since 1943, Kober had cataloged and analyzed the characters and symbols found in very limited materials, and created extensive concordances and indexes that helped her study the distribution of symbols and patterns. She analyzed the occurrences of various characters and combinations in the texts. By studying the frequencies and relationships between symbols, she aimed to identify recurring patterns that might provide insights into the structure and grammar of the underlying language.

In 1945, Kober noted that many symbols occurred in consistent patterns across different inscriptions, suggesting that they might represent grammatical elements. She also recognized that some symbols exhibited variations in form, which hinted at their potential **inflectional** roles—a change in the form to express a grammatical function or attribute such as tense, mood, person, number, case, and gender. She grouped together some sets of three words that have the same syllables in the beginning but different ones at the end, later known as "Kober's triplets".

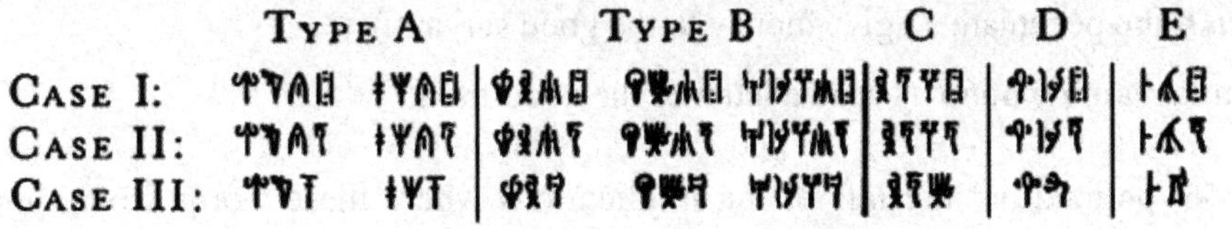

Figure 5.5   Sets of "Kober's triplets"
Source: Chackwick, 1970: 35

Of these triplets Case III is the shortest form, whereas Case I and Case II regularly add the signs -❏ and -❡ respectively; in this process the -❥ of all the Type A words is changed to -∧- , and the -❧ of Type B to- ⋀- ; similar changes are seen in Types C, D and E.

A highly skilled linguist, Kober began to discern patterns of possible inflectional endings. She drew on Latin second **declension**, which involves masculine nouns, neuter nouns, and adjectives that agree with these nouns in case, gender and number. For example, the forms of the masculine nouns *servus* (servant), *amicus* (friend), and the adjective *bonus* (good) for nominative, accusative, genitive and dative in singular are demonstrated through word endings -us, -um, -i, -o.

nominative singular:	*servus*	*amicus*	*bonus*
accusative singular:	*servum*	*amicum*	*bonum*
genitive singular:	*servi*	*amici*	*boni*
dative singular:	*servo*	*amico*	*bono*

The nominative case is used for the subject of the sentence. For example:

Servus bonus laborat. (The good servant is working.)

Amicus bonus venit. (The good friend is coming.)

The accusative case is used for the direct object of the sentence. For example:

Dominus **servum bonum** laudat. (The master praises the good servant.)

Video **amicum bonum**.(I see the good friend.)

The genitive case is used to show possession. For example:

Liber **servi boni** est in mensa. (The book of the good servant is on the table.)

Domus **amici boni** magna est. (The house of the good friend is large.)

The dative case is used for the indirect object of the sentence. For example:

Dono **servo bono** pecuniam. (I give money to the good servant.)

Mitto epistulam **amico bono**. (I send a letter to the good friend.)

Kober (1946) pointed out the interesting implications where these words would appear in syllabic spelling as:

ser-vu-s	*a-mi-cu-s*	*bo-nu-s*
ser-vu-m	*a-mi-cu-m*	*bo-nu-m*
ser-vi	*a-mi-ci*	*bo-ni*
ser-vo	*a-mi-co*	*bo-no*

Like the dative endings -vo, -co, -no, so too the series of parallel endings 𐀀 𐀂 𐀄 𐀆 𐀈 might be expected to share the same vowel but different consonants; whereas 𐀀/𐀉 𐀂/𐀊 etc. are probably pairs sharing the same consonant but different vowels, like vo/vu, co/cu and no/nu. This result can be tabulated in a diagrammatic form, labelled by Kober "the beginning of a tentative phonetic pattern," and known familiarly as "the grid" among the team of decoders (Chadwick, 1970: 16).

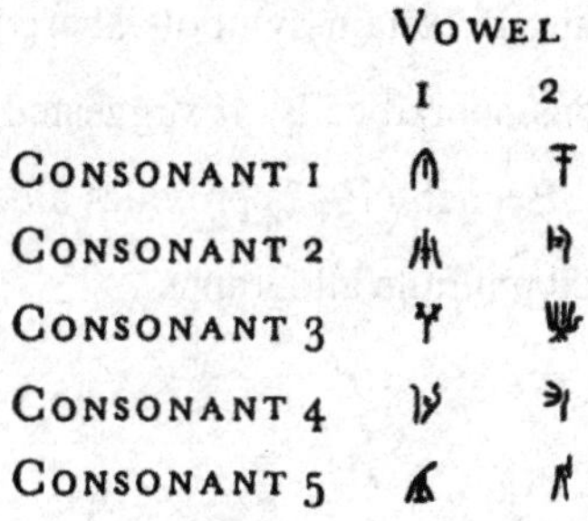

VOWEL

	1	2
CONSONANT 1	∧	千
CONSONANT 2	州	ㄐ
CONSONANT 3	Υ	Ψ
CONSONANT 4	))>	ㅋ
CONSONANT 5	∢	↑

Figure 5.6   Kober's grid
Source: Chadwick, 1970: 16

Of course, such a writing system was not suitable for Latin in which closed syllables and consonant clusters occur frequently. If it had to be used, strategies must be devised to treat word-final consonants and sequences of consonants: either a consonant is omitted or a consonant preceding another is written with CV symbol whose vowel is empty or "dead" and receives the coloring of vowel in the following syllable (cf. Further reading).

Through her grid, Kober developed hypotheses about the relationships between certain signs. Tragically, her life was cut short by her premature death in 1950 at the age of 43. Her legacy was carried forward by Michael Ventris, who built upon her sturdy work and eventually deciphered the script. In recent years, Kober's role in the decipherment has been likened to that of Rosalind Franklin, the English scientist now considered the unsung heroine of one of the most signal intellectual feats of the modern age, the mapping of the molecular structure of DNA by Francis Crick and James Watson (e.g., Robinson, 2002:16). "It is clear that without her work Linear B would never have been deciphered when it was, if at all." (Fox, 2013:14)

5.2.2   Emmett Bennett: expanding with data

A parallel analysis of the Pylos material was conducted by Emmett Bennett (1918—2011), an American linguist and epigrapher. Former doctoral student of Blegen, Bennett worked on the Pylos tablets and cleared the ground for orderly analysis of the vast array of data. He classified the documents primarily according to the ideograms appearing on them. For instance, A and B Class tablets all have ideograms for people (men and women), C and D tablets deal with livestock, J with bronze, G with wine and spices, and so forth. Moreover, he identified distinct signs and variations of the same sign by comparing their appearances, contexts, and potential meanings. If certain symbols appeared in similar contexts and were consistently associated with specific meanings or words, it suggested that those symbols were distinct and had consistent linguistic functions. If certain symbols shared a common core while having additional strokes or modifications sporadically, it suggested that they are variations of the same sign. Through minute work, Bennett (1947) provides a descriptive catalogue of about 80 graphemes, many of which showed multiple allographs.

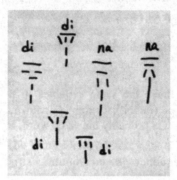

Figure 5.7   Signs for *di* and *na* written by different scribes
Source: Bendall, 2003: 52

Bennett's analysis supported and expanded upon some of Kober's hypotheses, providing valuable validation for her initial insights. His work added more evidence to the idea that Linear B was a syllabic script with potential inflectional features.

Kober and Bennett began their correspondence in June 1948, exchanging materials and working together to compile a comprehensive sign list of all the characters used in both the mainland and Cretan versions of the Linear B script. By 1951, a year after Kober's death, the signary was finalized by Bennett and Michael Ventris, who would later go on to decipher the script (cf. Fox, 2013: 213—216). The first established signary for Linear B—involving 89 graphemes, arranged by character shape, with simpler, straighter characters coming first and more complex, curvier ones coming later—was introduced in 1951 in Bennett's book *The Pylos Tablets: A Preliminary Transcription.*

5.2.3   Michael Ventris: assigning sound values

Kober and Bennett's insights and contributions paved the way for Michael Ventris (1922—1956), a British architect, who had shown a precocious interest in Linear B since his teens. His interest was piqued by the challenges posed by the script's unknown language and its connection to the ancient Mycenaean civilization.

Ventris drew heavily on Kober's linguistic grid. He extended it to the entire set of glyphs for

Linear B with additional triplets from the Pylos data and constructed a "syllabic grid." In addition, he conducted a frequency analysis, sorting the characters into three groups: Frequent, Average, and Infrequent. Much as Kober had done with the Knossos inscriptions, he also tabulated their use in various positions in Linear B words. In this way, Ventris determined that ⌐ⵑ was likely to be a pure vowel, say [a], because it is very frequent at the beginning of words, whereas in the middle or end the vowel would be likely to be joined to a consonant to form syllables, thus written with a different sign.

Ventris' choice to start with the hypothesis that this pure vowel was [a] was likely influenced by a combination of factors, including linguistic context of the Aegean region, phonetic analysis, and his own familiarity with known languages, particularly Greek, in which [a] is a common vowel sound that frequently appears at the beginning of words. Also, the open front unrounded vowel [a] is one of the most common vowel sounds found in a wide range of languages. However, it's important to clarify that it is not truly universal in all languages, and the probability of usage can vary significantly. For example, [a] is absent in some languages with small vowel inventories, though they usually include a subset of the common vowel sounds [i], [e], [a], [o], and [u].

"To go further would require a mind like his that combined her perseverance, logic and method," Robinson (2002: 91) has written, "with a willingness to take intellectual risks." The choice of [a] as a pure vowel was a starting point for further testing and validation.

The "Work Notes" Ventris circulated to a group of scholars recorded the main line of his progress between the start of 1951 and the middle of 1952. He cross-referenced his findings with known words worked out by other researchers, and it fit well. The ending of the feminine adjectives in Kober's Case I in −𐀀𐀁, etc., might well be -i-ja (since derivative women's names in -ia occur in Greek, Lycian and Etruscan): in this case Vowel 3 in Figure 5.6 (in 𐀂, 𐀃, etc.) was -i, and Vowel 1 was -a. Vowel 2 might be -e, if the very numerous men's names in

−𐀤𐀍 −𐀱𐀍 −𐀲𐀍, etc., were ancestral to Greek -ε𝘶ς (Note 16); and Vowel 4 might then be left with the value -o.

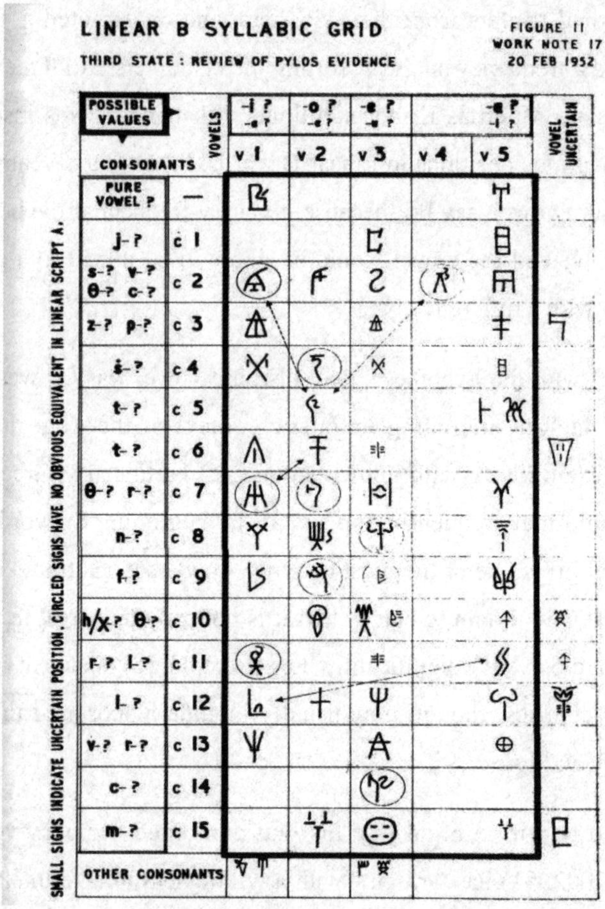

Figure 5.8   The state of the "grid" prior to decipherment (February 1952)
Source: Galanakis, et al. 2017: 22

The value of the consonants was much more difficult to guess. By comparing the content of Cretan tablets with those from mainland Greece, Ventris noticed that certain words seemed to occur only in headings on Knossos tablets. This observation led him to speculate that these unique words might be place names associated with locations specific to Crete, as place names were relevant in administrative records for identifying where goods were stored, transactions occurred, or other activities took place. A certain sequence of characters occurring repeatedly, which was also included in a set Kober had published in her 1946 paper on declension, goes as follows:

It was at this moment that Ventris made an intuitive leap by allowing himself to experiment with the Cypriot syllabary, "the only external clue in existence to the possible identities of some Linear B characters" (Fox, 2013: 271). The Cypriot syllabary, deciphered in the 1870s, was used to record the indigenous Cypriot language from approximately the 11th century BCE to the 4th century BCE. After the Hellenization of Cyprus, it was retained for a time to write Greek, especially the Arcadocypriot dialect. Investigators had long noticed the resemblance between a handful of Cypriot characters and Linear B signs, but had refrained from using the Cypriot script as a direct clue. Fox (2013: 273) lists several reasons: The Cypriot syllabary was a millennium younger than Linear B, and a lot can happen to a script in a thousand years; Similar-looking scripts often record extremely dissimilar languages; Even in related languages, identical characters can have entirely different sound-values.

Cypriot sign	Cypriot sound value	Linear B sign
+	"lo"	†
T̄	"na"	Ȳ
⊦	"ta"	⊦
↑	"ti"	∧

Figure 5.9   Examples of Cypriot characters and Linear B signs that resemble each other

Ventris turned to the Cypriot sign T̄, "na." If the Linear B sign had the same value, then he could insert "na" into the grid where Row C8 and Column V5 intersected, given ᵀ⁄ identified as [a] (Ventris draws the character as ᵀ̄, an acceptable variant form). Then he assigned the sound value "ti" to ∧, which he had already placed at the intersection of C6 and V1. Now the grid's web of interdependencies truly began to pay dividends: if Ȳ is "na" and "∧" is "ti," then Ÿ must be "ni." So far, the sequence can be read as [a]—[ni]—, which led him to the name of an important harbor town "Amnissos" (Αμνίσσος).

$$\text{ᵀ⁄–mi–}^{xx}\text{Ÿ–so}$$

This discovery triggered a chain reaction—if Ÿ were ni, then signs in the same row would share the consonant value n-, and those in the same column to have the vowel value -i. The same would work for m-, s-, -o.

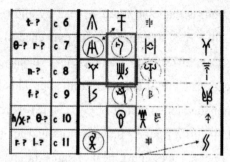

Figure 5.10   Chain reaction triggered by ɣ

Then another possible place name:

would be read as ?o- no-so. Knossos! The name of the archaeological site on Crete! With "Amnissos" and "Knossos," Ventris could now identify characters representing the sounds [m], [k], [n], and [s]. This expanded his repertoire of phonetic values and allowed him to decipher additional words and sequences that shared these sounds. The more values were deduced, the more words could be "read", and the more values could be filled in on the grid. Eventually he identified possible phonetic values for individual glyphs and created phonetic renderings for various Linear B words. For example, The first two sets of Kober's triplets mentioned above corresponded with Greek pronunciations for the Cretan place names of *Luktos* and *Amnisos*. Additional declensions indicated citizens, both masculine (-ijos) and feminine (ija).

ru ki to	a mi ni so
ru ki ti jo	a mi ni si jo
ru ki ti ja	a mi ni si ja
luktos	amnisos
luktijos	amnisijos
luktija	amnisija

Now let's come back to the groups of syllabic signs in Figure 5.3. What do they mean? Evans had already guessed that the sign-groups following the ideogram in tablet Aa 62 might refer to children. Ventris' values gave ko-wa and ko-wo, which are plausible syllabic spellings of the archaic Greek words for girls (korwai) and boys (korwoi), and the term before the ideogram turns out to be *me-re-ti-ri-ja* = *meletriai* "flour-grinders." Recording work-groups of women, girls, and boys, Aa 62 reads: "7 women, 1 girl and 6 boys as flour-grinders."

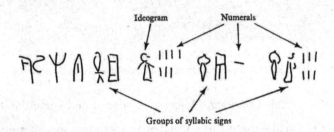

Within a few months, the results pointed him to an unexpected conclusion:

> During the last few weeks, I have come to the conclusion that the Knossos and Pylos tablets must, after all, be written in Greek—a difficult and archaic Greek, seeing that it is 500 years older than Homer and written in a rather abbreviated form, but Greek nevertheless (July 1st, 1952, in a talk on BBC radio).

5.2.4   John Chadwick: supporting, refining, documenting

Listening to the broadcast was John Chadwick (1920—1998), a British classical philologist and a specialist in early Greek dialects. He was struck by Ventris' suggestion that the Linear B might after all have been used for writing Greek, a possibility most people until then had thought highly unlikely. Chadwick visited Myres, who let him copy some of Ventris' *Work Notes* and put him in touch with Ventris. Chadwick knew what a version of Greek some 500 years earlier than Homer should look like, something of which Ventris had little idea. In his first letter back to Chadwick, Ventris asked him to consider collaborating in the publication of the decipherment. From then on, Ventris and Chadwick corresponded with one another almost daily, from July 1952 until shortly before Ventris' death in a car accident on September 6, 1956.

In 1953, a significant archaeological discovery took place at the site of Pylos in Greece. Excavations led by Carl Blegen uncovered a cache of clay tablets inscribed with Linear B script. Blegen examined the new Pylos tablets in detail, and sent Ventris and Chadwick exciting news of a tablet which "evidently deals with pots, some on three legs, some with four handles, some with three, and others without handles. The first word 𝕄 ; (by your system seems to be *ti-ri-po-de*, and it recurs twice as *ti-ri-po* (singular?). The four-handled pot 𝕎 is preceded by *qe-to-ro-we*, the threehandled ♀ by *ti-ri-o-we-e* or *ti-ri-jo-we*, the handleless pot ♀ by *a-no-we*."(Chadwick, 1970: 81)

Figure 5.11   The tripod tablet (Pylos tablet 641), hand-drawn by Ventris
Source: https://konosos.net/2013/12/21/the-decipherment-of-linear-b-py-ta-641/ (accessed Sept. 5, 2024)

These newly discovered tablets provided additional evidence and served as held-out data that allowed Ventris and Chadwick to further verify and validate their hypothesis that the underlying language was Greek.

Understanding Linear B provides valuable insights into pre-historic Greek civilization and its interactions with neighboring cultures in the Eastern Mediterranean. In the Middle Bronze Age period (ca. 2000 BCE—1550 BCE), the Minoan civilization on Crete dominated the Aegean (Braun, 2020). Cretan hieroglyphic was invented, as the first script used in Europe, around 2000 BCE and was in use to 1650 BCE. Co-existing with Cretan hieroglyphic for 200 years, Linear A was used from about 1850 BCE—1450 BCE, during the height of Minoan culture, when Minoans were traveling and trading throughout the Eastern Mediterranean. Around the Late Minoan period (ca. 1400 BCE—1300 BCE) the Minoan civilization fell under the control of the ever-expanding Mycenaean population, and Linear B was adapted from Linear A to write a different language: Greek. It was used from 1400 BCE to 1200 BCE to keep administrative records.

In the Spring of 1953, the announcement that Ventris had deciphered Linear B appeared right next to the headline of Edmund Hillary scaling Everest in Nepal. Linear B became known as "the Everest of Greek archaeology." As with the Egyptian hieroglyphs, Linear B was deciphered at the right time to get caught up in nationalistic fervor. Also as with Egyptian hieroglyphs, it is best described as a collaborative effort.

Chadwick, as Robinson (2002: 14) observed, played the dogged Watson to Ventris's inspired Holmes. Together, Ventris and Chadwick co-authored several significant papers and books. One of their most important works was *Documents in Mycenaean Greek* (1956/1973), which presented the decipherment comprehensively and provided a thorough analysis of the Linear B script and the Mycenaean administrative system. After the death of Ventris, Chadwick continued to decipher and interpret additional Linear B tablets, contributing to a more comprehensive understanding of the Mycenaean economy, administration, and society.

5.3   Frequency, entropy, and more

In the context of Linear B, the character representing the sound [a] can be considered more predictable and therefore contains less information. A statistical parameter which measures how much information is produced on the average for each letter of a text in the language is called entropy in Claude Shannon's information theory.

> In a previous paper the entropy and redundancy of a language have been defined. The entropy is a statistical parameter which measure in a certain sense, how much information is produced on the average for each letter of a text in the language. If the language is translated into binary digits (0 or 1) in the most efficient way, the entropy H is the average number of binary digits required per letter of the original language. The redundancy on the other hand, measures the amount of constraint imposed on a text of the language due to its statistical structure, e.g., in English the high frequency of the letter E, the strong tendency of H to follow T or of U to follow Q. It was estimated that when statistical effects extending over not more than eight letters are considered the entropy is roughly 2.3 bits per letter the redundancy about 50 per cent. (Shannon, 1950: 50)

In other words, **entropy** refers to the measure of uncertainty or randomness in a sequence of symbols. Lower entropy indicates a higher level of predictability, meaning that certain symbols or sequences are more likely to occur than others. Higher entropy implies more randomness and less predictability.

In the case of decipherment, identifying highly predictable characters or symbols can be a crucial step. For example, if a particular character consistently represents a common sound at the beginning of words (like [a]), decipherers can use this predictability as a starting point for identifying other characters and sounds. This process helps establish a foundation for deciphering more complex or less predictable elements.

Frequency analysis employed by Ventris is a standard codebreaking method. In the case of simple codes where the language is known it can be used to break the code. For instance, if you happen to know over a collection of sentences in English the letter *e* generally emerges as the most common, then if a code has used *z* to represent *e* you could find this out simply by noting that *z* is the most frequent in the text.

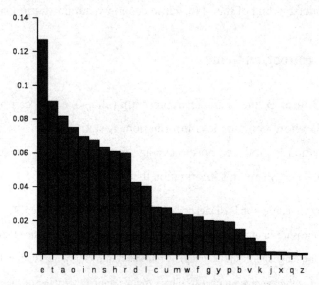

Figure 5.12   Relative frequency of occurrence of English alphabets
source: https://en.m.wikipedia.org/wiki/File:English_letter_frequency_(frequency).svg (accessed Sept. 5, 2024)

When it comes to the most common English words, *the, of, and, in, a, to, is, was, for, as, on, by, with, he, that, from, it, his, are, an* are the top twenty. When ranked across huge corpora or single books, word frequency also follows a predictable pattern:

–Second most common word in corpus appears half as often as the first
–Third most common word in corpus appears a third as often as the first
–Etc…

This is called Zipf's law.

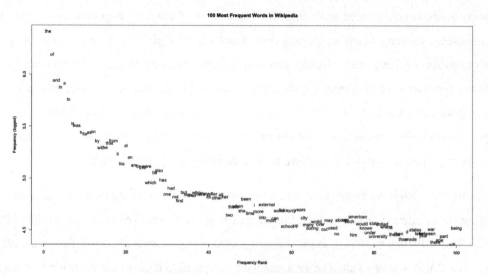

Figure 5.13   100 most frequent words in Wikipedia
Source: http://wugology.com/zipfs-law/ (accessed Sept. 5, 2024)

In writing, information is encoded by symbols under grammatical and semantic constraints. Montemurro and Zanette (2011) used entropy to quantify the contribution of different organizational levels to the overall statistical structure of language. They studied entropy of word ordering across eight languages belonging to five linguistic families and a language isolate (Indo-European: English, French, and German; Finno-Ugric: Finnish; Austronesian: Tagalog; Isolate: Sumerian; Afroasiatic: Old Egyptian; Sino-Tibetan: Chinese). Their analysis, as illustrated by the following figure, shows that a measure of relative entropy between a real text (H) and a disordered version (Hs) of it where word order has been destroyed presents an almost constant value (Ds) across different linguistic families.

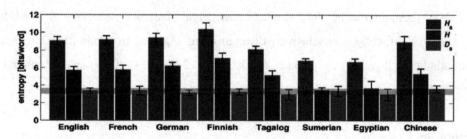

Figure 5.14   Entropy of word ordering across eight languages
Source: Montemurro and Zanette, 2011
Note: For each language, bars on the left in each group represent the average entropy of the random texts (Hs), bars in the middle show the average entropy of the original texts (H), and bars on the right show the difference between the entropies for the random and original texts (Ds).

Entropy analysis can involve analyzing the frequencies of different **n-gram**s, i.e., sequences of *n* consecutive items (such as characters or words) from a given text. N-grams are used to analyze patterns within text, identify common sequences of symbols, and understand how different symbols tend to appear together. By counting the occurrences of n-grams in a text, researchers can gain insights into the structure of language and the likelihood of certain sequences occurring. In essence, n-grams provide a way to analyze local patterns within text, while entropy provides a global measure of predictability across the entire text.

Attempts have been made to prove if some unknown script represents a language by the application of entropy and n-grams, including Linear A Script, Voynich manuscript, Indus Valley Script, Pictish symbols, and Rongorongo Script (e.g., Lee et al., 2010; Rao et al., 2009; Rao, 2010, 2018). Entropy values of the script were compared to those of known natural languages and non-linguistic sequences to assess whether the script exhibits linguistic properties. Additionally, the application of computational methods, including machine learning and AI, has become more prevalent in recent years to aid decipherment attempts for unknown scripts.

Figure 5.15   Indus script on stamp seals, amulets, and small tablets
Source: Rao et al., 2010

Nonetheless, these approaches face similar fundamental challenges: shortage of large, high-quality datasets; difficulty in conclusively distinguishing linguistic from non-linguistic patterns without additional linguistic insights (cf. Sproat, 2010: 266; 2014, 2015); lack of cultural and historical context.

Summing-up

Decipherment involves not only understanding the script's symbols and their possible phonetic or semantic values but also establishing a connection to a known language or languages. This connection is vital for making sense of the inscriptions' content, context, and meaning. The

Indus Valley script is a prime example of a script that remains undeciphered despite extensive research efforts. Regardless of progress in understanding its structural features and patterns, scholars have not yet been able to definitively associate the script with a known language. Lack of a known linguistic key makes it challenging to interpret the script's inscriptions in a meaningful way.

In decipherment efforts, the identification of a linguistic match often requires a combination of linguistic, historical, archaeological, and contextual evidence. Without these key elements, the decipherment process can stall or result in multiple speculative interpretations. While AI and computational methods have the potential to aid decipherment by analyzing large datasets and identifying patterns, the ultimate breakthrough often comes from a combination of interdisciplinary collaboration.

Deciphering ancient scripts involves more than just establishing linguistic patterns; it requires understanding the historical, cultural, and geographical context that can connect the script to a specific language and culture. Until all these pieces come together, certain scripts will remain enigmatic and undeciphered.

References

Bendall, Lisa M. 2003. *The Decipherment of Linear B and the Ventris-Chadwick Correspondence: An Exhibition to Celebrate the 50th Anniversary of the Publication of the Decipherment. Organized by the Mycenaean Epigraphy Group, Faculty of Classics, Cambridge, at the Fitzwilliam Museum, 9 September—21 December 2003. Exhibition Catalogue.* Cambridge: Fitzwilliam Museum.

Bennett, Emmett L. 1947. *The Minoan Linear Script from Pylos.* PhD diss., University of Cincinnati.

Bennett, Emmett. 1951. *The Pylos Tablets: A Preliminary Transcription.* Princeton: Princeton University Press for University of Cincinnati.

Braun, Graham. 2020. Women in Mycenaean Greece: The Linear B Textual Evidence. *The Ascendant Historian.* Vol. 7 (1): 6—19.

Chadwick, John. 1970. *The Decipherment of Linear B.* Second Edition. Cambridge: Cambridge University Press.

Evans, Arthur. 1909. *Scripta Minoa: The Written Documents of Minoan Crete with Special Reference to the Archives of Knossos.* Vol. 1, Oxford: Clarendon Press.

Evans, Arthur. 1952. *Scripta Minoa: The Written Documents of Minoan Crete with Special Reference to the Archives of Knossos.* Vol. 2, edited by John L. Myres, Oxford: Clarendon Press.

Fox, Margalit. 2013. *The Riddle of the Labyrinth.* London: Profile Books.

Galanakis, Yannis, Anastasia Christophilopoulou and James Grime. 2017. *Codebreakers and Groundbreakers.* Cambridge: The Fitzwilliam Museum, University of Cambridge.

Kober, Alice. 1945. Evidence of Inflection in the 'Chariot' Tablets from Knossos. *American Journal of Archaeology* Vol. 49 (2): 143—151.

Kober, Alice. 1946. Inflection in Linear Class B: 1—Declension. *American Journal of Archaeology,* Vol. 50(2): 268—276.

Lee, Rob, Philip Jonathan, and Pauline Ziman. 2010. Pictish Symbols Revealed as a Written Language through Application of Shannon Entropy. *Proceedings of the Royal Society A: Mathematical, Physical and Engineering Sciences,* Vol. 466 (2121): 2545—2560.

Montemurro, Marcelo A. and Damián H. Zanette. 2011. Universal Entropy of Word Ordering Across Linguistic Families. PLOS ONE, *Public Library of Science,* vol. 6(5): 1—9.

Rao, Rajesh. 2010. "Probabilistic Analysis of an Ancient Undeciphered Script." *IEEE Computer,* 43(4): 76—80.

Rao, Rajesh. 2018. "The Indus Script and Economics: A Role for Indus Seals and Tablets in Rationing and Administration of Labor." In *Walking with the Unicorn: Social Organization and Material Culture in*

Ancient South Asia, edited by D. Frenez, G. M. Jamison, R. W. Law, M. Vidale & R. H. Meadow, 518—525, Oxford: Archaeopress.

Rao, Rajesh, et al. 2009. "Entropic Evidence for Linguistic Structure in the Indus Script." *Science*, 324(5931): 1165.

Rao, Rajesh, et al. 2015. "On Statistical Measures and Ancient Writing Systems." *Language*. Vol. 91(4): 198—205.

Robinson, Andrew. 2002. *The Man Who Deciphered Linear B: The Story of Michael Ventris*. London: Thames & Hudson.

Robinson, Andrew. 2009. *Lost Languages: The Enigma of the World's Undeciphered Scripts*. London: Thames & Hudson.

Sproat, Richard. 2010. *Language, Technology, and Society*. Oxford: Oxford University Press.

Sproat, Richard. 2014. "A Statistical Comparison of Written Language and Nonlinguistic symbol Systems." *Language* 90, no. 2: 457—481.

Sproat, Richard. 2015. "On Misunderstandings and Misrepresentations: A Reply to Rao et al." *Language* 91, no. 4: e206—208.

Shannon, Claude E. 1950. "Prediction and Entropy of Printed English." *Bell System Technical Journal*, Vol. 30(1): 50—64.

Ventris, Michael and John Chadwick. 1956. *Documents in Mycenaean Greek*. Cambridge: Cambridge University Press.

Ventris, Michael and John Chadwick. 1973. *Documents In Mycenaean Greek*. 2nd ed. Cambridge: Cambridge University Press.

Further reading: excerpt from *Linear B: An Introduction*

Hooker, James Thomas. 1980. "Part One Chapter 4 The Linear B Inscriptions." In *Linear B: An Introduction*, 49—53. London: Bristol Classical Press.

Chapter VI   Writing, Literacy, and Society

Jumping-in

Below are two pages from a copy of *The Nihon Shoki* (《日本書紀》)—the second oldest book of classical Japanese history, finished in 720. Study the pages and then share your initial observations when looking at them in a short paragraph.

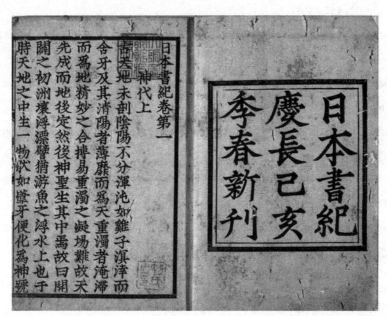

Figure 6.1   Two pages from a copy of *The Nihon Shoki*
Source: https://www.loc.gov/item/2021666419 (accessed Sept. 5, 2024)

The historical example of Linear B, a writing system borrowed from the Minoan civilization and used to write Ancient Greek, illustrates that literacy can take different forms and have different implications in different cultural and historical contexts.

In the case of Linear B, the Mycenaean Greeks adapted an existing writing system, likely of Minoan origin, to write their own language. The adaptation required Mycenaean scribes to develop strategies to accommodate the phonological differences between the Minoan language (which Linear B was initially developed for) and the Greek language. The scribes had to apply certain rules to make Linear B suitable for writing Greek. For instance, they dropped consonants at the end of syllables to approximate Greek phonology. Despite the adaptation, Linear B was not a perfect match for the Greek language's phonology and morphology. Some linguistic features of Greek could not be accurately represented within the constraints of the Linear B script.

In contrast, the historical use of writing systems in various regions of Asia, for example, in countries like Japan, Korea, and Vietnam, was not adaptation but rather adoption of an existing script, specifically the Chinese script, to represent their own languages. *The Nihon Shoki* (The Chronicles of Japan) shown in the Jumping-in above was written in pure Classical Chinese, as was common for official Japanese documents at that time. The Chinese script was imported to Japan in the 5th century through the transmission of Buddhist texts and teachings from China. From the 5th to the 9th century, the Chinese script was used for various purposes, including official documents, religious texts, historical records, and literature. Those who sought literacy had to learn Classical Chinese, making China the dominant culture in East Asia.

Analogous to this situation was Latin in medieval Europe. Spanning from the Late Antiquity to the Middle Ages, Latin remained a written *lingual franca* in Europe. Though the Renaissance period witnessed a significant expansion of writing in vernacular languages in literature, showcased by renowned works like Dante Alighieri's *Divine Comedy* (1472), Geoffrey Chaucer's *The Canterbury Tales* (1476), and Giovannni Boccaccio's *Decameron* (ca. 1353), Latin continued to be used and preferred well into the early modern period for academic, scientific, and religious contexts. Here are a few examples: *De Humani Corporis Fabrica* (On the Fabric of the Human Body) by Andreas Vesalius (1543), *Novum Organum* (The New Organon) by Francis Bacon (1620), *De Veritate Religionis Christiane* (The Truth of the Christian Religion) by Hugo Grotius (1627), *Meditationes de Prima Philosophia* (Meditations on First Philosophy) by René Descartes (1641), *Principia Mathematica* (Mathematical Principles of Natural Philosophy) by Isaac Newton (1687), *Systema Naturae* (System of Nature) by Carl Linnaeus (1758), *Theoria Philosophiae Naturalis* (A Theory of Natural Philosophy) by Roger Joseph Boscovich (1758).

6.1　Literacy: the multifaceted nature

From the above discussion, you might have captured an important aspect of literacy and the complexities associated with defining it. Literacy indeed goes beyond a simple binary of being able to read and write; it encompasses various contexts, languages, and levels of proficiency.

A society may be considered "**literate**" based on the existence of a written tradition and the ability of a select few to read and write. However, literacy in such societies is often highly restricted, typically limited to a small elite or privileged segment of the population who enjoyed social status, wealth, or positions of power. In cases of ancient Japan and medieval Europe where language shift was involved, specialized education demanded years of hard work. Therefore, there have been instances throughout history where even individuals who had access to education were not necessarily proficient in literacy. The samurai (侍) class in feudal Japan, for example, were trained in various martial skills, and their literacy levels might have varied.

In ancient societies, the control over literacy and its dissemination was often closely guarded. The elite classes, such as nobility, clergy, and scholars, used literacy as a means of maintaining their positions of power and reinforcing social hierarchies. The ability to read and write was seen as a mark of refinement and education, setting the literate apart from the general population. By restricting access to education and literacy, the elite could maintain a barrier to upward social mobility. Ancient Egypt, early Mesopotamia, Mycenae, early China boasted trained elites who resisted simplification or change of traditional scripts. Furthermore, those who controlled literacy also controlled access to information, enabling them to manage and manipulate information to their advantage. In societies where Latin religious texts held great importance, religious leaders who were literate gained significant authority. They could interpret and communicate religious teachings, exerting influence over spiritual matters. The selling of indulgences by the Roman Catholic Church in the 16th century is a well-known example of how monopoly over Latin religious texts and their interpretation could be used for financial gain.

As societies progressed, efforts were made to broaden access to literacy and education, leading to shifts in power dynamics and social transformation. During the late Qing Dynasty and early Republic of China, the "Baihua Movement" (白话运动, Vernacular Language Movement) , which advocated for writing in the vernacular Chinese instead of Classical Chinese, demonstrated how linguistic changes can spark significant social and cultural debates. The proponents of the movement sought to democratize education and make written communication more accessible to the general population by using the spoken language in writing. The opponents saw the shift to vernacular as a departure from a centuries-old tradition and expressed concerns about the loss of cultural heritage, the erosion of language purity, and the potential undermining of their social status. These debates and tensions provoke broader discussions about language, identity, culture, and societal change during a period of political and cultural transformation in China.

The 20th century witnessed a shift in the emphasis and understanding of what constitutes a literate society. For one thing, the focus switched from the mere presence of literacy to the proportion of the population that possessed literacy skills, recognizing that the size of the literate population is a crucial indicator when assessing the overall literacy of a society. For another, the definition of literacy evolved further to encompass a broader range of competencies beyond basic reading and writing, acknowledging the multi-faceted nature of literacy in a rapidly changing world where written, visual, and digital forms of communication are intertwined.

The shift is reflected in the stance on a "**literate person**" and "**literate society**" by United Nations Educational, Scientific and Cultural Organization (UNESCO) over the decades. In the 1950s and 1960s, UNESCO focused on basic literacy, and worked to eradicate illiteracy through campaigns and initiatives. The definition of literacy was relatively simple, emphasizing the ability to read and write. In the 1970s, it expanded its definition of literacy to encompass the concept of "functional literacy"—the ability to read and write in order to comprehend and engage with practical information relevant to one's daily life. In the 1980s and 1990s, it further developed the concept of functional literacy to emphasize comprehension and understanding, moving beyond basic reading and writing skills. From the 2000s on, it has placed increasing emphasis on the ability to communicate effectively across various mediums and contexts in a globalized world and on the concept of continuum of learning and proficiency. As of September 17, 2024, UNESCO defines literacy as follows,

> Acquiring literacy is not a one-off act. Beyond its conventional concept as a set of reading, writing and counting skills, literacy is now understood as a means of identification, understanding, interpretation, creation, and communication in an increasingly digital, textmediated, information-rich and fast-changing world. Literacy is a continuum of learning and proficiency in reading, writing and using numbers throughout life and is part of a larger set of skills, which include digital skills, media literacy, education for sustainable development and global citizenship as well as job-specific skills. Literacy skills themselves are expanding and evolving as people engage more and more with information and learning through digital technology. (https://www.unesco.org/en/literacy/need-know)

6.2　Literate society vs. oral society

When discussing the advantages of a literate society, there is often an implicit or explicit comparison being made with oral societies.

Oral societies are those in which cultural knowledge, traditions, and history are primarily transmitted through spoken language and oral communication rather than through written texts. Oral societies were studied by early anthropologist and ethnographers in the late 19th and early 20th centuries, but their approaches were often influenced by evolutionary theories that classified societies along a linear progression from "primitive" to "advanced" (e.g.,Tylor, 1871; Morgan, 1877; Frazer, 1890). This biased perspective hindered a thorough understanding of the complexity and value of oral traditions. The mid-20th century marked a significant shift in anthropological and ethnographic research, with scholars like Jack Goody (1919—2015), Claude Lévi-Strauss (1908—2009), and others contributing to the emergence of more systematic comparative analyses and theoretical frameworks in the following decades.

While his work was not exclusively focused on oral societies, Lévi-Strauss conducted extensive fieldwork in regions with oral traditions, such as parts of Africa and indigenous communities in the Americas. Lévi-Strauss ([1955] 1970) introduces the concepts of "cold societies" and "hot societies" to challenge the idea that oral and literate societies were fundamentally different or that one was more advanced than the other.

I would say societies studied by ethnologists, compared to our large society, our large modern societies, are a little bit like "cold" societies opposed to "hot" societies, something like horologe compared with a steam engine. These "cold societies" produce extremely little disorder, that physicists call "entropy", and they tend to preserve themselves in their initial state. Incidentally, it explains why they seem to us as societies without history or without progress (Charbonnier, 1969: 38).

In cold societies, knowledge and cultural traditions are primarily transmitted orally, through myths, stories, and rituals. Lévi-Strauss exams the underlying patterns of myths (1955, [1964] 1971), kinship systems (1949), and symbolic structures (1966) to illustrate the logic and coherence within apparently diverse cultural practices and demonstrates that these practices reflected deep cognitive processes and cultural organization.

In *The Savage Mind* (1962), Lévi-Strauss highlights how oral societies conceptualize and transmit their understanding of the past. Instead of a linear progression of events, oral cultures often view time as cyclical, where events repeat in patterns and cycles. Historical narratives are often interwoven with myth and legend which serve as repositories of historical memory, encoding cultural experiences, and the collective past. Knowledge is passed down through generations via storytelling and communal practices.

The oral narratives can lead to unique characteristics and perspectives in how history is understood, remembered, and conveyed. As history is often conveyed through storytelling, the narratives can be fluid and adaptable, changing over time to suit the needs of the audience or the context, and the focus might be on personal experiences and emotions rather than chronological details. This can lead to variations in the retelling of historical events. Moreover, narratives as such are often intertwined with cultural values, beliefs, and mythologies. The telling of history is not just about recounting events but also about conveying the cultural identity and collective memory of the community. Over time, oral traditions can lead to the accumulation of multiple layers of history. Events, anecdotes, and interpretations from different time periods might become meshed, enriching the complexity of the historical narrative.

A classic example is Homer, who lived in the "oral tradition era" in Greek history, a period after Linear B records were buried underneath burning palaces. His epic poem *The Iliad* features the use of repetition, formulaic phrases, and other mnemonic devices. Here is an excerpt from Book 1 (Translation by Samuel Butler), where we can observe some of these features:

Sing, O goddess, the anger of Peleus' son Achilles, that caused

the Greeks untold pain and hurled many strong souls of heroes to

Hades, leaving their bodies the prey of dogs and birds, as the will

of Zeus was accomplished. Begin from the moment of clash

between Agamemnon, the son of Atreus, and godlike Achilles.

Which god set them at odds? Apollo, the son of Zeus, and Leto.

Displeased with the king, he rained arrows down on the Greek

forces, and the men fell to illness. For Agamemnon had

dishonored Chryses, the priest of Apollo, and refused his

ransom for his daughter Chryseis, whom he loved, and Chryses,

the priest, prayed to Apollo.

Goody, on the other hand, focused on studying oral traditions, literacy, and the impact of writing on societies, often by comparing oral and literate cultures. He examined how the advent of writing systems affected societies' modes of communication, knowledge transmission, and social structures.

In *The Domestication of the Savage Mind* (1977), Goody argues that writing, as a technology and a cultural practice, profoundly transformed human cognition and led to significant shifts in modes of thinking and expression. Goody proposes that writing serves as an external memory aid, enabling information to be recorded and stored outside of individual memory. By externalizing the thought or the language in a linear spatial dimension, patterns become visible, as in anagrams, in the diagonals of matrices, the realization of gaps in tables or the emergence of the whole field of geometry, cartography and the related skills of navigation. It promotes abstract thought and analytical reasoning by allowing for the separation of language from its immediate context.

[List-making] it seems to me is an example of the kind of decontextualization that writing promotes, and one that gives the mind a special kind of lever on 'reality'. I mean by this that it is not simply a matter of an added 'skill', as is assumed to be the case with mnemonics, but of a change in 'capacity' (...) my intended meaning seems similar to George Miller's when he writes 'the kind of linguistic recoding that people do seems (...) to be the very life-blood of the thought processes (1956: 95). Writing, list making, involve linguistic recoding. (Goody, 1977: 109)

In Goody's discussion, lists, tables, and formulas are special forms of linguistic activity associated with developments in particular kinds of problem-raising and problem-solving. He saw them as a manifestation of the broader trend toward abstraction, organization, and systematic thinking facilitated by writing.

In *The Interface Between the Written and the Oral* (1987), Goody investigates how the introduction of writing and literacy affected Akan society in the region of Ghana. He observed the transformation of oral traditions, rituals, and cultural practices as they interacted with the written word. On the other hand, elements of oral communication, such as formulaic expressions, mnemonic techniques, and patterns of speech, can leave traces in written texts. This suggests that oral traditions can persist in written forms, leading to a fusion of both modes of communication. With these observations, he argues against the notion of a simple transition from oral to literate societies.

6.3   Alphabetic literacy vs. logographic literacy

Goody (1977) also touches upon alphabetic writing systems and their role in shaping cognitive processes, a topic tracing back to Goody and Ian Watt's collaborative work *The Consequences of Literacy* (1968) in which they claim alphabetic literacy as a catalyst to the rise of analytical philosophy, science, and democracy in Ancient Greece. The basic premise goes as follows: alphabet writing involves mapping distinct symbols with segmental phonemes. This process inherently requires analytical thinking because phonemes are not intuitive linguistic units like whole words or pictures. Writers must break down language into its smallest sound components, which demands a level of abstraction and analysis. Typically having a smaller number of symbols compared to logographic or syllabic systems, alphabet writing is easier to learn and disseminate. As a result, more people in Ancient Greece could acquire literacy skills, which were essential for engaging with written texts. This, in turn, allowed citizens to engage with a wide range of written materials, including laws, constitutions, and philosophical treatises related to governance and citizenship.

In fact, the idea had been around for years that alphabetic literacy played a crucial role in fostering creative and analytical thinking. As early as 1953, Moorhouse had aired the alleged "cognitive superiority" in his book title *The Triumph of the Alphabet: A History of Writing*. Since Goody and Watt (1968) popularized and furthered discussions on this topic, various scholars and researchers had supported this concept in their works, among which are Walter J. Ong (1982), Brian Stock (1983), Eric Havelock (1986), Kerckhove and Lumsden (1988), David R. Olson (1994), and Deborah Brandt (2001).

The boldest and most sweeping one of such claims was probably William Hannas (2003). In his book *The Writing on the Wall: How Asian Orthography Curbs Creativity*, Hannas perceives the logographic writing systems used in East Asia as the root cause of its technological creativity gap with the West. He presents two major arguments: first, these systems center around syllable, thus requiring less analysis from learners compared with those of the alphabetic system; second, to master thousands of characters often involves substantial rote memorization, an intensive process that hinders problem-solving and creativity.

Hannas' arguments are obviously fallacious. As stated in earlier chapters, Chinese characters are largely semantic-phonetic in nature. Readers commonly infer the pronunciation of unfamiliar characters by recognizing the phonetic component and associating it with characters they already know. This process of phono-semantic matching is an essential aspect of reading and writing in Chinese. Learning Chinese characters involves much more than simple rote memorization. It's a complex process that requires analysis, interpretation, and a deep understanding of the characters' structure and components. Furthermore, spoken syllables almost never map in a trivial fashion to individual symbols in syllabary. The spoken language often includes variations, stress patterns, and other nuances that are not fully captured by the writing system. A Beijing local may pronounce the first two syllables in "xī hóng shì" (西红柿, tomato) as something closer to "xiong" (胸, breast). To transcribe the phrase "西红柿炒鸡蛋"(scrambled eggs and tomatoes) as dictated by a Beijing local, one has to revert the contracted and reduced sounds to correct characters by referring to the context of a dish name in Chinese cuisine. This process involves contextual, morphological and phonetic analysis.

The relationship between writing systems and cognitive processes is complex, and it is difficult to draw direct causal links between the writing system used and technological creativity. Multiple variables such as education systems, cultural attitudes toward innovation, economic policies, and historical developments play more significant roles in disparities. Making broad claims without robust empirical evidence is risky. Moreover, it's worth noting that East Asian countries have made significant technological advancements in recent decades, challenging the notion of a creativity gap. Factors such as investment in education, research and development, and global collaboration have contributed to these advancements.

Another point to note is when Goody made the claim that the alphabet literacy was a catalyst to Greek analytical philosophy, science and democracy, he ignored the question of how many people were actually literate and who were these people. According to Sara Forsdyke (2021), At the high point of Greek civilization, fewer than one-third of the adult population could read or write. Moreover, literate population in Ancient Greece often included slaves to handle clerical work for their masters instead of the masters themselves. Places like Athens were far from egalitarian, and the concept of "democracy" was restricted to a subset of the population, excluding women, slaves, and non-citizens. While the impact of literacy on society may have been influenced by the spread of ideas from this educated class to a broader audience, it is just one element among many that shaped the historical trajectory of Ancient Greece.

6.4   Script reform and literacy rate: the Chinese case

Script reforms have been a common approach to promote literacy throughout history. Script reforms may involve simplifying or modifying existing writing systems to make them more accessible, or replacing an existing script with a different type, such as transitioning from a logographic script to an alphabetic one.

A linguistically diverse country, China is home to numerous dialects, which are classified into somewhere from seven (cf. Zhan 1981; Yuan 1983; Zhan et al., 2001) to ten (cf. Li, 1985; Li et al., 1987；Xiong and Zhang, 2012) major groups: Mandarin (cf. Further reading), Yue (Cantonese), Min, Wu, Xiang, Gan, and Kejia (Hakka), plus Jin, Hui and Ping, with Standard Mandarin Chinese, known as "Putonghua"(普通话, common speech) serving as the official language.

In China, two main types of attempts have been made to increase literacy through script reform: romanization and simplification. **Romanization** involves representing a language's sounds using a phonetic alphabet. Simplification refers to the process of reducing the number of strokes and simplifying the forms of Chinese characters to make them easier to write and learn.

6.4.1 Foreign attempts to romanize Chinese

The first recorded romanization attempts can be attributed to Jesuit missionaries in China during the late Ming and early Qing dynasties. One of the most notable figures in this context is Matteo Ricci (利玛窦，1552—1610), an Italian Jesuit priest and scholar who arrived in China in the late 16th century. To help others learn Chinese, Ricci and his Jesuit colleague Michele Ruggieri (罗明坚，1543—1607) compiled a 189-page Portuguese-Chinese word list in manuscript form, with the Chinese pronunciations written out phonetically in Latin letters. This is the earliest known effort at representing spoken Mandarin Chinese in Latin letters (Chung, 2016: 758). The system, later refined with tone marks, survives in Ricci's 1606 collection of religious essays widely known as *Xǐzì Qíjī* (《西字奇迹》 "The Miracle of Western Writing") (Yin, 1994: 5). Ricci's system was adopted by scholars and missionaries in the following decades. The figure below illustrates Ricci's romanization transcription side by side with the Classical Chinese.

萬	*uań*
曆	*lyě*
三	*sān*
十	*xǎ*
三	*sān*
年	*niên*

Figure 6.2　万历三十三年 '33rd year of the Wànlì era' (of the Ming dynasty emperor Shenzong),
accompanied with Romanization notations
Source: Chan and Minett, eds. 2016: 486

6.4.1.1 Wade-Giles system

The 19th century witnessed a significant surge in Protestant activity which led to the production of English-Chinese dictionaries and pedagogical works on the Chinese language for foreigners, including *Peking Syllabary* (1859) and *Yü-yen Tzu-erh Chi: A progressive course designed to assist the student of colloquial Chinese* (1867) by Thomas Wade (威妥玛，1818—1895), a British diplomat in China. In the former, he shifted from up to then Nanjing Mandarin to Beijing Mandarin as the Standard Chinese, and in the latter, he used a Roman alphabet of his own divising. From these works evolved the romanization scheme that was later set down in *A Chinese-English Dictionary* (1892) by Herbert Giles (翟理斯，1845—1935), thereby known as Wade-Giles system.

The following figure illustrates a distinct feature of and a common complaint about Wade-

Giles system: the use of the apostrophe to distinguish aspirated from unaspirated initial stops and affricates.

Initials		Some finals	
Pinyin	Wade–Giles	Pinyin	Wade–Giles
b	p	-ie	-ieh
c	ts', tz'	ye	yeh
ch	ch'	er	erh
d	t	you	yu
g	k	yong	yung
j	ch	-ong	-ung
k	k'	-ian	-ien
p	p'	-iong	-iung
q	ch'	yan	yen
r	j	yi	i
t	t'		
x	hs		
z	ts, tz		
zh	ch		

Figure 6.3   Romanization: The initials and some finals that differ in Pinyin and Wade-Giles
Source: Taylor and Taylor, 2014:145

Wade–Giles received wide acceptance and remained the undisputed standard for Romanization of Chinese in English-language writing until officially supplanted by Pinyin in 1979. Today, it is still seen in a small number of established loanwords in English, such as *tofu, Kungfu, Taichi, Kungpao* Chicken, and *I-ching*—though probably more are in Romanized Cantonese than Mandarin, and some Chinese place names and personal names in publications, now mostly restricted to Taiwan province.

6.4.1.2   Post Office system

In 1896, The Imperial Post Office (大清邮政总局) was established. By 1921, It developed a system of transliterating Chinese place names by using a combination of local dialects, Nanjing Mandarin and Beijing Mandarin, and the retention of some pre-existing romanizations and ancient usages (Harris, 2008). One of the primary goals of using a combination of regional dialects, local pronunciations, and established romanizations in the context of a postal system would be to approximate the local pronunciation of place names so as to facilitate postal workers and officials to correctly identify and handle mail. Below are examples of county names used in postal spelling after 1931.

Old Chinese Name	Old Romanization	New Chinese Name	New Romanization
蘇州	Soochow	吳縣	Wuhsien
揚州	Yangchow	江都	Kiangtu
太原	Taiyüan	陽曲	Yangku
西安	Sian	長安	Changan
蘭州	Lanchow	皋蘭	Kaolan
哈爾濱	Harbin	濱江	Pinkiang
溫州	Wenchow	永嘉	Yungkia
廈門	Amoy	思明	Szeming
福州	Foochow	閩侯	Minhow
廣州	Canton	番禺	Panyü

Figure 6.4   Examples of County Names used in Postal Spelling after 1931
Source: Harris, 2008

The system was in common use in post office until the 1980s when replaced by Pinyin. For major cities and other places that already had been widely accepted overseas, postal spellings were retained, as seen in "Peking University," "Tsinghua University," and "Soochow University." In addition, The International Air Transport Association (IATA) codes for airports are often based on former postal spellings of the cities: PEK for Peking, CAN for Canton, NKG for Nanking, TAO for Tsingtao, TSN for Tientsin, HKG for Hong Kong, and TPE for Taipei.

6.4.2   Native attempts to romanize Chinese

During the late Qing Dynasty to the mid-Republic of China period, Chinese intellectuals engaged in deep reflection on China's defeat in the First Sino-Japanese War (1894—1895) and the broader challenges facing their nation. One of the issues that came under scrutiny was the Chinese writing system based on Chinese characters, which many saw as a significant barrier to modernization and progress (e.g., Lu,1892; Fu, 1919; Qian, 1922; Lu, 1934; Li, 1936).

6.4.2.1   Qieyinzi

In response to the concerns, various campaigns were made to romanize Chinese. In 1892, Lu Zhuangzhang (卢戆章, 1854—1928) published a scheme of *Qieyin Xinzi* "phonetic alphabet" in his book *First Steps in Being Able to Understand at a Glance: Chinese New Phonetic Script in the Amoy Topolect* (《一目了然初阶 (中国切音新字厦腔)》) , marking the beginning of the Qieyinzi Movement that lasted till the fall of the Qing dynasty. Among dozens of phonetic scripts created in the movement, the more influential ones are as follows: Chuanyin

Kuaizi "Shorthand symbols for transmitting sounds" by Cai Xiyong (蔡锡勇，1847—1898)，
Guanhua Hesheng Zimu "Mandarin Phonetic Alphabet" by Wang Zhao (王照，1859—1933),
and Hesheng Jianzi "phonetic simplified characters" by Lao Naixuan (劳乃宣, 1843—1921)
(cf. Li, 2015: 387—406).

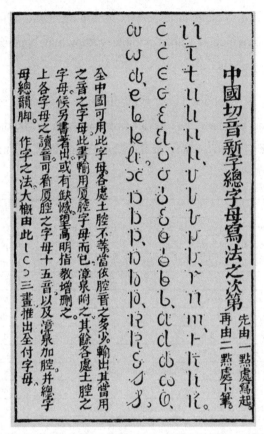

Figure 6.5   Phonetic alphabet designed by Lu Zhuangzhang
Source: Lu, 1892: 1

Opposing to reform the Chinese writing system through phonetic symbols, Zhang Taiyan
(章太炎, 1869—1936), a prominent scholar and reformer, did recognize the need to make
Chinese characters easier to read and understand. Taking the form of the ancient seal scripts,
he improved upon Fanqie (反切, lit., "reverse cut")—a method in traditional Chinese
lexicography to indicate the pronunciation of a character by using two other characters, one
with the same initial consonant and one with the same rest of the syllable, and formulated
the program of Niuwen (纽文, consonants) and Yunwen (韵文, rhymes), which was the
predecessor of *Zhuyin Zimu* (注音字母，lit., "sound-notating alphabet").

6.4.2.2 Zhuyin Zimu

In 1913 Zhuyin Zimu was proposed to be the national standard for transcribing Mandarin Chinese and was officially adopted as such in 1928. In 1930, it was renamed Zhuyin Fuhao (注音符号, lit., "sound-notating symbols"), and was in wide use until 1958 when replaced by Pinyin. While still included in dictionaries from Chinese mainland, Zhuyin Fuhao is now only widely used in Taiwan province of China, popularly known as bopomofo ("ㄅㄆㄇㄈ") after the names of the first 4 symbols.

Zhuyin Fuhao contains 39 symbols. These symbols were developed from Chinese characters and use parts of characters that have the relevant pronunciation in Mandarin. For example, ㄅ(b) comes from 勹, part of 包 (bāo). Many of the Zhuyin symbols are modelled on obsolete or cursive characters.

Zhuyin	origin	IPA	Hanyu Pinyin
ㄅ	From 勹, the ancient form and current top portion of 包 bāo	p	b
ㄆ	From "攵", the combining form of 攴 pū	ph	p
ㄇ	From 冂, the archaic character and current radical ⼍ mì	m	m
ㄈ	From ⼖ fāng	f	f
ㄉ	From archaic form of 刀 dāo	t	d
ㄊ	Upside-down form of 子 zǐ	th	t
ㄋ	From the archaic form of 乃 nai	n	n
ㄌ	From the archaic form of 力 lì	l	l
ㄍ	From the obsolete character 浍 guì/kuài, means river	k	g
ㄎ	From the archaic character 丂 kǎo	kh	k
ㄏ	From the archaic character and current radical 厂 hàn	x	h
......			
Zhuyin	Resources	IPA	Hanyu Pinyin
ㄧ	From Chinese character 一 yī	i	i
ㄨ	From 乂, ancient form of 五 wǔ	u	u
ㄩ	From the ancient character ㄩ qū	y	ü
ㄚ	From 丫 yā	a	a
ㄛ	From 呵 hē	o	o
ㄜ	Derived from its allophone in Standard Chinese, ㄛ e	ɤ	e
ㄝ	From 也 yě	ɛ	ê
......			

Figure 6.6   Origin of some Zhuyin symbols
Source: Xing and Feng, 2016: 103

6.4.2.3   Gwoyeu Romatzyh

To connect with the international world, in 1928 the Committee on Unification of National Language (国语统一委员会) adopted Gwoyeu Romatzyh "国语罗马字，National Language Romanization", a system for writing Mandarin Chinese in Latin alphabet, as the official national romanization system.

Gwoyeu Romatzyh (GR) was conceived by Chao Yuen Ren (赵元任，1892—1982), a celebrated linguist, phonologist, theorist, poet, composer and scholar of Chinese music. He published a textbook and a phonetic dictionary in the early 1920s, in order to support studies of this system. Its most distinctive feature is tonal spelling, i.e., showing the four tones of Mandarin via slight variations in spelling, an idea that westerners are thoroughly accustomed to.

However, GR involves an overtly complex system that can be challenging to learn:

For the 1st tone:

(1) Use the 'Basic Form.' For instances, hua 花, shan 山. The Basic Form also includes neutral tones, onomatopoeia and auxiliaries, e.g., ma 嗎, aia 啊呀.

(2) For initials of m, n, l, r, add h, e.g., mhau 貓, lha 拉.

For the 2nd tone:

(3) Add r after open finals, e.g., char 茶, torng 同, parang 旁

(4) If the first letter of finals is i or u, change i to y and u to w, e.g. chyn 琴, hwang 黄, yuan 元; but when the entire final is i or u, then change i to yi, u to wu, e.g., pyi 皮, hwu 胡, wu 吳.

(5) When initials are m, n, l, r, use the 'Basic Form,' e.g., ren 人, min 民, lian 連.

For the 3rd tone:

(6) Double the single vowels, e.g., chii 起, faan 反, eel 耳.

(7) For multiple vowels, change i to e, u to o, e.g., jea 假, goan 管, sheu 許, hae 海, hao 好; but do not change the final vowel if the first vowel is changed already, e.g., neau 鳥, goai 拐.

(8) Double vowels of ei, ou, ie, uo follow the Rule 6th, e.g. meei 美, koou 又, jiee 解, guoo 果.

For the 4th tone:

(9) Change the finals from -i to -y, from -u to -w, from -n to -nn, from -ng to -nq, from -l to -ll or from -(none) to -h. E.g., tzay 在, yaw 要, bann 半, jenq 正, ell 二, chih 器. (Chao, 1929: 42—43)

Due to the complexity of the system, GR was never extensively used. Yet, the vestigial of tonal spelling lives in the official English name for Shǎnxī (陕西) province—Shaanxi, to distinguish it from Shanxi (山西) .

6.4.2.4   Latinxua Sin Wenz

In the 1930s, a fledging competitor to GR was Latinxua Sin Wenz "Latinized New Script" (拉丁新文字), a set of romanizations based on principles developed by Chinese and Russian scholars headed by Qu Qiubai (瞿秋白, 1899—1935), a writer, poet, translator, and one of the most prominent leaders of the first generation of the Chinese Communist Party.

Considering GR a brainchild of an overtly academic endeavor, Qu contended that the new Chinese Script should be designed with simplicity and accessibility in mind so as to increase literacy among the general population, especially the proletarians who were not well educated. Tones, accordingly, should not be indicated unless necessary for disambiguation.

In 1930, Qu published *Chinese Latinized Alphabet* (《中国拉丁化的字母》) based on Northern dialect. In the following year, the First Congress on the Latinization of the Chinese was held, and the proposed Latinization based on Qu's scheme was adopted. A precursor to Pinyin, the scheme was distinct in the following major aspects:

1. It distinguishes two opposing groups in sibilant consonants, i.e., [ts], [tsʰ], [s] (Pinyin: z, c, s) and [tɕ], [tɕ ʰ], [ɕ] (Pinyin: j, q, x; Latinxua Sin Wenz: g, k, x), when they are followed by the sound [i] or [y] (Pinyin: i , ü). For example, giou (九) , ziou (酒).

2. It does not write the so-called "empty rhymes" in traditional Chinese phonetics, i.e., the sound -i after certain initial consonants like zi ci si zhi ri. For example, z (字).

3. h in Pinyin is written as x, e.g., Latinxua.

4. ü in Pinyin is written as y, e.g., ny (女).

5. er in Pinyin is written as r, e,g, re (二).

6. Loan words are written in their original form, e.g., Latinxua. (cf. Qu, 1989: 432—440).

Though the scheme chose to transcribe Mandarin, Qu argued for linguistic equality of other dialects. Instead of representing one privileged variety, the script should be dialect-friendly, accessible and phonetically consistent for all Chinese speakers. Between 1934 and 1937 alone, on top of Mandarin thirteen dialects developed their own writing systems in accordance to *Sin Wenz* principles, covering major dialect groups such as Wu, Min, and Cantonese (cf. Ni, 1948: 9—37). As a result, "the Latinization Movement created a dynamic discourse in which the script revolution lent voices to the people and made possible their dissemination in writing" (Zhong, 2014: 156).

6.4.2.5 Hanyu Pinyin

Partly based on the experiments of Sin Wenz, Hanyu Pinyin (previously in this chapter and hereafter, simply Pinyin) "the Chinese language sound spelling" (汉语拼音), the romanization system used so far for conversion of or comparison with other systems, was drafted in the 1950s by the Committee of the Chinese Script Reform (中国文字改革委员会), of which a prominent member was Zhou Youguang (周有光，1906—2017), a renowned Chinese linguist credited as "Father of Pinyin." It was promulgated in 1958 and adopted as the official romanization system in 1979.

One of the primary purposes of Pinyin was to improve literacy rate by providing a standardized system for representing the sounds of Modern Standard Mandarin, which was first codified in 1932 and also called Putonghua since 1955, a common language that came about as an effort by intellectuals and politicians to aid communications among speakers of different dialects used across the country.

Another primary purpose was to integrate China with the world. Pinyin utilizes the 26 letters of the Latin alphabet (though "v" is not generally used for any Chinese words, and on many Pinyin keyboards simply produces the letter ü) in the same order using approximately the same sounds (or at least possible sounds) as in European languages. Diacritics are used to mark the four tones of Mandarin. It makes Standard Mandarin more accessible, both within and without, contributing to the spread of the language as a global communication tool.

6.4.3 Character simplification

Along with the development of Pinyin were efforts to simplify Chinese characters by eliminating certain variants and reducing the number of strokes in many of those remaining to make writing easier and faster.

The first round of simplification was officially promulgated and implemented in 1956. To incorporate simplifications in a way rational and consistent while retaining continuity with written tradition, the scheme followed some general principles:

1. simplifying commonly occurring parts of characters, especially semantic-phonetic components of compounded characters

   e.g, 說 (shuō) "say" was simplified to 说, and 話(huà) "speech", to 话, where the radical 言, referring to speech, was reduced to two strokes.

2. replacing whole characters with simpler cursive forms, usually a kind of calligraphic shorthand

   e. g., 衛 (wèi) "guard" was simplified to 卫, quite a different character, but one that had served in south coastal China as a shorthand for 衛 for many generations.

3. retaining simplified characters that are already in common use, as far as possible

   a. g., 蟲 (chóng) "worm" was simplied to 虫, a historical convention for centuries.

The simplification occurred in rounds and in steps over decades. Pinyin and simplified characters often go hand in hand, the former providing a phonetic guide to the pronunciation of the latter. The simplified characters are primarily used in Chinese mainland, Singapore, and Malaysia, while traditional characters are primarily used in regions like Taiwan, Hong Kong and Macau of China, and by Chinese communities worldwide.

Summing-up

Though oral traditions encapsulate rich and intricate systems of knowledge, memory, and cultural expression, the impact of modernization, education, technology, and cultural change has influenced the way oral traditions are preserved and transmitted. In many cases, oral societies are indeed adapting to the changing world by incorporating written and digital media as tools for preserving and transmitting their oral traditions.

As societies transition from primarily oral to written traditions, the question whether one type of writing is "better" depends on the language and context being considered. Ultimately, the writing system that fits the language is the one better. The alphabetic hypothesis is, after all, a product of alphabetic culture. It was produced by scholars who, owing to their upbringings, were most familiar with alphabetic writing and thus tended to overemphasize differences and advantages distinguishing it from other writing systems, especially those in East Asia. A deeper look at Chinese writing dispels the long-lasting biases that often portray logography as inferior to alphabet.

To increase national literacy rate, government-sponsored script reform is a common practice. In the case of Chinese, the motives for Zhuyin Zimu and Gwoyeu Romatzyh were to remove characters, and those for Pinyin, wavered between replacing and assisting characters. Concerns for preserving tradition, history, culture and identity eventually led it to the latter, as an auxiliary to the simplified characters. These reforms may be one of the factors that have improved national literacy rates, as Chinese mainland literacy grew from less than 20% before 1949 to over 99.83% in 2021, according to GlobalData (accessed Oct. 12, 2024). But meanwhile, economic situation has improved immensely and expenditure on education has increased greatly. Education policy such as the implementation of nine-year compulsory education, narrowing of urban-rural disparities in facilities, changes in teaching methods and learning styles are probably stronger parameters at play, given the multifaceted nature of literacy.

It is hard to measure how successful these script reforms were, but one assurance is that the outcome of the reforms—Pinyin—has been almost directly responsible for allowing modern China to take advantage of the power of the computer.

References

Brandt, Deborah. 2001. *Literacy in American Lives*. Cambridge: Cambridge University Press.

Chan, Sin-Wai, and James Minett, eds. 2016. *The Routledge Encyclopedia of the Chinese Language*. London: Routledge.

Charbonnier, Georges. 1969. *Conversations with Claude Lévi-Strauss*. Translated by John and Doreen Weightman. London: Cape Ltd.

Chung, Karen Steffen. 2016. "Wade-Giles Romanization System." In *The Routledge Encyclopedia of the Chinese Language*, edited by Sin-Wai Chan and James Minett, 1025—1028. London: Routledge.

de Kerckhove, Derrick, and Charles J. Lumsden, eds. 1988. *The Alphabet and the Brain*. Berlin: Springer-Verlag.

Forsdyke, Sara. 2021. *Slaves and Slavery in Ancient Greece*. Cambridge: Cambridge University Press.

Frazer, James George. 1890. *The Golden Bough: A Study in Magic and Religion*. London: Macmillan and Co.

Giles, Herbert. 1892. *A Chinese-English Dictionary*. Shanghai: Commercial Press.

Goody, Jack. 1977. *The Domestication of the Savage Mind*. Cambridge: Cambridge University Press.

Goody, Jack. 1987. *The Interface Between the Written and the Oral*. Cambridge: Cambridge University Press.

Goody, Jack, and Ian Watt. 1968. "The Consequences of Literacy." *Comparative Studies in Society and History* 10 (3): 304—345.

Hannas, William C. 2003. *The Writing on the Wall: How Asian Orthography Curbs Creativity*. Philadelphia: University of Pennsylvania Press.

Harris, Lane J. 2008. "A 'Lasting Boon to All': A Note on the Postal Romanization of Place Names, 1896—1949." *Twentieth-Century China* 34 (1): 96—109.

Havelock, Eric A. 1986. *The Muse Learns to Write: Reflections on Orality and Literacy from Antiquity to the Present*. New Haven: Yale University Press.

Homer. *The Iliad*. Translated by Samuel Butler. Project Gutenberg. https://www.gutenberg.org/ebooks/2199 (accessed October 18, 2024).

Lévi-Strauss, Claude. 1949. *Les structures élémentaires de la parenté (The Elementary Structures of Kinship)*. Paris: Presses Universitaires de France.

Lévi-Strauss, Claude. 1962. *La pensée sauvage (The Savage Mind)*. Paris: Plon.

Lévi-Strauss, Claude. 1966. *Du miel aux cendres (From Honey to Ashes)*. Paris: Plon.

Lévi-Strauss, Claude. [1955] 1970. *A World on the Wane*. Trans. John and Doreen Weightman. New York: Atheneum. Originally published as Tristes tropiques.

Lévi-Strauss, Claude. [1964] 1971. *The Raw and the Cooked: Introduction to a Science of Mythology, Volume 1*. Trans. John and Doreen Weightman. New York: Harper & Row. Originally published as *Le Cru et le cuit*.

Li, Yuming. 2015. *Language Planning in China*. Berlin and Beijing: Mouton de Gruyter and Commercial Press.

McLuhan, Marshall. 1964. *Understanding Media: The Extensions of Man*. New York: McGraw-Hill.

Moorhouse, A. C. 1953. *Triumph of the Alphabet*. London: Sidgwick & Jackson.

Morgan, Lewis Henry. 1877. *Ancient Society: Or Researches in the Lines of Human Progress from Savagery through Barbarism to Civilization*. London: Macmillan & Company.

Olson, David R. 1994. *The World on Paper: The Conceptual and Cognitive Implications of Writing and Reading*. Cambridge: Cambridge University Press.

Ong, Walter J. 1982. *Orality and Literacy: The Technologizing of the Word*. London: Methuen.

Stock, Brian. 1983. *The Implications of Literacy*. Princeton: Princeton University Press.

Taylor, Insup, and M. Martin Taylor. 2014. *Writing and Literacy in Chinese, Korean, and Japanese*. 2nd ed. Amsterdam: John Benjamins Publishing Company.

Tylor, Edward Burnett. 1871. *Primitive Culture: Researches into the Development of Mythology, Philosophy, Religion, Language, Art, and Custom*. London: John Murray.

Wade, Thomas. 1859. *Peking Syllabary*. Shanghai: Educational Mission Press.

Wade, Thomas. 1867. *Yü-yen Tzu-erh Chi: A Progressive Course Designed to Assist the Student of Colloquial Chinese*. Shanghai: Educational Mission Press.

Xing, Huang, and Feng Xu. 2016. "The Romanization of Chinese Language." *Review of Asian and Pacific Studies*, Vol. 41: 99—111.

Zhong, Yurou. 2014. *Script Crisis and Literary Modernity in China, 1916—1958*. Ph.D. dissertation, Columbia University.

傅斯年，1919，《汉语改用拼音文字的初步谈》，载《新潮》，第 1 卷第 3 号，391。

黎锦熙，1936，《建设的"大众语"文学（国语运动史纲序）》，上海：商务印书馆。

李荣，1985，《官话方言的分区》，载《方言》，1985 年第 1 期，2—5。

李荣等编，1987，《中国语言地图集》，香港：朗文出版（远东）有限公司。

卢戆章，[1892] 1956，《一目了然初阶（中国切音新字厦腔）》，北京：文字改革出版社。

鲁迅，[1934] 2005，《汉字和拉丁化》，载《鲁迅全集》第五卷，北京：人民文学出版社。

倪海曙，1948，《中国拼音文字运动史简编》，上海：时代书报出版社。

钱玄同，1922，《注音字母与现代国音》，载《国语月刊》，第 1 卷第 1 期，1—7；第 2 期，1—4；第 3 期，1—4；第 4 期，1—7。

瞿秋白，1989，《瞿秋白文集》文学编第三卷，北京：人民文学出版社。

熊正辉、张振兴，2012，《汉语方言的分区》，载《中国语言地图集》第二版，北京：商务印书馆。

尹斌庸，1994，《第一个拉丁字母的汉语拼音方案是怎样产生的？》，载 *Sino-Platonic Papers* 50，1—7。

袁家骅等，1983，《汉语方言概要》第二版，北京：文字改革出版社。

詹伯慧，1981，《现代汉语方言》，武汉：湖北人民出版社。

詹伯慧等，2001，《方言及方言调查》第二版，武汉：湖北教育出版社。

赵元任，1929，《国语罗马字拼音法式》。收录于 A. A. 米尔恩，1929，《最后五分钟》，赵元任译，
　　上海：中华书局。收录于赵元任，2012，《赵元任全集》第 12 卷，北京：商务印书馆。

Further reading: excerpt from "What is Mandarin? The Social Project of Language Standardization in Early Republican China"

Weng, Jeffrey. "What Is Mandarin? The Social Project of Language Standardization in Early Republican China." *The Journal of Asian Studies*, Vol. 77, no. 3 (2018): 611—633. Excerpt, 613—615.

Chapter VII   Printing, Stability, and Variability

Jumping-in

Type into the search bar of a Chinese search engine "印刷术的发明" and then in an English one, its counterpart "the invention of printing." Compare the two sets of results and summarize your findings in a short paragraph.

Mass reproduction of texts is a crucial step to improve literacy and disseminate knowledge. The earliest such technology is printing. Printing had such wide ranging social effects that no single change is agreed to have been so expansively influential until the advent of the Internet.

However, the East and the West reckon the invention of printing from different time. When you search online for terms related to the invention of printing in Chinese (e.g., "印刷术的发明"), it's likely that you come across references to block printing, which has a long history in China and East Asia. In contrast, searching for their counterparts in English or other Western languages often brings up references to a German goldsmith Johannes Gutenberg and the movable type printing press.

The differences in search results are a reflection of the dominant historical narratives and cultural contexts associated with the development of printing technology in different regions. As pointed out by Thomas Carter (1931: 23), "Europe reckons the invention of printing from the time when **typography** was invented, and considers block printing as merely an important step in preparation. The Far East reckons the invention of printing from the time when block printing began, and considers movable type as a rather unimportant later addition."

Why the East and the West have varying views on what constitutes the invention of printing? The answer lies, fundamentally, in the distinction between logographic writing and phonographic writing. Chinese, as well as other East Asian languages like Japanese and Korean (prior to the 15th century) and Vietnamese (prior to the 20th century), uses logographic writing system, where each character typically represents a word or a morpheme. Such writing systems consist of thousands of unique characters, for which the use of movable type had long remained impractical and uneconomical. European languages, on the other hand, use phonographic writing systems based on an alphabet ranging from 21 to 33 letters, for which Gutenberg's development of the movable type printing press, particularly the "hand-mould" that industrialized the making of typefaces, made printing accessible and cost-effective. East to West, *the* invention of printing, therefore, is *the* form of printing that fits in with the writing system in use.

7.1 Printing in China

Printing is one of the four great inventions of early China. According to Lu Shen (陆深, 1477—

1544), a Ming Dynasty politician, the first recorded mentioning of printing is an imperial decree from 593 CE, in which the emperor Wen of Sui orders Buddhist images and scriptures to be printed ("敕废像遗经，悉令雕版"[engrave and print destroyed Buddha images and mutilated sutras], cited in Lv, 1992: 264).

In fact, engraving and printing was practiced long before the Sui Dynasty. **Engraving**, as a technique for creating images or inscriptions on various materials, has a long history that predates its use in printing. It was based on the long-standing practices of seal-making and stone carving. The earliest surviving seals can be traced back to the Shang Dynasty (c. 1600 BCE—1046 BCE), and stone carvings, to Qin Dynasty (221 BCE—207 BCE).

Seals in ancient China were divided into yin and yang types. **Yin seal**s had characters or symbols engraved into them in such a way that the impression left on paper or other materials appeared as white characters on a black background. In contrast, **yang seal**s had the characters engraved in reverse, resulting in black characters on a white background. The transition from yin to yang seals and the development of techniques to obtain positive written text reproductions from reverse-engraved yang seals were significant steps in the history of engraving and printing.

Also time-honored was the **rubbing of stone** tablet carvings. In this technique, a wetted rice paper is placed on a stone with sunken characters and tamped into every depression with a brush, then ink is carefully tapped over the entire sheet of paper to reproduce an image of the text. A paper is inked around the characters which stand out as white. This is practically a negative image of writing with a brush where dark-inked characters are on the white paper.

The historical use of engraving as a printing technique, particularly for mass-producing texts and images, is exemplified by the stone rubbings employed to replicate Buddhist sutras during the Han Dynasty (202 BCE—220 CE) and the use of engraved plates for reproducing incantations and spells during the Eastern Jin Dynasty (317—420).

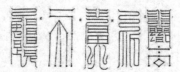

Figure 7.1   Amulet for entering mountains, from the *Baopuzi* (《抱朴子》) written
by Ge Hong in the 4th century
Source: Zhang et al., 1999: 27

Drawing inspiration from the practice of transferring texts by stone rubbing, people began carving the desired text onto wooden boards to create printing plates. These plates were then used to create relief impressions. The process involved a combination of techniques from seal making and stone rubbing. Those skilled in the art of woodcutting initially engraved the characters in reverse, following the approach used in yang seal making, and later applied ink to the plates before brushing paper onto them, akin to the process of stone rubbing. Through this innovative approach, a refined printing technique known as **woodblock printing** naturally emerged. Zhang et al. (1999: 32) infer that woodblock printing had existed by the time of the Liang Dynasty (502—557).

Yet, the destruction of temples, burning of scriptures, and the impact of wars throughout the ensuing centuries left many early printed materials and artifacts in ruins. The scarcity of surviving physical evidence from this era makes it difficult to provide concrete details about the extent and nature of early printing practices. Consequently, much of our knowledge about early Chinese woodblock technology relies on later historical accounts, archaeological discoveries, and surviving examples of printed texts, such as the *Diamond Sutra* from the Tang Dynasty (618—907).

Known as the world's oldest surviving printed book, *Diamond Sutra* dates to 868 CE, the ninth year of Xiantong of the Tang Dynasty. The book is a 5-meter scroll containing one of the most important Buddhist texts The Diamond Sutra, made for free distribution by a man named Wang Jie on behalf of his parents. The scroll includes seven sheets, each printed separately by using a single woodblock and then joined to the others.

Figure 7.2　Frontispiece of the Chinese Diamond Sutra, printed in the 9th year of the Xiantong ear of the Tang Dynasty
Source: https://www.bl.uk/collection-items/the-diamond-sutra (accessed Sept. 1, 2023)

7.1.1   Block printing

The method of block printing has largely remained the same through its long history. Craftsmen carve characters and pictures into wooden blocks, ink them, and then brush paper onto the blocks. Each block consists of an entire page of text and illustrations.

> The wood chosen for woodblocks was generally pear wood. The woodblock was finely planed and squared to the shape and dimensions of two pages. The surface is then rubbed over with a paste which renders it smooth and prepares it for the reception of characters. The future pages which have been finely transcribed by a professional person on thin transparent paper, are delivered to the block cutter, who, while the above-mentioned application is still wet, unites them to the block so that they adhere; but in an inverted position, the thinness of the paper displaying the writing perfectly through the back. This paper being subsequently rubbed off, a clear impression in ink of the inverted writing still remains on the wood. The workman then with his sharp graver cuts away extraordinary neatness and dispatch all the portion of the wooden surface which is not covered by the ink, leaving the characters in fairly high relief. The printer holds in his right hand two brushes at the opposite extremities of the same handle. With one he inks the face of the characters, and, the paper being then laid on the block, he runs the dry brush over it so as to take the impression. This is done with such expedition that one man can take off a couple of thousand copies in a day (Carter, 1931: 73).

When the Tang Dynasty came to a close, Feng Dao (冯道, 882—954), a prominent government official during the subsequent Period of the Five Dynasties and Ten Kingdoms, oversaw a significant project to engrave and print a revised version of the Nine Confucian Classics at Guozijian (国子监), the Imperial Academy. This ambitious project, which spanned from 932 to 953, marked the first instance of a large-scale publication sponsored by the government in Chinese history. However, the primary aim of this initiative was to establish a standardized canon for these Classics rather than to make them widely accessible to the general public.

During the Song Dynasty, woodblock printing underwent a transformative expansion, particularly in the production of books for mass consumption. This era marked a significant shift in Chinese governance, with power transitioned from military and aristocratic clans to civil officials. The civil service examination system was regularized, public schools proliferated, the merchant class rose, and popular culture grew. These interconnected developments created the perfect conditions for a publishing and printing boom. Many merchants chose book printing as a cultural investment—they hired skilled artist-craftsmen to produce elegant editions of classics, poetry books, and collections of tales. The books they produced were of such high quality that they set a standard for all time.

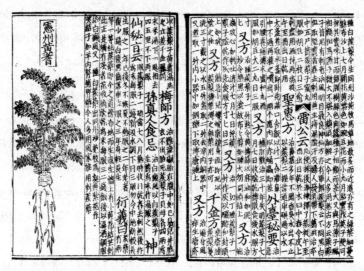

Figure 7.3　Book of traditional Chinese medicine (《重修政和经史证类备用本草》)
printed with woodblock in 1249
Source: commons.wikimedia.org (accessed Sept. 5, 2024)

7.1.2　Movable type printing

During the medieval Song Dynasty, Bi Sheng (毕昇, 972—1051), a woodblock carver from Hangzhou, invented **movable type**, i.e., one piece of type for each character, made of an amalgam of clay and glue hardened by baking. His method was accounted by Shen Kuo (沈括, 1031—1095), a Chinese polymath and statesman, in *Essays from the Torrent of Dreams* (《梦溪笔谈》) as follows:

> He took sticky clay and cut in it characters as thin as the edge of a cash. Each character formed as it were a single type. He baked them in the fire to make them hard. He had previously prepared an iron plate and he had covered this plate with a mixture of pine resin, wax and paper ashes. When he wished to print, he took an iron frame and set it on the iron plate. In this he placed the type, set close together. When the frame was full, the whole made one solid block of type. He then placed it near the fire to warm it. When the paste at the back was slighted melted, he took a perfectly smooth board and rubbed over the surface, so that the block of type became as even as a whetstone. (Vol. 18)

Based on Shen Kuo's account, Zhou Bida (周必大, 1126—1204), a government official during the Southern Song Dynasty, successfully replicated movable types. He arranged these types in a copper plate and printed his own book titled *Yutang Miscellany* (《玉堂杂记》) (cf. *The*

Complete Works of Zhou Wen Zhong, Vol. 198). Unfortunately, no surviving examples of books printed by Bi Sheng or Zhou Bida have endured the passage of centuries.

Contemporary to the Song Dynasty in the central plains, Xi Xia (1038—1227), a Tangut-led Buddhist imperial dynasty in what is today the northwest of China, drew on the use of clay movable type to print books in their own script. In 1987, physical artifacts in the form of books printed as such were discovered in Wuwei, a region associated with Xi Xia. These discoveries provided tangible evidence of early movable type printing techniques and added valuable historical context to the broader history of printing in China.

Figure 7.4   A torn page from Vimalakirti-nirdesa printed with moveable clay type in Xi Xia
Source: photo taken by the author, in June 2023 at The Wuwei Confucian Temple

Since the Song Dynasty, there were ongoing efforts to create more robust and durable types, which led to the development of wooden type and eventually metal type. A significant contributor to wooden type was Wang Zhen (王祯, 1271—1368), an official and author of a masterpiece agronomic book during the Yuan Dynasty. He designed a device called the "revolving wheel" for arranging and setting the types, facilitating the transition of typesetting from manual to mechanical operations. Characters were organized into corresponding positions on the wheel based on the five tones and rhyme sections as outlined in the *Book of Rhymes*. However, under the elite ideal to esteem literacy and to despise craftmanship, the revolving wheel typesetting method did not see widespread use in his time.

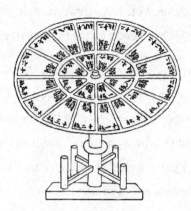

Figure 7.5　Revolving wheel for movable type described by Wang Zhen (活字板韵轮图)
Source: Wang, 1313: vol. 22

Further development was made in Qing Dynasty, when Jin Jian (金简, ?—1794) , the Editorial Grand Minister of the Imperial Household Department, systemized and standardized the style of working for *Prints with Moveable Types from the Hall of Military Glory* (《武英殿聚珍版书》), a series of collectanea compiled on the order of Qianlong emperor. In a short handbook written in 1776, Jin provides a comprehensive guide to the intricate craft of printing. These procedures are outlined as follows, each accompanied by an illustration and a brief description of the tool size standard: making of wood (成造木子), carving (刻字), type case (字柜), groove board (槽板), clamping strip (夹条), top wood (顶木), center wood (中心木), class grid (类盘), set frame (套格), set the book (摆书), pad plate (垫板), proofreading (校对), printing (刷印), categorization (归类), and day-by-day working schedule (逐日轮转办法).

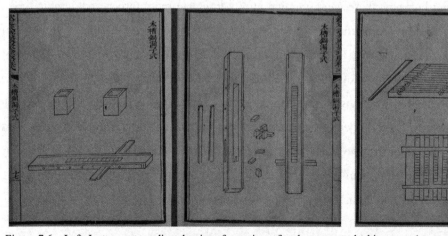

Figure 7.6　Left: Instrument to adjust the size of raw pieces for characters and white space (mucao, tong louzi shi 木槽、铜漏子式)
Right: Bed for fixing wood pieces during the carving process (kezi muchuang shi 刻字木床式)
Source: Jin, 1776

Metal movable types come in various forms based on the materials used, including tin movable type, bronze movable type, lead movable type, and other variations. Among these, tin movable type was the earliest form to appear, while bronze movable type found the most extensive application.

Bronze movable type probably appeared in Song Dynasty, following the use of tin movable type, which is documented in Wang Zhen's book. By the Hongzhi and Zhengde years of the Ming Dynasty, i.e., from 1488 to 1511, bronze movable type was already very popular in Wuxi, Changzhou, Suzhou and Nanjing, Jiangsu Province. At that time, many wealthy merchants used bronze type in printing books, the most famous of which was Hua Sui (华燧, 1439—1513), a scholar and printer from Wuxi. Apart from Jiangsu Province, bronze movable type printing sprouted in Zhejiang, Fujian and Guangdong. Printing with metal type continued through the 18th century.

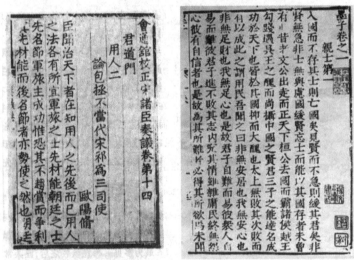

Figure 7.7　Left: A page from one of Hua Sui's books (《宋诸臣奏议》) printed in 1490,
the earliest surviving example of Chinese bronze movable type printing
Source: https://en.wikipedia.org/wiki/Hua_Sui#/media/File:Removeable_type_book.jpg (accessed Sept. 5, 2024)
Right: A page from *Mozi* (《墨子》) printed by Yao Kui from Zhi Cheng, Fujian, in Qing Dynasty
Source: http://www.kepu.net.cn/gb/civilization/printing/evolve/evl44301b_pic.html (accessed Sept. 5, 2024)

During the Qing Dynasty, particularly during the Yongzheng period, bronze movable type printing experienced a resurgence and reached a new peak. One of the most notable achievements during this time was the production of the *Ancient and Modern Books* (《古今图书集成》), a series of 10,000 volumes, typeset using bronze movable type. The use of bronze movable type allowed for the efficient and high-quality printing of this extensive collection, setting a standard that remained unrivaled in Asia.

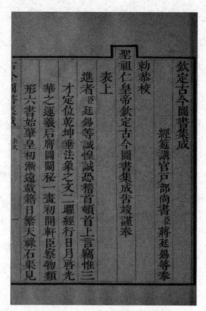

Figure 7.8　A page from *Ancient and Modern Books*
Source: https://en.dpm.org.cn/dyx.html?path=/tilegenerator/dest/files/image/8831/2009/0185/img0010.xml
(accessed Sept. 5, 2024)

However, movable type was never widely used in China. Apart from practical and economic concerns caused by the large grapheme inventory of the Chinese script, large-scale formation of literati culture took place at the same time that woodblock printing was spreading widely and movable type was being invented (Ze, 1995: 218). For the literati, a printed book was a piece of art that combines literary learning, block layout, style of calligraphy, and carving skill. Printing and possession of such books were marks of culture distinction. In block printing each character and line was subtly designed on a woodblock to ensure the artistic quality of a whole page, while the assembly of separately made types into one page in movable type printing would undermine a book's aesthetic value, and thus an important element of the social significance of the book was lost.

7.2　Printing in Europe

About four hundred years later after Bi Sheng invented the movable type, Johannes Gutenberg (c.1400—1468), a German goldsmith, introduced printing to Europe with his mechanical movable type printing press.

7.2.1 Manuscripts and scribes

Until then, books in Europe had been generally hand-copied by scribes, a tradition dating back to the time of Roman Empire where slaves were trained for book copying. Marjorie Plant describes the cost efficiency of slave-scribes as follows (1974: 17),

> The abundance of slaves specially trained for the work of copying manuscripts would have rendered the printing press unnecessary even had it been known, for it was claimed that a whole edition of a work could be finished within a day of the delivery. The edition ranged as a rule from five hundred to a thousand copies and the only expenses were for the provision of simple writing materials and for the bare maintenance of the slaves.

There is no doubt that the idea of creating text by reusing individual types had been floating in Europe long before the invention of the printing press, as missionaries and merchants who returned from China to Europe would not fail to spread reports of the flourished book culture there. Also, there are various claims about the technologies that Marco Polo (1254—1324) brought back from China, among which were compass, paper currency and printing. Yet, following the fall of the Roman Empire, Europe entered the long period of the Middle Ages, during which the demand for books was much less. Manuscript reproduction mainly took place in *scriptorium*, i.e., "a place for writing," in monasteries.

Since the 12th century, a revived interest in ancient Greek writings and the rise of universities had generated higher demand for books. By the 15th century, demand for manuscripts had far exceeded what could be produced by monks in monastic system (de Hamel, 1992: 12). Entrepreneurs across Europe began opening *scriptoria*, and some workshops hired craftsmen to add decorative elements including rubrications, illuminations, and illustrations. These scriptoria served as the predecessors to the publishing houses that would populate Europe after the advent of Johann Gutenberg's printing press.

7.2.2 Gutenberg and the printing press

In the mid-14th century, Europe was struck by the most fatal pandemic recorded in human history—the Black Death. The disaster had diminished the European population by one third to one half. The massive reduction of workforce led to efficiency of traditional work processes, including mining and metallurgy. Improved methods were adopted and better techniques for working with metals were developed (cf. Nef, 2008: 723—726).

Trained as a goldsmith and metallurgist, Johann Gutenberg is commonly referred to as the "inventor of printing" in the west, though it is more accurate to call him the inventor of the printing press with movable type, and more accurate still to say that he adapted the right technologies at the right time to industrialize printing in Europe. By Gutenberg's time, screw press that allowed controlled application of pressure had been used in wine and olive oil making for thousand years; water-powered paper mills had widely appeared in Germany, providing an industrial advantage in paper production; the codex that allowed double-sided writing and reading had been widely adopted over the scroll.

Gutenberg's **printing press** modeled after the ancient screw press. The adaptation by Gutenberg was the introduction of a movable under-table with a plane surface so that when the long handle was turned pressure could be evenly exerted against the paper, which was laid over the type mounted on a chase. To print on both sides of the medium, he drew inspiration from artists' paints and developed an oil-based ink that would adhere well to metal type and stick long to vellum or paper.

Figure 7.9   Gutenberg's printing press
source: http://vrworld.com/2014/08/17/week-history-gutenbergs-bible/ (accessed Sept. 5, 2024)

Compared with the step of printing, probably Gutenberg's greater contribution lies in the step of typesetting. As a goldsmith who knew metals well, he developed an alloy of lead, tin, and antimony that melted readily and cooled quickly to form durable and reusable type. He invented a device called "**hand mould**" to industrialize the making of the type. The hand mould consisted of a punch, a matrix, and a chamber. He engraved the steel punch with a character on its end, then used the punch to strike an impression in matrix—a block of copper. Then, he fixed the matrix in the chamber and dropped the melted alloy in the mouth, and a type was casted. According to Gaskell (1972: 10), a hand caster could turn out some 4000 types a day.

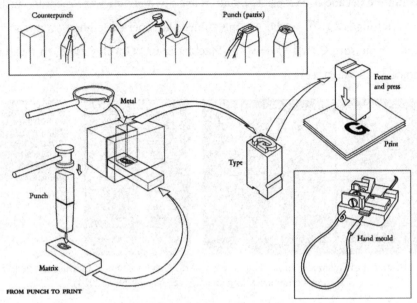

Figure 7.10   Gutenberg's hand mould
source: https://erenow.net/biographies/gutenberg-how-one-man-remade-the-world-with-words/6.php
(accessed Sept. 5, 2024)

There were strong power relations at playing determining the direction in which technology would develop (Ze, 1995: 87). When Gutenberg completed his first printing press by 1452, rapid economic and social development in late Middle Ages had led to emerging capitalism and rising middle class. The entire power structure of society was experiencing fundamental changes. There is evidence that reading and writing skills had become highly valued for different social groups during the fifteenth century (cf. Barron, 1996: 222—227). Rising literacy increased the demand for more books, cheaper books, and uniform books, making it possible for printing to become a commercial endeavor. By the end of 1500, printing press had taken root in major urban centers all over Europe.

7.2.3   Gutenberg and the Gothic type

Gutenberg began business by printing Latin grammars and thousands of indulgences. The press made printing works much faster and cheaper, but still an expensive undertaking for the printer. To print an entire book would be a very expensive investment. In 1452, he borrowed a sizable amount of money to produce a batch of printed Bibles, and in 1455 completed the first print of the Latin Bible, later known as 42-line Bible.

The one hundred and eighty copies of Gutenberg's Bible were disseminated widely throughout Europe within the decade it was printed, and at least two copies were recorded in London in this period (Hellinga, 2010). In the 42-line Bible, Gutenberg designed a typeface based on then-common manuscript, today known as blackletter or **"Gothic" type**, to mesh well with contemporary handwritten work.

Figure 7.11   Detail of Gutenberg Bible (Pelplin copy), Vol. 1. Pelplin Diocesan Museum, Pelplin, Poland
Source: commons.wikimedia.org (accessed Sept. 5, 2024)

Gutenberg trained a new generation of European printers, among which were Nicolas Jensen (c. 1420—1480) and Aldus Manutius (1449—1515). Jensen, former master of the French royal mint at Tours, established a printing house in Venice in 1470, and made Venice the commercial center of modern printing. He developed a typeface modelled on classical Roman letterforms that better suit spacing concerns, which became the basis of the Roman font that you are reading right now. Manutius, a Venetian printer, in 1500 designed a slanted font modeled on humanist cursive script. It condensed type for more compact printing, thus allowing the production of pocket-sized booklets. He patented the characters as Aldino font, but today we just call it italics.

Figure 7.12   Left: Typeface Roman
Source:https://upload.wikimedia.org/wikipedia/en/a/aa/Caslon_english_roman_sample.png
Right: Typeface italics (accessed Sept. 5, 2024)
Source: https://zh.wikipedia.org/wiki/File:Virgil_1501_Aldus_Manutius.jpg (accessed Sept. 5, 2024)

While the Gothic style dominated the German-speaking territories, the Roman one gained traction in other parts of Europe, including France, Italy, Spain, and the U.K. The rise of Roman fonts eventually led to a dispute in Germany over the use of the "**Antiqua**," a specific form of Roman style, in place of "**Fraktur**," a derivative of blackletter, especially in official and administrative contexts. Fraktur remained common in German academic and literary script until 1941, when Antiqua was promulgated for modernization and ease of communication.

Figure 7.13   Two typefaces: the German text uses Fraktur; numerals and Latin and French words are written in Antiqua (1768)
Source: https://de.wikipedia.org/wiki/Datei:Initialen.jpg (accessed Sept. 5, 2024)

7.2.4   *Printing and the standardization of English*

Within the next fifteen years after Gutenberg's first print of the 42-line Bible, printing houses opened throughout Europe (Steinberg, 1996: 18), in Strasbourg (1460), Bamberg (1461), Cologne (1465), at the Benedictine Abbey of Subiaco near Rome (1465), Basel (1468), Augsburg (1468), Venice (1469), Nuremberg (1469), Milan (1470), Naples (1470), and Sorbonne (1470). Apart from religious texts, a wide variety of books, ranging from classical literature, historical chronicles, humanist and philosophical works, scientific and medical treaties, legal and juridical texts, to pamphlets and broadsides, and to cookbooks and household manuals, were printed to meet diverse interests and needs. Printing press revolutionized the way information was disseminated and contributed significantly to the spread of knowledge throughout Europe. Elizabeth L. Eisenstein, in her influential work *The Printing Revolution in Early Modern Europe* (1979), made a compelling argument about how the printing press became an agent of change in numerous areas, including the Renaissance, the Reformation, Copernican revolution, medicine and anatomy, scientific publication, vernacular language, and language standardization.

7.2.4.1　Caxton and the first press in England

William Caxton (c. 1422—c. 1491), an English merchant who observed the new printing industry in Cologne, ventured into the business in 1473 in Bruges by printing his own translation of *The Recuyell of the Historyes of Troye*, the first book to be printed in the English language. Targeting at the English-speaking residents and traders in the Low Countries, this book served as a testing ground for Caxton to understand the tastes and preferences of his audience and to ascertain the probable sale for his productions. In 1476, Caxton set up a printing house and accompanying book shop in Westminster, London, which marked the establishment of the first printing press in England.

7.2.4.2　Printing in English as a marketing decision

By then, English had long existed as a vernacular alongside Latin, in a state of significant linguistic diversity and variation. It was spoken by the general population in such various dialects that individuals from regions could be mutually unintelligible. Some of the major dialect regions included Southern, Northern, East-Midland, West-Midland, and Kentish. When it came to the limited contexts of writing in English, such as personal letters and notes, there was a high degree of tolerance for spelling and grammatical variants.

Recognizing the growing demand for books among the increasing literate population in cities, Caxton focused on the production of vernacular books. Seventy-one of the 111 titles that Caxton published were either entirely or mostly written in English. He translated twenty-four of those books into English himself, mostly from French (Ford, 2020: 6). However, the trail blazer faced several challenging decisions: which dialect to use? What style to follow? Which variant to choose?

Caxton was astute enough to choose to print in what is often referred to as the "London dialect" or the "East Midland dialect" of Middle English. London dialect had several advantages for Caxton's printing endeavors: being associated with the capital city, it was used by the royal court, the government, and the educated elite, thereby contributing to the perception of authority and cultural significance; it aligned his printing with the heart of English commerce and governance, ensuring a broad audience and potential patrons among the influential residents of London; London dialect was understood not only in London but also in other cities of England, due in part to trade and mobility, and in part to Geoffrey Chaucer's use of London dialect in *The Canterbury Tales*, which was widely read and admired throughout England. As Ford explains, "the reading public served by publishers in and around London was national"(2020: 2).

To cater to the emerging middle class and the nobility of his era, Caxton had keen awareness of the issue of style. He defined his base variety in terms of audience and type of English, which represented the culmination of his views about English:

> And for as moche as this present booke is not for a rude vplondyssh man to laboure therein / ne rede it / but onely for a clerke & a noble gentylman … Therefor in a meane bytwene bothe, I haue reduced & translated this sayd booke in to our englysshe not ouer rude ne curyous, but in suche termes as shall be vnderstanden, by goddys grace, accordynge to my copye. (Caxton's prologue to *Enydos*, 1490: 3)

He sought a courtly style which was elegant but comprehensible, striking a balance between two extremes in his language choice. On the one hand, he avoided obsolete homely terms, which were likely Anglo-Saxon or Norse origin and might have seemed archaic to his readers. On the other hand, he refrained from excessive ornamentation, which often involved the use of modern words coined from French or Latin.

Caxton tried his powers by printing small pieces such as *Dictes and Sayings* (1477) and Morale Proverbes (1478), then Chaucer's *The Canterbury Tales* (1483) written in "ornate eloquence" (Caxton, preface to the morale proverbes 1478: 37), went on mainly with "joyous and pleysaunt historyes" of chivalry the "prynces, lordes, baron, knyghtes & gentilmen" were craving for (Blades, 1882: 84), devotional literature and hagiography that had a wider appeal, and scantily with poetry and history that required for more advanced mental education. He often took over constructions directly from the source text that he was translating when considering them fashionable and understandable. For example, the repeated adverb suffix -ly were taken over directly from -ment in the French original:

and dyd do pynte the hystoryes after somme points of our crystal faith Moche riche*ly* and repayred the places right delycyous*ly* (Caxton's transaltion of *Fierabras*, fol. B8r, cited in Blake, 1991: 125)

puys a paindre histoires selon aucuns poins de notre foy cristienne moult riche*ment* et les places réparer très délicieuse*ment* (*Fierabras*, fol. B8r)

Sometimes, Caxton included English equivalents or doublets alongside words borrowed from his source texts, making the text more accessible to his English-speaking audience while retaining some of the original flavor of the source language, for example, "*ancient and whyteheeryd*" (ancient and whitehaired) and "*digne and worthy*" (dignified and worthy). This practice may suggest "that Caxton's personal vocabulary was limited and generally of a prosaic and practical nature, but that when he translates he married over into English many words taken from his source" (Blake, 1991: 140).

Regarding typeface, spelling and punctuation, Caxton simply conformed to the manuscript traditions of his day. The typefaces used by him were subcategories of Gothic type, initially a form based on the more sumptuous French style called Bastard, and later, a more round and open one resembling most manuscripts of Middle English texts called Textura.

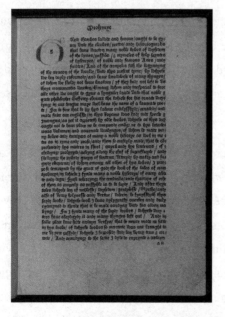

Figure 7.14   Caxton's illustrated second edition of *The Canterbury Tales*, 1483. Printed in Bastard
Source: https://www.bl.uk/collection-items/william-caxton-and-canterbury-tales (accessed Sept. 5, 2024)

The spelling and punctuation, both in his translations and in his original work, were featured by very much variability as they were in the English Chancery hands in the same period, who issued documents affixed by the king's Great Seal. He did not recognize one "correct" way to spell words and construct sentences, as seen from the prologue to *Enydos* published in the last year of his printing career: thai / theim, boke / booke/ bookys, dayly/dayli, axyd / axed, vsid/ vsed, eggys/egges, vnderstande/vnderstonden, wryton/wreton, etc. On the same page in the same paragraph the same word was spelled in different ways. Apparently, there appeared no uniformity or "standard" in the fifteenth century, nor was Caxton intentional to create one.

7.2.4.3   Variability and English standardization

In the textbooks of the history of the English language, Caxton and the standardization of English is a common theme. Some give credit to him for "standardizing" English. He is believed to "have it settled that one usage is generally current and will meet with acceptance everywhere" (Strang, 1970: 157), "settle the variant forms both of spelling and grammar" (Shaklee, 1980: 48), "resolve the dialect variants" (Fennell, 2001: 125), "give a currency to London English that assure more than anything else its rapid adoption" (Baugh and Cable, 2002: 182), and "deliver a standard spelling system" (Horobin, 2016: 81). Others, interestingly, blame him right for whimsical spelling or irregular orthography (e.g., Scragg, 1974: 66; Fisiak, 1994; Salmon, 1999: 24).

Despite the stark difference, both groups hypothesize there existed a "standard" type of English language which fits the descriptions of Standard English as it is understood today. However, this is anachronism of history, a practice of viewing the past through the prism of the present.

"**Standard**"—authoritative exemplar, unquestionable correctness—is a modern notion. In the fifteenth century, the ideology of "standardness as a virtue" (Lass, 1999: 8) did not exist and thus could not be put into practice. Conversely, variation—in spelling, punctuation, grammar, as well as the mixing of languages—was the default in a diffuse linguistic situation. Caxton showed such flexibility, so did other early English printers. Blake (1969:174) suggests that at first the printing press led to variety rather than uniformity.

The "confusion and disorder" in spelling variations prevailed so much so that in 1569 John Hart (c.1501—1574), the Chester herald of the College of Arms in London, published a book titled *An Orthographie* to address the problem of how the language should be spelled. He observes four types of "ills" in English spelling: "diminution," i.e., omitting or reducing letters or sounds from words; "superfluity," i.e., adding extra letters or sounds to words that were not originally present; "usurpation," i.e., inserting letters or sounds from one word into another word, often a result of confusion between homophones; "misplacing," i.e., changing the order of letters within a word (Hart, 1569: 146 ff.).

It is only from the mid-seventeenth century onwards that regularity in spelling is located. Yet, even in this period it was not the printers, but "orthoepists, orthographers and lexicographers" (Brengelman, 1980: 334) who were at the forefront in regularizing spelling. Successors to the 16th century orthoepists and orthographers, such as Alexander Gil (1565—1635) and Robert Robinson (1595?—1660+), continued in the efforts to reconstruct English pronunciation. Lexicographers like Thomas Blount (1618—1679) and Richard Hodges (1605?—1653+) published dictionaries that aimed to provide rules for spellings and definitions for English words. Following their guidance, grammar schools and educational institutions started emphasizing correct spelling. "Printed texts from the period demonstrate clearly that, during the middle half of the seventeenth century, English spelling evolved from near anarchy to almost complete predictability." (Brengelman, 1980: 334) In the 1660s, shortly after its founding, the Royal Society began to encourage discussions and debates on English spelling and the ways it could be improved. Publications by society members helped further shape the development of English spelling.

"Standards don't just happen—they are created." (Milroy, 2000, cited in Takeda, 2001: 43) English standards, no matter spelling or grammar, were codified and imposed through a top-down process rather than evolving spontaneously. Once printers began to follow language authorities, they disseminated and encouraged the developing standards in the widespread distribution of printed materials. Ultimately, standards are enforced through social acceptance—people tend to adopt the language norms promoted by institutions and authorities to ensure effective communication and social integration.

Though rooted in business opportunities, Caxton's decision to focus on vernacular shaped early book industry in England. The example that Caxton set encouraged other printers to produce work in English. According to Atkin and Edwards (cited in Kuskin, 2006: 199), about 59 percent of all book titles printed in England before 1501 were in the English language, while the comparable figure for other European vernaculars was less than 30 percent. Once a dialect gets a head start, it often builds up momentum—"the more important it gets, the more it is used; the more it is used, the more important it becomes" (Fromkin and Rodman, 1983: 257). In this sense, Caxton by "selecting" a variety of the East Midland dialect, which came to dominate London English as the type which became the later standard, albeit unconsciously, did cause the effect that the scholars are continuing the Anglo-Saxon linage of the English language and establishing a pedigree for the present-day standard.

7.2.4.4 Printing and the Great Vowel Shift

Printing happened to take place during the middle of a massive reorganization of the English vowel system—**the Great Vowel Shift**, a significant historical phonological change in the English language that drew out over several centuries, spanning roughly from the late Middle English period to the early Modern English period. During this shift, many vowels in English underwent significant transformations, resulting in the pronunciation of words changing over time (cf. Further Reading). By the mid-17th century, aided by the printing press, English writing system had largely stylized, though still not fully standardized. However, the Great Vowel Shift was still ongoing. Consequently, the written form of words often reflected earlier sounds rather than their current ones. For example, many of the words that today have the /i:/ sound used to have a different sound in the 15th century: the vowel in *meet* was more like the one in today's *mate*, the vowel in *leaf* was more like the one in today's *laugh* in American pronunciation.

Apart from helping fossilize old vowels, the printing press also preserved old consonants from Middle English that were no longer pronounced and French and Latin spellings of words borrowed into texts and translations. When the shift was over, "homophones, homographs, and silent letters littered the landscape" (Okrent, 2021: 161). While there were attempts to adjust spellings, entrenched "standard" in print and fluidity in pronunciation complicated these efforts. As a result, English spelling remains irregular and chaotic.

Dearest creature in creation

Studying English pronunciation,

I will teach you in my verse

Sounds like corpse, corps, horse and worse.

I will keep you, Susy, busy,

Make your head with heat grow dizzy;

Tear in eye, your dress you'll tear;

Queer, fair seer, hear my prayer.

Pray, console your loving poet,

Make my coat look new, dear, sew it!

Just compare heart, hear and heard,

Dies and diet, lord and word.

—The Chaos (Gerard Nolst Trenité, 1920)

Summing-up

Printing played a transformative role in both Eastern and Western societies. However, the timing of its development deeply influenced its function and societal impact. In China, printing supported education and governance by producing Confucian classics and administrative manuals that elevated literacy among the elite and reinforced hierarchy, social cohesion, and centralized state control. In Europe, by contrast, printing emerged during the Renaissance, when capitalism and the middle class were rising, along with a resurgence of interest in classical learning and individualism. It became a catalyst for diversity, sparking widespread change in religious, scientific, and political spheres.

In both regions, mass printing provided cultural continuity by establishing and maintaining standards. In China, printed texts like the Confucian classics were quickly seen as stable, authoritative sources. Printing enabled the dissemination of canonical texts, helping to maintain a coherent cultural identity and shared values across generations. In Europe, printing promoted linguistic continuity by elevating living languages—the vernaculars of each nation—over Latin. This shift empowered everyday languages in literature, science, and governance, gradually making knowledge accessible to broader audiences and reinforcing the distinct linguistic identities of emerging nation-states. Regarding English, printing helped homogenize vernaculars by adopting London dialect. The proliferation of printed texts contributed to a gradual shift from high variability to more regularized and standardized spelling and grammar.

References

Barron, Caroline. 1996. "The Expansion of Education in Fifteenth-Century London." In *The Cloister and the World: Essays in Medieval History in Honour of Barbara Harvey,* edited by J. Blair and B. Golding, 219—245. Oxford: Clarendon Press.

Baugh, Albert C., and Thomas Cable. 2002. *A History of the English Language.* 5th ed. London: Routledge.

Blades, William. 1882. *The Biography and Typography of William Caxton, England's First Printer.* New York: Scribner & Welford.

Blake, Norman Francis. 1969. *Caxton and His World.* London: Deutsch.

Blake, Norman Francis. 1991. *William Caxton and English Literary Culture.* London: Hambledon Continuum.

Brengelman, Frederick H. 1980. "Orthoepists, Printers, and the Rationalization of English Spelling." *Journal of English and Germanic Philology* 79: 332—354.

Carter, Thomas F. 1931. *The Invention of Printing in China and Its Spread Westward.* New York: Columbia University Press.

Chaucer, Geoffrey. 1483. *The Canterbury Tales.* Westminster: William Caxton.

Caxton, William. 1490/1913. "Prologue." *Caxton's Eneydos: Englisht from the French Liure des Eneydes, 1483.* Edited by Matthew T. Culley and Frederick J. Furnivall. London: Kegan Paul, Trench, Trubner & Co., Ltd.; Humphrey Milford: Oxford University Press.

Culley, M. T., and F. J. Furnivall, eds. 1890. *Caxton's Eneydos 1490.* London: Kegan Paul, Trench, Trübner & Co.

de Hamel, Christopher. 1992. *Scribes and Illuminators.* Toronto: University of Toronto Press.

de Pisan, Christine. 1478. *The Morale Proverbes of Cristyne.* Westminster: William Caxton.

de Voragine, Jacobus. 1483. *The Golden Legende.* Westminster: William Caxton.

Eisenstein, Elizabeth L. 1979. *The Printing Revolution in Early Modern Europe.* Cambridge: Cambridge University Press.

Fennell, Barbara. 2001. *A History of English: A Sociolinguistic Approach.* Oxford: Blackwell.

Fisiak, Jacek. 1994. "On the Writing of the History of Standard English." In *English Historical Linguistics 1992,* edited by Francisco Fernández, María Fuster, and Juan J. Calvo, 105—115. Amsterdam: John Benjamins.

Ford, Judy A. 2020. *English Readers of Catholic Saints: The Printing History of William Caxton's "Golden Legend."* London: Routledge.

Fromkin, Victoria, and Robert Rodman. 1983. *An Introduction to Language.* 3rd ed. New York: Holt.

Gaskell, Philip. 1972. *A New Introduction to Bibliography.* Oxford: Oxford University Press.

Hart, John. 1969 [1569]. *An Orthography.* Menston: Scholar Press Ltd.

Hellinga, Lotte. 2010. *William Caxton and Early Printing in England.* London: The British Library.

Hogg, Richard. 2006. *A History of the English Language.* Cambridge: Cambridge University Press.

Horobin, Simon. 2016. *A Short History of a Global Language.* Oxford: Oxford University Press.

ibn Fatik, Al-Mubashshir. 1477. *Dictes and Sayings of the Philosophers.* Westminster: William Caxton.

Kuskin, William, ed. 2006. *Caxton's Trace: Studies in the History of English Printing.* Notre Dame: University of Notre Dame Press.

Lass, Roger. 1999. "Introduction." In *The Cambridge History of the English Language, Volume III: 1476—1776,* edited by Roger Lass, 1—12. Cambridge: Cambridge University Press.

Love, Nicholas. 1483. *The Mirrour of the Blessed Lyf of Jesu Christ.* Westminster: William Caxton.

Milroy, Lesley. 2000. "Two Nations Divided by the Same Language: Contrasting Language Ideologies in Britain and the United States." Lecture presented at the 5th Conference for the European Society for the Study of English (ESSE).

Nef, John. 2008. "Mining and Metallurgy in Medieval Civilisation." In *The Cambridge Economic History of Europe, Volume 2,* 2nd ed., edited by Edward Miller et al., 691—761. Cambridge: Cambridge University Press.

Okrent, Arika. 2021. *Highly Irregular: Why Tough, Through, and Dough Don't Rhyme—And Other Oddities of the English Language.* Oxford: Oxford University Press.

Plant, Marjorie. 1974. *The English Book Trade: An Economic History of the Making and Sale of Books.* London: George Allen & Unwin.

Salmon, Vivian. 1999. "Orthography and Punctuation." In *The Cambridge History of the English Language, Volume III: 1476—1776,* edited by Roger Lass, 13—55. Cambridge: Cambridge University Press.

Scragg, Donald G. 1974. *A History of English Spelling.* Manchester: Manchester University Press.

Shaklee, Margaret. 1980. "The Rise of Standard English." In *Standards and Dialects in English,* edited by T. Shopen and J. M. Williams, 33—62. Cambridge, Mass.: Winthrop Publishers.

Steinberg, Sigfrid Henry. 1996. *Five Hundred Years of Printing.* London: British Library and Oak Knoll Press.

Strang, Barbara M. H. 1970. *A History of the English Language.* London: Methuen.

Takeda, Reiko. 2001. "The Question of the "Standardisation" of Written English in the Fifteenth Century." PhD diss., The University of Leeds.

Trenité, Gerard Nolst. 1920. "Appendix III The Chaos." In *Drop Your Foreign Accent*, 110—118. London: George Allen & Unwin Ltd.

Ze, David Wei. 1995. *Printing as an Agent of Social Stability: The Social Organization of Book Production in China during the Sung Dynasty.* PhD diss., Simon Fraser University.

(清) 金简，1776，《钦定武英殿聚珍版程式》（《钦定武英殿聚珍版书》卷一），https://old.shuge.org/ebook/wu-ying-dian-ju-zhen-ban-cheng-shi/。(accessed Oct. 1, 2023)

吕思勉，1992，《吕著中国通史》，上海：华东师范大学出版社。

(宋) 沈括，2015，《梦溪笔谈》，上海：古典文学出版社。

(元) 王祯，1313，《农书》卷二十二，https://zh.wikisource.org/wiki/王祯農書/卷二十二。(accessed Oct. 1, 2023)

张树栋等，1999，《中华印刷通史》，北京：印刷工业出版社。

(宋) 周必大，《益国周文忠公全集》卷一百九十八，https://zh.m.wikisource.org/wiki/文忠集_(周必大,_四庫全書本)/卷一百九十。(accessed Oct. 1, 2023)

Further reading: excerpt from *The Cambridge History of the English Language*

Lass, Roger. 2000. "Chapter 3 Phonology and Morphology." In *The Cambridge History of the English Language* Vol. 3, 72—77. Cambridge: Cambridge University Press.

Chapter VIII　Typewriter, Mind, and Style

Jumping-in

Use a simulated typewriter app (eg., "shifthappens": https://shifthappens.site/typewriter/) to write a paragraph without the ability to backspace or delete. Focus on getting your thoughts out in one go. Then discuss if using typewriter has affected your thought process and writing style.

Despite all the changes brought by the printing press, printing had remained a huge industrial operation and a large investment until the 19th century. When works went out of print, it was easier to just hand-copy. The work of the scribe did not end with the printing press. It ended with the typewriter.

The 19th century had witnessed various attempts to create writing machines. Some significant pioneers include William Austin Burt, Charles Grover Thurber, Alfred Ely Beach, Samuel Francis, Giuseppe Ravizza, Xavier Progin, Pierre Foucalut, and Peter Mitterhofer. Finally, two inventors created machines that were commercially produced in a series. One was Rasmus Malling-Hansen of Denmark, and the other was Christopher Sholes of the United States.

8.1   Malling-Hansen and Writing Ball

In the 1870s, the Danish pastor Hans Rasmus Johan Malling-Hansen (1835—1890) produced a *Skrivekugle*, or Writing Ball. Like many earlier attempts, his device was conceived largely as an aid for the sight-impaired writers. The machine helped the blind integrate into the society, and was thus "the tactile/visual interface" between the blind and the sighted (Lyons, 2021: 27).

The Writing Ball features a semi-sphere with radial pistons, which can be severally pushed down to the center of the sphere, where the type is printed on a paper surface. The semicircular arrangement of the keys prevented a view of the paper, making typewriting itself a blind activity.

Figure 8.1   Hansen's Writing Ball, c.1878
Source: http://www.malling-hansen.org/the-writing-ball.html (accessed Feb. 3, 2023)

On the webpage of Malling-Hansen Society, Dieter Eberwein and Sverre Avnskog, vice presidents of the society, introduce the function of the writing ball:

> The whole apparatus is mounted on a stationary foundation plate in such a way that it can be moved down against a spring, when the writing ball or one of its pistons are forced down by the finger. The foundation plate has an upright anvil under the center of the ball and directly under the paper frame. When a knob of a type piston is depressed, the paper resting on the anvil, below the same receives an impression. When the finger pressure on the type piston knob is removed, the instrument swings into its normal position. The escapement mechanism moved the paper frame that held the paper on space until the end of the line was reached. By pushing the button on the left in front of the ball all the way down, the carriage was turned concentrically back to the beginning of the line and moved one line to the left.

The most famous customer of Hansen's Writing Ball was the German philosopher and writer Friedrich Nietzsche (1844—1900), who ordered one in 1881 when suffering from worsening sight during his final decade. Shortly after receiving the machine, Nietzsche wrote a poem on his Writing Ball, in capital letters because that was all that the machine provided:

Figure 8.2　A facsimile of Nietzsche's Malling Hansen poem, 1882
Source: Kittler, 1999: 207

It reads,

THE WRITING BALL IS A THING LIKE ME: MADE OF

IRON

YET EASILY TWISTED ON JOURNEYS.

PATIENCE AND TACT ARE REQUIRED IN ABUNDANCE

AS WELL AS FINE FINGERS, TO USE US.

Unfortunately, the happiness did not last long. A few months later, in the humidity of rainy spring in Genoa, Nietzsche found that the ink ribbon became wet and sticky and the keys got stuck, making the machine unusable. By 1890, Hansen's Writing Ball had lost the commercial competition and was never made again later.

8.2   Sholes and the QWERTY keyboard

Sholes' invention was much more influential. A newspaperman, printer, and politician, Christopher Latham Sholes (1819—1890) launched a century-long industry, introduced the term "typewriter" for the device into English, and created the QWERTY keyboard that is still in wide use today.

In the 1860s, Sholes and his colleagues Carlos Glidden (1834—1877) and Samuel Soule (1830—1875) began working on a more practical typewriter for general purpose. By then, both in Europe and America there were many inventors competing for the same goal, but options remained open on the shape of the keyboard and the arrangement of the keys.

8.2.1   Theories on the QWERTY rationale

In 1873, after many trials, Sholes and his team decided on the prototype for later commercial success. E. Remington and Sons, a gun manufacturer based in New York, which also had a side business in sewing machines, purchased the patent to the invention and developed Sholes' design into a mass-producible typewriter in the next year. In the course of refining Sholes' machine, Remington did various modifications, but one of the things that remained unchanged was the keyboard layout. Below is the layout of Remington No. 10 keyboard. Some symbols on contemporary keyboards were lacking, but otherwise it is essentially the same.

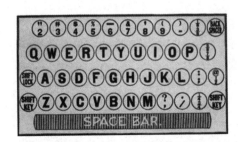

Figure 8.3   The Remington No.10 keyboard, c. 1910
Source: Cutler and SoRelle, 1910: 26

Figure 8.4   The Remington No.10 typewriter
Source: *Remington Notes*, Vol 3, No.10, 1915

8.2.1.1 Jamming theory

One plausible theory about how Sholes came up with the arrangement is that he was trying to separate frequently used pairs of keys so as to avoid **jamming** problem (David, 1985). As shown in the picture, Remington No. 10 is basically an open black box, with a roller for holding the paper, a ribbon and ribbon spools, and a keyboard with attached type levers and type bars. Each key is attached to a type lever, which in turn is connected to a type-bar with the letter mounted on the end. When a key is struck, the type-bar would swing up and hit the ink-coated tape which would transfer the image onto paper. If frequently used letters were in proximity, the type-bars would clash and jam when typed. Therefore, the design of QWERTY—this name comes from the first six letters in the top alphabet row—is a result of the key jamming problem.

The design of QWERTY was based on statistics corpus, i.e., **bigram** frequency usage of letter pairs in English. Sholes realized that he should fashion a keyboard that could maximize typebar distances between the jam-causing bigrams. According to Sproat (2010: 158), Sholes's financial backer James Densmore had a brother Amos Densmore, who was a schoolteacher. Sholes asked Amos Densmore to compile a list of common English letter pairs. Not knowing what text Amos Densmore used to compute the list, Sproat lists the ten most frequent letter bigrams with their counts from the King James Bible, the most widely printed book in the 19th century.

th 189,406

he 153,362

an 90,152

nd 75,799

in 55,925

er 54,690

ha 52,187

re 48,998

of 44,124

or 41,882

Six of them—the first five plus *of*—would remain on the list if we use Wikipedia as corpus in which the most common ten words are *the*, *of*, *and*, *in*, *a*, *to*, *is*, *was*, *for*, *as*, with the other four replaced by *to*, *is*, *was*, *as*. If we examine these six pairs and consider the layout of the QWERTY keyboard, we'll see all these bigrams are set apart from each other. The rest four each has one exception—the pair of *e* and *r* in the list derived from the King James Bible, and the pair *a* and *s* in the list based on Wikipedia.

Yet, there is a condition for this popular theory to be a good answer: the corresponding type-bars were not next to each other if the keys were adjacent. A close-up of the type-bars of the earliest model Remington No.1, where 44 type-bars were arranged in a circle or "type basket", will show that for any pair of keys adjacent in the top two or bottom two rows on the keyboard, the corresponding type-bars were separated by the type-bar for the key either above or below the two and in the middle. It confirms that the most common letter bigrams, *th*, *he*, *an*, *nd*, *in*, *of* are all set far apart, with one notable exception of *re/er*. How come he overlooked this pair?

Figure 8.5   Remington No.1 (The Sholes-Glidden Typewriter) top view
Source: National Museum Scotland Blog
https://blog.nms.ac.uk/2018/08/11/re-typing-history-the-sholes-glidden-typewriter-and-the-qwerty-keyboard/
(accessed Sept. 5, 2024)

The illustration of Sholes' 1872 trial model prior to the commercial one might strike one with an interesting clue—the keys for *r* and *e* were not next to each other, and the dot "." was in place of *r*. In other words, in the 1873 commercial model the placement of letter *r* and the dot were swapped, somewhat inexplicably.

Figure 8.6　The Type Writer, *Scientific American*, Vol. 27, No.6 (August 10, 1872), front page
Source: https://www.scientificamerican.com/issue/sa/1872/08-10/ (accessed Sept. 5, 2024)

A popular speculation is that the swap was made to allow the word "typewriter" to be typed using only the top row of keys, which was likely intended to showcase the typewriter's effectiveness and make a strong marketing point.

8.2.1.2　Functional theory

The jamming theory has been questioned by Yasuoka and Yasuoka (2011). By tracking the evolution of the typewriter keyboard along the history of telegraph apparatus (cf. Chapter IX), they conclude that the mechanics of the typewriter did not influence the keyboard design. Rather, the QWERTY system evolved over several years as a direct result of how the first typewriters—telegraph operators who needed to quickly transcribe messages—were used.

The early keyboard of typewriter was derived from Hughes-Phelps Printing Telegraph, and it was developed for Morse receivers (Yasuoka and Yasuoka, 2011: 161). In 1868, five years before finalizing the Remington prototype, Sholes and his colleagues shipped out a product to their first customer—Edward Payson Porter, the principal of Porter's Telegraph College, Chicago. In 1870, they reached out to the American Telegraph Works in New York. During 1868 to 1872, Sholes made several adjustments to the keyboard based on feedback from telegraph operators, turning it from a 28-key design resembling a piano to a 42-key, four-row arrangement, which was featured on the frontpage of American Science shown in Figure 8.6.

The QWERTY layout, which placed commonly used letters apart from each other on the keyboard, may have been developed to reduce errors caused by rapid typing. In telegraphy, misinterpreting a single letter could lead to significant communication errors.

The code represents Z as '....' which is often confused with the digram SE, more frequently-used than Z.

Sometimes Morse receivers in United States cannot determine whether Z or SE is applicable, especially in the first letter(s) of a word, before they receive following letters. Thus S ought to be placed near by both Z and E on the keyboard for Morse receivers to type them quickly (by the same reason C ought to be placed near by IE. But, in fact, C was more often confused with S) (Yasuoka and Yasuoka, 2011: 164).

The Functional Theory argues that keyboard arrangement accidently grew into QWERTY among the different requirements: first to receive telegraphs, then to thrash out a compromise between inventors and producers, and at last to evade old patents. As for the first requirement, it catered to both the need for accuracy in understanding Morse code signals and the need for efficiency in typing the correct letters once they were identified. The placement of keys was thus optimized to support the practical workflow of Morse code operators, balancing the dual goals of accuracy and speed.

Regardless of how he developed it, it seems Sholes himself wasn't convinced that QWERTY was the ultimate solution. Although he sold his designs to Remington early on, he continued to explore alternative keyboard layouts for the rest of his life. In 1889, a year before his death, he filed a patent for the following design.

Figure 8.7   U.S. Patent 568630A, issued to C. L. Sholes posthumously
Source: https://patents.google.com/patent/US568630A/en (accessed Oct. 1, 2024)

8.2.2 Head start and path dependency

After the introduction of Remington No. 1, which marked the beginning of practical typewriters, many other manufacturers entered the market to capitalize on the growing demand for typewriting machines. In the period between 1879 and 1889, several successful typewriting machines appeared on the market, beginning with The Caligraph, Remington's first competitor. It was soon followed by Hammond, Yost, Smith Premier, Williams, Crandall, and Hall (Casillo, 2017: 36). Competition led to a wide variety of typewriter designs—some focused on improved typing speed, others on portability, and still, others on cost-effectiveness, each seeking to establish themselves in the emerging industry.

Despite the competition, QWERTY layout became entrenched, largely due to its head start in office environments and the subsequent development of touch typing methods. In the 1870s, the primary customers of Remington typewriters were mostly stenographers in office environments. They typed via "hunt and peck" sight method. Soon after Remington N0. 2 was released, "touch typing" methods were introduced and courses on touch typing were taught. In 1882, Remington reached an exclusive agreement with Wyckoff to sell typewriters and set up a training company called Wycokoff, Seamans & Benedict (WS&B) to teach touch typing (Kafaee, et al. 2022). Since then, Remington started building programs with colleges, universities, and The World Young Women's Christian Association (YWCA), offering them free or discounted typewriters with a ready-made "touch typing" course (Hoke, 1979; Davies, 2010; Roemmele, 2019). The "touch typing" course used the QWERTY keyboard and required the typist to memorize the keys and to type without looking at the keyboard.

Typists who received this training became skilled touch typists on QWERTY keyboards, and their proficiency with this layout locked it into their minds. This made the QWERTY layout the de facto standard in typing and created a self-reinforcing cycle. When these well-trained typists entered office typing pools, they naturally preferred Remington typewriters with the QWERTY layout, and employers often provided them with the tools they were most skilled with.

In 1893, the manufacturers of the Remington Standard machine merged with several other large makers of the day to form Union Writing Machine Company (later renamed Union Typewriter Company), an early "typewriter trust" with the purpose of fixing prices and restricting competition. As part of the agreement, the Union decided to adopt the QWERTY keyboard layout as the standard for their machines. This decision further solidified the position of the QWERTY layout as the dominant keyboard standard for typewriters. By 1898, the QWERTY layout had captured over 70% of the typewriter market share.

Nevertheless, the QWERTY keyboard was open to challenges. It was accused of straining the left hand, overloading the small finger, and underutilizing the home row—the second-from-the-bottom row where one rests his fingers when preparing to type. The home row of nine letters includes two of the least used (J and K) but none of the three most frequently used (E, T, and O) and only one of the five vowels (A), though about 40% of all letters in a typical English text are vowels. The user's fingers must not only reach from the home row to the top or bottom but must at times hurdle completely over the home row, travelling directly from top to bottom and back again.

To increase efficiency, many competing keyboard designs concentrated the most common English letters onto the home row. One of the most famous is the Dvorak Simplified Keyboard designed in the 1930s by August Dvorak (1894—1975), an American educational psychologist at the University of Washington. The Dvorak keyboard devotes the home row to nine of the twelve most common letters, including all five vowels and the three most common consonants (T, H, N), while the six rarest letters (V, K, J, X, Q, and Z) are relegated to the bottom row.

Figure 8.8   Dvorak's Simplified Keyboard
Source: https://patents.google.com/patent/US2040248 (accessed Oct. 1, 2024)

Theoretically the Dvorak keyboard should beat the QWERTY keyboard by a large margin, but Light and Anderson's research (1993) shows that it makes far less improvement than expected. In their study, they proposed a "cost" metric for evaluating keyboard layouts, which could be broken down into three components: first, the relative frequency of letter pair for English; second, the "travel times" between positions on the key board; third, the mapping of the letters to the keys. The first and third are easy to compute. The second needs empirical data, as it is based on such considerations as the strength of the individual fingers. Light and Anderson base their estimate of travel times on previous work in human factors. They determine the cost of a given keyboard configuration as a sum, over every pair of letters, of the product of the frequency of the letter pair, and the travel time between the positions of the two letters. A lower cost is a more efficient keyboard. By this measure, QWERTY gets a cost of 1542, and Dvorak gets 1502. It turns out that the QWERTY keyboard is neither horribly inefficient as it is usually believed nor notably efficient, and that the Dvorak keyboard is better but not that much better. Not a disruptive innovation, the Dvorak keyboard was unable to create a new market and value network to overthrow King QWERTY.

In the 1970s, when commercial personal computers became popular, the first generation of consumers were at the same time the QWERTY keyboard typewriter users. The past model, too ingrained in a culture zeitgeist to change, survived. When it comes to virtual keyboard for smartphones, QWERTY was adopted in IOS and Android in 2007 and 2008 respectively. Such phenomenon is known as a "path dependency" (cf. Arthur, 1989; Liebowitz and Margolis, 1995; Vergne and Durand, 2010), often occurring due to factors like user habits, infrastructure, institutional support, and the costs associated with transitioning to a new solution, all of which can make it challenging to move away from the established path. Today, QWERTY enjoys its enduring popularity despite the presence of more theoretically efficient alternatives, such as Colemak, Maltron and ErgoDox. To most of us—the nonprofessional typists, "Qwerty is about as good a design as any alternative" (Liebowitz and Margolis, 1990: 1).

8.3　Typewriter and writing style

Though Nietzsche used Hansen's Writing Ball for no more than one season, he wrote that "our writing tools are also working on our thoughts" (quoted in Kittler, 1999: 204). Kittler (1999) studies Nietzsche's *The Wanderer and His Shadow* and suggests that typing changed Nietzsche's way of writing and thinking from sustained argument and prolonged reflection to aphorism, puns, and "telegram style."

Whether the typewriter led Nietzsche to a laconic style or not, modernist poets such as E. E. Cummings (1894—1962), T. S. Eliot (1888—1965), and Guillaume Apollinaire (1880—1918) were convinced that the typewriter had changed their writing style. They all explored the typographical effects that a typewriter could produce, and requested their publishers to strictly follow their layouts and punctuations, as these were very important for the sense. Lyons reviews the contribution of the machine to the development of freer verse forms by modernist poets, and concludes that "the typewriter assisted them to break with traditional rhyme and metre; it could create a *mise-en-page* that, for them, resembled a musical score" (2021: 76).

The following poem "l(a" by E. E. Cummings demonstrates how mechanical composition expresses the required-spatial relationships between its various components. The phrase "a leaf falls" is placed parenthetically within the word "loneliness", forming a slender strip that drops slowly.

l(a

le

af

fa

ll

s)

one

l

iness

In another poem "I Have Found What You Are Like," E. E. Cummings shaped the poem in the way that the readers may feel like seeing the woods stutter, even though it is not describing a realistic occurrence. Blank space became a vital and dynamic part of the poem, and "the typewriter was indispensable to measure it with the desired accuracy" (Lyons, 2021: 81).

i have found what you are like
the rain,

       (Who feathers frightened fields
with the superior dust-of-sleep. wields

easily the pale club of the wind
and swirled justly souls of flower strike

the air in utterable coolness

deeds of green thrilling light
                  with thinned

newfragile yellows

       lurch and.press

—in the woods

　　　　which

　　　　　　stutter

　　　　　　　　and

　　　　　　　　　　sing

And the coolness of your smile is

stirringofbirds between my arms;but

i should rather than anything

have(almost when hugeness will shut

quietly)almost,

　　　　　　your kiss

While Cummings could theoretically achieve similar effects by writing with a ruler in hand, the typewriter, as a medium structure, mechanizes the creative process and enables the poet to manipulate space as a visual aesthetic, which contributes to the meaning and emotional impact.

Martin Heidegger (1889—1976), a prominent German philosopher, had a critical perspective on the impact of the typewriter on human existence and the act of writing. He argued that the machine "tears writing from the essential realm of the hand, i.e., the realm of the word" (quoted in Kittler, 1999: 198). To him, the typewriter disrupted the more traditional and intimate connection between the act of writing and the physical, human hand. Perhaps it was this mechanical irruption that made Nietzsche aware of the toll that the writing ball was taking on his linguistic mind.

Yet, the interaction between humans and their writing tools is a deeply personal and variable aspect of creative and productive work. In the case of Henry James (1843—1916), the heralded nineteenth-century American novelist, the typewriter was quite positive. In 1907 he hired Theodora Bosanquet as his personal secretary and typist. For seven years, until his death, James dictated massive amounts of narrative to her. In an article titled "Typewriter Psyche: Henry James' Mechanical Mind" (2013: 14), Matthew Schillemann argues:

The mental model found in Henry James' late works derives from his switch to typewritten dictation …. Through careful investigation, it can be demonstrated that the properties of typewritten dictation play a crucial role in forming the dynamic system of drives, compulsions, repetitions, and displacements for which James's late works are famous.

It appears that the sounds of the typewriter acted as a motivational and creative stimulus, leading to more diffuse and productive writing. The "click" of the typewriter may have provided a sense of forward momentum and engagement with language, a positive spur for his writing.

This probably explains why mechanical keyboards are still favored by some people while modern computer keyboards come in various forms, including membrane and chiclet keyboards. Their preference can be related to some of the same principles that influenced Henry James' positive experience with the typewriter' sounds: a distinctive tactile feedback when a key is pressed, offering a satisfying "click" or "clack" sound and a noticeable physical actuation point.

8.4   Chinese typewriter

As early as the 1870s, the typewriter became known in China. With the globalization of the Western typewriter, efforts were made to build a Chinese typewriter. The logographic nature of the Chinese writing system would require designers to depart from the conventional typewriter form that caters to alphabetic writing at a time when this form enjoyed prestige and popularity. However, this task is anything but simple.

8.4.1   Characters of common usage and movable typewriter

According to Mullaney (2017), two approaches had been taken to create a Chinese typewriter. The first approach seizes upon characters of common usage. It dates back to Devello Sheffield (1841—1913), an American Presbyterian missionary to China, who designed a machine in 1897. He carefully selected characters for common usage and settled on a set of 4,662 characters. However, other than a curiosity-inducing prototype, the machine was never manufactured.

In the same line was Zhou Houkun (周厚坤, 1891—?), an overseas Chinese student studying Mechanical Engineering and Naval Architecture at MIT, who reduced the total number to about 3,000 and built the first model of his machine in 1914. Zhou's machine contained a cylinder measuring roughly sixteen to eighteen inches in length and six inches in diameter, on which a set of approximately three thousand characters slugs was arranged in accordance with the Kangxi **radical-stroke system**, a method of classifying and organizing characters in the *Kangxi Dictionary* published in 1716 and then widely adopted in traditional Chinese dictionaries. In this system, each character falls under one of the 214 radicals, i.e., common graphical components of characters, within which characters are ordered by the total number of additional strokes beyond the radical itself.

Figure 8.9   Zhou Houkun and his typewriter in *Popular Science Monthly* (1917, April)
Source: https://archive.org/details/popularsciencemo90newyuoft/page/598/mode/2up (accessed Oct. 1, 2024)

Zhou's invention caught the attention of The Commercial Press, which brought him and his device to Shanghai. However, The Commercial Press did not put Zhou's machine into production. The reasons were not clearly identified, but one undoubted consideration was that "the characters on Zhou's machine were completely fixed, impossible to adjust to a different terminological needs and contexts" (Mullaney, 2017: 166).

The first mass-produced Chinese typewriter was Shu-style typewriter invented by Shu Zhendong (舒振东, ?—?), an engineer who joined The Commercial Press in 1919. Shu abandoned the Chinese character cylinder in Zhou's design and replaced it with a flat, rectangular bed within which character slugs would sit loosely and interchangeably, so that the machine can be customized to fit different terminological contexts. This movable typewriter was advanced by The Commercial Press as "part competitor, part complement to both the human hand and the printing press" (Mullaney, 2017: 171).

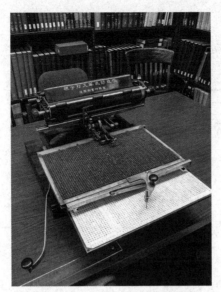

Figure 8.10   Shu-style Chinese typewriter, Huntington Library
Source: Mullaney, 2017: 162

Shu-style typewriter was mass-produced beginning in 1920. It became "indispensable for government offices, educational institutions, companies and factories" (Zhou, 2009) in the 1930s and 1940s, and continued to be used in some publishing houses until the 1960s and 1970s.

8.4.2   Divisible type and combinatorial typewriter

Radically different from the first approach, the second approach focused on divisible type and combinatorial machine. The first prototype of its kind was built by Qi Xuan (祁暄, ?—?) in 1915, an overseas Chinese student in New York who undertook the invention almost at the same time with Zhou Houkun. Through analyzing Qi's United States patent and one of the surviving photos of the inventor, Mullaney (2017: 149) points out the profound difference: in addition to the 4,200 common usage characters on his cylinder, Qi also included a set of 1,327 pieces of Chinese characters that the operator could use to assemble or "spell" out less frequent characters piece by piece, in a manner akin to composing an English-language word letter by letter.

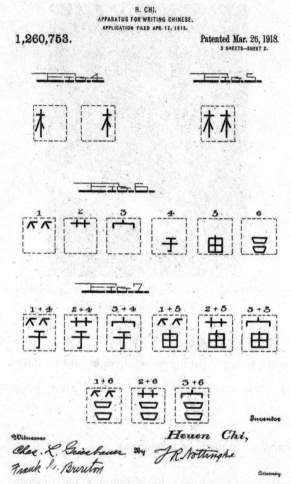

Figure 8.11   Qi Xuan (Heuen Chi) apparatus for writing Chinese United States patent
Source: https://patentimages.storage.googleapis.com/62/e0/c1/f10e60bcfc3c28/US1260753.pdf
(accessed Oct. 1, 2024)

Qi's invention was a significant departure from earlier typewriter designs, allowing for greater versatility and flexibility for typing Chinese characters, especially those that were not included on the standard typewriter cylinder. He challenged the idea that characters had to be individual, stand-alone units. Instead, "he thought of them as more modular, like alphabet-based words, things that could be recycled to compose different characters" (Tsu, 2022: 82). As with many innovations, unfortunately, it struggled to gain wide recognition, particularly in the Chinese circles, due to practical inertia and aesthetic concerns.

8.4.3   Search-writing and MingKwai typewriter

In 1946, Lin Yutang (林语堂，1895—1976), the world renowned Chinese linguist, novelist, philosopher, and translator, offered an alternative to radical system in his "MingKwai"("clear" and "quick") Chinese typewriter.

Lin drew his inspiration from a language reform debate known as the "character retrieval problem" (检字法问题) taking place in China from the 1910s through the 1930s, in which scientists, educators and linguists fought over and experimented with systems of organizing Chinese dictionaries, library catalogues, indexes, name lists, and telephone books. As early as 1918, in a paper published in *New Youth* "A Chinese Index System: An Explanation," Lin challenged the time-honored tradition of radical-based character classification by breaking them down into strokes. He identified five different stroke types: horizontal, vertical, diagonal, point, and hook, each as a broad category, following the direction of the stroke execution rather than the style of any specific stroke. From that, he created a second-level taxonomy, coupling the first with a second stroke, and identified a set of twenty-eight first-plus-second-stroke patterns that accounted for almost all characters. This index scheme was the compositional logic of MingKwai. Thus, the black box below was not a typewriter in the conventional sense, but a device designed primarily for the retrieval of Chinese characters.

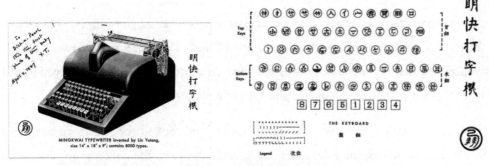

Figure 8.12   Keyboard of the MingKwai Chinese typewriter
Source: Mullaney, 2017: 246

All the mechanisms of selection and retrieval were factored into the design of the keyboard. Mullaney (2017: 246) explains how the machine worked:

Seated before the device, an operator would see seventy-two keys divided into three banks: upper keys, lower keys, and eight number keys. First, the depression of one of the thirty-six upper keys triggered movement and rotation of the machine's internal gears and type complex—a mechanical array of Chinese character graphs contained inside the machine's chassis, out of view of the typist. The depression of a second key—one of the twenty-eight lower keys—initiated a second round of shifts and repositionings within the machine, now bringing a cluster of eight Chinese characters into view within a small window on the machine—a viewfinder Lin Yutang called his "Magic Eye." Depending upon which of these characters one wanted—one through eight—the operator then depressed one of the number keys to complete the selection process and imprint the desired character on the page.

Thus, to type the character "题", just depress "目日" in top keys and "㇏" in bottom keys. Then press the number key corresponding to the correct character within the Magic Eye's display. This process is analogous to the way modern input method editors (IMEs) work when we type Chinese on laptops or cell phones: every character is assigned an index according to strokes or Pinyin; an input of strokes or Pinyin reduces the pool of potential characters from thousands to a few dozen or fewer. The difference is that now the built-in frequency data and user history would help prioritize the most likely characters based on general usage patterns and individual user behavior, making the selection process faster and more intuitive. By breaking down the input process into manageable steps and narrowing choices through a systematic approach, Lin's interface design anticipated the logic behind modern input systems well before the invention of computers. In this sense, his invention is a visionary step towards future development.

Also, Lin's typewriter was designed to be accessible to a wide range of users, both Chinese and Westerners, regardless of whether they knew Chinese characters or not. Every piece of information for locating a character was encoded on those seventy-two keys, which were simply labeled with character components instead of alphabet letters.

Lin filed an application with the U.S. Patent Office and looked for American companies that would develop the machine for commercial sale. However, the concerns for uncertainty for production and sales during an all-out civil war period of China halted any significant investment. The only existing prototype, whose development left Lin bankrupt, was nowhere to be found.

8.5   Typewriter and women's entrance into office

During the late 19th and early 20th centuries, the growth of office work, facilitated by the typewriter, significantly altered the landscape of employment and gender roles in the U.S. The statistics provided by Hoke (1979: 77) should suffice to prove typewriter triggered an influx of women into the labor force: in 1870, while the typewriter was still a model in a machine shop, there were seven women stenographers, by 1900 there were 200,000, and by 1930, there were 2,000,000.

Unlike many other jobs of the time, typewriting did not have a strong gender bias, and women were readily accepted as typists and stenographers. This provided new employment opportunities for women beyond traditional roles such as homemakers, caregivers, agricultural workers, factory labors, and handmaids. Moreover, the rise of typewriting and office work coincided with the growth of women's organizations and the suffrage movement. Women working in offices had opportunities to network, organize, and advocate for women's rights and equality, expanding society's view of what women could achieve outside the home.

The role of women typists extended beyond simply performing clerical tasks; they actively participated in streamlining business communication practices. As they became integral to the office environment, they collaborated in the formulation of new conventions for business correspondence and reshaped the appearance and structure of written communication. As Walker (2018) has shown on the basis of a study of typing manuals, it were women typists who introduced wider margins and more paragraph indentations into the text, and adopted as standard a fully "blocked" layout in which every line began at the left-hand margin.

For some time, the association between the typewriter and the woman was so strong that the word "typewriter" denoted the female typist rather than the machine itself. While ushering women into office, the typewriter also subjected them to underpayment, immobility and male gaze in a dead-end job (cf. Further reading). It took many years for substantial progress to be made in addressing these issues.

Similarly in Asia, women's progress through the formal economy has been closely intwined with the typewriter. During China's Republican era, the expanding administrative needs of a rapidly developing economy gave rise to the profession of typists. Concurrently, progress on women's emancipation and girls' access to education opened doors for Chinese women to pursue professional work. According to Zhang and Jiang (2023), by the 1930s, women began to gain traction as clerks in companies, particularly in roles as typists and stenographers. From 1932 to 1948, women made up 70 percent of typist trainees. Typists combined with elementary school teachers constituted two-thirds of the professional women workforce. Mirroring their counterparts in the U.S., they were seen on the one hand as symbols of modernity, competence, and independence—emblematic of the "New Woman" breaking free from traditional shackles, on the other hand sometimes trivialized as mere "eye candy" or portrayed as potential "office mistress." The historical association between women and the typewriter serves as a reminder of the complex relationship between technology, societal norms, and the empowerment of marginalized groups.

Summing-up

For long, the typewriter had been a missing piece in techno-linguistic historiography. Small as it is, this piece magnifies colours and details giving our picture of "information infrastructure journey" an extra punch. It links printing and computer, in the U.S. with the legacy of QWERTY, and in China with unyielding struggles to integrate Chinese characters into text mechanization devices. Fitting in this piece adds another layer to our understanding of information globalization: the path toward a more interconnected world was shaped by gradual, often challenging adaptations at the intersection of global forces and local realities.

Beyond its technical significance, the typewriter also served as a catalyst for social change, particularly in the lives of women. In both the U.S. and China, this seemingly modest machine reshaped gender roles and labor dynamics, opening up new opportunities for employment and independence. In the U.S., the typewriter became a symbol of the emerging female workforce, empowering women to enter offices in unprecedented numbers. In China, it was entwined with the broader narrative of women's emancipation, helping to bridge the gap between traditional roles and modern aspirations. Thus, the typewriter's impact reverberates not only through the realms of technology and language but also through the very fabric of society, echoing the struggles and triumphs of women as they navigated a rapidly changing world.

References

Arthur, W. Brian. 1989. "Competing Technologies, Increasing Returns, and Lock-In by Historical Events." *The Economic Journal* 99, no. 394: 116—131.

Casillo, Anthony. 2017. *Typewriters: Iconic Machines from the Golden Age of Mechanical Writing.* San Francisco: Chronicle Books.

Cutler, Ida McLenan, and Rupert P. SoRelle. 1910. *Rational Typewriting: A New Idea in Teaching Touch Typewriting.* New York: Gregg Publishing Company.

Davies, Margery. 2010. *Women's Place is at the Typewriter.* Philadelphia: Temple University Press.

David, Paul A. 1985. "Clio and the Economics of QWERTY." *The American Economic Review* 75, no. 2: 332—337.

Hoke, Donald. 1979. "The Woman and the Typewriter: A Case Study in Technological Innovation and Social Change." *Business and Economic History* 8, Papers Presented at the Twenty-Fifth Annual Meeting of the Business History Conference: 76—88.

Kafaee, Mahdi, Elahe Daviran, and Mostafa Taqavi. 2022. The QWERTY Keyboard from the Perspective of the Collingridge Dilemma: Lessons for Co-construction of Human-Technology. *AI & SOCIETY* (2024) 39:1229—1241. https://doi.org/10.1007/s00146-022-01569-5.

Kittler, Friedrich. 1999. *Gramophone, Film, Typewriter.* Translated by Geoffrey Winthrop-Young and Michael Wutz. Stanford, CA: Stanford University Press.

Liebowitz, Stan J., and Stephen E. Margolis. 1990. "The Fable of the Keys." *Journal of Law and Economics* 33, no. 1: 1—26.

Liebowitz, Stan J., and Stephen E. Margolis. 1995. Path Dependence, Lock-In, and History." *Journal of Law, Economics, & Organization* 11, no. 1: 205—226.

Light, Lisa, and Peter G. Anderson. 1993. "Typewriter Keyboards via Simulated Annealing." *AI Expert,* September 1993.

Lyons, Martyn. 2021. *The Typewriter Century: A Cultural History of Writing Practices.* Toronto: University of Toronto Press.

Mullaney, Thomas S. 2017. *The Chinese Typewriter: A History.* Cambridge, MA: MIT Press.

Remington Notes 1915. 3, no. 10. https://oztypewriter.blogspot.com/2014/08/not-again-from-miss-remington-to-peter.html. (accessed July 4, 2023)

Roemmele, Brian. 2019. "Why Was the QWERTY Keyboard Layout Invented?" *Forbes,* January 10, 2019. https://www.forbes.com/sites/quora/2019/01/10/why-was-the-qwerty-keyboard-layout-invented/. (accessed Feb. 1, 2023)

Schillemann, Matthew. 2013. "Typewriter Psyche: Henry James' Mechanical Mind." *Journal of Modern Literature* 36, no. 3: 14—30.

Sproat, Richard. 2010. *Language, Technology, and Society.* Oxford: Oxford University Press.

Tsu, Jing. 2022. *Kingdom of Characters: The Language Revolution that Made China Modern.* New York: Riverhead Books.

Vergne, Jean-Philippe, and Rodolphe Durand. 2010. "The Missing Link Between the Theory and Empirics of Path Dependence: Conceptual Clarification, Testability Issue, and Methodological Implications." *Journal of Management Studies* 47, no. 4: 736—759.

Walker, Sue. 2018. "Modernity, Method, and Minimal Means: Typewriters, Typing Manuals, and Document Design." *Journal of Design History* 31, no. 2: 138—153.

Yasuoka, Koichi, and Motoko Yasuoka. 2011. "On the Prehistory of QWERTY." *ZINBUN* 42: 161—174.

林玉堂[①]，1918，《汉字索引制说明》，载《新青年》，1918年第4卷第2号，128—131。

章梅芳、姜心玉，2023，《民国时期大众报刊中的女打字员形象阐释》，载《北京科技大学学报（社会科学版）》，第39卷第3期，353—361。

周楠，2009，《"舒式打字机"发明者后人讲述与世博八十年的情缘》，载《解放日报》，2009-11-17。

Further reading: excerpt from *Typewriter Century: A Cultural History of Writing Practices*

Lyons, Martyn. 2018. "Chapter 3 Modernity and the 'Typewriter Girl.'" In *Typewriter Century: A Cultural History of Writing Practices*, 54—58. Toronto: University of Toronto Press.

---

① Commonly known by the later name "林语堂".

Chapter IX   Telegraph, Morse Code, and Global Connectivity

Jumping-in

In 2018, a hiker in California was rescued after using Morse code to signal for help. The hiker had become lost and was unable to call for help on his cell phone, so he used a flashlight to signal "SOS" in Morse code to a rescue helicopter flying overhead. The helicopter crew spotted the signal and were able to rescue the hiker.

Do you know how to signal SOS with a flashlight? Now tap the flashlight icon on your cell phone and have a try.

Like the typewriter, and many seminal inventions of the industrial era, the electric telegraph was not the invention of one person. Instead, it was the result of collaborative efforts by multiple inventors and innovators who built upon each other's work.

Several people contributed vital parts of the system, but it was William Fothergill Cooke (1806—1879) and Charles Wheatstone (1802—1875) in England, and Samuel F. B. Morse (1791—1872) and Alfred Vail (1807—1859) in the United States who first built practical, working telegraph lines of substantial length and transmitted messages over them.

Cooke and Wheatstone's system was first put into commercial use in 1837, when the first telegraph line was installed between Euston Square Terminus and Camden Town Station in England, a short stretch on the North-Western Railway. The line was a success, and it was soon extended to other parts of the railway network. By 1845, there were over 500 miles of telegraph wire in England (cf. Fyfe, 1863: 190—192). In 1846 the Electric Telegraph Company was incorporated, and after twenty years had elapsed, the total number of telegraph in operation in Britain was no less than 16,000 miles (Western Union Telegraph Company, 1869: 30).

Despite its early success, Cooke and Wheatstone's telegraph system was later superseded by Morse's system, which was put into commercial use in the United States in 1844, when the first telegraph line was established between Washington, D.C. and Baltimore. Compared to Cooke and Wheatstone's multi-wire system, Morse's system used a single wire, which made it easier and cheaper to install and maintain. Eventually, it was Morse's cost-effective system and, especially, his highly efficient code that became the standard.

9.1　The semiotic architecture: Morse Code

In October 1832, Morse, then a portrait painter by profession, was on an American-bound ship out of France. His interest in telegraphy was sparked by a conversation with a fellow passenger Charles Jackson (1805—1880), a Boston physician, on the latest scientific insights into electromagnetism (cf. Prime, 1875: 251—252). Soon after, he began working on developing a system that could transmit language instantaneously by electricity to any distance.

Essential to his idea, as he had set forth in notes written in 1832, were that signals would be sent by opening and closing of an electrical circuit, that the receiving apparatus would, by electromagnet, record signals as dots and dashes on paper, and that there would be a code whereby the dots and dashes would be translated into numbers and letters (McCullough, 2011). In other words, he would need to formulate a **binary-based** combinatorial system.

The figure below illustrates Morse and Vail's receiving device for recording transmitted code. Avery (1895: 565) explains its mechanism:

> The Morse register is represented [here]. The armature, A , is supported at the end of a lever, and over the cores of the magnet bobbins, M. A spring, S, lifts the armature when the cores are demagnetized on the breaking of the circuit by the operator at the key. When A is pulled down by M, a style or pencil at P is pressed against R, a paper ribbon that is drawn along by clock work. this style may be made to record upon the paper a dot-and-dash communication sent by the operator at a key, perhaps hundreds of miles away.

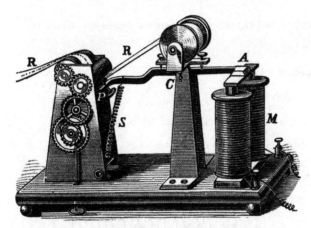

Figure 9.1   Morse and Vail's receiving device for recording transmitted code
Source: Avery, 1895: 565

When Morse set about devising the dot-and-dash code for the English alphabet, like Sholes, he took into consideration the frequency of a letter's occurrence in the language's writing system in order to assign shorter sequences of dots and dashes to more common letters, and longer sequences to less common letters. To figure out the frequency of each letter, Morse and his associates visited a local newspaper printing office, and recorded the quantity of sorts for each letter in the compositor's type case (Burns, 2004: 84). They assigned shorter codes to sorts used most often, and longer codes to sorts used most seldom. As shown in the following figure, the letter "E" is the most frequently used letter, so it is represented by a single dot. The letter "T" is the second most frequently used letter, so it is represented by a single dash. In contrast, less common letters like "Q" and "Z" are represented by longer sequences of dots and dashes.

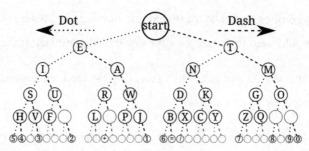

Figure 9.2   A binary tree of the Morse Code adapted from the dichotomic search table in the en: morse code Wikipedia entry

Source: https://commons.wikimedia.org/wiki/File:Morse-code-tree.svg (accessed Oct. 1, 2024)

In addition to dot representing one time unit and dash representing three time units, the original version of the Morse Code include a number of rules about space, as shown in Figure 9.3.

1. intra-character gap (standard gap between the dots and dashes in a character)

2. short gap (between letters)

3. medium gap (between words)

4. long gap (between sentences)

5. long intra-character gap (longer internal gap used in C, O, R, Y, Z and &)

6. "long dash" (the letter L)

7. even longer dash (the numeral 0)

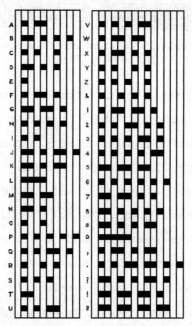

Figure 9.3   1911 Chart of the Standard American Morse Characters

Source: https://en.wikipedia.org/wiki/American_Morse_code#/media/File:Amercode.png (accessed Sept. 5, 2023)

Beyond English, Morse code could be easily adapted for languages written with an alphabet or syllabary. The basic principles remain the same, but some modifications may be necessary to account for differences in the frequency of letters and the unique characteristics of each writing system. In German, French, Italian, which use the same Latin alphabet but with a few additional letters with diacritical marks, the letters with diacritical marks are represented by additional dots and dashes. For example, in French the letter "é" is represented by "..-..", "è" by ".-..-", and "ê" by "-..-.". In a syllabary like Japanese, Morse Code has been adapted to work by assigning unique sequences of dots and dashes to each kana character. For example, the kana character "あ" (pronounced "a") is represented by "--.--", while the character " か " (pronounced "ka") is represented by ".-..".

In 1848, Friedrich Clemens Gerke (1801—1888), a German writer and pioneer of telegraphy, revised the American Morse Code to facilitate international communication and eliminate confusion. He included letters with diacritical marks as well as additional punctuation marks and symbols, eliminated multiple representations for some letters and numbers, and standardized timing for spaces. Gerke's revised version gave rise to the International Morse Code.

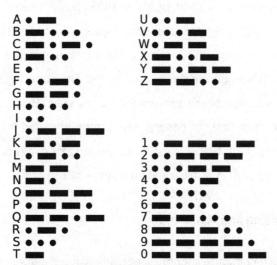

Figure 9.4   International Morse Code by Rhey T. Snodgrass & Victor F. Camp 1922
Source: https://commons.wikimedia.org/wiki/File:International_Morse_Code.svg (accessed Sept. 5, 2023)

Here's an example of how International Morse Code works:

Let's say you want to send the message "SOS" in Morse code by using the telegraph. The Morse code for "S" is three dots (· · ·) and the Morse code for "O" is three dashes (− − −). So, to send "SOS" in Morse code, you would send:

· · · − − − · · ·

When the recipient receives this message, they would decode it by listening for the duration of the dots and dashes. A dot is a short sound, while a dash is a longer sound. So, to decode "SOS", the recipient would hear:

Short sound, short sound, short sound, long sound, long sound, long sound, short sound, short sound, short sound

Which they would then interpret as the letters "SOS."

If expressed in binary, where 0 means no data and 1 means data and a dash is three times the length of a dot, then we have:

(101010)000(111011101110)000(101010)

The distress signal SOS was officially introduced by the German government radio regulations in 1905, and was later adopted as the worldwide standard under the second International Radiotelegraphic Convention, which was signed in 1906 and became effective on July 1, 1908. Despite popular beliefs, SOS does not stand for phrases like "Save Our Ship" or "Save Our Souls." It was adopted simply because it was easier to recognize and transmit. Perhaps the most famous use of SOS was during the sinking of the Titanic on April 14—15, 1912 after striking an iceberg. According to the surviving wireless man (Bride, 1912), The operators switched between SOS and CQD, a general call commonly used by British telegraphers. Unfortunately, the Titanic sank before most of the passengers could be saved. However, the incident cemented the use of SOS as the standard distress call.

9.2 Logographic writing and Morse Code

A language written with logographs, Chinese apparently requires a different approach. To devise a particular dot-and-dash sequence for every symbol in the large character repertoire, though theoretically possible, is practically infeasible for both the sender and receiver.

In 1871, an undersea cable between Shanghai and Hong Kong was laid by the Great Northern Telegraph Company of Denmark, which connected the Qing Empire to the rapidly expanding global telegraph network for the first time. Morse Code was thereby brought into contact with a writing system it was ill-equipped to handle.

In 1872, the Great Northern published *New Book for the Telegraph* (《电报新书》), a standard Chinese telegraph codebook listing 6899 most commonly used characters, each assigned a unique four-digit number from 0000 to 9999 (cf. Baark, 2000: 136—137). The characters were categorized under 214 radicals listed according to the number of their strokes, and the characters selected under each radical were also arranged according to the number of their strokes. Encoding a message required finding a Chinese character and its corresponding number according to the radicals and strokes in the same way as looking up a word in the Chinese dictionary. Then the four-digit codes would be transmitted using standard Morse signals. Using numbers as a middle stage, it was the first coding table to turn Chinese characters into electronic signals.

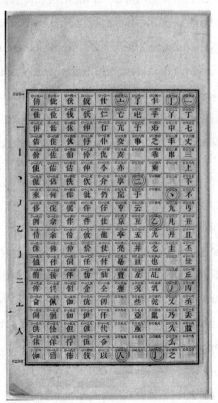

Figure 9.5   A sample page from *New Book for the Telegraph*

Source: Sheet 13 of the electronically reproduced Viguier, Dianbao xinshu, archived in Det Kongelige Bibliotek (Royal Library of Denmark), Oriental and Judaica Collections, Copenhagen (http://www5.kb.dk/permalink/2006/manus/340/eng/13/?var=1) (accessed Oct. 1, 2024)

In 1881, the Qing government established the Imperial Telegraph Administration (ITA) at the request of Li Hongzhang (李鸿章，1823—1901), Governor General of Zhili province and Minister of Beiyang trade, at the culmination of a massive telegraph construction campaign (cf. Further reading). In the same year, ITA issued a codebook titled *New Compilation for the Telegraph* (《电报新编》), which was basically a reproduction of the *New Book For the Telegraph*, using four-digit numbers to represent single characters selected from the *Kangxi Dictionary*. In 1897, confidential codebook was released for local officials "to add or subtract number" to prevent information leaks (Zhang, 2018). *New Book For the Telegraph* remained in effect until the Ministry of Transportation and Communications printed a new book in 1929. In 1933, a supplement for Zhuyin Fuhao, Latin alphabet, Cyrillic alphabet, and various symbols including special symbols for months, days in a month, and hours was added to the book.

After the founding of the People's Republic of China in 1949, the codebook forked into two different versions, due to revisions made in the Chinese mainland and Taiwan separate from each other. The mainland version, the third edition of *Standard Telegraph Codebook* compiled and printed in 1983, embraced the use of simplified Chinese characters, streamlined the content by excluding variant characters and infrequently used ones, introduced a small number of commonly-used characters, and standardized the Chinese character font. The original arrangement of radicals was retained in the first part of the book, while the second part was organized in the phonetic order of Pinyin, with a total collection of 7,294 Chinese characters, alphabets and symbols.

Apparently, the Standard Telegraph Code (STC) functions as a Chinese character **input system**. When sending a telegram, the Chinese characters are changed into telegraphic codes and sent out in Morse signals, and the other party who receives the signal converts the telegram number into Chinese characters for comprehension. Notably, both Hong Kong and Macau Resident Identity Cards display the STC for the holder's Chinese name. The codes help to input Chinese characters into a computer. Also, non-Chinese speaking countries use STC in their visa and immigration applications such as the DS-160 form for the U.S. visa.

Figure 9.6   Sample of Hong Kong Identity Card
Source: https://www.consumptionvoucher.gov.hk/en/faqs_hkid-sample.html (accessed Sept. 5, 2023)

The STC is extensively used in law enforcement and immigration control worldwide for Chinese name identification (Daye, 1996: 31). Of course, there are phonetic representations of Chinese such as Pinyin, pronunciation may vary depending on dialects. For instance, Mr. Wu in Mandarin becomes Mr. Ng in Cantonese (吴先生); while Mr. Wu in Cantonese would become Mr. Hu in Mandarin (胡先生). Even with the Standard Mandarin, there are various romanization schemes, including the classic Wade-Giles system as well as Pinyin. The confusions can be remedied by application of the STC. For instance, investigators following a subject in Taiwan named Hsiao Ai-Kuo might not know this is the same person known in Chinese mainland as Xiao Aiguo and Hong Kong as Siu Oi-Kwok until codes are checked for the actual Chinese characters to determine all match as: 5618/1947/0948 for 萧爱国 (simplified) / 蕭愛國 (traditional) (cf. Daye, 1996: 351—353).

Inspired by the four-digit telegraph code, in 1925 Wang Yunwu (王云五, 1888—1979), then the editor-in-chief at The Commercial Press, created Four-cornered Numbering System（四角号码）, also referred to as the Four-corner Method (四角检字法). He broke away from the traditional radical system to overcome the problem that it is often hard to determine which part of the character is a radical. For example, for the character "鹰", some dictionaries take "广" as the radical, while others take "鸟" as the radical. In addition, it is time-consuming to use the radical system, as one has to find the radical first, and then select the character from a number of characters with the same radical. Giving up the radicals altogether, Wang focused on the four corners of the Chinese character. By observing the shapes of strokes at the four corners, he directly converted them into four digits to retrieve the character.

Specifically, the shapes of strokes at the four corners are categorized into 10 types, and each type is given a number from 0 to 9, with the order upper left—upper right—lower left—lower right. These numbers represent certain graphical elements:

0 the top element 亠

1 horizontal strokes

2 vertical strokes

3 dots

4 crosses (vertical and diagonal)

5 double-crossed lines

6 Boxes

7 Corners

8 diverging structures of two parts

9 structures with three diverging parts

In addition to these basic structures, 1 also stands for elements tending to the right, 2 for elements tending to the left, 3 also for slants to the lower right, and so on. The exact rules can be found in the table below.

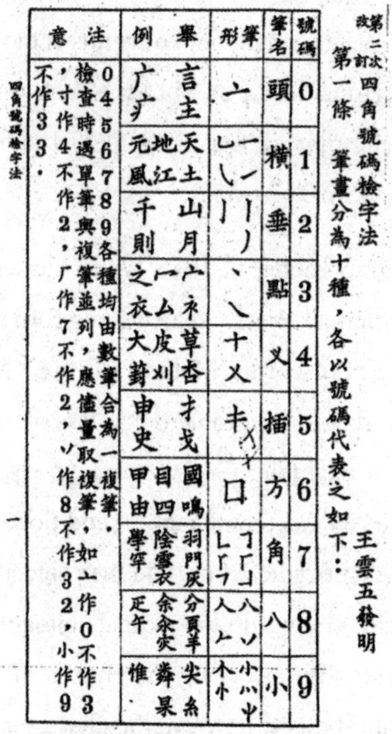
第二次改訂 四角號碼檢字法 王雲五發明

第一條 筆畫分為十種，各以號碼代表之如下：

號碼	筆名	筆形	舉例
0	頭	亠	言主广疒
1	橫	一 ㇀ ㇄ ㇂	天土地江元風
2	垂	丨 丿 亅	山月千則
3	點	丶 ㇏	宀礻冖厶之衣
4	叉	十 乂	草杏皮刈大葤
5	插	扌	才戈申史
6	方	口	國鳴目四甲由
7	角	㇆ 「 」 ㇗ ㇕	羽門灰陰雪衣學罕
8	八	八 人 ㇒ 𠂉	分頁羊余籴災疋午
9	小	小 𣥂 忄	尖糸粦杲惟

注意：0456789各種均由數筆合為一複筆．檢查時遇單筆與複筆並列，應儘量取複筆，如亠作0不作3，寸作4不作2，厂作7不作2，ソ作8不作32，小作9不作33．

四角號碼檢字法

Figure 9.7 Explanation of the number system in the dictionary *Sijiao haoma xuesheng zidian* (《四角号码学生字典》)
Source: Lu and Fang, eds.1928: 1

Accordingly, the characters 四角号码 are indexed 6021/2722/6121/1162 respectively. These days the Four-corner Method has been largely neglected, but it nourished later creations of computer input method, including Cangjie Input Method (仓颉输入法) and Five-Stroke Input Method (五笔字型输入法). Cangjie Input Method, developed in the 1970s by Chu Bong-Foo (朱邦复，born 1937) uses a set of 24 basic components to represent different character shapes and structures. Users input characters by breaking them down into these components. Similarly, Five-Stroke Input Method, invented by Wang Yongmin (王永民，born 1943) in 1983, is based on stroke count and stroke order. It simplifies the input process by categorizing characters according to the number of strokes they contain.

9.3   "Communication" reconceptualized

Communications theorist and historian James W. Carey (1934—2006) argues that the effect of the telegraph on modern life and its role as a model for the future developments in communications have gone unexplored. He takes such neglect to be unfortunate for a number of reasons (2009[1983]: 155—157): First, the telegraph, in conjunction with the railroad, provided the setting in which modern techniques for the management of complex enterprises were first worked out, though for the telegraph in what was eventually monopolistic circumstances; Second, the telegraph was the first product—really the foundation—of the electrical goods industry and thus the first of the science-and-engineering-based industries; Third, the telegraph brought about changes in the nature of language, of ordinary knowledge, of the very structures of awareness; Fourth, the telegraph was a watershed in communication: it permitted for the first time the effective separation of **communication** from **transportation**.

The last two points are of particular interest to our topic. Before Morse received his first patent for the electro-magnetic telegraph in 1840, news traveled as quickly as the swiftest horse, boat, or carrier pigeon. Komor (2015) records a vivid story how in 1843 the printers of a New York newspaper *The Sun* waited aboard a steamboat for the text of the governor's New Year's message. "When it arrived by rail from Albany at Piermont in Rockland County, the printers set up type on the boat as they headed down river to New York City. The next day, *The Sun* proclaimed: 'By the Sun's Exclusive Express. From Albany Through by Horse and Sleigh in 10 Hours and ½'." The telegraph revolutionized this situation by enabling near-instantaneous communication across great distances, permitting the effective separation of communication from transportation.

… before the telegraph, "communication" was used to describe transportation, as well as the transmission of information, when messages moved on foot, on horseback, or on railroad tracks. The telegraph freed communication from its geographic constraints and thus changed not only the relationship between communication and transportation, but also the basic way people thought about the word "communication" –the mode of transmission. (Carey, 2009[1983]:157).

This shift led to a more abstract form of language, where messages were often reduced to their most essential elements to convey meaning quickly and efficiently. News became more about immediacy, fostering a form of knowledge that was fragmented and more focused on events rather than explanations. The change in the flow of information altered how people perceived the world, as they were now exposed to a broader, more immediate stream of data.

The value of instantaneous communication was embodied in the high cost of early telegrams—they were charged by the word—in 1860, according to Dodson (2013), a ten-word telegram sent from New York to New Orleans cost $2.70 (about $105 in 2024 currency, calculated using measuringworth.com), in 1866 a ten-word telegram sent from the U.S. to England cost about $100 (about $2043 in 2024 currency). The high cost led to many expedients to reduce the word count, which were later labeled "telegraphic" or "cablese" jargon. Pfrehm (2018: 87) provides some examples:

First, words that were not essential to a message's content were left out. Such words include articles (e.g., *the, a, an*), demonstrative pronouns (e.g., *this*, *that*, *these*, *those*), auxiliary verbs (conjugated forms of *be* and *have*), and even prepositions (e.g., *to, of*). Second, verbs with a fixed preposition and written as two words, like "check out" or "hold down" were reversed and written as one: *outcheck* and *downhold*. Third, prefixed and suffixes were use in abundance, and augmented by drawing from existing propositions in English and other languages. The prefix un-, for example, did a lot of heavy lifting. Essentially, you could stick it onto any verb or adjective and it would mean "not". So, *unsend, unsaw, and unupblown* were to be read, respectively, as "do not send," "did not see," and "not blown up." The Latin prepositions *cum* ("with") and *ex* ("out of" or "from") were fused to any noun: *cumluggage*, for example, meant "with luggage," while *exParis* signified that something or someone was "from Paris." French found its way into the mix, too: the prepositions *dans* ("in") and *sur* ("on") showed up in chimeras like "danshouse" ("in the house") and "surplains" ("on the plains"). Suffixes were also slung around profligately. English -ed, -ing, and -ly made appearances all over the place. If you got a telegram with the words *Olivered*, *efforting*, and *otherhandedly*, you were supposed to interpret them as "Oliver had," "making an effort," and "on the other hand."

Other than finance, confidentiality was also a concern. "Telegrams were generally, though unfairly, regarded as less secure than letters, since you never knew who might see them as they were transmitted, retransmitted, and retranscribed on their way from sender to receiver," Tom Standage explains in his book *The Victorian Internet* (1998: 88). Hence, many large companies created their own secret code books. For example, the message "What is the best price delivered here for axle steel? How long does the quotation hold good? Disposed to accept any reasonable offer. Anxiously awaiting your reply. Rodgers." in the private code of the U.S. Steel company would read "QKKMA AFBEH QPXFL QRURH QSWKU Rodgers" (Dodson, 2013). However, such telegrams would not be permitted to send overseas after The International Telegraph Convention of St. Petersburg in 1903, which introduced stricter regulation on the use of private codes in international telegrams. Specifically: The telegrams must be written in plain language that offers an intelligible sense in one or more of the languages authorized; the words, whether genuine or artificial, must be formed of syllables capable of pronunciation according to the usage of one of the authorized language (cf. Twisaday and Neilson, 1904: 14—15).

9.4   Journalistic style, news objectivity, and information consumption

The constraints of the telegraph medium created a unique linguistic environment for a concise and "telegraphic" style, but for many individuals it might be a one-off or occasional experience, which would not be carried over to other language registers. In contrast, journalistic style influenced by the telegraph, had a more widespread and enduring impact on language. This influence extended beyond telegraph users to a broader readership, shaping expectations for how information, especially news, is presented in written form.

In May 1846, the Associated Press (AP) was founded, when five daily newspapers in New York City agreed to share the economy of transmitting telegraphic news of the Mexican-American War (1846—1848). Its on-site reporters were instructed to send matter of facts with "no coloring, no personal preferences or opinions" (Blondheim, 1994: 195). Brevity and accuracy as its soul, the telegraphic news demanded economical and direct written language, lean with bare facts, unadorned with details and analysis, a language of "strict denotation in which the connotative features of utterance were under rigid control" (Carey, 2009[1983]: 162):

If the same story were to be understood in the same way from Maine to California, language had to be flattened out and standardized. The telegraph, therefore, led to the disappearance of forms of speech and styles of journalism and storytelling—the tall story, the hoax, much humor, irony, and satire—that depended on a more traditional use of the symbolic, a use I earlier called the fiduciary.

The telegraph thus altered the style of journalism writing. A well-known story is how cablese influenced Ernest Hemingway (1899—1961), the American novelist, short-story writer, and journalist. As a European cable correspondent for the *Toronto Star* from 1922 to 1924, Hemingway stripped down language used to file stories for overseas transmission. His colleagues George Seldes and Lincoln Steffens recalled that Hemingway came in one night and said: "Stef, look at this cable: no fat, no adjectives, no adverbs—nothing but blood and bones and muscle. It's great. It's a new language" (Meyers, 1985: 94). Cablese transformed his writing so much that later he told Steffens that he had to quit being a correspondent because of "getting too fascinated by the lingo of the cable" (Steffens, 1958: 834). But his time as a correspondent left an indelible mark on him. Carlos Baker, his first biographer, believes that Hemingway learned "how to get the most from the least, how to prune language and avoid waste motion, how to multiply intensities, and how to tell nothing but the truth in a way that always allowed for telling more than the truth" (Baker, 1972: 117). These principles became integral to his distinctive style and had a lasting impact on the landscape of 20th-century literature.

When the terse, compressed and expressive telegraphic dispatches arrived at the newsroom, editors used them as raw materials to write longer and detailed stories for widespread consumption without altering the concise and matter-of-fact language of the correspondents. As the telegraph spread nationwide in the U. S., AP established arrangements for selling telegraphic news to subscribing newspapers. As a result, the telegraph led to a fundamental change in news. "It snapped the tradition of partisan journalism by forcing newsmen to generate 'objective' news, news that could be used by papers of any political stripe" (Carey, 1969: 164).

In the face of what was a real glut of occurrences, news judgment had to be routinized and the organization of the newsroom made factory-like. The reporter who produced the new prose moved into prominence in journalism by displacing the editor as the archetype of the journalist. The spareness of the prose and the sheer volume of it allowed news—indeed, forced news—to be treated like a commodity: something that could be transported, measured, reduced, and timed. In the wake of the telegraph, news was subject to all the procedures developed for handling agricultural commodities. It was subject to "rates, contracts, franchising, discounts and thefts." (Carey, 2009[1983]: 163)

Now, the principle of "journalism objectivity" has found its way into journalism education and ethical norms around the world, though its definition and possibility are now confronting challenges across cultures, with objections based on ethical/political values, scientific hollowness, bias and irresponsibility, source dependence, frame-blindness, contradiction in terms, etc. (cf. Maras, 2013: 58—81). A way to manifest this principle in practice is to employ "**the inverted pyramid**," a structure model in which a journalist lines the facts up from the most important to the least important, accommodating the readers' need to grasp the main points.

Figure 9.8   The inverted pyramid technique of journalism writing (The Air Force Departmental Publishing Office)
Source: https://commons.wikimedia.org/wiki/File:Inverted_pyramid_2.svg (accessed Sept. 5, 2023)

"Hemingway Dead of Shotgun Wound"—the headline on *The New York Times* front page on July 3, 1961—serves as a powerful example of how the "telegraphic" style communicates a weighty and impactful piece of news. Concise, straightforward, without embellishment and sensationalism, it packed up the literary giant's life into a five-word message.

Figure 9.9   The front page of *The New York Times* on July 3, 1961
Source: https://archive.nytimes.com/www.nytimes.com/books/99/07/04/specials/hemingway-obit.html
(accessed Sept. 5, 2023)

9.5 Cable adventure, a thread across the ocean, and global connectivity

On January 27, 2006, the world's most famous telegraph company Western Union announced the termination of telegram service, ending an era that began with Morse 162 years ago.

The word telegraph, literally "to write from a distance," to many of us is simply a relic of the past, an artifact from a bygone era that is no longer useful. However, its synonym cable, a new sense that the word gained in the 1850s from telegraphic cable—an insulated wire having a protective casing and used for transmitting telecommunication signals, proves essential in the development of modern network industries.

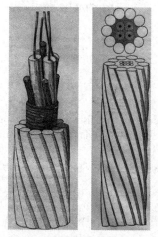

Figure 9.10   Diagrams of the component parts of the Dover to Calais cable, laid in September 1851 from St. Margaret's Bay, England to Sangatte, France (four 16-gauge conductors, gutta percha insulation, ten iron armoring wires with right-hand lay)
Source: https://atlantic-cable.com/Cables/1851DoverCalais/index.htm (accessed Oct. 1, 2024)

Before the invention of telegraphy, *cable* only meant "a large, strong rope or chain used on a ship". As nearly three-quarters of the surface of the Earth is covered by water, it was not long before men began to consider how to extend telegraphy across these bodies of water. A big reel of telegraphic wire was loaded onto a ship—henceforth "cable", with one end of the cable connected to land, and the crew began paying out the cable behind the ship as it moved, using a complex system of pulleys and brakes to control the speed and tension of the cable. As the cable was paid out, it would sink to the ocean floor, where it would settle into the mud. Between 1846 and 1854, submarine telegraph cables were laid across the shallow and narrow seas between Britain and France, Holland, and Ireland.

The success in Europe ignited the interest of American entrepreneur Cyrus Field (1819—1892) in cabling messages between North America and Europe. By 1854, at the age of 34, Field had already secured financial independence, being restless and in search of a new venture. Seizing on the potential to unite distant continents, he embarked on forming the Atlantic Telegraph Company, bringing together a group of investors from New York and London, including the renowned inventor Samuel Morse. The project was fraught with challenges: manufacturing a cable strong enough to withstand the ocean's currents; overcoming the technical difficulties of laying it across such an immense distance. Yet, Field and his team persevered. In 1858, they laid the first transatlantic cable, although it ceased functioning after only a few weeks. Undeterred by this setback and three subsequent failures, they finally succeeded on September 2, 1866. The new cable proved to be a reliable means of communication, heralding a new era of global connectivity (cf. Gordon, 2002: 72—310).

Today, approximately 99% of global internet traffic is transmitted through undersea cables. These cables are laid on the ocean floor and connect continents, countries, and islands, allowing for global communication and data transfer. Undersea cables are preferred over satellite communication for internet traffic because they offer much higher bandwidth and lower latency.

The cables, now commonly consisting of optical fibers, are designed to be durable and withstand harsh ocean conditions, and they are constantly monitored and maintained to ensure uninterrupted communication. Without undersea cables, global communication and the Internet as we know it today would not be possible. According to SimilarWeb, as of June 2024 Google and YouTube account for approximately 25.28% of global web traffic. These two companies, together with other social media giants in the top 50, including Facebook, Instagram, X (formerly Twitter), Tiktok, WhatsApp, and Reddit account for over 38% of all internet traffic. As these websites and apps are global, data centers were built first and it is the undersea cables that connect them to ensure smooth searching and video playing.

These companies then have a strong motivation to lay undersea cables for security and stability. Since early 2000s Silicon Valley giants like Google, Meta, Amazon and Microsoft began investing fortunes in building massive submarine cables. From then to now, about one fourth of the global subsea cable system has been built and operated by Google and Meta, and 45% of new cables to be completed between 2023 and 2025 are owned by these two companies.

Summing-up

Morse Code stands among the earliest systematic implementations of a binary encoding system in a technological context. By representing information through combinations of simple symbols, it set the stage for the development of computers, which subsequently digitalized language. The expansion of the telegraphic network to China brought it into contact with the logographic world that it was not designed to handle. To mediate Chinese writing within its semiotic system, four-digit codes were used to represent characters and then transmitted as Morse Code signals. This makeshift, along with subsequent influx of energy for improvement, became a source of inspiration for various Chinese input methods in the information age.

The telegraph, emerging alongside the railway, fundamentally transformed communication by decoupling it from transportation vehicles, including the fastest trains. Its ability to facilitate near-instantaneous communication introduced a more abstract form of language, where messages were often reduced to their most essential elements to convey meaning economically and efficiently. This shift led to a "telegraphic style" in news writing— direct, nonpersonal, lean with bare facts, unadorned with details and analysis. The change in the flow of information altered how people perceived the world and organized experiences.

As telegraphy extended across the oceans, it rendered the term "cable" to mean "telegraphic cable," referring to the wires laid under the seabed. Today, few can live without the Internet. Miles of undersea cables, which are constantly breaking and continually being maintained, tie us on one end to the future, and on the other, to the lost technology—the telegraph.

References

Avery, Elroy M. 1895. *School Physics: A New Text-Book for High Schools and Academies*. New York: Sheldon & Company.

Baark, Erik. 2000. "Wires, Codes and People: The Great Northern Telegraph Company in China 1870—90." In *China and Denmark: Relations Since 1674*, edited by Kjeld Erik Brødsgaard and Mads Kirkebæk, 119—152. Copenhagen: Nordic Institute of Asian Studies.

Baker, Carlos. 1972. *Hemingway: The Writer as Artist*. 4th ed. Princeton: Princeton University Press.

Blondheim, Menahem. 1994. *News over the Wires: The Telegraph and the Flow of Public Information in America, 1844—1897*. Cambridge: Harvard University Press.

Bride, Harold. 1912. "Thrilling Story by Titanic's Surviving Wireless Man." *The New York Times*, April 19. https://www.nytimes.com/1912/04/19/archives/thrilling-story-by-titanics-surviving-wireless-man-bride-tells-how.html. (accessed Feb. 1, 2023)

Burns, Russel W. 2004. *Communications: An International History of the Formative Years*. London: Institution of Electrical Engineers.

Carey, James W. 1969. "The Communications Revolution and the Professional Communicator." *The Sociological Review Monograph* 13: 23—38.

Carey, James W. [1983] 2009. "Technology and Ideology: The Case of the Telegraph." In *Communication as Culture: Essays on Media and Society*, 155—177. New York: Routledge.

Daye, Douglas D. 1996. *A Law Enforcement Sourcebook for Asian Crime and Cultures: Tactics and Mindsets*. New York: Routledge.

Dodson, Brian. 2013. "Plug Pulled on the World's Last Commercial Electric Telegraph System." *New Atlas*, July 17, 2013. https://newatlas.com/last-telegraph-message/28314/. (accessed Feb. 1, 2023)

Fyfe, James Hamilton. 1863. *The Triumphs of Invention and Discovery*. London: T. Nelson.

Gordon, John Steele. 2002. *A Thread Across the Ocean: The Heroic Story of the Transatlantic Cable*. New York: Walker & Company.

Komor, Valerie S. 2015. "How the Mexican-American War Gave Birth to a News-Gathering Institution: The Associated Press Was Built for Speed and Straight Facts." *Zócalo Public Square*, September 4, 2015. https://www.zocalopublicsquare.org/2015/09/04/how-the-mexican-american-war-gave-birth-to-a-news-gathering-institution/chronicles/who-we-were/. (accessed Feb. 3, 2024)

Maras, Steven. 2013. *Objectivity in Journalism*. Cambridge: Polity Press.

McCullough, David. 2011. "Samuel Morse's Reversal of Fortune." *Smithsonian Magazine*, September 2011. https://www.smithsonianmag.com/history/samuel-morses-reversal-of-fortune-49650609/ (accessed Feb. 3, 2024)

Meyers, Jeffrey. 1985. *Hemingway: A Biography*. New York: Harper & Row.

Pfrehm, James. 2018. *Technolingualism: The Mind and the Machine.* London and New York: Bloomsbury Publishing.

Prime, Samuel Irenæus. 1875. *The Life of Samuel F. B. Morse, LL.D.: Inventor of the Electro-Magnetic Recording Telegraph.* New York: D. Appleton & Company.

Standage, Tom. 1998. *The Victorian Internet: The Remarkable Story of the Telegraph and the Nineteenth Century's On-line Pioneers.* New York: Walker & Company. [Reprinted 2007].

Steffens, Lincoln. 1958. *The Autobiography of Lincoln Steffens*. New York: Harcourt, Brace & World.

Twisaday, Charles E. J., and Geo. R. Neilson. 1904. *The International Telegraph Convention of St. Petersburg, and the International Telegraph Service Regulations. London Revision, 1903.* London: The "Electrician" Printing and Publishing Co.

Western Union Telegraph Company. 1869. *The Proposed Union of Telegraph and Postal Systems: Statement of the Western Union Telegraph Company.* Cambridge: Welch, Bigelow, and Company.

Zhang, Wenyang. 2018. "The Grammar of the Telegraph in the Late Qing." *Journal of Modern Chinese History* 12 (2): 227—245.

陆尔奎、方毅编，1928，《四角号码学生字典》，上海：商务印书馆。

中华人民共和国邮电部编，1983，《标准电码本》修订本，北京：人民邮电出版社。

Further reading: excerpt from *Quest for Power: European Imperialism and the Making of Chinese Statecraft*

Halsey, Stephen R. "Chapter 7 Communication." In *Quest for Power: European Imperialism and the Making of Chinese Statecraft*, 213—216. Cambridge: Harvard University Press.

Chapter X   Linguistics, Rationalism, and Rule-Based Machine Translation

Jumping-in

Now translate the following expressions or sentences into either English or Chinese. Focus on the process you go through and then summarize the key steps in the translation process.

1. 苏式月饼
2. 猝则费，费则匮 。
3. He would not answer when spoken to.
4. He recovered the lost umbrella and had it re-covered.
5. a little man with a puffy say-nothing-to-me-or-I'll-contradict-you sort of countenance

To undertake the translation task, you have to know both Chinese and English. As a Chinese college student, you have learned English as a foreign language for more than ten years. Over the years, you have memorized many words and learned some sentence patterns through plenty of exercises—some are passive activities, e.g., reading and listening, and some are active, e.g., speaking and writing.

You begin by thoroughly understanding the source text—for example, you want to figure out: What is "苏式" in "苏式月饼," and what is "猝" in "猝则费，费则匮"? What does "puffy" or "countenance" mean, and what does the structure "when spoken to" modify? What is the relation between the prepositional phrase "with a puffy Say-nothing-to-me-or-I'll-contradict-you sort of countenance" and the noun phrase "a little man"? This step involves grasping the meaning, context, and nuances, including cultural references and idioms, through analyzing the structure, grammar, and style of the source text. If you don't understand, you would clarify by conducting research or ask for help.

After you break the source text down into its constituent parts while understanding the relationships between them, you may generate a translation, either by mainly keeping the content and form of the original or by mainly keeping the ideas without much concern for the exact words or structure of the original, so as to maintain the intended meaning, style, and tone.

Throughout this process, you draw on your linguistic competence, cultural knowledge, and cognitive abilities to produce accurate, meaningful, and contextually appropriate translations. It's a skill that involves both analytical and creative thinking to convey the richness and subtleties of the source language into the target language.

The first approaches to Machine Translation (MT), to a large extent, modelled this process. In these approaches, the step analogous to "learning a foreign language" is the "setup stage," in which translation lexicon is built and grammar rules are made; the step aligning with "translation" is the "decoding stage," in which a given sentence, viewed as a sequence of words, is automatically analyzed in order to determine its possible underlying syntactic structures, and then a translation is generated based on the predefined rules and the translation lexicon created during the training stage.

As rules form the core of these approaches, they are in general called Rule-based Machine Translation (RBMT).

How humans do translation	How machines do translation
Learn a foreign language	Setup stage
*Memorize words	*Develop lexicon
*Learn patterns	*Create rules
Do translation	Decoding stage
*Understand the sentence	*Conduct parsing
*Choose between a literal and a flexible translation	* Produce literal translation at word/phrase level

Figure 10.1   A broad comparison between human translation and RBMT

RBMT is a marriage of linguistics and computer science, founded on a collaboration between linguists, who contribute their understanding of the intricacies of language, and computer scientists, who implement these linguistic rules in computational models. In the following part, I will describe basic linguistic rules in these approaches and provide simple examples to give some ideas of how they work.

10.1   Formal grammar and MT

The history of MT dates back to a widely circulated memorandum written in 1949 by Warren Weaver (1894—1978), an American mathematician and science administrator, shortly after the electronic computer was invented (Hutchins, 1986: 13). In this memorandum, titled "Translation", Weaver envisions the possibility of using computers to do translation and lays out the long-term goal of pursuing "an approach that goes so deeply into the structure of languages as to come down to the level where they exhibit common traits" (Weaver, 1955[1949]: 23).

Weaver's conception was greeted with much interest and research funding. During the next few years, individuals and groups began MT studies at a number of locations in the U.S. Notable early projects included the Georgetown-IBM experiment conducted in 1954, with a Russian-English dictionary of about 250 words and a set of basic grammatical rules. From the mid-1950s onwards, research on MT was pursued with great vigor in the UK, the USSR and elsewhere by numerous groups.

However, it took years for them to go deep into linguistic structure, as computer science itself was in its infancy, struggling to formalize and develop programming "language" that abstracted the instructions further away. In computer science, formalization refers to the process of precisely defining concepts, structures, rules, and operations within a system using mathematical notation or other rigorous methods. The goal is to create a clear and unambiguous representation of the system, making it amenable to analysis, verification, and implementation. During the 1950s, computers had extremely limited computational power compared to modern systems. The available hardware constraints made it challenging to develop sophisticated programming languages and implement complex algorithms. It was not until the 1960s and 1970s that significant advances in computing capacity were made.

When it comes to computational analysis of linguistic structure, **formalization** assumes that language is a well-defined system. A formal grammar consists of a collection of rules that specify how elements of the language, e.g., words, may be combined to form sentences, and how sentences are structured. Rules may be concerned with purely syntactic information, such as grammatical functions, subject-verb agreement, word ordering, etc., but some models may also incorporate issues such as lexical semantics. These rules were manually crafted by linguists who had expertise in the languages involved.

In the early years of RBMT, linguistic studies in the U.S. was heavily influenced by the approach of American linguist Leonardo Bloomfield (1887—1949). Shaped by the practical need of analyzing diverse and disappearing aboriginal languages of the Americas, Bloomfield's method was primarily descriptive and taxonomic, aiming to catalog and analyze language structures based on empirical observation. The influence of Bloomfieldian structural linguistics declined in the late 1950s and 1960s as the theory of transformative-generative grammar developed by American linguist Noam Chomsky (born 1928) came to predominate. In the mid-1960s and early 1970s, researchers in MT began drawing on Chomsky's insights. Shortly thereafter, they also began incorporating dependency grammar, developed by French linguist Lucien Tesnière (1893—1954). Chomsky and Tesnière's grammars became the backbone of RBMT, providing the formal structure necessary for effective computational translation.

10.2   Parsing: constituency vs. dependency

There is a wide range of grammatical formalisms, which depend on various syntactic theories in linguistics, and the structures that result from the process of automatic syntactic analysis, or *parsing*, may differ substantially between one such formalism and another. Among these, two are especially important tools for RBMT. One specifies the syntactic analysis in terms of constituency structure, and the other, in terms of dependency structure.

10.2.1   Constituency structure

In 1957, Noam Chomsky published *Syntactic Structures*, a seminal work featuring on the concept of **recursive structure** in natural language. A hallmark of human languages, recursive structures refer to the ability of a language to embed linguistic elements within similar or identical structures, creating a hierarchical and potentially infinite set of expressions. These recursive structures can be represented and implemented using rewriting rules, a set of instructions that define how one sequence of symbols can be replaced by another sequence of symbols. These rules are used to generate strings in a language.

In Chomsky (1957), rewriting rules are called "phrase structure" rules. **Phrase structure** (PS) is an ordered, labelled tree that expresses hierarchical relations among certain groups of words called phrases, or syntactic constituents. Specifically, constituency refers to a relation between a linguistic unit, i.e., **constituent**, and the larger unit that it is a part of. Constituents are formed directly from the part-of-speech sequences of the words in the sentence, e.g., noun (N), verb (V), adjective (A), and Adverb (Adv), or from higher order constituents, e.g., noun phrase (NP), verb phrase (VP), and prepositional phase (PP) until a full sentence (S) is constructed. Each phrase structure has a *head* that determines the main properties of the phrase, as N in NP, V in VP and P in PP.

PS rules capture the transformation of one syntactic structure into another. For example, a simple PS rule might be expressed as "S → NP VP", indicating that a sentence can be generated by combining a noun phrase and a verb phrase.

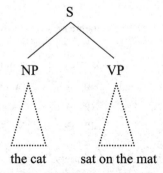

Figure 10.2   Tree diagram for PS rule "S→NP VP", exemplified by the sentence "the cat sat on the mat"

Increasingly complex sentences can be produced by each time adding another layer of "S→NP VP" to S. For instance,

Pat saw the cat sat on the mat.

Nat said Pat saw the cat sat on the mat.

Matt knew Nat said Pat saw the cat sat on the mat.

The power of recursive structure comes from the ability to apply rewriting rules repeatedly. If a rule allows for the replacement of a constituent with a structure that includes the same type of constituent, recursion occurs. Through the recursive application of rewriting rules, generative grammars can theoretically generate an infinite number of sentences. Rewriting rules, therefore, provide a formal mechanism to express the recursive nature of language, allowing for the generation of complex sentences with nested structures. This formalization has had a substantial impact on constituency structure analysis, which became an essential tool in RBMT.

Aligning with constituency-based framework, Phrase Structure Grammar (PSG) dominated natural language processing (NLP) during the 20th century, with the Penn Treebank initially released in 1992 as a notable contribution. The following figure shows the lexicon and the rules for a sample PSG and the PS tree generated by applying the grammar rules.

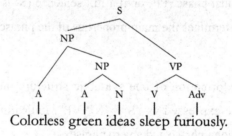

Figure 10.3　Example PSG and tree

Lexicon: Grammar:

colorless	A			
green	A	S	→	NP VP
ideas	N	NP	→	A NP
sleep	V	NP	→	A N
furiously	Adv	VP	→	V Adv

The sentence "Colorless green ideas sleep furiously," which might have successfully aroused your curiosity, is a classic linguistic example introduced by Chomsky (1957). It is designed to illustrate the distinction between syntax and semantics—the juxtaposition of seemingly unrelated or contradictory words highlights that a sentence can be syntactically correct without being semantically meaningful. As far as RBMT is concerned, it foresees the limitations of purely rule-based approaches to understanding language that we will come to in 10.4.

10.2.2 Dependency structure

An alternative representation of sentence structure is provided by dependency grammar, developed by Lucien Tesnière in his book *Éléments de syntaxe structural* (*Elements of Structural Syntax*), published posthumously in 1959 (English translation, 2015).

Dependency is the notion that linguistic units are connected to each other by directed links, emphasizing binary grammatical relations between words in a sentence. In Dependency Grammar (DS), each word in a sentence is associated with a dependency relationship with another word, where one word is the *head* or governor, and the other is the *dependent*. Thereby, dependency structures focus on capturing the relationships between words rather than grouping them into hierarchical constituents.

In contrast to constituency structure, the dependency structure is more motivated by the semantic relations between individual words. In this framework, the verb is reckoned the driving force, all other syntactic units being either directly or indirectly connected to the verb, as participants of the action or their features or the circumstances where the action takes place. In other words, all other words are depending either directly on the root verb or on another word in the sentence which they form a close relation with. In a NP, the head noun determines the form of its dependent adjectives, reflecting various agreement features, which is particularly apparent in languages with grammatical gender, number and case inflections, such as French, German and Russian. These relationships form a directed graph structure where the head noun is the central node, and the adjective is connected to it.

The following figure shows the dependency tree for the same sentence in Figure 10.3, in order to contrast the two different representations.

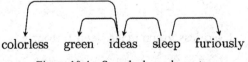

Figure 10.4   Sample dependency tree

By comparing the trees, we can see that dependency structures are flatter than phrase structures in that they tend to overlook phrasal nodes. While constituency trees typically show neighboring node groupings that reflect the hierarchical organization of phrases, dependency trees show the link of each word to its head or "parent," thus are well suited for parsing languages with a free word order, such as German and Czech. The development of corpora with dependency-based annotation schemes, such as the Prague Dependency Treebank initially published in 2001, has contributed to the popularity of dependency-based tools in the early 21st century. These resources provide annotated data that allow for training and evaluating dependency parsers.

In the context of RBMT, the choice between constituency and dependency structures depends on several factors, including the linguistic theory adopted, the nature of the languages being translated, and the specific requirements of the translation task. Though Chomsky's influence is more prominent in constituency-based approaches, the field of machine translation has explored both constituency and dependency structures. Some RBMT systems utilize constituency structures to leverage the hierarchical organization of phrases. Others adopt dependency structures for a more direct representation of word relationships. Each formalism has its strengths and weaknesses, and the choice can impact how syntactic information is represented and utilized in the translation process.

10.2.3　Trees and brackets

Both constituency-based trees and dependency-based trees can be presented in bracketed expressions. Each node in the tree corresponds to one pair of brackets. Thus, trees and brackets provide the same amount of information. It is always possible to convert a tree into a bracketing structure, and vice versa. The correspondence between trees and bracketed expressions is illustrated as follows:

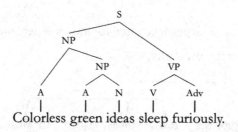

The above constituency tree may be converted to the bracketed expression:

(1) *a*. [[colorless] [[green] [ideas]]] [[sleep] [furiously]]

Part-of-speech categories may be added to the node labels:

(1) *b*. [NP [A colorless] [[A green] [N ideas]]] [VP [V sleep] [Adv furiously]]

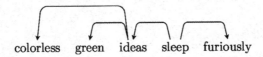

colorless   green   ideas   sleep   furiously

The above dependency tree may be converted to the following bracketed expression:

(2) *a*. [sleep [idea [colorless][green]] [furiously]]

Part-of-speech categories may be added to the node labels:

(2) *b*. [V sleep [N idea [A colorless] [A green]] [Adv furiously]]

The structure of dependency trees directly reflects the syntactic relationships between words in a sentence, making them ideal for functional and grammatical analysis. The edges in a dependency tree typically represent grammatical relations such as subject, object, modifier, and other syntactic functions. This makes dependency trees well-suited for capturing the functional categories of words within a sentence. Dependency tree is especially suitable for functional categorizations, as in (2) *c* where PRED stands for Predicate, SUB for Subject, ATTR for Attribute, and ADJUN for Adjunct.

(2) *c*. [PRED sleep [SUBJ idea [ATTR colorless] [ATTR green]] [ADJUN furiously]]

Both functional and morphosyntactic categories can be merged. Word order, which is not inherent in the tree, can be depicted by additional labelling, e.g., by the symbol "<" for "left of the head" and ">" for "right of the head".

(2) *d*. [PRED sleep V [< SUBJ idea N [< ATTR colorless A] [< ATTR green A]] [> ADJUN furiously] Adv]

Though trees are visually appealing and much easier to process, bracketed structures are preferable, especially in large syntactically annotated corpora such as the Penn Treebank. Two major considerations are: for one thing, they are cheaper to typeset; for another, once labelled they are searchable using dedicated query languages or string manipulation languages. When desired, the bracketed structures can be converted into trees by graphic interface programs, or they can be formatted as in (1) *c*. and (2) *c'*. to facilitate human processing.

(1) *c*.

[[[colorless]

[[green]

[ideas]]]

           [[sleep]

           [furiously   ]]

(2) *c'*.

[sleep

      [idea

           [colorless]

           [green]]

      [furiously   ]]

10.3　Types of RBMT

RBMT systems can be categorized into three types based on the level of abstraction applied during the translation process, namely, direct translation approach, transfer approach, and interlingual approach. The relationships between these approaches are commonly visualized using the **Vauquois Triangle** (Vauquois, 1968).

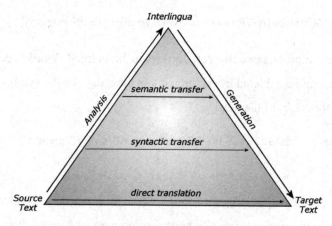

Figure 10.5　The Vauquois triangle
Source: Vauquois, 1968

The Vauquois Triangle matches the theory of stratification in natural languages and is well suited to the realization of computable models:

> By a simple example we can imagine as many levels as we wish from the zero level (level of the text considered as a string of characters), asymptotically towards a level of understanding. At each level a formalization of the input sentence can be defined. Then, it may be assumed that the deeper the level chosen, the easier the transfer is. At the limit, if the ideal level of understanding could be reached for a given sentence in one language, the same structural specifier would represent all the paraphrases of this sentence in all languages. (Vauquois 1976: 130)

At the base of the Vauquois Triangle is the direct translation approach. In this approach, translation is done directly between the source and target languages without an intermediate representation. Each word or phrase is translated individually, and a substantial amount of transfer knowledge is required for each word. This can involve detailed rules for each word or phrase in the source language. Above the direct translation approach is the transfer approach, which requires transfer rules only for parse trees or semantic roles. While there is still a need for transfer knowledge, it becomes more abstract and less language-specific than in the direct approach. The focus is on transferring meaning and structure rather than individual words. The interlingual approach, situated at the top of the Vauquois Triangle, envisions a scenario where translation occurs through a language-independent interlingua. In this idealized approach, there is no specific transfer knowledge required for individual languages. The interlingua captures the underlying meaning and semantic structure common to both languages, allowing for more versatile and scalable translation across various language pairs.

10.3.1   Direct translation approach

Until the late 1960s, the general strategy employed in nearly all MT systems was the "direct translation" approach: words of the text to be translated, i.e., the source language (SL), were analyzed morphologically; the identified morphemes or the entire words were looked up in a large bilingual dictionary; the equivalent words of the target language (TL) were directly mapped; and the results were printed out.

A notable example was the Mark II system for Russian-English translation developed and implemented at the Foreign Technology Division of the U.S. Air Force and was in use from 1964 until 1970 (Hutchins, 1979: 32). The following example shows rules for translating *much* or *many* into Russian in Mark II.

Function DIRECT TRANSLATE MUCH/MANY (word) **returns** Russian translation

    if preceding word is *how* **return** *skol'ko*

    else if preceding word is *as* **return** *stol'ko zhe*

    else if word is *much*

    if preceding word is *very* **return** nil

    else if following word is a noun **return** *mnogo*

    else /* word is many */

    if preceding word is a preposition and following word is a noun **return** *mnogii*

    else return *mnogo*

Figure 10.6   A procedure for translating "much" and "many" into Russian
Source: Bessou, 2015: 53

However, the translation exercise in Jumping-in should have clued you into the fact that translation is more than word-for-word replacement. The unfavorable results generated by such systems for real examples led to extreme skepticism and pessimism in an MT assessment report issued by The Automatic Language Processing Advisory Committee (ALPAC) in 1966. A significant setback to MT, the *ALPAC Report* immediately dampened the funding in the U.S.

Yet, the field did not halt. The following decade witnessed the emergence of "indirect" approaches, which incorporated additional linguistic knowledge, such as phrasal and structural information, into the translation process.

10.3.2 Transfer approach

Transfer approach is characterized by a transfer component that performs the translation on a linguistic abstraction level such as syntax or semantics. It involves three phases: analysis, transfer, and generation. In the first phase, an analysis component is applied to the surface words of the SL, resulting in an intermediate representation as a SL syntactic tree or semantic representation. In the second phase, transfer rules are applied to transform the SL representation into the corresponding representation of the TL. Finally, in the third phase, a generation component produces the TL sentence.

The analysis and generation components are referred to as the grammar of the translation system. They encode the monolingual knowledge of word morphology and how to construct sentences from words. Typically, analysis and generation perform inverse operations, only that analysis operates on the SL and generation on the TL. The lexicon contains the rules that perform the mapping of words and abstract representations between the SL and the TL. The higher up in the triangle the transfer takes place, the more complex analysis and generation are, and the more abstract and language-independent the representation for transfer is.

The following is a simple transformation that reorders adjectives and nouns from "*blue house*" to its French equivalent "*maison bleue.*"

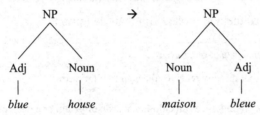

Figure 10.7   A simple transformation that reorders adjective and noun

The following is a further sketch of the transfer approach.

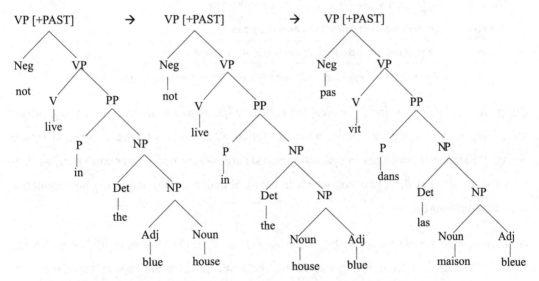

Figure 10.8   A further sketch of the transfer approach

The resulting prototype of the transfer approach, the TAUM-MÉTÉO system, an English-to-French weather forecast translation system used between 1977 and 2003 in Canada, indicates a level of reliability and success in the targeted domain (cf. Further reading).

On top of syntactic transfer there may require semantic transfer. Verbs in natural language play a crucial role in both structuring the syntactic components of a sentence and imposing semantic restrictions on those components. The semantic roles, often referred to as ***thematic roles*** (theta roles) represent the specific functions that different noun phrases, often referred to as *arguments*, play in relation to the action or state described by the verb (cf. Fillmore, 1968). Common theta roles include roles like Agent (the entity performing the action), Patient (the entity affected by the action), Theme (the entity involved in the action), Experiencer (the entity experiencing a state), etc. For example, in the sentence "The cat chased the mouse," the verb "chased" imposes the structural requirement of having a subject (the cat) and an object (the mouse). Semantically, *the cat* is the Agent, and *the mouse* is the Theme. The following figure lists some commonly used thematic roles with their definitions.

Agent	the volitional causer of an event
Theme	the entity that directly receives the action of the verb
Experiencer	the entity that undergoes an emotion, a state of being, or a perception expressed by the verb
Instrument	the entity by which the action of the verb is carried out
Benefactive	the entity that receives a concrete or abstract element as a result of the action of the verb
Location	the location where the action of the verb takes place
Source	the direction from which the action originates
Goal	the direction towards which the action of the verb moves

Figure 10.9　Some commonly used thematic roles with their definitions

Thematic role analysis helps to unravel the relationships between the verb and its arguments, identifying who is doing the action, what the action is, and who or what is affected by the action. Dependency structures in syntactic analysis are closely tied to thematic roles, as they represent the relationships between words in terms of dependencies, capturing both syntactic and semantic connections.

A transfer-based system for translating Chinese to English might have rules to deal with theta roles. For example, in Chinese PPs that fill the theta role Goal tend to appear before the verb, while in English these Goal PPs must appear after the verb. In order to build a transformation to deal with this and related PP ordering differences, the parser of the Chinese must include thematic structure, so as to distinguish Benefactive PPs (which must occur before the verb) from Locative PPs (which preferentially occur before the verb) and from Recipient PPs (which occur after).

Let's use "墙上钉钉子" ("Hammer a nail into the wall.") to illustrate the point. 墙上(on the wall) is Goal, the direction towards which the action of the verb "钉" (hammer) moves, and钉子 (nail) is the theme, the entity that directly receives the action of the verb. When translating this sentence into English, where Goal PPs generally appear after the verb, a transformation is needed to ensure grammatical and natural-sounding English. Incorporating theta roles into the translation process like this is commonly referred to as semantic transfer.

(3) *a.* [墙上 [钉 [钉子]]]

(3) *b.* [Hammer [a nail] [into [the wall]]]

Many of the dominant research and commercial systems of the 1960s through the 1990s were variants of the analysis-transfer-generation approach. Examples of such systems include Logos, METAL, and Systran.

10.3.3   *Interlingual approach*

The third major approach in RBMT took the motivation behind the analysis-transfer-generation methods to its logical conclusion, attempting to remove the need for a transfer phase by proposing the use of truly interlingual intermediate representations. This approach models the MT process as two phases. The SL text is first subjected to a deep semantic analysis, resulting in a language-independent intermediate representation. Because the intermediate representation is language-independent, no transfer phase is needed, and the second phase directly generates the TL text from the intermediate representation. These two phases respectively correspond to the downward and upward arrows in the Vauquois triangle (see Figure 10.5).

One example of an interlingual is event-based representation, in which events are linked to their arguments via a small fixed set of theta roles, providing a common semantic representation that is shared across different languages. Consider the English sentence "The cat chased the mouse." In event-based representation, the focus would be on the event of chasing, and participants like "the cat" and "the mouse" would be linked to the event through theta roles like Agent and Theme. The same event-based representation could be used for the corresponding French sentence, "Le chat a poursuivi la souris," with the same underlying event structure and theta roles.

Such a scheme presupposes the existence of language-independent representation, i.e., representing the "same" meanings in the same way, regardless of the language they happen to be in. Conceptually elegant as it is, in practice the actual intermediate representations used fell short of this ideal. Languages differ widely in the way they break down concepts. For example, Chinese has two words for brother: one for an elder brother, and one for a younger brother (哥哥 vs. 弟弟); German has two words for wall: one for an internal wall, and one for a wall that is outside (Wand vs. Mauer); Spanish has two words for leg: one for a human's leg, and one for an animal's leg, or the leg of a table (pierna vs. pana). Thus, an interlingual system is generally only possible in relatively simple and specific domains based on a small set of data, as described by Levin et al. (1998) who present an interlingual for the translation of task-oriented dialogues in the travel domain for six languages, where the database definition determines the possible entities and relations.

10.4 Achievements and limitations

RBMT has demonstrated success in certain specialized domains where the language is highly structured and constrained. The TAUM-MÉTÉO system used between 1977 and 2003 in Canada (cf. Further reading), for instance, excelled in translating weather forecasts from English to French due to the specific and predictable nature of weather-related language.

RBMT systems, by nature, demands a high degree of linguistic precision. Linguists design explicit rules that capture specific terminology, syntactic structures, and semantic features. Precision can be advantageous in domains where accuracy and adherence to specific guidelines are critical and controlled and predictable output is valuable.

Nevertheless, language is so rich and complex that it could never be fully analyzed and distilled into a set of rules, which are then encoded into a computer program. The meaning of words and phrases often depends on the broader context of the discourse which defy rule-based analysis, requiring an understanding of cultural and contextual nuances. Furthermore, languages evolve, and maintaining an extensive set of linguistic rules becomes an ongoing, resource-intensive process. Due to challenges in handling the complexity and variability of natural language, RBMT went into an era of stagnancy in the 1990s.

No longer the mainstream, RBMT systems still have niche applications and can be part of hybrid systems, particularly in contexts involving low-resource or no-resource languages—languages for which there is little to no publicly available bilingual or monolingual data. A recent example is the development of a translation system for Owens Valley Paiute (OVP), a critically endangered indigenous American language. Researchers from the University of Southern California have created LLM-Assisted RBMT tool that combines rule-based methods with large language models (LLMs) to translate OVP into English and vice versa (Coleman et al., 2024). This system would be particularly useful for language revitalization and educational purposes, as it helps users create grammatically correct sentences in OVP, despite the lack of extensive language data.

Summing-up

RBMT systems explicitly model the human translation process in particular languages. The basic idea is that an infinite number of sentences can be generated by a finite set of rules.

For one thing, a system based on this approach relies heavily on hand-crafted rules for each new language pair, and therefore is costly to build. Formation of rules in a language pair belonging to distant families is especially daunting. Moreover, it is often difficult to maintain large-scale rules, as new rules are prone to compatibility problems with existing rules.

For another, the accuracy of such a system is dependent on the size of the grammatical knowledge base. Yet, there are linguistic phenomena that are hard to formalize, and there are linguistic rules over which linguists' views differ. Handling of exceptional cases leads to an increase in the size and the complexity of the knowledge base. As the size of the knowledge base increases the accuracy increases up to a certain threshold. If the size increases above certain threshold then accuracy may reduce due to conflicting rules. Thus a system based on this approach has to balance accuracy and the number of exceptions it can handle.

Addressing these challenges has been a driving force behind the shift toward data-driven approaches such as Statistical Machine Translation (SMT) and Neural Machine Translation (NMT), which can automatically learn patterns from large datasets, thereby promising greater adaptability and improved performance.

References

Bessou, Sadik. 2015. "Contribution au Niveau de l'Approche Indirecte à Base de Transfert dans la Traduction Automatique." PhD diss., Ferhat Abbas University of Setif.

Chomsky, Noam. 1957. *Syntactic Structures*. The Hague: Mouton.

Coleman, Jared, et al. 2024. "LLM-Assisted Rule-Based Machine Translation for Low/No-Resource Languages." In *Proceedings of the 4th Workshop on Natural Language Processing for Indigenous Languages of the Americas (AmericasNLP 2024)*, 67—87. Mexico City: Association for Computational Linguistics. https://ar5iv.labs.arxiv.org/html/2405.08997.

Fillmore, Charles J. 1968. "The Case for Case." In *Universals in Linguistic Theory*, edited by E. Bach and R. T. Harms, 1—25. London: Holt, Rinehart and Winston.

Hutchins, John. 1979. "Linguistic Models in Machine Translation." *UEA Papers in Linguistics* 9 (January): 29—52.

Hutchins, John. 1986. *Machine Translation: Past, Present, Future*. Chichester: Ellis Horwood.

Levin, Irwin, et al. 1998. "An Interlingua Based on Domain Actions for Machine Translation of Task-Oriented Dialogues." In *Proceedings of ICSLP-98: The 5th International Conference on Spoken Language Processing Sydney, Australia.* https://dblp.uni-trier.de/db/conf/interspeech/icslp1998.html#LevinGLW98 (accessed May. 4, 2023)

Slocum, Jonathan. 1984. "Machine Translation: Its History, Current Status, and Future Prospects." In *10th International Conference on Computational Linguistics and 22nd Annual Meeting of the Association for Computational Linguistics*, 546—561. Stanford: Association for Computational Linguistics.

Tesnière, Lucien. 1959. *Éléments de Syntaxe Structurale*. Paris: Klincksieck.

Tesnière, Lucien. 2015. *Elements of Structural Syntax*. Trans. Timothy John Osborne and Kahane Sylvain. Amsterdam and Philadelphia: John Benjamins Publishing Company.

Vauquois, Bernard. 1968. "A Survey of Formal Grammars and Algorithms for Recognition and Transformation in Mechanical Translation." In A. J. H. Morrel (Ed.), *Proceedings of the IFIP Congress,* Edinburgh, UK, 5—10 August 1968 , Vol. 2: 1114—1122.

Vauquois, Bernard. 1976. "Automatic Translation—A Survey of Different Approaches." *Statistical Methods in Linguistics*, 127—135.

Weaver, Warren. [1949] 1955. "Translation." Reprinted in *Machine Translation of Languages*, edited by William N. Locke and A. Donald Booth, 15—23. Cambridge, MA: MIT Press.

Further reading: excerpt from *An Introduction to Machine Translation*

Hutchins, W. John and Harold L. Somers. 1992. "Chapter 12 Météo." In *An Introduction to Machine Translation*, 212—215. London: Academic Press Ltd.

Chapter XI Corpora, Empiricism and Data-driven Machine Translation

Jumping-in

You are translating from Chinese to English the title of Shen Kuo's book《梦溪笔谈》. After thinking hard, you would like to know how it has been done before. Then you are provided with the following examples:

Dream Pool Essays

Dream Brook Notes

Dream Brook Essays

Dream Torrent Essays

Brush Talks from Dream Brook

Essays from the Torrent of Dreams

What will you do? Write down your reaction in a short paragraph.

When confronted with the task in the Jumping-in, of course, you may go on banging your head for a perfect rendering. But if you want to save time, you could simply take the example that you like or modify the one that you think usable. Usually there are many acceptable translations of a particular expression or sentence, the choice among them being largely a matter of taste. When making your choice, probably you would balance between two basic criteria: adequacy, i.e., matching the meaning of the SL expression, and fluency, i.e., arranging the words in the right way to ensure fluent output.

Similarly, machines may approach the problem of translation by focusing on the result rather than the process. Taking this perspective, the task of MT is to estimate the most probable translation by maximizing some value function that represents the importance of adequacy and fluency.

In the early 1990s—the midst of "a severe funding winter" (cf. Further reading), focus was shifted to observed data and real-world examples. Since then, the pendulum has swung from deep analysis of restricted domain using reason and logic, to broad coverage of unrestricted texts relying on inductive observation. The data-driven paradigm encompasses various approaches, each with its characteristics and methodologies. In general, these approaches can be categorized into two main types: Statistical Machine Translation (SMT) and Neural Machine Translation (NMT).

In the following part, I will give a quick sketch of the two types, with a focus on SMT. Please note that my goal is not to provide highly technical details, but to provide some basic insights into how they work and where some of their main stumbling blocks lie, through either simple examples or analogies.

11.1 Text, corpora, and SMT

SMT started to gain traction in the late 1980s when corpora became available like never before. The term *corpus* (plu. *corpora*) comes from Latin, meaning literally "a body." It has been used to refer to "a collection of facts or things" since the early 18th century.

In linguistics and language-related disciplines, corpus occupies an esteemed status with an orientation towards the large and systematic collection of natural occurring categories of texts, both written and spoken. Before the age of computers, such collections were made laboriously by hand. For example, in the 19th century in order to compile *The Oxford English Dictionary* (OED), the editors had to compile a large collection of authentic texts which constituted the database where they could collect entry words and sort citations to illustrate their usage. In the age of information technology, corpus is closely connected to the use of computers. It is by default a collection of texts "computerized and searchable by computer programs" (Friginal and Hardy, 2014: 20). McEnery et al. (2006: 5) provide the following comprehensive definition of **a modern corpus**:

> A corpus is a collection of (1) *machine-readable* (2) *authentic* texts (including transcripts of spoken data) which is (3) *sampled* to be (4) *representative* of a particular language or language variety.

The first computer-readable corpus was The Brown Corpus of Standard American English (Brown Corpus), which was developed in 1961 by Nelson Francis and Henry Kučera at the Brown University, USA. The corpus is small-sized by today's standard, consisting of one million words of American English texts printed during the calendar year 1961. The texts were sampled from different subjects that were composed by speakers of American English. Following the Brown Corpus, within a span of six decades, a large number of corpora were developed in various parts of the world. Among those most referred to for the study of the English language are The Lancaster-Oslo/Bergen Corpus (LOB) released in 1978, The Helsinki Corpus (HC) published in 1991, The British National Corpus (BNC) completed in 1994, the Humanities Text Initiative of the University of Michigan (HTI) accessible since 1994, and The Corpus of Contemporary American English (COCA) available and continuously updated since 2008, Corpus of Historical American English (COHA) released in 2010, Google Books Ngram Viewer developed in 2010, and Corpus of Global Web-Based English (GloWbE) launched in 2013.

Dash and Arulmozi (2017) divide corpora into various categories by following different criteria: genre of text (e.g., written, spoken), nature of data (e.g., general, special), type of text (e.g., monolingual, bilingual), purpose of design (e.g., unannotated, annotated), and nature of text application (e.g., parallel, reference). By these criteria, COCA, one of the larger and more comprehensive, is a written (based on written texts), general (from various subject fields), monolingual (in a single language variety), annotated (word or sentence features, e.g., part of speech [POS], marked with tags) and reference (designed to provide comprehensive information) corpus.

A monolingual corpus can be a valuable resource for testing or training language fluency, especially when it comes to understanding collocations, word usage, and syntactic patterns. For instance, if you are interested in finding the right verb in collocation with the word "knowledge" to describe learning, here is what COCA reveals:

+ VERB		NEW WORD	?
54962	3.33	share	
49633	4.67	gain	
36770	2.19	require	
29246	2.46	apply	
28092	2.55	develop	
21687	4.57	acquire	
17101	3.71	demonstrate	
15349	3.51	expand	
13009	2.31	test	
11568	2.11	experience	
10393	4.30	possess	
9051	2.96	enhance	

Figure 11.1   Top 12 verbs that collocate with the word "knowledge"
Source: COCA (accessed Nov. 22, 2023)

So *gain* is the most common way to phrase this concept, winning over its synonym *acquire* more than two times, *expand* more than three times, and *enhance* more than five times. It is worth noticing that l*earn*, a likely choice for many Chinese EFL students, is not on the list at all. Monolingual corpora like COCA help language models understand and generate text that flows naturally, and adheres to native speaker patterns.

Yet, what is at the core of SMT is **parallel corpus**: texts in one language paired with their translations in a second language. Two parallel corpora are especially important for the thriving of SMT: The Canadian Hansard Corpus and The Europarl Parallel Corpus. The Canadian Hansard Corpus consists of official records of the proceedings of the Canadian Parliament, published by law in the country's two official languages, English and French, thus limited to legislative discourse. it spans a broad assortment of topics and the stylistic range includes spontaneous discussion and written correspondence along with legislative propositions and prepared speeches (Roukos et al., 1995). Similarly, The Europarl Parallel Corpus consists of the proceedings of the European Parliament upon laws and votes. It includes versions in 11 official languages of the European Union (EU) between 1996 and 2004, and in increasing number of languages after the enlargement of the EU in 2004, 2007 and 2013.

A parallel corpus is particularly useful for assessing adequacy, ensuring that the model captures the meaning and context of the source text. Koehn (2020: 12) explains its mechanism by using counts of the German word *Sicherheit* in the Europarl Parallel Corpus. *Sicherheit* has three main possible translations into English: *security*, *safety*, and *certainty*. The distinction between *security* and *safety* is arguably subtle, but in most cases, only one of the choices is a correct translation. For instance, *job security* and *job safety* mean very different things—the former is concerned with not losing a job, the second with not getting harmed while working. Their respective counts are:

Sicherheit → *security*: 14,516

Sicherheit → *safety*: 10,015

Sicherheit→ *certainty*: 334

How is a computer to know which translation to use? Without other further information, the counts indicate *security* is the best shot, but *safety* is a close second, so we would be wrong very many times. In this case, surrounding words would help the computer do better. Adding a preceding noun (which in German is merged into a compound), Koehn (2020: 12) finds:

Sicherheitpolitik→ *security policy*: 1, 580

Sicherheitpolitik→ *safety policy*: 13

Sicherheitpolitik→ *certainty policy*: 0

Lebensmittelsicherheit → *food security*: 51

Lebensmittelsicherheit→ *food safety*: 1,084

Lebensmittelsicherheit→ *food certainty*: 0

Rechtssicherheit → *legal security*: 156

Rechtssicherheit → *legal safety*: 5

Rechtssicherheit → *legal certainty*: 723

This example highlights that "to know a word is to know the company it keeps." Contextual information can make predictions of the correct translation of words highly reliable, though there will always be a chance of error.

According to Koehn (2005), acquisition of a parallel corpus for the use in a SMT system typically takes five steps:

1. Obtain the raw data

2. Extract and map parallel chunks of text (document alignment)

3. Break the text into sentences (sentence splitting)

4. Prepare the corpus for SMT systems (normalization; tokenisation)

5. Map sentences in one language with sentences in the other (sentence alignment)

Alignment is the process of finding corresponding matches between elements in the SL and the TL, which can be done at various levels—document, sentence, phrase and word. **Normalization** is the process of standardizing the text before it undergoes further processing, involving converting all characters to lowercase, removing punctuation, handling diacritics, or normalizing different forms of the same word (e.g., converting "running" to "run"). Proper normalization can reduce superficial differences for SMT systems to focus on the core content. **Tokenization** is the process of breaking down a text into smaller units, i.e., *tokens*, which are often words or subwords. For languages that use spaces to separate words, e.g., English, tokenization is relatively straightforward. However, for languages like Chinese or Japanese, which do not use spaces to separate words, tokenization is more complex and may involve identifying meaningful word boundaries. In some SMT systems, tokenization may also include splitting compound words or handling special cases like numbers and dates. The figure below shows an extract from the Canadian Hansard corpus aligned at sentence level.

French Text	English Text
J'ai fait cette comparaison et je tiens à m'arrêter sur ce point.	I have looked at his and I want to talk about it for a second.
L'article 11 du projet de loi crée tellement d'exceptions qu'il va bien au-delà de l'article 21 de la convention, au point de carrément compromettre l'objet même de celle-ci.	Clause 11 in the bill creates so many exceptions that it goes well beyond article 21 of the treaty and basically completely undercuts the intention of the convention itself.
Je cite l'article 21 de la convention.	I will read what article 21 says.
C'est assez simple:	It is pretty straightforward:

（ continued ）

French Text	English Text
Chaque État partie encourage les États non parties à la présente Convention à la ratifier, l'accepter, l'approuver ou y adhérer […]	Each State Party shall. Encourage States not party to this Convention to ratify, accept, approve or accede to this Convention […]
Chaque État notifie aux gouvernements de tous les États non parties à la présente Convention.	Each State Party shall notify the governments of all States not party to this Convention.

Figure 11.2　An extract from the Hansard corpus aligned at sentence level
Source: Poibeau, 2017: 142

11.2　Probability and SMT

SMT is the name for a class of approaches that attempt to build probabilistic models of adequacy and fluency, and then combine these two models to choose the most probable translation.

Such attempts originate with the foundational work of Brown et al. (1993: 264) at IBM, which used the Canadian Hansard, 1.7 million sentences of 30 words or less in length, as a training set of translation examples to estimate the probability that a French word will be translated into a particular English word. Brown et al. explain the basic idea of **probability** and SMT as follows:

> In statistical translation, we take the view that every French string, f, is a possible translation of e. We assign to every pair of strings $<e, f>$ a number $\Pr(f \mid e)$, which we interpret as the probability that a translator, when presented with e, will produce f as his translation. We further take the view that when a native speaker of French produces a string of French words, he has actually conceived of a string of English words, which he translated mentally. Given a French string f, the job of our translation system is to find the string e that the native speaker had in mind when he produced f. We minimize our chance of error by choosing that English string $\hat{e}$ for which $\Pr(e \mid f)$ is greatest.

Thus, the job of MT is turned into a statistical optimization problem. The best translation combines $\Pr(f \mid e)$ i.e., probabilistic model of accuracy, and $\Pr(e)$, i.e., probabilistic model of fluency. In Brown's description, $\Pr(f \mid e)$ is called the translation model probability and $\Pr(e)$, the language model probability. The translation model assigns high probability to English sentences that have the necessary words in them in roughly the right place to account for the French, and the language model assigns high probability to well-formed English strings regardless of their connection to the French.

The following figure illustrates how the two models interact when translating the French sentence *John est passé a la tele*. The cross marks indicate which sentences pass each model by being assigned a high probability.

	P(e)	P(f|e)
Jon appeared in TV.		x
Appeared on Jon TV.		
In Jon appeared TV.		x
Jon is happy today.	x	
Jon appeared on TV.	x	x
TV appeared on Jon.	x	
TV in Jon appeared.		
Jon was not happy.	x	

Figure 11.3   Interaction of language and translation model probabilities
Source: AI-Onaizan et al., 1999

"John appeared on TV," which has passed both models, is thus the most probable translation. In terms of probability, choosing the product of adequacy and fluency can be written in a formula which Brown et al. (1993) called "Fundamental Equation of Machine Translation":

$$\hat{e} = \arg \max_{e} P(e|f)$$

Where:

$\hat{e}$ is the translation hypothesis, which is the best possible translation of the foreign sentence f into the English sentence e. $P(e|f)$ is the probability of the English sentence e given the foreign sentence f.

Brown et al. apply Bayes' theorem to rewrite this as:

$$\hat{e} = \underset{e}{\text{argmax}}\, \Pr(e)\, \Pr(f|e).$$

Here:

$\Pr(e)$ is the language model, which estimates the probability of the English sentence e occurring in the language. $P(f|e)$ is the translation model, which estimates the probability of the foreign sentence f being generated by the English sentence e. The idea is to find the English sentence e that maximizes this product, thus giving us the most likely translation of the foreign sentence f.

11.3　IBM models: groundwork of SMT

A language model models the fluency of the generated target sentence by estimating the probability of a sentence being a good representative of the TL. The most common type in SMT are n-gram language models. The concept of n-grams, i.e., contiguous sequences of n items (usually words or characters), was first introduced by Claude Shannon (1948) and then applied to probabilistic language models by researchers such as Frederick Jelinek and Robert Mercer in 1980s.

In Brown et al. (1993), an n-gram language model is a collection of statistics on the distribution of TL n-grams in large monolingual corpora in the TL. It estimates the probability of a word given its context, where the context consists of the preceding (n-1) words. For example, a bigram language model considers the probability of a word given its immediately preceding word, as illustrated in the Europarl German example afore. After training, the language model can provide a probability for individual words as well as complete sentences. For each word in a sentence, the n-gram probability takes the history of n-1 previous words into account. The probability of a sentence s consisting of words $w1$, $w2$, $w3$... is calculated as the product of the individual n-gram probabilities.

What Brown et al. (1993) focus on is translation modeling component. They elaborate a series of five models, numbered 1 through 5, for Pr $(f \mid e)$ which are known collectively as the IBM models. Each model in the series improves on its predecessor, with the earlier models used to provide initial parameter estimates for later models. They first parameterize string rewriting into four components: word fertilities (i.e., the probability that a word will expand into a number of words in the TL), word-for-word (i.e., the probability that a TL word is the translation of a SL word), target positions for word reordering (i.e., the probability that a target position will be chosen for a SL word), and spurious word insertion (i.e., the probability that an extra word will be inserted at any point in a sentence). They use these parameters to define alignments between sentences and their translations. The following figure gives a graphical representation of the alignment between a pair of strings, indicating for each word in the French string that word in the English string from which it arose.

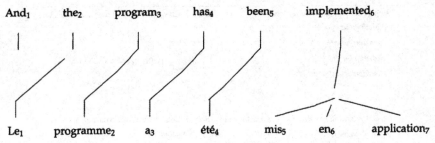

Figure 11.4   An alignment with independent English words
Source: Brown et al., 1993

The probability of an alignment $P(a, f \mid e)$ is calculated as the product of the fertility probabilities of each of the words in the English sentence, times the product of the translations between each pair of connected words, times the target positions selected for each of the French words.

Knight (1999) describes the incremental models used by Brown et al. to estimate the parameters of the translation model. The first model, IBM Model 1, ignores distortion (i.e., re-ordering) probabilities and spurious word introduction, and requires that each word have a fertility of one. Given the simplifications, the only thing that bears on the alignment probabilities are the word-for-word translation parameter values.

The following figure shows how IBM Model 1 can be used to estimate the translation parameters for four words contained in the two sentence pairs <*maison bleue, blue house*> and <*maison, house*>. The translation probabilities are initially uniformly set. Then through a process of iterative re-estimation, which involves changing the weight of the two possible alignments for <*maison bleue, blue house*> given the one alignment for <*maison, house*>, the translation probabilities for the four words are made more linguistically plausible. This method allows to bootstrap better translation probabilities by examining the likelihood of all possible alignments.

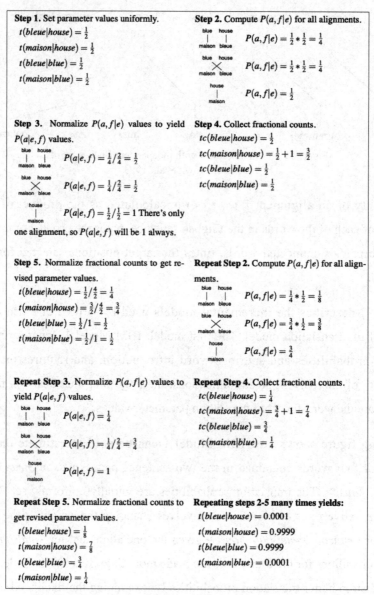

Figure 11.5   Using Expectation-Maximization to estimate translation values from two sentences
Source: Callison-Burch, 2002: 15, based on Knight, 1999: §22

The translation values t estimated from IBM Model 1 are then given as the starting conditions to IBM Model 2 which adds further complexity of the distortion probabilities d to the calculation of the probability of alignments. The t and d values produced are transferred to Model 3. Model 3 introduces the concept of fertility, the ability that allows one word in the SL to generate several words in the TL. The fertility value is then equal to the number of target words that a source word induces. Model 4 adds an alignment model with relative positions which encourage reordering of whole constituents and also introduces word classes for obtaining better probability estimates. Model 5 fixes deficiencies introduced in previous models which allowed multiple assignment of the same target position. The IBM Models are foundational in the history of SMT and form the basis of many translation systems.

11.4 Scope of SMT: from word to sentence

the IBM series model the lexical correspondences on the word level in a cascaded form with increasing complexity of each model. However, each source word is aligned with at most one target word or the null word. This one-to-one alignment assumption simplifies the modeling process but may not fully capture more complex relationships, such as one-to-many alignments.

In order to enable one-to-many or many-to-many translations, one should take more context into account by changing translation units from words to phrases that contain a number of consecutive words. Such a change signals the shift from word-based SMT to phrase-based SMT.

In phrase-based SMT a source sentence is segmented into a sequence of phrases which are then mapped one-to-one to target counterparts and reordered to form a fluent target sentence. It is worth noticing that phrases refer to any contiguous sequences of words, not necessarily linguistic entities.

There are a variety of phrase-based SMT approaches. Here let us focus on Koehn et al. (2003) to get the basic idea. Koehn et al. (2003) estimate phrase models from The Europarl Parallel Corpus that were annotated with word alignments. The following figure shows how German-English phrase-based models work.

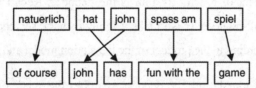

Figure. 11.6   Phrase-based machine translation: the input is segmented into phrases, translated one-to-one into phrases in English and possibly reordered
Source: Koehn et al., 2003: 8

The German word *natuerlich* best translates into *of course*. To capture this one would like to have a translation table that maps not words but phrases. A phrase translation table of English translations for the German *natuerlich* may look like the following:

Translation	Probability $p(e|f)$
of course	0.5
naturally	0.3
of course ,	0.15
, of course ,	0.05

Figure 11.7　A phrase translation table of English translations for the German *natuerlich*
Source: Koehn et al., 2003: 8

The core of a phrase-based SMT is the phrase translation table. Koehn et al. (2003) present one method to acquire such as table: first, create a word alignment between each sentence pair, then extract phrase pairs that are consistent with this word alignment. IBM Model 1 was used to build word alignments on the training set, and phrase pairs that are consistent with the word alignment are extracted.

However, since Model 1 cannot generate a German phrase from multiple English words, Model 1 cannot align a multiword phrase in the SL with a multiword phrase in the TL. A method called symmetrizing is introduced to extend Model 1 to produce phrase-to-phrase alignments: first, train two separate aligners, an English-to-German aligner and a German-to-English aligner; then, align (f, e) using both aligners; finally, combine these alignments in clever ways to get an alignment that maps phrases to phrases. Each phrase, together with its maximum likelihood estimate for the phrase translation probability of a particular pair, is stored in a large phrase translation table. This phrase translation table will be used to compute the translation probability by a decoding algorithm.

The remaining component of a SMT system is the decoder. Recall the equation introduced above (§ 11.3), the job of the decoder is to take a foreign source sentence f and produce the best English translation e according to the product of the translation model and the language model.

In order to find the best translation, the decoder searches the space of all possible translation hypotheses that are incrementally built during the translation process. This task has a complexity which is exponential in the length of the input sentence, so that an exhaustive search is computationally too expensive. Heuristic search methods, i.e., rules of thumb, are applied, in order to limit search errors and focus on the most promising translation hypotheses while introducing reordering restrictions. The search space for finding the best translation is built incrementally by expanding it with possible translation hypotheses from the phrase table and controlling its size by hypothesis recombination and pruning. In order to compare intermediate translations, the future costs for translating the rest of the sentence can be included. Finally, the translation hypothesis with the highest score is chosen as the best translation.

Subsequent work in SMT focuses on ways to move further up the Vauquois hierarchy, from simple phrases to larger and hierarchical syntactic structures. It turns out that it doesn't work just to constrain each phrase to match the syntactic boundaries assigned by traditional parsers (Yamada and Knight, 2001). Instead of relying solely on phrase-based approaches, SMT models attempt to align sentences at a deeper level by assigning parallel syntactic tree structures to pairs of sentences in different languages. This involves capturing the hierarchical relationships within sentences. The goal is to translate sentences by applying reordering operations on the syntactic trees, acknowledging that languages may have different word orders. The mathematical model used for representing these parallel syntactic structures is referred to as a transduction grammar or synchronous grammar. These transduction grammars can be viewed as "generating pairs of aligned sentences in two languages" (Jurafsky and Martin, 2024: 229), i.e., an explicit implementation of the syntactic transfer systems but based on a modern statistical foundation.

11.5   Neural MT and beyond

With the launch of Google's Multilingual NMT System in 2016, Neural Machine Translation (NMT) has replaced SMT to become the state of the art. The term *neural* expresses inspiration from neurons in the brain—information messengers, using electrical impulses and chemical signals to transmit information between different regions of the brain and between the brain and the rest of the nervous system. The complexity and interconnectedness of neurons contribute to the brain's ability to process information, learn, and perform various cognitive functions.

Figure 11.8 illustrates the core elements of a real neuron—the human brain contains about 86 billion of them, according to Azevedo et al. (2009). Each neuron receives as input signals from other neurons via its dendrites, i.e., the short branched extensions of the cell. If the combined signals are strong enough, the neuron becomes activated and passes a signal via its axon, i.e., the long threadlike part of the cell, to the various axon terminals that are connected to other dendrites of other neurons.

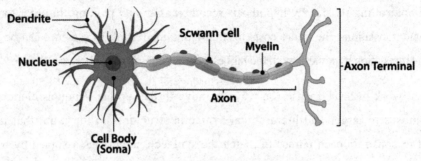

Figure 11.8　Neuron anatomy
Source: https://mhanational.org/neurons-how-brain-communicates (accessed Oct. 1, 2024)

Gaining insight from their interconnected and layered structure, artificial neural networks take the idea of combining inputs (by a weighted sum), an activation function, and an output value (Koehn, 2020: 31). They typically learn their weights by supervised training. In an NMT model, the parameters between artificial neurons are like the synapses connecting nerve cells. During training, the model learns the strength and patterns of these connections, adjusting them to improve the translation performance based on the training data.

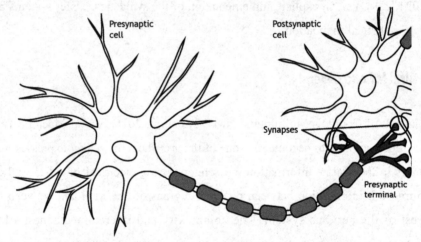

Figure 11.9　The terminal of a presynaptic neuron comes into close contact with a postsynaptic cell at the synapse
Source: "Synapse" by Casey Henley, licensed under a Creative Commons Attribution Non-Commercial Share-Alike (CC BY-NC-SA) 4.0 International License. https://openbooks.lib.msu.edu/neuroscience/chapter/synapse-structure/ (accessed Oct. 1, 2024)

It is worth noticing that this analogy is only to help conceptualize the basic idea. NMT models are not exact replicas of the biological processes in the brain. The actual mechanisms are more mathematical and abstract, with artificial neurons connected in orderly architectures and grouped into layers that are processed in a sequence of steps (Koehn, 2020: 31).

The past decade has witnessed NMT undergo rapid advancements through various architectural innovations, marked with milestones like Recurrent Neural Networks (the early 2010s), Long Short-Term Memory (the mid 2010s), Gated Recurrent Unit (the mid 2010s), Sequence-to-Sequence Models (around 2014—2015), Convolutional Neural Networks (the mid to the late 2010s), Attention Mechanisms (around 2014—2015), and The Transformer (in 2017). As of 2024, the Transformer model remains a foundational architecture in NMT and broader NLP tasks, including pre-trained language models such as Generative Pretrained Transformer (GPT) series. A detailed description of the evolution is a daunting task beyond this chapter, so here I will focus on the differences between NMT and SMT to shed light on the leaps made and the challenges it addresses.

As expounded earlier, in SMT a potential translation of a sentence is represented by a set of features—e.g., fertility, distortion, spurious insertion in IBM models—and each feature is weighted by a parameter to obtain an overall score. In other words, "it assumes all instances, represented as points in the feature space, are linearly separable" (Koehn, 2020: 68). The following figure illustrates a linear model as a network, where feature values are input nodes, arrows are weights, and the score is an output node.

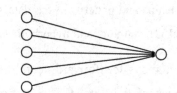

Figure 11.10   A linear model as a network
Source: Koehn, 2020: 68

Such models have a significant drawback: they do not allow us to define more complex relationships between the features, such as dependence between features and a nonlinear relationship between the feature value and its impact on the final score. This is where NMT comes in. According to Koehn (2020: 67—70), neural networks modify linear models in two important ways: the first is the introduction of hidden layers to structure. These layers act as intermediaries that process the input data in stages. Instead of computing the output value directly from the input values, computation is processed in two steps: First, a linear combination of weighted input nodes is computed to produce each hidden node value; Second, a linear combination of weighted hidden nodes is computed to produce each output node value. Figure 11.11 illustrates a neural network with one hidden layer, where x stands for a **vector**—

a mathematical object that represents a list of numbers arranged in a specific order—of input nodes, h for a vector of hidden nodes, y for a vector of output nodes, and arrows for weights connecting input nodes to hidden nodes and hidden nodes to output nodes.

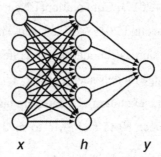

Figure 11.11   A neural network with a hidden layer
Source: Koehn, 2020: 69

The second step is the use of a nonlinear activation function. After each linear combination, a nonlinear activation function is applied. Mathematically, the activation function is denoted as $a=f(z)$, where a is the output of the activation function, f is the activation function, and z is the result of linear combination of the weighted feature values. This output is then passed as input to the next layer of the neural network. This introduces nonlinearity into the model, allowing it to capture more complex relationships and patterns in the data. Common activation functions include Rectified Linear Unit (ReLU), sigmoid, and hyperbolic tangent (tanh).

The **Transformer** architecture employs feedforward neural networks as a key component, on top of which the attention mechanism is added. The feedforward networks process each position in the sequence independently, while the **attention mechanism** allows the model to focus on and weigh different parts of the sequence based on content, providing a more contextually aware understanding of the input. To make an analogy, the neural networks in the Transformer are akin to members in a project team, each working independently with individual skills and expertise (the hidden layers and nonlinear activation functions). They gather in a meeting room (attention mechanism) to adjust their understanding (model positions) based on the contributions of their peers (sequence positions) when making decisions. In the overall project, the combination of individual expertise (neural networks) and collaborative discussions (self-attention mechanism) leads to a more effective and informed team.

Though the original Transformer, introduced in the seminal paper by Vaswani et al. (2017), is still highly relevant, now the cutting-edge of NMT are models that extend, optimize, or build on the Transformer architecture, e.g., mBART (Facebook AI), mT5 (Google Research), M2M100 (Facebook AI), NLLB (Meta), etc. However, their use is primarily targeted at individuals with programming and machine learning expertise.

The general public, instead, typically relies on more accessible services that may incorporate similar underlying technologies, such as Google Translate, DeepL or ChatGPT. Built on extensive parallel corpora, Google Translate and DeepL are more fine-tuned on translation-specific data. They may provide more precise outputs, especially for supported language pairs. In contrast, ChatGPT is trained on a broad and diverse corpus, which includes multilingual content but is not specifically tailored to translation. It excels in adapting translations contextually and interactively, even in complex or ambiguous scenarios.

Summing-up

The basic idea of SMT is to use a parallel corpus as a training set of translation examples. SMT systems rely not on linguistic knowledge but on the distributional properties of words and phrases in order to establish their most likely translation. Probabilities are assigned to different translation options based on their observed frequencies in the training data. This allows the system to estimate the likelihood of a particular translation given a specific source language input.

Instead of relying on explicitly defined statistical paremeters, NMT systems learn complex, non-linear mappings between source and target language sequences through the training process on large datasets. Despite differences in mechanisms, NMT is shaped by foundational principles of SMT: data-driven learning—exposure to diverse language pairs allows the models to generalize and make accurate predictions on unseen data; probabilistic modeling—the idea of assigning probabilities to translations based on observed patterns in the data has influenced the thinking behind how NMT models learn to generate translations, even though the mechanisms are different; feature engineering—In SMT, feature engineering involves defining and selecting relevant features that contribute to translation quality. While NMT doesn't explicitly use handcrafted features, the idea of learning representations that capture relevant information from the data can be seen as an evolution of this principle.

In both cases, the quality and effectiveness of the predictions are influenced by the quality and size of the training data. Larger and more diverse datasets often lead to better models, as they enable the systems to capture a broader range of language patterns and nuances. Both SMT and NMT benefit from leveraging extensive and relevant training data to enhance their translation capabilities.

The craze for data has no end in sight. Yet, if we put it in the history of philosophy and science which shows a salient trend of oscillation between rationalism and empiricism every couple of decades, a possible future might be: "Going forward, we should expect Machine Translation research to make more and more use of richer and richer linguistic representations" (Church, 2007).

References

Al-Onaizan, Yaser, et al. 1999. *Statistical Machine Translation: Final Report, JHU Summer Workshop*. Baltimore: Johns Hopkins University.

Azevedo, Frederico A. C., et al. 2009. "Equal Numbers of Neuronal and Nonneuronal Cells Make the Human Brain an Isometrically Scaled-up Primate Brain." *Journal of Comparative Neurology* 513: 532—541.

Brown, Peter F., et al. 1990. "A Statistical Approach to Machine Translation." *Computational Linguistics* 16 (2): 79—85.

Brown, Peter F., et al. 1993. "The Mathematics of Statistical Machine Translation: Parameter Estimation." *Computational Linguistics* 19 (2): 263—311.

Callison-Burch, Chris. 2002. "Co-training of Statistical Machine Translation." M.A. Thesis, University of Edinburgh.

Church, Kenneth W. 2007. "A Pendulum Swung Too Far." *Linguistic Issues in Language Technology* 2 (1): 1—27.

Dash, Niladri Sekhar, and Sujatha Arulmozi. 2017. *History, Features, and Typology of Language Corpora*. Singapore: Springer.

Friginal, Eric, and Jack A. Hardy. 2014. *Corpus-Based Sociolinguistics: A Guide for Students*. New York: Routledge.

Jelinek, Frederick, and Robert L. Mercer. 1980. "Interpolated Estimation of Markov Source Parameters from Sparse Data." In *Proceedings of the Workshop on Pattern Recognition in Practice*, 381—397. Amsterdam: North-Holland.

Jurafsky, Daniel and James H. Martin. 2024. *Speech and Language Processing: An Introduction to Natural Language Processing, Computational Linguistics, and Speech Recognition with Language Models*. 3rd Edition draft (Draft of August 20, 2024) https://web.stanford.edu/~jurafsky/slp3/ed3book.pdf (accessed Oct. 1, 2024)

Knight, Kevin. 1999. *A Statistical MT Tutorial Workbook*. Prepared for the 1999 JHU Summer Workshop. https://kevincrawfordknight.github.io/papers/wkbk.pdf. (accessed May. 4, 2023)

Koehn, Philipp. 2005. "Europarl: A Parallel Corpus for Statistical Machine Translation." In *Proceedings of the 10th Machine Translation Summit X*, 79—86. Phuket, Thailand.

Koehn, Philipp, et al. 2007. "Moses: Open Source Toolkit for Statistical Machine Translation." In *Proceedings of the 45th Annual Meeting of the Association for Computational Linguistics (ACL 2007)*, 177—180. Prague, Czech Republic.

Koehn, Philipp. 2020. *Neural Machine Translation*. Cambridge: Cambridge University Press.

Koehn, Philipp, Franz Josef Och, and Daniel Marcu. 2003. "Statistical Phrase-Based Translation." In *Proceedings of the 2003 Conference of the North American Chapter of the Association for Computational Linguistics on Human Language Technology (HLT-NAACL 2003)*, 48—54. Edmonton, AB: Association for Computational Linguistics.

McEnery, Tony, Richard Xiao, and Yukio Tono. 2006. *Corpus-Based Language Studies: An Advanced Resource Book*. New York: Routledge.

Mercer, Robert L. 1993. "The Mathematics of Statistical Machine Translation." *Computational Linguistics* 19 (2): 263—313.

Och, Franz Josef, and Hermann Ney. 2003. "A Systematic Comparison of Various Statistical Alignment Models." *Computational Linguistics* 29 (1): 19—51.

Poibeau, Thierry. 2017. *Machine Translation*. Cambridge: The MIT Press.

Roukos, Salim, et al. 1995. *Hansard French/English LDC95T20*. Web Download. Philadelphia: Linguistic Data Consortium.

Shannon, Claude E. 1948. "A Mathematical Theory of Communication." *The Bell System Technical Journal* 27: 379—423, 623—656.

Vaswani, Ashish, et al. 2017. "Attention Is All You Need." *Proceedings of the 31st International Conference on Neural Information Processing Systems (NeurIPS)*, 5998—6008. Long Beach, CA: Curran Associates, Inc.

Williams, Philip, Chris Quirk, and Kristina Toutanova. 2017. "Syntax-Based Statistical Machine Translation." *Computational Linguistics* 43 (4): 791—829.

Yamada, Kenji, and Kevin Knight. 2001. "A Syntax-Based Statistical Translation Model." In *Proceedings of the 39th Annual Meeting of the Association for Computational Linguistics (ACL 2001)*, 523—530. Toulouse, France.

Further reading: excerpt from "A Pendulum Swung Too Far"

Church, Kenneth. 2007. "A Pendulum Swung Too Far." *Linguistic Issues in Language Technology – LiLT.* Vol. 2, no. 4: 1—26. Excerpt, 5—9.

Chapter XII   MT Literacy and MT Ethics

Jumping-in

Otto Jespersen (1860—1943) was a Danish linguist who had great influence in several linguistic fields. The following is an excerpt from his book *Growth and Structure of the English Language* (1982. 10th ed. Chicago: The University of Chicago Press). Now, translate the excerpt into Chinese by using an online translator, then evaluate its performance from different perspectives (e.g., lexical, syntactic, discoursal) by referring to advancement made and limitations remained in the development of MT. Write your evaluation in a short passage.

Our scholarly tradition has a long and distinguished line in popular one-volume treatments of English linguistic history. Jespersen's great little book of 1905 was, for example, preceded in 1904 by Henry Bradley's *Making of English* and followed in 1907 by Henry Cecil Wyld's *Growth of English*. And succeeding generations of philologists have contributed their own distillations in similar-sized vessels down the years. One that comes close to Jespersen's work in profundity and interest is the *Esquisse d'une histoire de la langue anglaise* (1947) by another non-native 'amateur' of English, the late Fernand Mossé.

Each has had its day, enjoyed a fair hearing, been duly tried out with the latest crop of sixth-formers and undergraduates. Each in turn has yielded place, not only (unremarkably) to its successor, but also to that excellent predecessor of 1905, for—alone in the long list of such studies—*Growth and Structure of the English Language* has retained its appeal. I have been challenged in this Foreword to explain why.

How do you feel about the performance of your online translator? You might have been amazed by some good jobs it did, while confused or amused by some other errors it made. Assessing its performance from different aspects by referring to how MT systems process information provokes thoughts about whether, when, why, and how to use MT. Such awareness and competence will turn one into an informed and critical user of this technology, an ability that Bowker and Ciro (2019) term "**MT literacy**."

The advent of internet has largely shifted our reading, writing and communicating to various digital platforms, thus expanded the skills that form the foundation of conventional concept of literacy to a reasonable knowledge that people make use of as a means to "identify, understand, interpret, create, and communicate in an increasingly digital, text-mediated, information-rich and fast-changing world" (UNESCO). Technology therefore led to a proliferation of literacy: digital literacy, library literacy, corpus literacy, hyper-literacy, media literacy, MT literacy, to name a few. The set of literacies affect the ability to "communicate effectively, think critically and act conscientiously" required by global citizenry (Shulsky et al., 2017).

12.1 Ambiguity, thy name is language

Despite great strides made in both rationalistic approaches and empirical approaches, MT is faced with the challenge encapsulated in one word: ambiguity. Natural language is inherently ambiguous on every level: lexical, morphological, syntactic, and discoursal. Humans, to some extent, navigate this ambiguity by considering broader context and background knowledge. However, even among humans, misunderstandings are common. These ambiguities present obstacles to enhancing MT performance.

12.1.1 Lexical ambiguity

Lexical ambiguity is the most common, but nevertheless, challenging type of ambiguity. It is caused either as a result of **homonymy**, i.e., when two or more words have the same form, or a result of **polysemy**, i.e., when a word has more than one meaning. A classic example of lexical ambiguity in English is *bank*.

1) I will meet you by the bank.

2) I will meet you by the bank, in front of the automatic teller machine.

3) I will meet you by the bank. We can jump in for a swim in the river.

1) is ambiguous in that it may mean "I'll meet you by the financial institution." or "I'll meet you by the riverside." Humans can leverage their background knowledge, situational context, and common sense to infer the intended meaning. Machines heavily relies on the context provided in the immediate linguistic surroundings, as in 2) and 3), to determine which meaning to assign to it. While advancements in NLP and machine learning have improved MT systems, they still face challenges when it comes to nuanced contextual understanding and common-sense reasoning, which humans naturally excel at.

In Chinese what may cause ambiguity are grammatical homonyms, words capable of playing different functions that have link in lexical meanings. For example, 锁 in 4) can serve as both noun and verb, and 热 in 8), adjective and verb.

4) 我的自行车没锁。

5) 我的自行车没锁。我去锁一下。

(I didn't lock my bicycle. I'll go lock it.)

6) 我的自行车没锁。锁坏了，让我给拆了。

(My bicycle has no lock. The lock was broken, so I removed it.)

7) 饭不热了。

8) 饭不热了。温度正好。

(The rice is not hot anymore. The temperature is just right.)

9) 菜热过了。饭不热了，就这么吃吧。

(The dishes are reheated. I won't reheat the rice. Let's just eat like this.)

12.1.2   Morphological ambiguity

In English, morphological ambiguity arises when morphological elements can be combined in different hierarchies. Typical examples are some trimorphemic adjectives that contain the prefix *un-* and the suffix *-able*, e.g., *untieable, unlockable, undoable, unbuttonable, unwrappable*. In these cases, the verb may either first combines with *-able* and then the resulting adjective combines with *un-* on a higher level, or first combines with *un-* and then the resulting verb combines with *-able* on a higher level. The two processes are illustrated by tree diagrams:

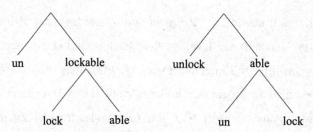

Figure 12.1   Tree diagrams illustrating morphological ambiguity of *unlockable*

10) The door is unlockable.

11) The door is unlockable! I got the wrong key!

12) The door is unlockable! I cannot lock it!

10) is ambiguous in that it may mean "the door cannot be unlocked" as in 11) or "the door cannot be locked" as in 12), though the latter is much less common.

In Chinese, similar problems may arise when words and morphemes are of the same form. For example,

13) 人才是海淀最美的风景。

It could have two interpretations. In the first case, 人 is a free morpheme, a standalone word. 才 functions with 是 ("is") to form a part of the predicate, expressing something like: "People are truly/only the most beautiful scenery in Haidian." In this reading, 才 emphasizes that people are what makes Haidian special, implying "people alone" or "only people."

人(才是)

In the second case, 人才 is a compound word formed from two free morphemes, referring to "talented people" as a whole concept, expressing the idea "Talent is the most beautiful scenery in Haidian."

(人才)是

Likewise, the following example is morphologically ambiguous:

14) 冬天能穿多少穿多少，夏天能穿多少穿多少。
(In winter, wear as much as you can; in summer, wear as little as you can.)

In the former part, "多少" is a measure word, meaning *many* or *much*; in the latter, "多" is an adverb modifying the adjective "少" (little), indicating h*ow*. To illustrate the difference with bracketing,

(多少)

(多(少))

Morphological ambiguity in synthetic languages like German and Russian is more complicated, and in Arabic, "a notorious problem" (Kiraz, 1998). As these languages have a relatively free word order, they use morphological changes, i.e., inflections, to mark clear the relationship between words. When translating these languages into English, which mostly uses word order to mark the relationship between words, morphological ambiguity interweaves with syntactical ambiguity.

12.1.3 *Syntactical ambiguity*

Syntactical ambiguity occurs when the words in a phrase or a sentence can be grouped in more than one way. A classic example for syntactic ambiguity is prepositional phrase attachment. For instance, *The boy saw the man with the telescope* allows two interpretations. In the first case, the noun in the prepositional phrase belongs to the subject while in the second case it is connected to the object. When translating into Chinese, Google Translate assigns the prepositional phrase to the subject (这个男孩用望远镜看到了那个男人), while DeepL assigns it to the object (男孩看到了那个拿着望远镜的人) (accessed Nov. 16, 2023). However, this problem does not matter much for translation into many languages such as French, German and Spanish, since they allow for the same ambiguous structure.

French: Le garçon a vu l'homme avec un téléscope.

German: Der Junge sah den Mann mit einem Teleskop.

Spanish: El niño vio al hombre con un telescopio.

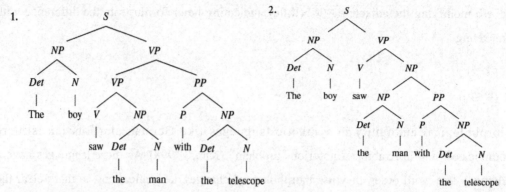

Figure 12.2   Tree diagrams illustrating syntactical ambiguity of *The boy saw the man with the telescope*

What matters more is structural divergence caused by different ways of encoding syntactic roles in different languages. For example, noun phrases can serve as the subject or object of a sentence, among others. In German, the role is marked by grammatical case; in English, by word order. Consider the following short German sentence, with possible translations for each word below it.

15) das behaupten sie   wenigstens
    that claim   they   at least
    the   she

There is a lot going on here. The first word *das* could mean *that* or *the*, but since it is not followed by a noun, the translation *that* is more likely. The third word *sie* could mean *she* or *they*. The verb *behaupten* means *claim*, but it is also morphologically inflected for plural. The only possible plural subject in the sentence is *sie* in the interpretation of *they*.

So, the closest English translation *they claim that at least* requires the reordering from object-verb-subject word order to subject-verb-object word order. Google Translate translates this sentence as *at least that's what they claim* (accessed Nov. 16, 2023), which avoids some of the reordering (*that* is still in front of the verb). This is also a common choice of human translators who would like to retain the emphasis on *that* by placing it early in the English sentence.

12.1.4   Discoursal ambiguity

Discoursal ambiguity arises when words of a given sentence requires information beyond the sentence in order to be understood. **Anaphora**, i.e., references to items mentioned earlier in a discourse, often poses this problem. The most prevalent type of anaphora is the pronominal anaphora, in which a pronoun (anaphor), such as *he*, *she*, *it*, or *they*, refers to a concept mentioned earlier in the text (antecedent). Anaphora poses a challenge for MT, as the reference has to be detected in the source text and has to be held true in the translation. For instance, in the example below *it* refers back to entity *the car*.

16) She had seen the car which met with an accident. It was an old white Ambassador.

Both humans and machines tend to look for the antecedent within a reasonable and coherent span of the text. This span could be limited to the same sentence, extend to the previous sentence or sentences, or even encompass a broader discourse context, depending on the complexity of the language and the specific linguistic structures involved. The difficulty increases when the anaphor is far apart from its antecedent, as shown in the excerpt of Jespersen's book in the Jumping-in—the pronoun *each* refers back to any of the books mentioned in a previous paragraph.

The demands for agreement between anaphor and antecedent can vary strongly between languages. For some pronouns, the reference is very clear in one language but highly ambiguous in another. For example, where the English refers to an antecedent noun in French that is feminine, the pronoun's feminine gender must be reflected in a French translation.

17) It was small.

   Il/elle était petit.

18) The left slipper remained stuck. *It* was small.

   La pantoufle gauche est restée coincée. Elle était petit.

In 17) the translation of the English pronoun *it* to French is ambiguous to either *il* (masculine *it*) or *elle* (feminine *it*) depending on the gender of the antecedent object. To avoid the problem, Google Translate is now clever enough to translate it into *ce*, the impersonal, indefinite demonstrative pronoun which can mean *this* or *it*. In 18) the antecedent *slipper* is mentioned in a previous sentence, without which the MT system cannot translate *it* into *elle* correctly.

Very similar to anaphora is **coreference**, i.e., words or phrases referring to a single unique entity (or union of entities) in an operating environment (Sukthanker et al., 2020). Compared with anaphora, coreference has a much broader scope and involves much more world knowledge. Koehn (2020: 7) provides the following example that involves co-reference resolution.

19) Whenever I visit my uncle and his <u>daughters</u>, I can't decide who is my favorite cousin.

The English word *cousin* is gender neutral, but there is no gender-neutral translation of the word in languages such as German and Chinese. In this case, there is even more complex inference required to detect that the cousin is female—because it is the daughter of my uncle. This requires world knowledge about facts of family relationships, in addition to the need for co-reference resolution (*cousin* and *daughters* are connected) and knowledge of grammatical gender of German nouns.

Other examples include **ellipses** of various kinds, i.e., linguistic phenomena in which parts of a sentence are omitted, and have to be retrieved from discourse. For instance, one sentence might refer to *ear of the corn*, while the following sentences might refer to it simply as the *ear*.

20) The female inflorescence is the <u>"ear" of the corn</u>. The <u>ear</u> develops along the stalk, near the middle of the plant, growing from a leaf node. The immature ear of corn has a cob, with many tiny ovaries that will develop into kernels after they are pollinated. The kernels are arranged in the familiar pairs of rows, which we enjoy eating. For each ovary/egg, a hair-like structure extends outward. This is the "silk" that we traditionally remove before eating. Each strand of silk will grow until it emerges from the top of the protective husk of leaves around the cob. This cluster of silk is what we know as the tassel at the end of the <u>ear</u>.

Greater hurdles are posed by metaphors whose meanings depend heavily upon cultural awareness or pragmatic knowledge. The translation of metaphors relies on the recreation of various logical and inferential properties of the source text in the target text (cf. Gutt, 1992). For example, the English idiom *see red* alludes to anger due to a cultural association between the emotion and the color, a conception not apparent in any literal sense. Merely replacing the word for *red* with its counterpart 红 in Chinese would not convey the intended meaning to a Chinese speaker.

21) The rival team saw <u>red </u>when they realized they had been pranked.

Furthermore, metaphors are typically rich with aesthetic and expressive values particular to a cultural community. The translation of metaphors to a large extent depends on the successful representation of these values. Some metaphors are beautiful in English, but their direct translation into Chinese becomes bland or unintelligible, as illustrated in examples 22), 23) and 24). To ensure the reader is aesthetically entertained in the same way as in the original, even human translators have to work against lots of odds on a case-by-case basis, let alone machines.

22) Her beauty blew me away.

23) Philologists have contributed their own distillations in similar-sized vessels down the years.

24) Of no development could it be more aptly said that the rest is history.

Similarly, idioms, jargons, and colloquialism—typically loaded with colorful metaphors—need to be addressed with care when translating into other languages. They are challenging for machine translations partly due to the complexity of identifying a phrase as idiomatic and generating its correct non-literal translation, and partly to the fact that they are rarely encountered in the standard datasets used for training the systems.

12.2 MT ethics

Bias is one of the largest ethical issue surrounding MT. Friedman and Nissenbaum (1996) developed three overarching categories of bias in computer systems: pre-existing bias, technical bias, and emergent bias. Pre-existing bias is rooted in social institutions, practices and attitudes. Technical bias arises from technical constraints or decisions. Emergent bias arises in a context of use.

Regarding MT, massive amounts of data that a machine learns from are susceptible to **pre-existing bias**. As machines build predictive models on the training data, biases that existed in the training data will be learned, reinforced and replicated. It is also not unusual for the machine to overcorrect—strengthening existing patterns and creating an algorithm that is even more biased than reality. The Europarl Corpus, which was used extensively as benchmark for SMT (Koehn, 2005) and Google NMT (Wu et al., 2016), contains only 30% of sentences uttered by women (Vanmassenhove et al., 2018). Gender imbalance in such training data led to biased prediction in grammatical gender languages, such as French, German and Spanish, where each noun pertains to a gender class such as masculine, feminine and neuter (if present) and several parts of speech beside the noun (e.g., verbs, determiners, adjectives) carry gender inflections. Since its birth in 2006 until today, Google Translate consistently provides "masculine default" translations when asked to translate English gender-ambiguous nouns and pronouns such as *I*, *cook*, *professor*, *designer*, and *doctor* to grammatical gender languages.

English	French	German
I'm happy.	Je suis heureux.	Ich bin glücklich.
I'm a cook.	je suis un cuisinier.	Ich bin ein Koch.
I'm a professor.	je suis professeur.	Ich bin Professor.
I'm a designer.	je suis un créateur.	Ich bin Designer.
I'm an engineer.	Je suis un ingénieur.	Ich bin Ingenieur.
I'm a doctor.	je suis un médecin.	Ich bin Arzt.

Figure 12.3   French and German outputs of Google Translate when given gender-neutral English
(accessed Sept. 1, 2024)

Technical bias comprises aspects related to data creation, model design, and training and testing procedures (Savoldi et al, 2021). If data with pre-existing bias are not carefully managed via means such as pragmatic analysis (Sap et al., 2020) or annotation practices (Gaido et al., 2020), balancing the number of speakers in existing data itself does not guarantee a fairer representation of gender in MT outputs. Furthermore, architectural choices in multilingual MT (Costa-jussa, 2020) may disfavor the generation of feminine forms. Finally, MT evaluation metrics such as BLEU or TER are rather insensitive to specific linguistic phenomena (Sennrich, 2017), and test sets containing the same gender imbalance present in the training data can reward biased predictions (Savoldi et al, 2021). As a consequence, when asked to translate from German to French, Google Translate renders *Die Präsidentin* (the female president) to "*le président*" (the male president) and *Die Historikerin* (female historian) to *l'historien* (male historian)(retrieved Sept. 1, 2024).

Emergent bias arises typically after a design is completed, as a result of changing societal knowledge, population, or cultural values (Friedman and Nissenbaum, 1996). A case in point is why Google Translate translates English gender-ambiguous word *nurse* in French with *infirmière* (female nurse) and in German with *Krankenschwester* (female nurse). Though today the nursing profession remains dominated by the female, the picture of nursing workforce is changing. According to State of the World's Nursing Report 2020 issued by the World Health Organization (WHO), male nursing personnel account for 13% in Americas, 22% Eastern Mediterranean, and 24% in Africa. The percentage is even higher in advanced practice registered nurses, for example, the proportion of male certified registered nurse anesthetists exceeded 40% in 2008 in the US (Wakefield et al., 2021), in contrast to 2.7 % of male nurses in general in 1970 in the US (Fogel and Woods, 2008: 31).

| I'm a nurse. | Je suis une infirmière. | Ich bin eine Krankenschwester. |
| I'm a programmer. | Je suis programmeur. | Ich bin Programmierer. |

Figure 12.4   Google Translate's French and German outputs when given English
(accessed Sept. 1, 2024)

Crawford (2017) defines two main categories of harms produced by a biased system: 1) Representational harms (R) (i.e., detraction from the representation of social groups and their identity, which, in turn, affects attitudes and beliefs); and 2) Allocational harms (A) (i.e., a system allocates or withholds certain groups an opportunity or a resource. Savoldi et al (2021) further distinguishes R into under-representation and stereotyping. The outputs of Google Translate shown above are liable to cause harms of both types. As one of the most popular free online translators, its strong tendency toward male defaults, in particular for fields typically associated to unbalanced gender distribution or stereotypes such as science, technology, engineering and mathematics jobs (Prates et al., 2019), will shape how we see the world and thus further perpetuate and exaggerate gender stereotypes.

Efforts confronting gender bias in MT are rapidly emerging (Stanovsky et al., 2019; Tomalin et al., 2021). For example, DeepL is now trying to mitigate these biases by identifying potentially gendered phrases and offering multiple possible translations side-by-side, though the user has to know the TL before making a choice.

Ethical considerations in MT extend beyond bias to "a call for transparency of how such systems reach decisions has echoed within academic and policy circles" (Felzmann et al., 2020). **Transparency** refers to the ability to peer into the workings of an AI model and understand how it reaches its decisions. The complexity of deep neural networks, especially in advanced models, makes it difficult to fully understand their internal workings, which are buried in a so-called "black box." Improving the interpretability of NMT models is not only important for understanding how they work but also for building trust in their use, especially in sensitive applications such as healthcare or legal translation (cf. Prithwijit, et al., 2018; Vieira et al., 2021; Mehandru et al., 2022). As the field advances, finding a balance between model complexity and interpretability will be crucial for the responsible development and deployment of MT systems. While solving the "black box" issue may take time, transparency in other aspects of the machine learning pipeline is achievable—the data it is trained on, the process of categorizing the types and frequency of errors and biases, and the ways of communicating these issues to developers and users. It helps users make informed choices and fosters trust.

Another concern is how MT systems may process sensitive or personal information. When we use an online translator, the text we input may be processed and stored on the service provider's servers. Part of Google terms of service (effective January 22, 2019) reads:

> When you upload, submit, store, send or receive content to or through our Services, you give Google (and those we work with) a worldwide license to use, host, store, reproduce, modify, create derivative works (such as those resulting from translations, adaptations or other changes we make so that your content works better with our Services), communicate, publish, publicly perform, publicly display and distribute such content. The rights you grant in this license are for the limited purpose of operating, promoting, and improving our Services, and to develop new ones. This license continues even if you stop using our Services (for example, for a business listing you have added to Google Maps). Some Services may offer you ways to access and remove content that has been provided to that Service. Also, in some of our Services, there are terms or settings that narrow the scope of our use of the content submitted in those Services. Make sure you have the necessary rights to grant us this license for any content that you submit to our Services.

Regarding privacy, we should consider the implications of the license and understand our content may be used by the service provider. Additionally, we should be mindful of the types of content we upload or submit to ensure they have the necessary rights to grant the provided license.

On the other hand, disclosure of MT in various scenarios, including academic or professional contexts, is a growing concern. If a published translation has been primarily generated or significantly influenced by MT, shall the author disclose this fact in the work? Who owns the authorship? Was the MT verified by a human? Creating a byline for translation or language editing will normalize the acknowledgment of these critical services, provide scientists with an alternative option to exchanging authorship for editing assistance, and provide a language contact to whom translation questions can be directed (Steigerwald et al., 2022). Some academic journals and publishers have specific policies regarding the use of MT. Authors should be aware of these policies and adhere to any requirements for disclosure.

Furthermore, when using MT for academic work, it's crucial to cite and reference original ideas, regardless of the language in which they were initially presented. Even if translated into a different language, those ideas are still the intellectual property of the original author, and failing to credit them constitutes plagiarism.

12.3   MT literacy in the scholarly community

Having set the linguistic stage that challenges MT, now we can consider how as text creators and users of MT we may interact more effectively with these systems for scholarly communication.

Scholarly communication is the process by which academics, scholars, graduate students and other researchers share and publish their findings so that they are available to the wider research community and beyond (Bowker and Ciro, 2019: 7). Since the second world war, English has growingly asserted itself as the international language for such communication. Now most articles accepted by international journals are in English, thus professionals and specialists as well as students in the field need to read, write and understand papers in English.

12.3.1 As text creator

Bowker and Ciro (2019) suggest that all researchers and journals, regardless of their native tongue, write in a plain language that is both reader-friendly and translation-friendly. They offer ten guidelines:

- Use short sentences.
- Use the active voice rather than the passive voice.
- Avoid long noun strings or modifier stacks.
- Use relative pronouns such as "that" and "which".
- Avoid wordiness.
- Use nouns instead of personal pronouns.
- Use terminology consistently.
- Choose unambiguous words.
- Avoid abbreviated forms.
- Avoid idiomatic expressions, humor, and cultural references.

By adhering to these strategies, authors can create content that is easier to understand and more accurately translated, thus broadening its impact and fostering global engagement. Writing with clarity and consistency not only benefits non-native speakers but also ensures that the ideas are preserved across different languages and cultural contexts.

12.3.2　As MT user

Recently, significant advancements have been made in the scope of context-awareness in language models. A test using the excerpt from Jumping-in revealed the following: as of December 2023, eight translation services (non-professional versions)—including Baidu, Tencent, Youdao, LingoCloud, Sogou, Iciba, Google Translate, and DeepL—all failed in detecting the antecedent of *each* in "Each has had its day"; as of August 2024, three has succeeded in connecting *each* to either *book* or *work*: Youdao (每一本), Google Translate (每本书), and DeepL (每部作品).

In contrast, Baidu and Sogou stand out in translating poems by masters and phrases frequently used in China's national newspapers. This proficiency is likely due to the incorporation into their training data of translated documents from diplomatic or news archives. A few examples (accessed September 2, 2024) should suffice:

25) 不忘初心，牢记使命。

Baidu: Remain true to our original aspiration and keep our mission firmly in mind.

Sogou: Remain true to our original aspiration, and keep our mission firmly in mind.

Google: Don't forget your original intention and keep your mission in mind.

DeepL: Don't forget your beginnings and keep your mission in mind.

26) 绿水青山就是金山银山。

Baidu: Lucid waters and lush mountains are invaluable assets.

Sogou: Lucid waters and lush mountains are invaluable assets.

Google: Green waters and green mountains are invaluable assets.

DeepL: Green water and green mountains are golden mountains.

27) 苟利国家生死以，岂因祸福避趋之。

Baidu: In line with the conviction that I will do whatever it takes to serve my country even at the cost of my own life, regardless of fortune or misfortune to myself.

Sogou: In line with the conviction that I will do whatever it takes to serve my country even at the cost of my own life, regardless of fortune or misfortune to myself.

Google: If it is beneficial to the country, we will not avoid it because of misfortune or fortune.

DeepL: If you want to live and die for the sake of your country, will you not avoid it because of misfortune or happiness?

28) 各美其美，美人之美，美美与共，天下大同。

Baidu: Appreciate the values of others as do to one's own, and the world will become a harmonious whole.

Sogou: Each has its own beauty, and the beauty of others is in harmony with the world.

Google: Each one has his own beauty, and everyone appreciates the beauty of others. All beauty can be shared and the world will be united.

DeepL: To each his own, the beauty of the beauty of the beauty of the beauty of the beauty of the beauty of the beauty of the beauty of the beauty of the beauty of the beauty of the beauty of the beauty of the world.

With these observations, I would like to offer the following tips for MT users:

- Include relevant context or additional information. Context helps NMT generate more accurate translations.
- Use multiple MT tools to compare translations, especially for critical or nuanced texts.
- Choose a MT service that aligns with the context of your text. Some MT systems may perform better in specific domains or industries.
- Maintain proper punctuation. Incorrect punctuation can lead to tokenization errors which impact the quality of the MT output.
- Explore customization options if available. Some MT systems allow customization based on specific terminologies or preferences.
- Keep yourself updated about advancements in MT technology. The knowledge can help you understand the capabilities of different systems.

Summing-up

MT is an invaluable tool, but it's neither infallible nor impeccable. User involvement is crucial for achieving accurate and contextually appropriate translations. The collaboration between human translators and MT systems leverages the strengths of both, with human translators providing the necessary expertise, cultural understanding, and quality assurance, and MT aiding in efficiency and speed.

MT literacy, therefore, is "primarily a cognitive issue rather than a techno-procedural one" (Bowker et al., 2022: 37). A comparison of MT results and my alternative translations, for examples as simple as 29), 30), 31) and 32), should clue you into the fact that MT literacy indeed requires a strong understanding of both the SL and the TL.

29) 儿子的眼睛像我。

Baidu: My son's eyes are like mine.

Youdao: My son has my eyes.

Google: My son's eyes are like mine.

DeepL: My son's eyes look like mine.

Alternative: My son has my eyes.

30) 明天我有事情要做。

Baidu: I have something to do tomorrow.

Youdao: I have something to do tomorrow.

Google: I have things to do tomorrow.

DeepL: I have things to do tomorrow.

Alternative: I'm tied up tomorrow.

31) 我不会跳舞。

Baidu: I can't dance.

Youdao: I can't dance.

Google: I can't dance.

DeepL: I can't dance.

Alternative: I'm no dancer.

32) 我下周要出门几天。

Baidu: I'm going out for a few days next week.

Youdao: I'm going away for a few days next week.

Google:I'm going to be away for a few days next week.

DeepL: I'm going away for a couple days next week.

Alternative: I'll be out of town for a few days next week.

Ultimately, the reality of MT as a technological system will depend on how it is socially constructed. The adoption, use, and perception of MT are influenced not only by technological advancements but also by the social and cultural contexts in which these technologies are embedded. As the historian of technology David Nye describes, the social construction of technological system "emerges not only through its use as a functional device, but also through it being experienced as part of many human situations which collectively define its meaning" (Nye, 1991: 85).

References

Bowker, Lynne, and Jairo Buitrago Ciro. 2019. *Machine Translation and Global Research: Towards Improved Machine Translation Literacy in the Scholarly Community*. Bingley, UK: Emerald Publishing.

Bowker, Lynne et al. 2022. "Artificial Intelligence, Machine Translation, and Academic Libraries: Improving Machine Translation Literacy on Campus." In *The Rise of AI: Implications and Applications of Artificial Intelligence in Academic Libraries*, edited by Sandy Hervieux and Amanda Wheatley, 35—46. Chicago: Association of College & Research Libraries.

Costa-jussa, Marta R., Eva Vanmassenhove, and Marcello Federico. 2020. "Gender Bias in Multilingual Neural Machine Translation: The Architecture Matters." *Proceedings of the 28th International Conference on Computational Linguistics*. Barcelona: International Committee on Computational Linguistics.

Crawford, Kate. 2017. "The Trouble with Bias." *Conference on Neural Information Processing Systems (NIPS) – Keynote*, Long Beach, USA. https://blog.revolutionanalytics.com/2017/12/the-trouble-with-bias-by-kate-crawford.html. (accessed Aug. 1, 2024)

Felzmann, Heike et al. 2020. "Towards Transparency by Design for Artificial Intelligence." *Philosophy & Technology* 33, no. 2: 209—230.

Fogel, Catherine I., and Nancy Fugate Woods, eds. 2008. *Women's Health Care in Advanced Practice Nursing*. New York: Springer Publishing Company.

Friedman, Batya and Helen Nissenbaum. 1996. "Bias in Computer Systems." *ACM Transactions on Information Systems* 14, no. 3: 330—347.

Gaido, Marco, Alina Karakanta, and Luisa Bentivogli. 2020. "Breeding Gender-Aware Direct Speech Translation Systems." In *Proceedings of the 28th International Conference on Computational Linguistics*, 3951—3964. Online: International Committee on Computational Linguistics.

Gutt, Ernst-August. 1992. *Relevance Theory: A Guide to Successful Communication in Translation*. New York: Summer Institute of Linguistics and United Bible Societies.

Jespersen, Otto. 1982. *Growth and Structure of the English Language*. 10th ed. Chicago: The University of Chicago Press.

Kaplan, Frédéric, and Warren Sack. 2014. "Language, Writing and Automaticity: Software Studies in Front of Linguistic Capitalism." *AI & Society* 29, no. 2: 145—159.

Kiraz, George Anton. 1998. "Arabic Computational Morphology in the West." In *Proceedings of the 6th International Conference and Exhibition on Multi-lingual Computing*. Cambridge, UK.

Koehn, Philipp. 2005. "Europarl: A Parallel Corpus for Statistical Machine Translation." In *Proceedings of the 10th Machine Translation Summit X*, 79—86. Phuket, Thailand.

Koehn, Philipp. 2020. Neural Machine Translation. Cambridge: Cambridge Universing Press.

Lucas Nunes Vieira, Minako O'Hagan, and Carol O'Sullivan. 2021. "Understanding the Societal Impacts of Machine Translation: A Critical Review of the Literature on Medical and Legal Use Cases." *Journal of Information, Communication and Ethics in Society* 19, no. 1: 25—41.

Mehandru, Nikita, Samantha Robertson, and Niloufar Salehi. 2022. "Reliable and Safe Use of Machine Translation in Medical Settings." *Journal of Language and Technology in Medicine* 6, no. 2: 98—110.

Nye, David E. 1991. *Electrifying America: Social Meanings of a New Technology, 1880—1940*. Cambridge, MA: MIT Press.

Poibeau, Thierry. 2017. *Machine Translation*. Cambridge, MA: The MIT Press.

Prates, Marcelo O. R., Pedro H. C. Avelar, and Luis C. Lamb. 2019. "Assessing Gender Bias in Machine Translation: A Case Study with Google Translate." *Neural Computing and Applications* 32, 6363—6381.

Prithwijit, Debasis, et al. 2018. "Dangers of Machine Translation: The Need for Professionally Translated Anticipatory Guidance Resources for Limited English Proficiency Caregivers." *BMC Pediatrics* 18, no. 1: 21—32.

Sap, Maarten et al. 2020. "Social Bias Frames: Reasoning about Social and Power Implications of Language." In *Proceedings of the 58th Annual Meeting of the Association for Computational Linguistics*, 5477—5490. Online: Association for Computational Linguistics.

Savoldi, Beatrice et al. 2021. "Gender Bias in Machine Translation." *Transactions of the Association for Computational Linguistics* 9: 845—874. https://doi.org/10.1162/tacl_a_00401.

Sennrich, Rico. 2017. "How Grammatical is Character-Level Neural Machine Translation? Assessing MT Quality with Contrastive Translation Pairs." In *Proceedings of the 15th Conference of the European Chapter of the Association for Computational Linguistics: Volume 2, Short Papers*, 376—382. Valencia, ES: Association for Computational Linguistics. https://doi.org/10.18653/v1/E17-2060.

Shulsky, Debra, et al. 2017. "Cultivating Layered Literacies: Developing the Global Child to Become Tomorrow's Global Citizen." *International Journal of Development Education and Global Learning* 9, no. 1: 49—63.

Stanovsky, Gabriel, et al. 2019. "Evaluating Gender Bias in Machine Translation." *Proceedings of the 2019 Conference on Empirical Methods in Natural Language Processing*, 3003—3008. Brussels, BE: Association for Computational Linguistics.

Steigerwald, Emma, et al. 2022. "Overcoming Language Barriers in Academia: Machine Translation Tools and a Vision for a Multilingual Future." *Journal of Multilingual and Multicultural Development* 43, no. 5: 432—447.

Sukthanker, Rakesh, et al. 2020. "Anaphora and Coreference Resolution: A Review." *Information Fusion* 59: 139—162.

Tomalin, Marcus et al. 2021. "The Practical Ethics of Bias Reduction in Machine Translation: Why Domain Adaptation is Better than Data Debiasing." *Ethics and Information Technology* 23: 419—433. https://doi.org/10.1007/s10676-021-09583-1.

Vanmassenhove, Eva, Christian Hardmeier, and Andy Way. 2018. "Getting Gender Right in Neural Machine Translation." In *Proceedings of the 2018 Conference on Empirical Methods in Natural Language Processing*, 3003—3008. Brussels, BE: Association for Computational Linguistics.

Vieira, Lucas N., Minako O'Hagan, and Carol O'Sullivan. 2021. "Understanding the Societal Impacts of Machine Translation: A Critical Review of the Literature on Medical and Legal Use Cases." *Information, Communication & Society* 24, no. 11: 1515—1532.

Wakefield, Mary, et al. 2021. *The Future of Nursing 2020-2030: Charting a Path to Achieve Health Equity.* Washington, DC: The National Academies Press. https://doi.org/10.17226/25982.

WHO. 2020. *State of the World's Nursing Report 2020.* Geneva, Switzerland: World Health Organization.

Wu, Yonghui, et al. 2016. "Google's Neural Machine Translation System: Bridging the Gap between Human and Machine Translation." *arXiv* 1609.08144. https://arxiv.org/abs/1609.08144. (accessed Ang. 1, 2024)

Further reading: excerpt from *Fallacies Rising from Ambiguity*

Walton, Douglas. 1996. "Chapter 1 Ambiguity and Fallacies." In *Fallacies Arising from Ambiguity*, 2—7. Dordrecht: Springer-Science+Business Media, LLC.

Chapter XIII   Social Media and Language Play

Jumping-in

The figure below shows a snippet of a college students' group chat. Detect one feature and discuss how it affects language. Write your findings in one short paragraph.

Figure 13.1   Part of a college students' group chat

For a professor, who happens to catch a glimpse of Figure 13.1, the way college students communicate is neither like how they talk in person nor like how they write in assignments. Apparently, to make meaning of the "codes" and constructions, which they seem playing with, is a social process that involves in-group relationships. Language, in social media, is again reconceptualized.

13.1   Language: spoken vs. written

As pointed out in the very first chapter, the seemingly transparent term "language" can be defined in different ways from various perspectives. Taking the view that writing is the first technology devised for language, in early discussions I have emphasized that language is first and foremost vocal.

However, once established, writing is inherently and inextricably linked with language. It not only represents the concrete sounds, words, and grammatical structures that come out of our mouth, but also influences language through ideologies, lexical enlargement, syntactic complexity, hypercorrection and so on (cf. Pfrehm, 2018: 17—25) to such a degree that language has long been investigated as either spoken or written. Claiming that **written language** is an independent system that deserves a status equivalent to that of spoken language, Vachek (1989: 9) summarizes the differences between the two as follows:

> Written language is a system of signs which can be manifested graphically and whose function is to respond to a given stimulus (which, as a rule, is not urgent) in a static way, i.e., the response should be permanent (i.e., preservable), affording full comprehension as well as a clear survey of the facts conveyed, and stressing the intellectual side of the facts. On the other hand, spoken language is a system of signs that can be manifested acoustically and whose function is to respond to a given stimulus (which, as a rule, is urgent) in a dynamic way, i.e., the response should be quick, ready, and stressing the emotional as well as the intellectual side of the facts concerned.

This distinction between written language and spoken language reflects the idea that each mode serves specific purposes and is suited to different communicative contexts. Written language offers a preserved, detailed, and intellectually focused form of communication, while spoken language provides a dynamic, immediate, and emotionally expressive mode of interaction, often required in real-time situations. These two forms complement and influence each other, contributing to the richness and flexibility of human communication.

13.2   Language online: a third kind?

The advent of social media has brought changes to language and its use in unprecedented ways. Like "language," a clear-cut definition for "**social media**" is elusive. Here we take it as an umbrella term referring to "Internet-based sites and services that promote social interaction between participants" (Page et al., 2022: 5). It dates back to early channels such as mailing list and Bulletin Board System (BBS) in the late 1970s, though it is typically associated with forums, social networking sites, and content-sharing sites that began to be developed in the latter years of the 1990s.

The first decade of the 21st century marked a significant period of growth, diversification, and widespread adoption of social media. Various dedicated platforms, Facebook (founded in 2004), YouTube (established in 2005), Reddit (created in 2005), Twitter (launched in 2006, now rebranded as X), and Instagram (founded in 2010), among others, emerged and rapidly gained popularity, each catering to different forms of communication, content sharing, and social interaction. The 2010s and beyond continued this trend, with the introduction of platforms like Snapchat (founded in 2011), WeChat (launched in 2011),Telegram (founded in 2013), TikTok (founded in 2016), and the ongoing evolution of existing ones, shaping how individuals communicate, share, and connect in the digital age.

Interactive language in social media soon posed a question to researchers in linguistic and communication studies: is it spoken, written, or a third kind? Among earlier researches focusing on BBS, email or chatting room, some perceived it pro-written (e.g., Baron, 1984; Maynor, 1994; Crystal, 2001); some viewed it pro-spoken (e.g., Paolillo, 2001; Greenfield and Subrahmanyam, 2003). The former group highlighied that typing was physically a form of writing, retaining features of written language such as permanence and planning. The latter stressed the real-time, interactive and informal nature of chat aligning with spoken language.

At the turn of the 21st century, greatly increased bandwidth led to changing trends in, and new uses of, web technology and web design, such as participatory information sharing, user-generated content, and use of the web as a multimodal social platform. Instead of an either-or paradigm, now many researches tend to describe online communication in terms of a multipoint cline in a continuum (e.g., Baron, 2008; Crystal, 2011; Dürscheid and Frehner, 2013; Wikström, 2017). Crystal (2011: 19) explains it as follows:

It is more realistic to think of speech and writing as being the endpoints of a multidimensional continuum, within which varieties of language can be located as being "more or less like speech" or "more or less like writing." The varieties that form the Internet can be approached in this same way.

The blurring of spoken and written modes led to various labels for communication in social media: "computer-mediated communication," "Netspeak," "chatspeak," "textspeak," "cyber language," "Internet language," "Internet slang," "electronic language," "textual deformation," "digital discourse," "digitalk," "supervernacular," "conversational text," "oralized written text," etc. There is no consensus which one is the most suitable, as the decision lies in the perspective taken. Among these, **computer-mediated communication** (CMC) is more widespread than the others, partially due to its earlier introduction and partially due to an academic journal that bears the same name. In the following part, I will adopt the term CMC, for it sounds more neutral and encompassing. Of course, in contemporary usage "computer" refers no longer just to bulky desktop systems, but to a wide array of digital devices and platforms, including smartphones, tablets, wearable technologies, and Internet-based programs.

13.3　Features of CMC

One of the earliest traditions of CMC research is the identification and description of linguistic features that are not commonly found in spoken language and written language. Typical orthographic features of text-based CMC in English identified by Barton and Lee (2013: 5) include:

1) acronyms and initialisms (e.g. GTG for "got to go", LOL for "laugh out loud");

2) word reductions (e.g. *gd* for "good"; *hv* for "have");

3) letter/number homophones (e.g. U for "you" and 2 for "to");

4) stylized spelling (e.g. I'm s*ooooooooooo* happy!);

5) emoticons (such as :-) and :( );

6) unconventional/stylized punctuation (e.g. '!!!!!!!!!!!!!', '.................').

Similar features abound in Chinese social media. To list a few corresponding examples:

1) npy, Pinyin initials for "nan peng you" (boyfriend) or "nü peng you" (girlfriend);

2) 网红，abbreviation for "网络红人" (online influencer);

3) 7456 for "气死我了" (I'm furious); 油菜 for "有才" (talented);

4) 太太太太太太美了 for "太美了" (so beautiful);

5) ⊙ - ⊙ (Chinese emoticon for "surprise");

6) …………????????????! ！！…………. (unconventional/stylized punctuation).

However, it is worth noticing that except emoticons all these features predate the Internet. Abbreviations and word reductions were especially widespread in some discourses, e.g., post-it notes on the fridge (Thurlow and Poff, 2013: 173) or telegram and postcards (Page et al., 2022: 36) . Playful orthography like homophones is often used as a stylistic element in poetry and other literary genres. The reason these features are considered epitome of early CMC is not because they are Internet-born but because they are statistically popular when large quantities of online data were randomly collected and analyzed. The truth is that there are large differences between particular communities of users and platforms. More recent approaches have emphasized the many and varied linguistic practices within particular social media contexts and the way people use language to construct and negotiate their identities (cf. Stenström and Jørgensen, 2009; Zappavigna, 2012; Seargeant and Tagg, 2014; Djenar et al., 2015; Dovchin, 2019; Irwin-Turner, 2023).

In the following part, I will focus on college students' text-based CMC in WeChat, currently the most dominant mobile app and social media platform in China. WeChat is a "cross-platform service" featuring Chats, Moments, Subscription, WeChat Pay, etc. As for chat, one can exchange messages privately with an individual or join a group for gathering and discussions. WeChat groups are communication spaces shared among multiple users from the minimum size of three to the maximum of 500, who are not necessarily WeChat friends to each other. One can join a group by scanning a shared QR code or by asking someone to add him or her into the group. Therefore, a user's WeChat personal ties and group ties are independent from each other, yet they may have considerable overlap. My data are collected from various college students' WeChat groups. These groups are related to their work and life in college, including course learning groups, research program groups, students' association groups, recreational activity groups, information update groups, dormitory groups, etc. These groups are characterized by weak-tie intimacy according to the sociologist Mark Granovetter's foundational paper in social network "The Strength of Weak Ties" (1973), which contrasts the effectiveness of "strong" ties of family and close friends with "weak" ties of casual acquaintances or new people whom we meet.

13.4 Language play in WeChat group chat

"Enjoyment" is identified as the primordial factors influencing people's continuous social media usage (Lin and Lu, 2011). A large part of enjoyment comes from language play, which refers to "any local manipulation of elements and relations of language, creative of a specialized genre, code-variety, and/or style" (Kirshenblatt-Gimblett and Sherzer, 1976: 1). Language play on social media platforms typically involves multi-modality, ranging from puns, memes, neologisms, code switching, catchphrases, hashtags, emojis and emoticons, to GIFs, stickers, filters, and playful narratives.

In the following part, I will exam a few playful constructions employing bracketed annotations and explore how these constructions contribute to weak-tie intimacy by referring to in-group cooperation and politeness.

13.4.1 *Bracketed annotation and Cooperative Principle*

Construction with **bracketed annotation** has gone viral in Chinese text-based CMC in the past couple of years. In this construction, a sentence written in Chinese characters is followed by a fully bracketed or left-bracketed annotation written in either Chinese characters or Pinyin. For example:

1)

A: 老师刚才不是讲过了吗？

Didn't the teacher just talk about this?

B: (走神了…)

(I just zoned out …)

2)

姐姐!（喊破音

Sis! (voice cracked

3)

刚刚的表现真的很可爱啦～（笑）

You were really cute just now~ (laughs)

4)

（捂脸哭泣）（不知所措）（回什么呀）（捂脸哭泣）

(crying hand over face) (be at loss) (not know what to say) (crying hand over face)

The annotation adds paralinguistic features that are missing in non-face-to-face interaction such as facial expression, voice, tone, intonation, and gesture. It helps convey the speaker's emotion and intention clearly. In example 1, the brackets indicate a low voice. It is like the hand put in front of our mouth when we are whispering in class to our neighbor. In example 2, the bracketed annotation describes the shout was so loud that the voice broke. In example 3, the annotation supplements the facial expression that accompanies the comment.

This practice is reminiscent of traditional uses of brackets, yet it also introduces some distinct differences. Traditionally, brackets are used in writing to include additional information, clarify a point, or indicate editorial comments. For example, in this book brackets have been used from time to time to provide a citation or clarify a term within a quotation. In contrast, the bracketed annotations seen in Chinese CMC, such as "(laughs)" or "(voice cracked)," are used to inject **paralinguistic cues** that function similarly to stage directions in plays, where bracketed text describes an actor's emotions or actions. The key difference is that in play bracketed annotations are typically descriptive of physical actions or emotions that are to be enacted or imagined, but in CMC they are intended directly for the reader to interpret the writer's emotions or intentions.

Compared with emojis, which became popular during the middle of the 1990s, such annotations can avoid ambiguity caused by different interpretations of the same emoji. According to Emojipedia analysis of 1.68 billion tweets dated between June 1, 2018 and March 31, 2021, the use of 😂 (face with tears of joy) and 😭 (loudly crying face) had a wide emotional range, from laughter to sadness, or pride, joy, or relief (Broni, 2021). As of 2024, these trends have largely continued. The same is true for their use in Chinese social media:

5) 哈哈哈哈哈哈笑死我了😂
Hahahahaha laughing my ass off

6) 刚才实在太社死了😂
That' embarrassing as hell

7) 没事没事😂
It's Okay

8) 好好笑啊😂
It's so funny

A WeChat favorite, (facepalm) — said to be inspired on Hong Kong star Stephen Chow's classic role in the movie *Flirting Scholar* — has become known unknown. It varies from person to person to tell if the yellow face, with one hand covering part of it, is crying, or laughing, or a combination of both. Thus, it might convey emotions ranging from mild annoyance to self-deprecating humor, or even to an "Oh no!" moment. Such flexibility in interpretation allows it to be used in a wide array of situations, leading to its frequent appearance in conversations where the tone is ambiguous or where the user intentionally leaves the emotion open to interpretation. It showcases how certain digital symbols can take on a life of their own, with meanings that evolve based on cultural and social contexts.

9) 就是就是

Exactly

10) sry 我在肝作业

Sorry I'm flooded with work

11) 相反我这边的老师总会提前下课

Just the opposite, my teacher always end the class early

12) 群里有其实

It's actually in the group

Furthermore, like many sociolinguistic practices, emoji use evolves over time. The same emoji may generate completely different emotions for different age groups. In China, over the past few years secret meanings have been attached to some emojis by the internet savvy. For instance, the use of 🙂 (slightly smiling face) is breaking away from traditionally-ascribed emotions. The older generations may still use it to convey the positive, happy and friendly sentiments, while the younger generations almost always use it to convey a feeling of contempt. In the following interaction, friendliness attached to the emoji by the sender, a fifty-year old teacher, will arouse complicated emotions in the receiver, a twenty-year old student.

13)

A: 老师我能晚一点交作业吗?

Professor, can I submit my assignment a bit late?

B: 可以 🙂

Okay

Also, when one wants to express his feelings with an emoji, he may not be able to find a proper one or he may simply be lazy to look for it. An easy solution is to use Chinese character(s) plus ".jpg" in brackets, as illustrated in the following example:

14) 坐上那动车去乙楼（逃.jpg）

Get on the high-speed train to building B (escape.jpg)

15) 吃太饱了（打嗝.jpg）

So stuffed (burp.jpg)

16) 刚刚家三是江总吗（脸盲症.jpg）

Was that Mr. Jiang? on the third floor of Jiayuan Canteen (face blindness.jpg）

17) 不担心改签/退票成本的话可以考虑买机票（流下了贫穷的泪水.jpg）

You may consider taking a plane if you don't mind the fees to rebook or cancel your flight (shed tears of poverty.jpg)

The characters combined with the file extension for image format ".jpg" encourage the interactants to imagine an emoji by themselves. When one does not know what emoji to use, he may just use a left bracket to let the interactants imagine freely.

18) 马上考听力（.jpg）

taking the listening test right now (.jpg）

From the above examples, we can see paralinguistic features expressed by bracketed annotations stand out in two ways when compared with emojis: they carry more or less a cute feeling similar to that of pictorial emojis; they are more explicit than emojis. Their use is thus in accordance with the **Cooperative Principle** (CP) put forth by Paul Grice (1913—1988), a British philosopher of language. Effective communication involves not just conveying information but also making contributions that align with the expectations and purposes of ongoing conversation (Grice, [1975] 1989: 45):

> Make your conversational contribution such as is required, at the stage at which it occurs, by the accepted purpose or direction of the talk exchange in which you are engaged.

The CP describes the assumption that participants in a conversation normally attempt to be informative, truthful, relevant and clear. To be specific, it consists of four maxims:

Maxim of quantity

- make your contribution as informative as is required;
- Do not make your contribution more informative than is required.

Maxim of quality

- Do not say what you believe to be false;
- Do not say that for which you lack adequate evidence.

Maxim of relation

- Make sure that all the information you provide is relevant to the current exchange;
- Omit irrelevant information.

Maxim of manner

- Avoid obscurity;
- Avoid ambiguity;
- Be brief;
- Be orderly.

In other words, the CP aims at maximal efficiency with the least effort. However, sometimes being "informative, truthful, relevant and clear" may threaten the "face," a concept deriving from Chinese into English (Hinze, 2012), of the interactants. To save face, the speaker sometimes needs to violate the CP. Instead of maximizing efficiency for his own interests, he would choose to minimize the damage to the interactants by adopting an appropriate amount of politeness.

13.4.2 Bracketed annotation and Politeness Principle

To complement the CP, Geoffrey Leech (1936—2014), an influential British scholar who had shaped several fields of linguistics, proposed the **Politeness Principle** (PP) in 1983. The PP is particularly relevant in analyzing the pragmatic aspects of communication and how individuals navigate social interactions while considering the social norms and expectations of politeness. The PP consists of six maxims:

Maxim of Tact

- Minimize cost to others

Maxim of generosity

- Minimize benefit to yourself

Maxim of approbation

- Minimize dispraise of others

Maxim of modesty

- Minimize praise to yourself

Maxim of agreement

- Minimize disagreement between you and others

Maxim of sympathy

- Minimize antipathy between you and others

Leech (2005) re-presents these maxims as sub-strategies of a "General Strategy of Politeness" in order to study politeness in speech acts such as requests, offers, compliments, apologies, thanks, and responses to these acts. He introduces the concepts of positive politeness and negative politeness as two major types of politeness strategies within his Politeness Theory. Positive politeness involves the use of language to emphasize friendliness, camaraderie, and the speaker's connection to the hearer. It aims to affirm and enhance the positive relationship between the speaker and the hearer. Negative politeness, on the other hand, focuses on mitigating potential face-threatening acts by respecting the hearer's autonomy and minimizing intrusiveness. It involves acknowledging and addressing the hearer's need for personal space and freedom.

Under the guidance of the PP, when making a request we do not go straight to the point. In text-based CMC, a bracketed annotation may be good enough to compromise the needs of the CP and the PP, as illustrated by the following example:

19)

（突然）周末有空吗？能不能来做实验

(suddenly) are you free this weekend? Can you come over to the lab?

On the one hand, it provides a certain degree of "negative politeness," a buffer from a potentially more internal or private thought to an external communication, making the following request not abrupt to the point of rudeness. By adding "(suddenly)," the speaker signals awareness that the request might come unexpectedly or at an inconvenient time, subtly lessening the pressure on the listener. On the other hand, it is short and brief, meeting the demand of fast-paced online interaction.

Negative politeness is signified by Leech (2014) as a form of hedging or indirectness, to soften or mitigate the force of a statement or to reduce potential imposition or offense. Leech's concept of negative politeness can be traced back to the ideas of face and facework of Erving Goffman (1922—1982), a prominent American sociologist. In his work *Relations in Public: Microstudies of the Public Order*, published in 1971, Goffman defines **face** as an individual's publicly manifest self-esteem, an emotionally sensitive concept of the self. Face represents the positive social identity or value a person seeks to maintain in social encounters. He claims that social members have two kinds of face requirements: positive face (the desire for approval from others), and negative face (the desire not to offend others). He views social interactions as ritualistic performances where individuals engage in symbolic behaviors to maintain social order. Politeness, as a form of ritual, is part of the symbolic interactions that contribute to facework. Overall, Leech's negative politeness can be seen as an application and extension of Goffman's ideas into the realm of linguistic politeness. Leech's negative politeness strategies, such as using hedging and showing deference, aim to minimize potential threats to the hearer's positive face and manage the delicate balance of maintaining face while respecting the face of others.

Goffman's facework is an aspect of impression management within dramaturgy, a term adapted from theatre into sociology by Goffman in his 1956 book *The Presentation of Self in Everyday Life*. The **dramaturgical theory** is based on the analogy of social life as a theatrical performance, where individuals are actors on a stage, presenting themselves to others through various performances so as to shape the perception that others have of them. Thus "self" is not seen as a fixed entity but as a dynamic and fluid construction that emerges through interaction (cf. Further reading). He uses theatrical metaphors, specifically the stage: the front stage, where individuals actively perform and present their identities to others, and the back stage, where they can relax and momentarily step out of their character and where "the impression fostered by the performance is knowingly contradicted as a matter of course" (Goffman, 1959 [1956]: 112) when they take a glimpse into the authentic or private self.

20)

A: 计概是下周吗？

Is Introduction to Computing Exam next week?

B: 嗯嗯，看schedule上是这么写的（我最近水逆，啊啊要寄

Uh-huh. That's what the schedule says (I've been so down on my luck. Ah, I'm screwed…

In example 20, the left bracket acted as a stage curtain, signaling a shift from the front stage, where the interaction is more composed and matter-of-fact, to the back stage, where a deeper emotional state is exposed. The use of bracket becomes a form of non-verbal communication that adds layers to the interaction, serving as a visual cue for the audience (in this case, A and others in the chat group) to recognize the shift in the performance and acknowledge the hidden realities that lie behind the visible facade.

With bracketed annotation, B creates a dramatic effect, emphasizing the emotional turmoil behind the composed response. By revealing his anxiety and expressing a downcast mood, B could be reaching out for empathy, understanding, or advice from group members. Alternatively, B's decision to set himself on a down side might be a strategic move to provide support to A and others—a way of signaling to others that it's okay to express concerns or difficulties.

In an online group chat, where emotions can be conveyed through text, B's dual performance might be an attempt to create a shared emotional space within the group. Others in the group may relate to or empathize with B's feelings, fostering a sense of camaraderie. When individuals in a group share personal struggles, emotions, or experiences, it creates a sense of in-group intimacy. This shared vulnerability and openness contribute to the formation of a close-knit community within the group.

13.4.3 Bracketed annotation: playing by flouting maxims

Playfulness often involves a deviation from typical conversational norms. Group members may intentionally flout maxims to inject humor into interactions for a more relaxed and enjoyable atmosphere.

The following construction derives from Japanese manga reviews where the kanji "誤" (mistake) is often used in brackets at the end of a sentence when the author of the review deliberately distorts the original idea or deliberately expresses a bad personal thought, so as to remind the reader that the description of the sentence is wrong. In Chinese CMC, common alternatives of "误" include不是 (no), "bushi" (不是in Pinyin), 不 (no), or simply "x" (a cross), "。" (a period), or even nothing.

21)

建议开放甲乙同一楼层之间的大门

两楼统一（误

I suggest opening the doors between the same floors of Building A and B.

Unite the two buildings (mistake

22)

难道是你双胞胎弟弟（x

好像啊

Is he your twin brother? (x

Looks just like you!

23)

你居然又写完一篇！简直不是人（bushi

You finished another paper! You are simply inhuman! (no

24)

谁还不是个小公举（不是）

Who isn't a little princess? (mistake)

In example 21, what is said before the bracket, i.e., the annotated part, is a flouting of PP maxims: getting the two buildings united will bring higher cost to others (e.g., the janitors) and create tension between groups (e.g., those who agree and those who do not agree). Aware of these controversies, the speaker negates what is said with bracketed annotation, turning it into a witty and animated joking.

In example 22, the annotated is a flouting of the maxim of quality, for the speaker knows for sure that the interlocutor has no twin brother. Following the bracket, the speaker immediately admits being wrong. The bracketed annotation withdraws what is said to exaggerate the impression someone resembles the interlocutor so much that he knows his remark is pointless but he could not help making it.

In example 23, the annotated part is clearly a flouting of the maxim of approbation. The bracketed annotation reverses what is said, turning the impoliteness into a banter, i.e., playful and friendly exchange of teasing remarks, or "mock impoliteness" (Leech, 2014: 101). The annotated is offensive, but the annotation is intended to maintain comity. "简直不是人" (You are simply inhuman!) deliberately fails to observe the politeness strategies to express admiration of the other's ability. The drama created by the bracketed annotation reinforces the in-group solidary.

Example 24 involves a deliberate flouting of politeness maxims, particularly the maxim of modesty. The bracketed annotation withdraws what is said before the bracket, resulting in a balance between the self-aggrandizing and self-effacing. It creates a sense of banter by juxtaposing a potentially arrogant claim with an immediate acknowledgment of fallibility. In face-to-face interaction, banter is often associated with a special demeanor of tone or voice. In this case, the use of brackets becomes a valuable signal for a light and teasing tone. Facilitated with such cues, the speaker invites a specific interpretation from the audience, fostering a cohesive and engaging in-group dynamic.

Once the users are familiar with this construction, they may deliberately breach the rules to create a dramatic effect with an unexpected twist, as illustrated in the following example:

25)

A: 所以今天还是可以有作业的（无误）

So there still could be assignment today (no mistake)

B: 现在没有作业，所以只要我们保持对作业的观测，就会一直没有作业（。

There's no assignment right now, so as long as we watch out for the assignment, we'll stay free of all our assignments (。

In example 25, A changes the normal "误" into "无误" (no mistake), affirming rather than reversing the statement that there might be an assignment to do for today. This breakaway allows participants to reframe the situation in a way such that they experience it as entertaining, or intellectually stimulating and personally interesting.

Summing-up

Seeking fun, pursuing happiness, and engaging in playfulness are inherent aspects of human nature.

In the context of CMC, where nuances of tone and non-verbal cues are limited, playful language can help convey humor and lightheartedness, making interactions more intriguing. Playful engagement, in turn, can lead to the creation of neologisms, memes, and other innovative constructions and narratives. They not only add to the overall enjoyment but also contribute to one's aesthetic and intellectual pleasure.

"Discursive creativity in new media is often *poetic*, usually *playful* and always *pragmatic*", commented Thurlow (2012: 170, italics original). Language play is after all part of social human behavior, a tool for individuals to negotiate and construct their identity, a means of fitting in, challenging norms, or establishing a unique online persona.To maintain in-group intimacy, members must stay updated on the latest "codes" within the group. They need to catch up, practice, and become proficient in using the evolving language forms. If one falls behind or struggles to adapt, they may feel disconnected or left out. Mastery of these codes helps reinforce a shared identity and strengthens the bonds among members.

An example of Chinese creativity in social media—construction with annotated brackets in college students' CMC—exhibits a pragmatic richness that extends beyond mere playfulness to weak-tie in-group cooperation and politeness.

References

Baron, Naomi. 1984. "Computer-Mediated Communication as a Force in Language Change." *Visible Language* 18 (2): 118—141.

Baron, Naomi. 2008. *Always On: Language in an Online and Mobile World*. Oxford: Oxford University Press.

Barton, David, and Carmen Lee. 2013. *Language Online*. New York: Routledge.

Broni, Keith. 2021. "😭 Loudly Crying Becomes Top Tier Emoji." *Emojipedia Blog*, April 1, 2021. https://blog.emojipedia.org/loudly-crying-becomes-top-tier-emoji/. (accessed Aug. 1, 2024)

Crystal, David. 2001. *Language and the Internet*. Cambridge: Cambridge University Press.

Crystal, David. 2011. *Internet Linguistics: A Student Guide*. London: Routledge.

Djenar, Dwi Noverini, Ahmar Mahboob, and Ken Cruickshank. 2015. *Language and Identity Across Modes of Communication*. Berlin: De Gruyter Mouton.

Dovchin, Sender. 2019. *Language, Social Media, and Ideologies: Translingual Practices in Globalizing Spaces*. New York: Routledge.

Dürscheid, Christa, and Carmen Frehner. 2013. "Email Communication." In *Pragmatics of Computer-Mediated Communication*, edited by Susan C. Herring, Dieter Stein, and Tuija Virtanen, 35—54. Berlin: Mouton de Gruyter.

Goffman, Erving. [1956] 1959. *The Presentation of Self in Everyday Life*. Garden City, NY: Doubleday Anchor Books.

Goffman, Erving. 1971. *Relations in Public: Microstudies of the Public Order*. New York: Harper and Row.

Granovetter, Mark. 1973. "The Strength of Weak Ties." *American Journal of Sociology* 78 (6): 1360—1380.

Greenfield, Patricia Marks, and Kaveri Subrahmanyam. 2003. "Online Discourse in a Teen Chatroom: New Codes and New Modes of Coherence in a Visual Medium." *Journal of Applied Developmental Psychology* 24: 713—738.

Grice, Paul. [1975] 1989. *Studies in the Way of Words*. Cambridge, MA: Harvard University Press.

Hinze, Carl. 2012. "Chinese Politeness Is Not About 'Face': Evidence from the Business World." *Journal of Politeness Research* 8 (1): 11—27. https://doi.org/10.1515/JPLR.2012.002.

Irwin-Turner, Anthea. 2023. *Language, Media and Society*. London: Routledge.

Kirshenblatt-Gimblett, Barbara, and Joel Sherzer. 1976. "Introduction." In *Speech Play: Research and Resources for the Study of Linguistic Creativity*, edited by Barbara Kirshenblatt-Gimblett, 1—18. Philadelphia: University of Pennsylvania Press.

Leech, Geoffrey. 1983. *Principles of Pragmatics*. London and New York: Longman.

Leech, Geoffrey. 2005. "Politeness: Is There an East-West Divide?" *Journal of Foreign Languages* 160 (6):

3—31.

Leech, Geoffrey. 2014. *The Pragmatics of Politeness*. Oxford: Oxford University Press.

Lin, Kuo-Hsien, and Hsin-Yi Lu. 2011. "Why People Use Social Networking Sites: An Empirical Study Integrating Network Externalities and Motivation Theory." *Computers in Human Behavior* 27 (3): 1152—1161.

Maynor, Natalie. 1994. "The Language of Electronic Mail: Written Speech?" In *Centennial Usage Studies*, edited by Garland Little and Michael Montgomery, 48–54. Durham, NC: American Dialect Society.

Murray, Denise. 2000. *The Globalisation of English: ELT and the Mass Media*. London: Routledge.

Page, Ruth, et al. 2022. *Researching Language and Social Media: A Student Guide*. 2nd ed. London and New York: Routledge.

Paolillo, John. 2001. "Language Variation on Internet Relay Chat: A Social Network Approach." *Journal of Sociolinguistics* 5 (2): 180—213.

Pfrehm, James. 2018. *Technolingualism: The Mind and the Machine*. London: Bloomsbury Academic.

Seargeant, Philip, and Caroline Tagg. 2014. *The Language of Social Media: Identity and Community on the Internet*. London: Palgrave Macmillan.

Stenström, Anna-Brita, and Annette Myre Jørgensen. 2009. *Youngspeak in a Multilingual Perspective*. Philadelphia: John Benjamins.

Thurlow, Crispin. 2012. "Language Play in New Media Discourse." In *Discourse, Creativity and Technology: Explorations and Intersections*, edited by Rodney H. Jones, 169—190. London: Routledge.

Thurlow, Crispin, and Alexandra Poff. 2013. "Text Messaging." In *Handbook of Pragmatics of Computer-Mediated Communication*, edited by Susan Herring, 163—190. Berlin: Mouton de Gruyter.

Vachek, Josef. 1989. "Written Language and Printed Language." In *Written Language Revisited*, 47—68. Philadelphia: John Benjamins.

Wikström, Peter. 2017. "I Tweet Like I Talk: Aspects of Speech and Writing on Twitter." PhD diss., Karlstad University.

Zappavigna, Michele. 2012. *Discourse of Twitter and Social Media: How We Use Language to Create Affiliation on the Web*. London: Continuum.

Further reading: excerpt from *The Presentation of Self in Everyday Life*

Goffman, Erving. 1956. "Chapter VII Conclusion." In *The Presentation of Self in Everyday Life*, 252—255. Edinburgh: Edinburgh University Press.

Master Bibliography

Adkins, Lesley and Roy Adkins. 2000. *The Keys of Egypt: The Obsession to Decipher Egyptian Hieroglyphs.* New York: Harper Collins Publishers.

Åkerblad, Johan David. 1802. *Lettre sur l'inscription Égyptienne de Rosette: adressée au citoyen Silvestre de Sacy, Professeur de langue arabe à l'École spéciale des langues orientales vivantes, etc.; Réponse du citoyen Silvestre de Sacy.* Paris: L'imprimerie de la République.

Al-Onaizan, Yaser, et al. 1999. *Statistical Machine Translation: Final Report, JHU Summer Workshop.* Baltimore: Johns Hopkins University.

Allen, James P. 2010. *Middle Egyptian: An Introduction to the Language and Culture of Hieroglyphs.* 2nd Edition. Cambridge: Cambridge University Press.

Allen, Kathy. 2012. *Ancient Egyptian Hieroglyphs.* North Mankato: Capstone Press.

Arthur, W. Brian. 1989. "Competing Technologies, Increasing Returns, and Lock-In by Historical Events." *The Economic Journal* 99, no. 394: 116—131.

Avery, Elroy M. 1895. *School Physics: A New Text-Book for High Schools and Academies.* New York: Sheldon & Company.

Azevedo, Frederico A. C., et al. 2009. "Equal Numbers of Neuronal and Nonneuronal Cells Make the Human Brain an Isometrically Scaled-up Primate Brain." *Journal of Comparative Neurology* 513: 532—541.

Baark, Erik. 2000. "Wires, Codes and People: The Great Northern Telegraph Company in China 1870—1890." In *China and Denmark: Relations Since 1674*, edited by Kjeld Erik Brødsgaard and Mads Kirkebæk, 119—152. Copenhagen: Nordic Institute of Asian Studies.

Baker, Carlos. 1972. *Hemingway: The Writer as Artist.* 4th ed. Princeton: Princeton University Press.

Baron, Naomi. 1984. "Computer-Mediated Communication as a Force in Language Change." *Visible Language* 18 (2): 118—141.

———. 2008. *Always On: Language in an Online and Mobile World.* Oxford: Oxford University Press.

Barron, Caroline. 1996. "The Expansion of Education in Fifteenth-Century London." In *The Cloister and the World: Essays in Medieval History in Honour of Barbara Harvey*, edited by J. Blair and B. Golding, 219—

245. Oxford: Clarendon Press.

Barton, David, and Carmen Lee. 2013. *Language Online*. New York: Routledge.

Baugh, Albert C., and Thomas Cable. 2002. A *History of the English Language*. 5th ed. London: Routledge.

Bendall, Lisa M. 2003. *The Decipherment of Linear B and the Ventris-Chadwick Correspondence: An Exhibition to Celebrate the 50th Anniversary of the Publication of the Decipherment. Organized by the Mycenaean Epigraphy Group, Faculty of Classics, Cambridge, at the Fitzwilliam Museum, 9 September— 21 December 2003. Exhibition Catalogue*. Cambridge: Fitzwilliam Museum.

Bennett, Emmett L. 1947. *The Minoan Linear Script from Pylos*. PhD diss., University of Cincinnati.

———. 1951. *The Pylos Tablets: A Preliminary Transcription*. Princeton: Princeton University Press for University of Cincinnati.

Bessou, Sadik. 2015. "Contribution au Niveau de l'Approche Indirecte à Base de Transfert dans la Traduction Automatique." PhD diss., Ferhat Abbas University of Setif.

Blades, William. 1882. *The Biography and Typography of William Caxton, England's First Printer*. New York: Scribner & Welford.

Blake, Norman Francis. 1969. *Caxton and His World*. London: Deutsch.

———. 1991. *William Caxton and English Literary Culture*. London: Hambledon Continuum.

Blondheim, Menahem. 1994. *News over the Wires: The Telegraph and the Flow of Public Information in America, 1844—1897*. Cambridge: Harvard University Press.

Bossard, Antoine. 2022. "Ontological and Quantitative Analyses of the Kokuji Characters of the Japanese Writing System." *Journal of Chinese Writing Systems* 5(2): 115—124. https://doi.org/10.1177/251385022110509.

Bottéro, Françoise. 2004. "Writing on Shell and Bone in Shang China." In *The First Writing: Script Invention as History and Process*, edited by Stephen D. Houston. Cambridge: Cambridge University Press.

Bowker, Lynne et al. 2022. "Artificial Intelligence, Machine Translation, and Academic Libraries: Improving Machine Translation Literacy on Campus." In *The Rise of AI: Implications and Applications of Artificial Intelligence in Academic Libraries*, edited by Sandy Hervieux and Amanda Wheatley, 35—46. Chicago: Association of College & Research Libraries.

Bowker, Lynne, and Jairo Buitrago Ciro. 2019. *Machine Translation and Global Research: Towards Improved Machine Translation Literacy in the Scholarly Community*. Bingley, UK: Emerald Publishing.

Brandt, Deborah. 2001. *Literacy in American Lives*. Cambridge: Cambridge University Press.

Braun, Graham. 2020. Women in Mycenaean Greece: The Linear B Textual Evidence. *The Ascendant Historian*. Vol. 7 (1): 6—19.

Brengelman, Frederick H. 1980. "Orthoepists, Printers, and the Rationalization of English Spelling." *Journal of English and Germanic Philology* 79: 332—354.

Bride, Harold. 1912. "Thrilling Story by Titanic's Surviving Wireless Man." *The New York Times*, April 19. https://www.nytimes.com/1912/04/19/archives/thrilling-story-by-titanics-surviving-wireless-man-bride-tells-how.html.

Broni, Keith. 2021. "😭 Loudly Crying Becomes Top Tier Emoji." *Emojipedia Blog*, April 1, 2021. https://blog.emojipedia.org/loudly-crying-becomes-top-tier-emoji/.

Brown, Peter F., et al. 1990. "A Statistical Approach to Machine Translation." *Computational Linguistics* 16 (2): 79—85.

———., et al. 1993. "The Mathematics of Statistical Machine Translation: Parameter Estimation." *Computational Linguistics* 19 (2): 263—311.

Budge, E. A. Wallis. 1905. *The Nile, Notes for Travellers in Egypt*, 9th Edition, London: Thos. Cook and Son.

Burns, Russel W. 2004. *Communications: An International History of the Formative Years*. London: Institution of Electrical Engineers.

Callison-Burch, Chris. 2002. "Co-training of Statistical Machine Translation." M.A. Thesis, University of Edinburgh.

Carey, James W. 1969. "The Communications Revolution and the Professional Communicator." *The Sociological Review Monograph* 13: 23—38.

———. 1983. "Technology and Ideology: The Case of the Telegraph." In *Communication as Culture: Essays on Media and Society*, 155—177. New York: Routledge, 2009.

Carter, Thomas F. 1931. *The Invention of Printing in China and Its Spread Westward*. New York: Columbia University Press.

Casillo, Anthony. 2017. *Typewriters: Iconic Machines from the Golden Age of Mechanical Writing*. San Francisco: Chronicle Books.

Caxton, William. 1490/1913. "Prologue." *Caxton's Eneydos: Englisht from the French Liure des Eneydes, 1483*. Edited by Matthew T. Culley and Frederick J. Furnivall. London: Kegan Paul, Trench, Trubner & Co., Ltd.; Humphrey Milford: Oxford University Press.

Chadwick, John. 1970. *The Decipherment of Linear B*. Second Edition. Cambridge: Cambridge University Press.

Champollion, Jean-François. 1822. *Lettre à M. Dacier relative à l'alphabet des hiéroglyphes phonétiques*. Paris: Firmin-Didot.

Chan, Sin-Wai, and James Minett, eds. 2016. *The Routledge Encyclopedia of the Chinese Language*. London: Routledge.

Charbonnier, Georges. 1969. *Conversations with Claude Lévi-Strauss*. Translated by John and Doreen

Weightman. London: Cape Ltd.

Chaucer, Geoffrey. 1483. *The Canterbury Tales*. Westminster: William Caxton.

Chomsky, Noam. 1957. *Syntactic Structures*. The Hague: Mouton.

Chung, Karen Steffen. 2016. "Wade-Giles Romanization System." In *The Routledge Encyclopedia of the Chinese Language*, edited by Sin-Wai Chan and James Minett, 1025—1028. London: Routledge.

Church, Kenneth W. 2007. "A Pendulum Swung Too Far." *Linguistic Issues in Language Technology* 2 (1): 1—27.

Coleman, Jared, et al. 2024. "LLM-Assisted Rule-Based Machine Translation for Low/No-Resource Languages." In *Proceedings of the 4th Workshop on Natural Language Processing for Indigenous Languages of the Americas (AmericasNLP 2024)*, 67—87, Mexico City: Association for Computational Linguistics. https://ar5iv.labs.arxiv.org/html/2405.08997.

Collier, Mark and Bill Manley. 2003. *How to Read Egyptian: A Step-by-Step Guide to Teach Yourself*. Revised Edition. Berkeley, Los Angeles & London: University of California Press.

Costa-jussa, Marta R., Eva Vanmassenhove, and Marcello Federico. 2020. "Gender Bias in Multilingual Neural Machine Translation: The Architecture Matters." *Proceedings of the 28th International Conference on Computational Linguistics*. Barcelona: International Committee on Computational Linguistics.

Coulmas, Florian. 1999. *The Blackwell Encyclopedia of Writing Systems*. Malden, MA: Blackwell Publishing.

Crawford, Kate. 2017. "The Trouble with Bias." *Conference on Neural Information Processing Systems (NIPS) – Keynote*, Long Beach, USA. https://blog.revolutionanalytics.com/2017/12/the-trouble-with-bias-by-kate-crawford.html.

Crystal, David. 2001. *Language and the Internet*. Cambridge: Cambridge University Press.

———. 2011. *Internet Linguistics: A Student Guide*. London: Routledge.

Culley, M. T., and F. J. Furnivall, eds. 1890. *Caxton's Eneydos 1490*. London: Kegan Paul, Trench, Trübner & Co.

Cutler, Ida McLenan, and Rupert P. SoRelle. 1910. *Rational Typewriting: A New Idea in Teaching Touch Typewriting*. New York: Gregg Publishing Company.

Daniels, Peter. 1996. "The Study of Writing Systems." In *The World's Writing Systems*, edited by Peter Daniels and William Bright. Oxford: Oxford University Press.

Dash, Niladri Sekhar, and Sujatha Arulmozi. 2017. *History, Features, and Typology of Language Corpora*. Singapore: Springer.

David, Paul A. 1985. "Clio and the Economics of QWERTY" *The American Economic Review* 75, no. 2: 332—337.

Davies, Margery. 2010. *Women's Place is at the Typewriter*. Philadelphia: Temple University Press.

Davies, William Vivian. 1990. "Egyptian Hieroglyphs." In *Reading the Past: Ancient Writing from Cuneiform to the Alphabet*, edited by John Thomas Hooker, 75—136. London: British Museum Press.

Daye, Douglas D. 1996. *A Law Enforcement Sourcebook for Asian Crime and Cultures: Tactics and Mindsets*. New York: Routledge.

de Hamel, Christopher. 1992. *Scribes and Illuminators*. Toronto: University of Toronto Press.

de Kerckhove, Derrick, and Charles J. Lumsden, eds. 1988. *The Alphabet and the Brain*. Berlin: Springer-Verlag.

de Pisan, Christine. 1478. *The Morale Proverbes of Cristyne*. Westminster: William Caxton.

De Prémanre, Joseph Henri. 1831. *Notitia Lingua Sinicae*. Malacca: Cura Academiae Anglo-sinensis.

de Voragine, Jacobus. 1483. *The Golden Legende*. Westminster: William Caxton.

DeFrancis, John. 1989. *Visible Speech: The Diverse Oneness of Writing Systems*. Honolulu: University of Hawaii Press.

Djenar, Dwi Noverini, Ahmar Mahboob, and Ken Cruickshank. 2015. *Language and Identity Across Modes of Communication*. Berlin: De Gruyter Mouton.

Dodson, Brian. 2013. "Plug Pulled on the World's Last Commercial Electric Telegraph System." *New Atlas*, July 17, 2013. https://newatlas.com/last-telegraph-message/28314/.

Dovchin, Sender. 2019. *Language, Social Media, and Ideologies: Translingual Practices in Globalizing Spaces*. New York: Routledge.

Dürscheid, Christa, and Carmen Frehner. 2013. "Email Communication." In *Pragmatics of Computer-Mediated Communication*, edited by Susan C. Herring, Dieter Stein, and Tuija Virtanen, 35—54. Berlin: Mouton de Gruyter.

Eisenstein, Elizabeth L. 1979. *The Printing Revolution in Early Modern Europe*. Cambridge: Cambridge University Press.

Encyclopaedia Britannica. "Jean-François Champollion". Last revised and updated by Teagan Wolter. Accessed May 11, 2024. https://www.britannica.com/biography/Jean-Francois-Champollion

Evans, Arthur. 1909. *Scripta Minoa: The Written Documents of Minoan Crete with Special Reference to the Archives of Knossos*. Vol. 1, Oxford: Clarendon Press.

———. 1952. *Scripta Minoa: The Written Documents of Minoan Crete with Special Reference to the Archives of Knossos*. Vol. 2, edited by John L. Myres, Oxford: Clarendon Press.

Felzmann, Heike et al. 2020. "Towards Transparency by Design for Artificial Intelligence." *Philosophy & Technology* 33, no. 2: 209—230.

Fennell, Barbara. 2001. *A History of English: A Sociolinguistic Approach*. Oxford: Blackwell.

Fillmore, Charles J. 1968. "The Case for Case." In *Universals in Linguistic Theory*, edited by E. Bach and R. T.

Harms, 1—25. London: Holt, Rinehart and Winston.

Fischer-Bovet, Christelle. 2015. Social Unrest and Ethnic Coexistence in Ptolemaic Egypt and The Seleucid Empire. *Past & Present* No. 229: 3045.

Fisiak, Jacek. 1994. "On the Writing of the History of Standard English." In *English Historical Linguistics 1992,* edited by Francisco Fernández, María Fuster, and Juan J. Calvo, 105—115. Amsterdam: John Benjamins.

Fogel, Catherine I., and Nancy Fugate Woods, eds. 2008. *Women's Health Care in Advanced Practice Nursing.* New York: Springer Publishing Company.

Ford, Judy A. 2020. *English Readers of Catholic Saints: The Printing History of William Caxton's "Golden Legend."* London: Routledge.

Forsdyke, Sara. 2021. *Slaves and Slavery in Ancient Greece.* Cambridge: Cambridge University Press.

Fox, Margalit. 2013. *The Riddle of the Labyrinth.* London: Profile Books.

Frazer, James George. 1890. *The Golden Bough: A Study in Magic and Religion.* London: Macmillan and Co.

Friedman, Batya and Helen Nissenbaum. 1996. "Bias in Computer Systems." *ACM Transactions on Information Systems* 14, no. 3: 330—347.

Friginal, Eric, and Jack A. Hardy. 2014. *Corpus-Based Sociolinguistics: A Guide for Students.* New York: Routledge.

Fromkin, Victoria, and Robert Rodman. 1983. *An Introduction to Language.* 3rd Edition. New York: Holt.

———. 1998. *An Introduction to Language.* 6th Edition. Fort Worth, Philadelphia, San Diego, New York, Orlando, Austin, San Antonio, Toronto, Montreal, London, Sydney & Tokyo: Harcourt Brace College Publishers.

Fyfe, James Hamilton. 1863. *The Triumphs of Invention and Discovery.* London: T. Nelson.

Gaido, Marco, Alina Karakanta, and Luisa Bentivogli. 2020. "Breeding Gender-Aware Direct Speech Translation Systems." In *Proceedings of the 28th International Conference on Computational Linguistics,* 3951—3964. Online: International Committee on Computational Linguistics.

Galanakis, Yannis, Anastasia Christophilopoulou and James Grime. 2017. *Codebreakers and Groundbreakers.* Cambridge: The Fitzwilliam Museum, University of Cambridge.

Gaskell, Philip. *A New Introduction to Bibliography.* Oxford: Oxford University Press.

Giles, Herbert. 1892. *A Chinese-English Dictionary.* Shanghai: Commercial Press.

Goffman, Erving. [1956] 1959. *The Presentation of Self in Everyday Life.* Garden City, NY: Doubleday Anchor Books.

———. 1971. *Relations in Public: Microstudies of the Public Order.* New York: Harper and Row.

Goody, Jack. 1977. *The Domestication of the Savage Mind.* Cambridge: Cambridge University Press.

———.1987. *The Interface Between the Written and the Oral*. Cambridge: Cambridge University Press.

Goody, Jack, and Ian Watt. 1968. "The Consequences of Literacy." *Comparative Studies in Society and History* 10 (3): 304–345.

Gordon, John Steele. 2002. *A Thread Across the Ocean: The Heroic Story of the Transatlantic Cable*. New York: Walker & Company.

Granovetter, Mark. 1973. "The Strength of Weak Ties." *American Journal of Sociology* 78 (6): 1360—1380.

Greenfield, Patricia Marks, and Kaveri Subrahmanyam. 2003. "Online Discourse in a Teen Chatroom: New Codes and New Modes of Coherence in a Visual Medium." *Journal of Applied Developmental Psychology* 24: 713—738.

Grice, Paul. [1975] 1989. *Studies in the Way of Words*. Cambridge, MA: Harvard University Press.

Griffith, Francis Llewellyn. 1898. *A Collection of Hieroglyphs: A contribution to the History of Egyptian Writing*. London: Gilbert &Rivington Ltd.

Grube, Nikolai. 2021. "Writing with Heads: Animated Logographs and Syllabograms in Maya Writing." *Estudios Latinoamericanos* 41: 165—180. https://doi.org/10.36447/Estudios2021.v41.art9.

Gutt, Ernst-August. 1992. *Relevance Theory: A Guide to Successful Communication in Translation*. New York: Summer Institute of Linguistics and United Bible Societies.

Hannas, William C. 2003. *The Writing on the Wall: How Asian Orthography Curbs Creativity*. Philadelphia: University of Pennsylvania Press.

Harris, Lane J. 2008. "A 'Lasting Boon to All': A Note on the Postal Romanization of Place Names, 1896—1949." *Twentieth-Century China* 34 (1): 96—109.

Hart, John. [1569] 1969. *An Orthography*. Menston: Scholar Press Ltd.

Havelock, Eric A. 1986. *The Muse Learns to Write: Reflections on Orality and Literacy from Antiquity to the Present*. New Haven: Yale University Press.

Hellinga, Lotte. 2010. *William Caxton and Early Printing in England*. London: The British Library.

Hinze, Carl. 2012. "Chinese Politeness Is Not About 'Face': Evidence from the Business World." *Journal of Politeness Research* 8 (1): 11—27. https://doi.org/10.1515/JPLR.2012.002.

Hogan, Aidan, Pascal Hitzler, Krzysztof Janowicz. 2020. "The Semantic Web: Two Decades On." *Semantic Web*. Vol. 11 (1): 169—185.

Hogg, Richard. 2006. *A History of the English Language*. Cambridge: Cambridge University Press.

Hoke, Donald. 1979. "The Woman and the Typewriter: A Case Study in Technological Innovation and Social Change" *Business and Economic History* 8, Papers Presented at the Twenty-Fifth Annual Meeting of the Business History Conference: 76—88.

Homer. *The Iliad*. Translated by Samuel Butler. Project Gutenberg. Accessed October 18, 2024. https://www.

gutenberg.org/ebooks/2199.

Horobin, Simon. 2016. *A Short History of a Global Language*. Oxford: Oxford University Press.

Houston, Stephen, John Robertson, and David Stuart. 2000. "The Language of Classic Maya Inscriptions." *Current Anthropology* 41(3): 321—356.

Hu, Zhuanglin, and Jiang Wangqi, eds. 2002. *Linguistics: An Advanced Course Book*. Beijing: Peking University Press.

———, eds. 2014. *Linguistics: An Advanced Course Book*. 2nd ed. Beijing: Peking University Press.

Hutchins, John. 1979. "Linguistic Models in Machine Translation." *UEA Papers in Linguistics* 9 (January): 29—52.

———.1986. *Machine Translation: Past, Present, Future*. Chichester: Ellis Horwood.

ibn Fatik, Al-Mubashshir. 1477. *Dictes and Sayings of the Philosophers*. Westminster: William Caxton.

Irwin-Turner, Anthea. 2023. *Language, Media and Society*. London: Routledge.

Iwasaki, Shoichi. 2013. *Japanese*. Amsterdam and Philadelphia: John Benjamins Publishing Company.

Jelinek, Frederick, and Robert L. Mercer. 1980. "Interpolated Estimation of Markov Source Parameters from Sparse Data." In *Proceedings of the Workshop on Pattern Recognition in Practice*, edited by Edzard S. Gelsema and Laveen N. Kanal, 381—397. Amsterdam: North-Holland.

Jespersen, Otto. 1982. *Growth and Structure of the English Language*. 10th ed. Chicago: The University of Chicago Press.

Joshi, R. Malatesha, and P. G. Aaron, eds. 2013. *Handbook of Orthography and Literacy*. London and New York: Routledge.

Jurafsky, Daniel, and James H. Martin. 2024. *Speech and Language Processing: An Introduction to Natural Language Processing, Computational Linguistics, and Speech Recognition with Language Models*. 3rd ed. draft (Draft of August 20, 2024) https://web.stanford.edu/~jurafsky/slp3/ed3book.pdf

Kafaee, Mahdi, Elahe Daviran, and Mostafa Taqavi. 2022. "The QWERTY Keyboard from the Perspective of the Collingridge Dilemma: Lessons for Co-construction of Human-Technology." *AI & SOCIETY* 39, no. 3:1229—1241. https://doi.org/10.1007/s00146-022-01569-5.

Kaplan, Frédéric, and Warren Sack. 2014. "Language, Writing and Automaticity: Software Studies in Front of Linguistic Capitalism." *AI & Society* 29, no. 2: 145—159.

Kettunen, Harri, and Marc Zender. 2019. "On the Graphic and Lexical Origins of Maya Syllabograms." In *Tiempo detenido, un tiempo suficiente: Ensayos y narraciones mesoamericanistas en homenaje a Alfonso Lacadena García Gallo*, edited by Harri Kettunen, et al. Wayeb Publication Series, Vol. 1. Belgium: Wayeb.

Khan, Geoffrey. 1997. "Tiberian Hebrew Phonology." In *Phonologies of Asia and Africa*, edited by A. S. Kaye and P. T. Daniels, 85—102. Winona Lake, IN: Eisenbrauns.

Kiraz, George Anton. 1998. "Arabic Computational Morphology in the West." In *Proceedings of the 6th International Conference and Exhibition on Multi-lingual Computing*. Cambridge, UK.

Kirshenblatt-Gimblett, Barbara, and Joel Sherzer. 1976. "Introduction." In *Speech Play: Research and Resources for the Study of Linguistic Creativity*, edited by Barbara Kirshenblatt-Gimblett, 1—18. Philadelphia: University of Pennsylvania Press.

Kittler, Friedrich. 1999. *Gramophone, Film, Typewriter.* Translated by Geoffrey Winthrop-Young and Michael Wutz. Stanford, CA: Stanford University Press.

Knight, Kevin. 1999. *A Statistical MT Tutorial Workbook.* Prepared for the 1999 JHU Summer Workshop. https://kevincrawfordknight.github.io/papers/wkbk.pdf.

Kober, Alice. 1945. Evidence of Inflection in the 'Chariot' Tablets from Knossos. *American Journal of Archaeology* Vol. 49 (2): 143—151.

———.1946. "Inflection in Linear Class B: 1—Declension." *American Journal of Archaeology*, Vol. 50(2): 268—276.

Koehn, Philipp. 2005. "Europarl: A Parallel Corpus for Statistical Machine Translation." In *Proceedings of the 10th Machine Translation Summit X*, 79—86. Phuket, Thailand.

———. 2020. *Neural Machine Translation.* Cambridge: Cambridge University Press.

———., et al. 2007. "Moses: Open Source Toolkit for Statistical Machine Translation." In *Proceedings of the 45th Annual Meeting of the Association for Computational Linguistics (ACL 2007)*, 177—180. Prague, Czech Republic.

———., Franz Josef Och, and Daniel Marcu. 2003. "Statistical Phrase-Based Translation." In *Proceedings of the 2003 Conference of the North American Chapter of the Association for Computational Linguistics on Human Language Technology (HLT-NAACL 2003)*, 48—54. Edmonton, AB: Association for Computational Linguistics.

Komor, Valerie S. 2015. "How the Mexican-American War Gave Birth to a News-Gathering Institution: The Associated Press Was Built for Speed and Straight Facts." *Zócalo Public Square*, September 4, 2015. https://www.zocalopublicsquare.org/2015/09/04/how-the-mexican-american-war-gave-birth-to-a-news-gathering-institution/chronicles/who-we-were/.

Kuskin, William, ed. 2006. *Caxton's Trace: Studies in the History of English Printing.* Notre Dame: University of Notre Dame Press.

Ladefoged, Peter. 1962. *Elements of Acoustic Phonetics.* Chicago: University of Chicago Press.

Lass, Roger. 1999. "Introduction." In *The Cambridge History of the English Language, Volume III: 1476—1776,* edited by Roger Lass, 1—12. Cambridge: Cambridge University Press.

Lee, Rob, Philip Jonathan, and Pauline Ziman. 2010. "Pictish Symbols Revealed as a Written Language through Application of Shannon Entropy." *Proceedings of the Royal Society A: Mathematical, Physical and Engineering Sciences*, Vol. 466 (2121): 2545—2560.

Leech, Geoffrey. 1983. *Principles of Pragmatics*. London and New York: Longman.

———. 2005. "Politeness: Is There an East-West Divide?" *Journal of Foreign Languages* 160 (6): 3—31.

———. 2014. *The Pragmatics of Politeness*. Oxford: Oxford University Press.

Leibniz, Gottfried Wilhelm. 1677. "Preface to the General Science." Revision of Rutherford's translation in Jolley 1995: 234. In *The Cambridge Companion to Leibniz*, edited by Nicholas Jolley, 234. Cambridge: Cambridge University Press.

Lévi-Strauss, Claude. 1949. *Les structures élémentaires de la parenté (The Elementary Structures of Kinship)*. Paris: Presses Universitaires de France.

———. 1962. *La pensée sauvage (The Savage Mind)*. Paris: Plon.

———. 1966. *Du miel aux cendres (From Honey to Ashes)*. Paris: Plon.

———. [1955] 1970. *A World on the Wane*. Trans. John and Doreen Weightman. New York: Atheneum. Originally published as *Tristes tropiques*.

———. [1964] 1971. *The Raw and the Cooked: Introduction to a Science of Mythology, Volume 1*. Trans. John and Doreen Weightman. New York: Harper & Row. Originally published as *Le Cru et le cuit*.

Levin, Irwin, et al. 1998. "An Interlingua Based on Domain Actions for Machine Translation of Task-Oriented Dialogues." In *Proceedings of ICSLP-98:The 5th International Conference on Spoken Language Processing Sydney, Australia.* https://dblp.uni-trier.de/db/conf/interspeech/icslp1998.html#LevinGLW98

Li, Yu. 2020. *The Chinese Writing System in Asia: An Interdisciplinary Perspective*. London and New York: Routledge.

Li, Yuming. 2015. *Language Planning in China*. Berlin and Beijing: Mouton de Gruyter and Commercial Press.

Lieberman, Philip. 2007. "The Evolution of Human Speech: Its Anatomical and Neural Bases." *Current Anthropology* 48, no. 1: 39—66.

Liebowitz, Stan J., and Stephen E. Margolis. 1990. "The Fable of the Keys." *Journal of Law and Economics* 33, no. 1: 1—26.

———. 1995. Path Dependence, Lock-In, and History." *Journal of Law, Economics, & Organization* 11, no. 1: 205—226.

Light, Lisa, and Peter G. Anderson. 1993. "Typewriter Keyboards via Simulated Annealing." *AI Expert*, September 1993.

Lin, Kuo-Hsien, and Hsin-Yi Lu. 2011. "Why People Use Social Networking Sites: An Empirical Study Integrating Network Externalities and Motivation Theory." *Computers in Human Behavior* 27 (3): 1152—

1161.

Loprieno, Antonio. 1995. *Ancient Egyptian: A Linguistic Introduction*. Cambridge: Cambridge University Press.

———, and Matthias Müller. 2012. "Ancient Egyptian and Coptic." In *The Afroasiatic Languages*, edited by Zygmunt Frajzyngier and Erin Shay. Cambridge: Cambridge University Press.

Love, Nicholas. 1483. *The Mirrour of the Blessed Lyf of Jesu Christ*. Westminster: William Caxton.

Lucas Nunes Vieira, Minako O'Hagan, and Carol O'Sullivan. 2021. "Understanding the Societal Impacts of Machine Translation: A Critical Review of the Literature on Medical and Legal Use Cases." *Journal of Information, Communication and Ethics in Society* 19, no. 1: 25—41.

Lyons, Martyn. 2021. *The Typewriter Century: A Cultural History of Writing Practices*. Toronto: University of Toronto Press.

MacGinnis, John, et al. 2014. "Artefacts of Cognition: The Use of Clay Tokens in a Neo-Assyrian Provincial Administration." *Cambridge Archaeological Journal* 24(2): 289—306.

Maras, Steven. 2013. *Objectivity in Journalism*. Cambridge: Polity Press.

Maynor, Natalie. 1994. "The Language of Electronic Mail: Written Speech?" In *Centennial Usage Studies*, edited by Garland Little and Michael Montgomery, 48—54. Durham, NC: American Dialect Society.

McBrearty, Sally, and Alison S. Brooks. 2000. "The Revolution That Wasn't: A New Interpretation of the Origin of Modern Human Behavior." *Journal of Human Evolution* 39, no. 5: 453—563.

McCullough, David. 2011. "Samuel Morse's Reversal of Fortune." *Smithsonian Magazine*, September 2011. https://www.smithsonianmag.com/history/samuel-morses-reversal-of-fortune-49650609/

McEnery, Tony, Richard Xiao, and Yukio Tono. 2006. *Corpus-Based Language Studies: An Advanced Resource Book*. New York: Routledge.

McLuhan, Marshall. 1964. *Understanding Media: The Extensions of Man*. New York: McGraw-Hill.

McMahon, April. 2002. *An Introduction to English Phonology*. Edinburgh: Edinburgh University Press.

Meggs, Phillip B., and Alston W. Purvis. 2016. *History of Graphic Design*. 6th ed. Hoboken, NJ: Wiley.

Mehandru, Nikita, Samantha Robertson, and Niloufar Salehi. 2022. "Reliable and Safe Use of Machine Translation in Medical Settings." *Journal of Language and Technology in Medicine* 6, no. 2: 98—110.

Mercer, Robert L. 1993. "The Mathematics of Statistical Machine Translation." *Computational Linguistics* 19 (2): 263—313.

Metz, Cade. 2016. "Google Has Open Sourced SyntaxNet, Its AI for Understanding Language." *Wired*, May 12, 2016. https://www.wired.com/2016/05/google-open-sourced-syntaxnet-ai-natural-language/.

Meyers, Jeffrey. 1985. *Hemingway: A Biography*. New York: Harper & Row.

Milroy, Lesley. 2000. "Two Nations Divided by the Same Language: Contrasting Language Ideologies in

Britain and the United States." Lecture presented at the 5th Conference for the European Society for the Study of English (ESSE).

Montemurro, Marcelo A. and Damián H Zanette. 2011. Universal Entropy of Word Ordering Across Linguistic Families. PLOS ONE, *Public Library of Science*, vol. 6(5): 1—9.

Moorhouse, A. C. 1953. *Triumph of the Alphabet*. London: Sidgwick & Jackson.

Morag, Shelomo. 1972. *The Vocalization Systems of Arabic, Hebrew, and Aramaic*. The Hague: Mouton & Co.

Morgan, Lewis Henry. 1877. *Ancient Society: Or Researches in the Lines of Human Progress from Savagery through Barbarism to Civilization*. London: Macmillan & Company.

Mullaney, Thomas S. 2017. *The Chinese Typewriter: A History*. Cambridge, MA: MIT Press.

Murray, Denise. 2000. *The Globalisation of English: ELT and the Mass Media*. London: Routledge.

Nef, John. 2008. "Mining and Metallurgy in Medieval Civilisation." In *The Cambridge Economic History of Europe, Volume 2,* 2nd ed., edited by Edward Miller et al., 691—761. Cambridge: Cambridge University Press.

Nichols, Johanna. 1998. "The Origin and Dispersal of Languages: Linguistic Evidence." In *The Origin and Diversification of Language*, edited by Nina G. Jablonski and Leslie C. Aiello, 127—170. San Francisco, CA: California Academy of Sciences.

Niessen, Hans J., Peter Damerow, and Robert K. Englund. 1993. Translated by Paul Larsen. *Archaic Bookkeeping: Writing and Techniques of Economic Administration in the Ancient Near East*. Chicago and London: The University of Chicago Press.

Nye, David E. 1991. *Electrifying America*: *Social Meanings of a New Technology, 1880-1940*. Cambridge, MA: MIT Press.

O'Shaughnessy, Douglas. 2023. Trends and developments in automatic speech recognition research. *Computer Speech & Language*. Vol. 83 Issue C https://doi.org/10.1016/j.csl.2023.101538

Och, Franz Josef, and Hermann Ney. 2003. "A Systematic Comparison of Various Statistical Alignment Models." *Computational Linguistics* 29 (1): 19—51.

Okrent, Arika. 2021. *Highly Irregular: Why Tough, Through, and Dough Don't Rhyme—And Other Oddities of the English Language*. Oxford: Oxford University Press.

Olson, David R. 1994. *The World on Paper: The Conceptual and Cognitive Implications of Writing and Reading*. Cambridge: Cambridge University Press.

Ong, Walter J. 1982. *Orality and Literacy: The Technologizing of the Word*. London: Methuen.

Oppenheim, Leo. 1959. "On an Operational Device in Mesopotamian Bureaucracy." *Journal of Near Eastern Studies* 18(2): 121—128.

Page, Ruth, et al. 2022. *Researching Language and Social Media: A Student Guide*. 2nd ed. London and New

York: Routledge.

Paolillo, John. 2001. "Language Variation on Internet Relay Chat: A Social Network Approach." *Journal of Sociolinguistics* 5 (2): 180—213.

Parkinson, Richard. 1999. *Cracking Codes: The Rosetta Stone and Decipherment.* Berkeley: University of California Press.

———. 2005. British Museum Objects in Focus: The Rosetta Stone. London, British Museum Press.

Pfrehm, James. 2018. *Technolingualism: The Mind and the Machine.* London: Bloomsbury Academic.

Plant, Marjorie. 1974. *The English Book Trade: An Economic History of the Making and Sale of Books.* London: George Allen & Unwin.

Poibeau, Thierry. 2017. *Machine Translation.* Cambridge, MA: The MIT Press.

Pope, Maurice. 1999. *The Story of Decipherment, from Egyptian Hieroglyphs to Maya Script, Revised Edition.* Thames & Hudson.

Powell, Barry. 2009. *Writing: Theory and History of the Technology of Civilization.* Malden: Wiley-Blackwell.

Prates, Marcelo O. R., Pedro H. C. Avelar, and Luis C. Lamb. 2019. "Assessing Gender Bias in Machine Translation: A Case Study with Google Translate." *Neural Computing and Applications* 32, 6363—6381.

Prime, Samuel Irenæus. 1875. *The Life of Samuel F. B. Morse, LL.D.: Inventor of the Electro-Magnetic Recording Telegraph.* New York: D. Appleton & Company.

Prithwijit, Debasis, et al. 2018. "Dangers of Machine Translation: The Need for Professionally Translated Anticipatory Guidance Resources for Limited English Proficiency Caregivers." *BMC Pediatrics* 18, no. 1: 21—32.

Rao, Rajesh. 2010. "Probabilistic analysis of an ancient undeciphered script." *IEEE Computer*, 43(4): 76—80.

———. 2018. "The Indus Script and Economics: A Role for Indus Seals and Tablets in Rationing and Administration of Labor." In *Walking with the Unicorn: Social Organization and Material Culture in Ancient South* Asia, edited by D. Frenez, G. M. Jamison, R. W. Law, M. Vidale & R. H. Meadow, 518—525, Oxford: Archaeopress.

———, et al. 2009. "Entropic evidence for linguistic structure in the Indus script." *Science*, 324(5931): 1165.

———, et al. 2015. "On Statistical Measures and Ancient Writing Systems." *Language.* Vol. 91(4): 198—205.

Ravid, Dorit, and Sarit Haimowitz. 2006. "The Vowel Path: Learning about Vowel Representation in Written Hebrew." *Written Language and Literacy* 9(1): 67—93.

Remington Notes 1915. 3, no. 10. Accessed July 4, 2023. https://oztypewriter.blogspot.com/2014/08/not-again-from-miss-remington-to-peter.html.

Rendburg, Gary A. 1997. "Ancient Hebrew Phonology." In *Phonologies of Asia and Africa*, edited by A. S. Kaye and P. T. Daniels, 65—83. Winona Lake, IN: Eisenbrauns.

292　语言、技术与社会
Language, Technology, and Society

Robinson, Andrew. 2002. *The Man Who Deciphered Linear B: The Story of Michael Ventris*. London: Thames & Hudson.

———. 2007. *The Last Man Who Knew Everything: Thomas Young*. Oxford: Oneworld Publications.

———. 2009. *Lost Languages: The Enigma of the World's Undeciphered Scripts*. London: Thames & Hudson.

———. 2012. *Cracking the Egyptian code: the revolutionary life of Jean-François Champollion*. Oxford: Oxford University Press.

Roemmele, Brian. 2019. "Why Was the QWERTY Keyboard Layout Invented?" *Forbes,* January 10, 2019. https://www.forbes.com/sites/quora/2019/01/10/why-was-the-qwerty-keyboard-layout-invented/.

Rogers, Henry. 2005. *Writing Systems: A Linguistic Approach*. Malden, MA: Blackwell Publishing.

Roukos, Salim, et al. 1995. *Hansard French/English LDC95T20*. Web Download. Philadelphia: Linguistic Data Consortium.

Salmon, Vivian. 1999. "Orthography and Punctuation." In *The Cambridge History of the English Language, Volume III: 1476—1776,* edited by Roger Lass, 13—55. Cambridge: Cambridge University Press.

Sampson, Geoffrey. 1985. *Writing Systems: A Linguistic Introduction*. Redwood City: Stanford University Press.

Sap, Maarten et al. 2020. "Social Bias Frames: Reasoning about Social and Power Implications of Language." In *Proceedings of the 58th Annual Meeting of the Association for Computational Linguistics*, 5477—5490. Online: Association for Computational Linguistics.

Savoldi, Beatrice et al. 2021. "Gender Bias in Machine Translation." *Transactions of the Association for Computational Linguistics* 9: 845—874. https://doi.org/10.1162/tacl_a_00401.

Schillemann, Matthew. 2013. "Typewriter Psyche: Henry James' Mechanical Mind" *Journal of Modern Literature* 36, no. 3: 14—30.

Schmandt-Besserat, Denise. 1992. *Before Writing: From Counting to Cuneiform*. Austin: University of Texas Press.

Schmandt-Besserat, Denise. 1996. *How Writing Came About*. Austin: University of Texas Press.

Scragg, Donald G. 1974. *A History of English Spelling*. Manchester: Manchester University Press.

Seargeant, Philip, and Caroline Tagg. 2014. *The Language of Social Media: Identity and Community on the Internet*. London: Palgrave Macmillan.

Sennrich, Rico. 2017. "How Grammatical is Character-Level Neural Machine Translation? Assessing MT Quality with Contrastive Translation Pairs." In *Proceedings of the 15th Conference of the European Chapter of the Association for Computational Linguistics: Volume 2, Short Papers*, 376—382. Valencia, ES: Association for Computational Linguistics. https://doi.org/10.18653/v1/E17-2060.

Shaklee, Margaret. 1980. "The Rise of Standard English." In *Standards and Dialects in English,* edited by T. Shopen and J. M. Williams, 33—62. Cambridge, Mass.: Winthrop Publishers.

Shannon, Claude E. 1948. "A Mathematical Theory of Communication." *The Bell System Technical Journal* 27: 379—423, 623—656.

Shannon, Claude E. 1950. "Prediction and Entropy of Printed English." *Bell System Technical Journal*, Vol. 30(1): 50—64.

Shen, Ruiqing. "The Monosyllabicization of Old Chinese and the Birth of Chinese Writing: A Hypothesis on the Co-evolution of the Chinese Language and Its Writing System." *Journal of Language Relationship* 17(1—2): 44—54.

Shulsky, Debra, et al. 2017. "Cultivating Layered Literacies: Developing the Global Child to Become Tomorrow's Global Citizen." *International Journal of Development Education and Global Learning* 9, no. 1: 49—63.

Silvestre de Sacy, Antoine-Isaac. 1802. *Lettre au citoyen Chaptal au sujet de l'inscription égyptienne du monument trouvé à Rosette.* Paris: Imprimerie de la République.

Slocum, Jonathan. 1984. "Machine Translation: Its History, Current Status, and Future Prospects." In *10th International Conference on Computational Linguistics and 22nd Annual Meeting of the Association for Computational Linguistics*, 546—561. Stanford: Association for Computational Linguistics.

Sproat, Richard. 2010. *Language, Technology, and Society.* Oxford: Oxford University Press.

———. 2014. "A Statistical Comparison of Written Language and Nonlinguistic symbol Systems." *Language* 90, no. 2: 457—481.

———. 2015. "On Misunderstandings and Misrepresentations: A Reply to Rao et al." *Language* 91, no. 4: e206—208.

Standage, Tom. 1998. *The Victorian Internet: The Remarkable Story of the Telegraph and the Nineteenth Century's On-line Pioneers.* New York: Walker & Company. [Reprinted 2007].

Stanovsky, Gabriel, et al. 2019. "Evaluating Gender Bias in Machine Translation." *Proceedings of the 2019 Conference on Empirical Methods in Natural Language Processing*, 3003—3008. Brussels, BE: Association for Computational Linguistics.

Steffens, Lincoln. 1958. *The Autobiography of Lincoln Steffens*. New York: Harcourt, Brace & World.

Steigerwald, Emma, et al. 2022. "Overcoming Language Barriers in Academia: Machine Translation Tools and a Vision for a Multilingual Future." *Journal of Multilingual and Multicultural Development* 43, no. 5: 432—447.

Steinberg, Sigfrid Henry. 1996. *Five Hundred Years of Printing.* London: British Library and Oak Knoll Press.

Stenström, Anna-Brita, and Annette Myre Jørgensen. 2009. *Youngspeak in a Multilingual Perspective.*

Philadelphia: John Benjamins.

Stock, Brian. 1983. *The Implications of Literacy*. Princeton: Princeton University Press.

Strang, Barbara M. H. 1970. *A History of the English Language*. London: Methuen.

Strathern, Paul. 2009. *Napoleon in Egypt*. Reprint edition. New York: Bantam.

Sukthanker, Rakesh, et al. 2020. "Anaphora and Coreference Resolution: A Review." *Information Fusion* 59: 139—162.

Takeda, Reiko. 2001. "*The Question of the 'Standardisation' of Written English in the Fifteenth Century*." PhD diss., The University of Leeds.

Taylor, Insup, and M. Martin Taylor. 2014. *Writing and Literacy in Chinese, Korean, and Japanese*. 2nd ed. Amsterdam: John Benjamins Publishing Company.

Tesnière, Lucien. 1959. *Éléments de Syntaxe Structurale*. Paris: Klincksieck.

———. 2015. *Elements of Structural Syntax*. Trans. Timothy John Osborne and Kahane Sylvain. Amsterdam and Philadelphia: John Benjamins Publishing Company.

Thurlow, Crispin. 2012. "Language Play in New Media Discourse." In *Discourse, Creativity and Technology: Explorations and Intersections*, edited by Rodney H. Jones, 169—190. London: Routledge.

Thurlow, Crispin, and Alexandra Poff. 2013. "Text Messaging." In *Handbook of Pragmatics of Computer-Mediated Communication*, edited by Susan Herring, 163-190. Berlin: Mouton de Gruyter.

Tomalin, Marcus et al. 2021. "The Practical Ethics of Bias Reduction in Machine Translation: Why Domain Adaptation is Better than Data Debiasing." *Ethics and Information Technology* 23: 419—433. https://doi.org/10.1007/s10676-021-09583-1.

Trenité, Gerard Nolst. 1920. "Appendix III The Chaos." In *Drop Your Foreign Accent*, 110—118. London: George Allen & Unwin Ltd.

Trigault, Nicolas, and Matteo Ricci. 1615. *De Christiana expeditione apud Sinas Suscepta ab Societate Jesu*. Lyon: Horatij Cardon.

Tsu, Jing. 2022. *Kingdom of Characters: The Language Revolution that Made China Modern*. New York: Riverhead Books.

Twisaday, Charles E. J., and Geo. R. Neilson. 1904. *The International Telegraph Convention of St. Petersburg, and the International Telegraph Service Regulations. London Revision, 1903*. London: The "Electrician" Printing and Publishing Co.

Tylor, Edward Burnett. 1871. *Primitive Culture: Researches into the Development of Mythology, Philosophy, Religion, Language, Art, and Custom*. London: John Murray.

Vachek, Josef. 1973. *Written Language: General Problems and Problems of English*. The Hague: Mouton.

———. 1989. "Written Language and Printed Language." In *Written Language Revisited*, 47—68.

Philadelphia: John Benjamins.

Valério, Miguel, and Silvia Ferrara. 2019. "Rebus and Acrophony in Invented Writing." *Writing Systems Research* 11(1): 66—93. Published online March 16, 2020. https://doi.org/10.1080/17586801.2020.1724239.

Vanmassenhove, Eva, Christian Hardmeier, and Andy Way. 2018. "Getting Gender Right in Neural Machine Translation." In *Proceedings of the 2018 Conference on Empirical Methods in Natural Language Processing*, 3003—3008. Brussels, BE: Association for Computational Linguistics.

Vaswani, Ashish, et al. 2017. "Attention Is All You Need." *Proceedings of the 31st International Conference on Neural Information Processing Systems (NeurIPS)*, 5998—6008. Long Beach, CA: Curran Associates, Inc.

Vauquois, Bernard. 1968. "A Survey of Formal Grammars and Algorithms for Recognition and Transformation in Mechanical Translation." In A. J. H. Morrel (Ed.), *Proceedings of the IFIP Congress,* Edinburgh, UK, 5—10 August 1968 , Vol. 2: 1114—1122.

Vauquois, Bernard. 1976. "Automatic Translation—A Survey of Different Approaches." *Statistical Methods in Linguistics*, 127—135.

Ventris, Michael, and John Chadwick. 1956. *Documents in Mycenaean Greek*. Cambridge: Cambridge University Press.

———. 1973. *Documents In Mycenaean Greek*. 2nd Edition. Cambridge: Cambridge University Press.

Vergne, Jean-Philippe, and Rodolphe Durand. 2010. "The Missing Link Between the Theory and Empirics of Path Dependence: Conceptual Clarification, Testability Issue, and Methodological Implications" *Journal of Management Studies* 47, no. 4: 736—759.

Vieira, Lucas N., Minako O'Hagan, and Carol O'Sullivan. 2021. "Understanding the Societal Impacts of Machine Translation: A Critical Review of the Literature on Medical and Legal Use Cases." *Information, Communication & Society* 24, no. 11: 1515—1532.

Vinson, Steve. "Demotic: The History, Development and Techniques of Ancient Egypt's Popular Script." https://arce.org/resource/demotic-history-development-and-techniques-ancient-egypts-popular-script/ (accessed on June 3, 2024)

Wade, Thomas. 1859. *Peking Syllabary*. Shanghai: Educational Mission Press.

———. 1867. *Yü-yen Tzu-erh Chi: A Progressive Course Designed to Assist the Student of Colloquial Chinese*. Shanghai: Educational Mission Press.

Wakefield, Mary, et al. 2021. *The Future of Nursing 2020—2030: Charting a Path to Achieve Health Equity*. Washington, DC: The National Academies Press. https://doi.org/10.17226/25982.

Walker, Sue. 2018. "Modernity, Method, and Minimal Means: Typewriters, Typing Manuals, and Document Design" *Journal of Design History* 31, no. 2: 138—153.

Warburton, William. 1738—1741. *The Divine Legation of Moses*. London: Printed for A. Millar, and J. and R. Tonson.

Weaver, Warren. 1949. "Translation." Reprinted in *Machine Translation of Languages*, edited by William N. Locke and A. Donald Booth, 15—23. Cambridge, MA: MIT Press, 1955.

Wester, Mirjam. 2003. "Pronunciation modeling for ASR—knowledge-based and data-derived methods." *Computer Speech & Language*. Vol. 17 (1): 69—85.

Western Union Telegraph Company. 1869. *The Proposed Union of Telegraph and Postal Systems: Statement of the Western Union Telegraph Company*. Cambridge: Welch, Bigelow, and Company.

WHO. 2020. *State of the World's Nursing Report 2020*. Geneva, Switzerland: World Health Organization.

Wikström, Peter. 2017. "I Tweet Like I Talk: Aspects of Speech and Writing on Twitter." PhD diss., Karlstad University.

Williams, Philip, Chris Quirk, and Kristina Toutanova. 2017. "Syntax-Based Statistical Machine Translation." *Computational Linguistics* 43 (4): 791—829.

Woods, Christopher. 2015. "Introduction—Visible Language: The Earliest Writing Systems." In *Visible Language: Inventions of Writing in the Ancient Middle East and Beyond*, edited by Christopher Woods. Chicago: The Oriental Institute of the University of Chicago.

———. 2015. "The Earliest Mesopotamian Writing." In *Visible Language: Inventions of Writing in the Ancient Middle East and Beyond*, edited by Christopher Woods. Chicago: The Oriental Institute of the University of Chicago.

Wu, Yonghui, et al. 2016. "Google's Neural Machine Translation System: Bridging the Gap between Human and Machine Translation." *arXiv* 1609.08144. https://arxiv.org/abs/1609.08144.

Xing, Huang and Feng Xu. 2016. *"The Romanization of Chinese Language." Review of Asian and Pacific Studies*, Vol. *41*: 99—111.

Xu, Bing. 2014. *Book from the Ground: From Point to Point*. Cambridge, MA: MIT Press.

Yamada, Kenji, and Kevin Knight. 2001. "A Syntax-Based Statistical Translation Model." In *Proceedings of the 39th Annual Meeting of the Association for Computational Linguistics (ACL 2001)*, 523—530. Toulouse, France.

Yasuoka, Koichi, and Motoko Yasuoka. 2011. "On the Prehistory of QWERTY." *ZINBUN,* 42: 161—174.

Young, Thomas. 1819. "Egypt." In *Supplement to the Encyclopaedia Britannica*, Vol. IV, Part I, 1—60. Edinburgh: Archibald Constable and Company.

———. 1823. *An Account of Some Recent Discoveries in Hieroglyphical Literature and Egyptian Antiquities*. London: John Murray.

Ze, David Wei. 1995. *Printing as an Agent of Social Stability: The Social Organization of Book Production in*

China during the Sung Dynasty. PhD diss., Simon Fraser University.

Zhang, Hang. 2018. *Second Language Acquisition of Mandarin Chinese Tones: Beyond First-Language Transfer.* Leiden & Boston: Brill Rodopi.

Zhang, Wenyang. 2018. "The Grammar of the Telegraph in the Late Qing." *Journal of Modern Chinese History* 12 (2): 227—245.

Zhong, Yurou. 2014. *Script Crisis and Literary Modernity in China, 1916—1958.* Ph.D. dissertation, Columbia University.

傅斯年，1919，《汉语改用拼音文字的初步谈》，载《新潮》，第1卷第3号，391。

河北省文物研究所，2005，《战国中山国灵寿城——1975～1993年考古发掘报告》，北京：文物出版社。

(清) 金简，1776，《钦定武英殿聚珍版程式》（《钦定武英殿聚珍版书》卷一），https://old.shuge.org/ebook/wu-ying-dian-ju-zhen-ban-cheng-shi/。（accessed Oct. 1, 2023）

黎锦熙，1936，《建设的"大众语"文学（国语运动史纲序）》，上海：商务印书馆。

李荣，1985，《官话方言的分区》，载《方言》，1985年第1期，2—5。

李荣等编，1987，《中国语言地图集》，香港：朗文出版（远东）有限公司。

林玉堂，1918，《汉字索引制说明》，载《新青年》，1918年第4卷第2号，128—131。

卢戆章，[1892] 1956，《一目了然初阶（中国切音新字厦腔）》，北京：文字改革出版社。

鲁迅，[1934] 2005，《汉字和拉丁化》，载《鲁迅全集》第五卷，北京：人民文学出版社，615。

陆尔奎、方毅编，1928，《四角号码学生字典》，上海：商务印书馆。

吕思勉，1992，《吕著中国通史》，上海：华东师范大学出版社。

倪海曙，1948，《中国拼音文字运动史简编》，上海：时代书报出版社。

钱玄同，1922，《注音字母与现代国音》，载《国语月刊》，第1卷第1期，1—7；第2期，1—4；第3期，1—4；第4期，1—7。

瞿秋白，1989，《瞿秋白文集》文学编第三卷，北京：人民文学出版社。

（宋）沈括，2015，《梦溪笔谈》，上海：古典文学出版社。

（元）王祯，1313，《农书》卷二十二，https://zh.wikisource.org/wiki/王祯農書/卷二十二。（accessed Oct. 1, 2023）

熊正辉、张振兴，2012，《汉语方言的分区》，《中国语言地图集》第二版，北京：商务印书馆。

尹斌庸，1994，《第一个拉丁字母的汉语拼音方案是怎样产生的？》，载*Sino-Platonic Papers* 50，1—7。

袁家骅等，1983，《汉语方言概要》第二版，北京：文字改革出版社。

詹伯慧，1981，《现代汉语方言》，武汉：湖北人民出版社。

詹伯慧等，2001，《汉语方言及方言调查》第二版，武汉：湖北教育出版社。

章梅芳、姜心玉，2023，《民国时期大众报刊中的女打字员形象阐释》，载《北京科技大学学报（社会科学版）》，第39卷第3期，353—361。

张树栋等，1999，《中华印刷通史》，北京：印刷工业出版社。

赵元任，1929，《国语罗马字拼音法式》。收录于A. A. 米尔恩，1929，《最后五分钟》，赵元任译，上海：中华书局。收录于赵元任，2012，《赵元任全集》第12卷，北京：商务印书馆。

中华人民共和国邮电部编，1983，《标准电码本》修订本，北京：人民邮电出版社。

（宋）周必大，《益国周文忠公全集》卷一百九十八，https://zh.m.wikisource.org/wiki/文忠集_(周必大,_四庫全書本)/卷一百九十。（accessed Oct. 1, 2023）

周楠，2009，《"舒式打字机"发明者后人讲述与世博八十年的情缘》，载《解放日报》，2009-11-17。

Works Consulted

A Committee of the Soochow Literary Association. 1892. *Syllabary of the Soochow Dialect*. Shanghai: Presbyterian Mission Press.

Akmajian, Adrian, Richard A. Demers, Ann K. Farmer, and Robert M. Harnish. 2010. *An Introduction to Language and Communication*. 6th ed. Cambridge, MA: MIT Press.

Altmann, Gabriel, and Fan Fengxiang. 2008. *Analyses of Script: Properties of Characters and Writing Systems*. Berlin and New York: Mouton de Gruyter.

Ashby, Muata. 2006. *Ancient Egyptian Hieroglyphs for Beginners: Medtu Neter*. Miami: Cruzian Mystic Books.

Baines, John, John Bennet, and Stephen Houston. 2008. *The Disappearance of Writing Systems Perspectives on Literacy and Communication*. London: Equinox Publishing Ltd.

Baldwin, Rev. C. C. 1871. *Manuel of the Foochow Dialect*. Foochow: Methodist Episcopal Mission Press.

Baron, Naomi S. 2002. *Alphabet to Email: How Written English Evolved and Where It's Heading*. London and New York: Routledge.

———. 2015. *Words Onscreen: The Fate of Reading in a Digital World*. Oxford: Oxford University Press.

———. 2021. *How We Read Now*. Oxford: Oxford University Press.

———. 2023. *Who Wrote This? : How AI and the Lure of Efficiency Threaten Human Writing*. Redwood City: Stanford University Press.

Bazerman, Charles. 2008. *Handbook of Research on Writing: History, Society, School, Individual, Text*. New York and London: Lawrence Erlbaum Associates.

Beauchamp, Ken. 2001. *History of Telegraphy*. London: The Institution of Engineering and Technology.

Bender, Emily M., and Alex Lascarides. 2020. *Linguistic Fundamentals for Natural Language Processing II: 100 Essentials from Semantics and Pragmatics*. San Rafael, CA: Morgan & Claypool Publishers.

Bodde, Derk. 1991. *Chinese Thought, Society, and Science: The Intellectual and Social Background of Science and Technology in Pre-modern China*. Honolulu: University of away Press.

Bonea, Amelia. 2016. *The News of Empire: Telegraphy, Journalism, and the Politics of Reporting in Colonial*

India, c. 1830—1900. Oxford: Oxford University Press.

Borgwaldt, Susanne R., and Terry Joyce, eds. 2013. *Typology of Writing Systems*. Amsterdam and Philadelphia: John Benjamins Publishing Company.

Brokaw, Cynthia J., and Kai-Wing Chow, eds. 2005. *Printing and Book Culture in Late Imperial China*. Berkeley, Los Angeles, and London: University of California Press.

Brown, Nathan. 2021. *Rationalist Empiricism: A Theory of Speculative Critique*. New York: Fordham University Press.

Budge, E. A. Wallis. [1929] 1989. *The Rosetta Stone*. New York: Dover Publications, Inc.

———. [1895] 2003. *First Steps in Egyptian Hieroglyphics: A Book for Beginners*. Mineola, N. Y. : Dover Publications, Inc.

Busse, Beatrix. 2020. *Speech, Writing, and Thought Presentation in 19th-Century Narrative Fiction: A Corpus-Assisted Approach*. Oxford: Oxford University Press.

Carr, Caleb T. 2021. *Computer-Mediated Communication: A Theoretical and Practical Introduction to Online Human Communication*. London: Rowman & Littlefield.

Chambers, Deborah. 2013. *Social Media and Personal Relationships: Online Intimacies and Networked Friendship*. London: Palgrave Macmillan.

Charbonnier, Georges. 1961. *Entretiens avec Claude Lévi-Strauss*. Paris: Pion, Julliard.

Chenoweth, Kate. 2019. *The Prosthetic Tongue: Printing and the Rise of the French Language*. Philadelphia: University of Pennsylvanian Press.

Chia, Lucille, and Hilde De Weerdt, eds. 2011. *Knowledge and Text Production in an Age of Print: China, 900—1400*. Leiden and Boston: Brill.

Chow, Kai-Wing. 2004. *Publishing, Culture, and Power in Early Modern China*. Redwood City: Stanford University Press.

Coe, Michael D. 2012. *Breaking the Maya Code*. 3rd ed. London and New York: Thames & Hudson.

Cook, Vivian, and Benedetta Bassetti. 2005. *Second Language Writing Systems*. Clevedon, Buffalo, and Toronto: Multilingual Matters Ltd.

Coulmas, Florian. 2013. *Writing and Society: An Introduction*. Cambridge: Cambridge University Press.

Cruttenden, Alan. 2021. *Writing Systems and Phonetics*. London and New York: Routledge.

Crystal, David. 2012. *Spell it Out: The Singular Story of English Spelling*. London: Profile Books.

Culp, Robert. 2019. *The Power of Print in Modern China*. New York: Columbia University Press.

Danesi, Marcel. 2016. *Language, Society, and New Media: Sociolinguistics Today*. London and New York: Routledge.

de Hamel, Christopher. 1994. *A History of Illuminated Manuscripts*. London : Phaidon Press.

de Mul, Jos. 2005. "The Game of Life: Narrative and Ludic Identity Formation in Computer Games." Paper presented at *Digital Games Research Conference 2005, Changing Views: Worlds in Play, June 16—20, 2005*, Vancouver, British Columbia, Canada. https://doi.org/10.1057/9781137462534.0020.

DeFrancis, John. 1984. *The Chinese Language: Fact and Fantasy*. Honolulu: University of Hawaii Press.

Dehaene, Stanislas. 2009. *Reading in the Brain: The Science and Evolution of a Human Invention*. New York: Penguin Group Inc.

Di Cristofaro, Matteo. 2024. *Corpus Approaches to Language in Social Media*. New York and London: Routledge.

Dickinson, Oliver. 1994. *The Aegean Bronze Age*. Cambridge: Cambridge University Press.

Dolnick, Edward. 2021. *The Writing of the Gods: The Race to Decode the Rosetta Stone*. New York: Scribner.

Dyer, Harry T. 2020. *Designing the Social: Unpacking Social Media Design and Identity*. Singapore: Springer Nature.

Edkins, J. 1869. *A Vocabulary of the Shanghai Dialect*. Shanghai: Presbyterian Mission Press.

Farzindar, Anna Atefeh, and Diana Inkpen. 2020. *Natural Language Processing for Social Media*. 3rd ed. San Rafael, CA: Morgan & Claypool Publishers.

Fasold, Ralph, and Jeff Connor-Linton, eds. 2006. *An Introduction to Language and Linguistics*. Cambridge: Cambridge University Press.

Fernandez, Luke, and Susan J. Matt. 2019. *Bored, Lonely, Angry, Stupid: Changing Feelings about Technology, from the Telegraph to Twitter*. Cambridge, MA: Harvard University Press.

Fromkin, Victoria, Robert Rodman, and Nina Hyams. 2011. *An Introduction to Language*. 9th ed. Boston: Cengage Learning.

———. 2017. *An Introduction to Language*. 11th ed. Boston: Cengage Learning.

Frost, Ram, and Leonard Katz. 1992. *Orthography, Phonology, Morphology, and Meaning*. Amsterdam, London, New York, and Tokyo: North-Holland.

Fuchs, Christian. 2024. *Media, Economy and Society: A Critical Introduction*. London and New York: Routledge.

Genetti, Carol, and Allison Adelman, eds. 2014. *How Languages Work: An Introduction to Language and Linguistics*. Cambridge: Cambridge University Press.

Goody, Jack. 1986. *The Logic of writing and the Organization of Society*. Cambridge: Cambridge University Press.

———. 2000. *The Power of the Written Tradition*. Washington and London: Smithsonian Institution Press.

Grossman, Eitan, Martin Haspelmath, and Tonio Sebastian Richter, eds. 2015. *Egyptian-Coptic Linguistics in Typological Perspective*. Berlin, Munich, and Boston: Walter de Gruyter.

Halliday, M. A. K, and J. R. Martin. 1993. *Writing Science: Literacy and Discursive Power*. London and
Washington: The Falmer Press.

Handel, Zev. 2015. "Logography and the Classification of Writing Systems: a Response to Unger." *SCRIPTA* 7
(October 2015):109—150.

Headrick, Daniel R. 2000. *When Information Came of Age: Technologies of Knowledge in the Age of Reason
and Revolution, 1700—1850*. Oxford: Oxford University Press.

Hellinga, Lotte. 2014. *Texts in Transit: Manuscript to Proof and Print in the Fifteenth Century*. Leiden and
Boston: Brill.

———, and J,. B. Trapp, eds. 1999. *The Cambridge History of the Book in Britain, Volume III 1400—1557*.
Cambridge: Cambridge University Press.

Hooker, John Thomas. 1980. *Linear B: An Introduction*. London: Bristol Classical Press.

Horning, Alice S. 2012. *Reading, Writing, and Digitizing: Understanding Literacy in the Electronic Age*.
Newcastle upon Tyne: Cambridge Scholars Publishing.

Jepsen, Thomas C. 2000. *My Sisters Telegraphic: Women in the Telegraph Office, 1846—1950*. Athens: Ohio
University Press.

Ji, Qihao. 2024. *Social Media and Society*. London and New York: Routledge.

Johnson, Sally, and Astrid Ensslin, eds. 2007. *Language in the Media: Representations, Identities, Ideologies*.
London: Continuum International Publishing Group.

Judson, Anna P. 2022. "Learning to Spell in Linear B: Orthography and Scribal Training in Mycenaean Pylos."
The Cambridge Classical Journal 68 (2022):133—163. https://doi.org/10.1017/S1750270522000057.

Karaoke, Shin, and Cream Lee. 2008. "A System without a System: Cantonese Romanization Used in Hong
Kong Place and Personal Names." *Hong Kong Journal of Applied Linguistics* 11, no. 1: 79—98.

Kaźmierski, Kamil. 2015. *Vowel-Shifting in the English Language: An Evolutionary Account*. Berlin,
München, Boston: De Gruyter Mouton.

Knospe, Sebastian, Alexander Onysko, and Mail Goth. 2016. *Crossing Languages to Play with Words:
Multidisciplinary Perspectives*. Berlin and Boston: Walter de Gruyter GmbH.

Kraus, Richard Curt. 1991. *Brushes with Power: Modern Politics and the Chinese Art of Calligraphy*.
Berkeley: University of California Press.

Krijnen, Tonny, et al. eds., 2023. *Identities and Intimacies on Social Media: Transnational Perspectives*.
London and New York: Routledge.

Kuzuoğlu, Uluğ. 2018. "Chinese Cryptography: The Chinese Nationalist Party and Intelligence Management,
1927—1949." *Cryptologia* 42, no. 6: 514—539.

———. 2023. *Codes of Modernity: Chinese Scripts in the Global Information Age*. New York: Columbia

University Press.

Linell, Per. 2005. *The Written Language Bias in Linguistics: Its Nature, Origins and Transformations*. London and New York: Routledge.

Lyons, John. 1981. *Language and Linguistics: An Introduction*. Cambridge: Cambridge University Press.

McDermott, Joseph P. 2006. *A Social History of the Chinese Book: Books and Literati Culture in Late Imperial China*. Hong Kong: Hong Kong University Press.

McMillian, John. 2011. *Smoking Typewriters: The Sixties Underground Press and the Rise of Alternative Media in America*. New York: Oxford University Press.

Meletis, Dimitrios , and Christa Dürscheid. 2022. *Writing Systems and Their Use: An Overview of Grapholinguistics*. Berlin and Boston: Walter de Gruyter GmbH.

Meyerson, Daniel. 2004. *The Linguist and the Emperor: Napoleon and Champollion's Quest to Decipher the Rosetta Stone*. New York: Ballantine Books.

Milroy, James, and Lesley Milroy. 1985. *Authority in Language: Investigating Standard English*. 4th ed. London and New York: Routledge.

Minkova, Donka, and Robert Stockwell. 2009. *English Words: History and Structure*. 2nd ed. Cambridge: Cambridge University Press.

Morrison, Robert. 1828. *Vocabulary of the Canton Dialect*. Macao: East India Company Press.

Morrison, William T. 1876. *An Anglo-Chinese Vocabulary of the Ningpo Dialect*. Shanghai: American Presbyterian Mission Press.

Navas, Eduardo, Owen Gallagher, and Xtine Burroughs. 2021. *The Routledge Handbook of Remix Studies and Digital Humanities*. London and New York: Routledge.

Nickles, David Paull. 2003. *Under the Wire: How the Telegraph Changed Diplomacy*. Cambridge, MA: Harvard University Press.

Oppenheim, A. Leo. 1977. *Ancient Mesopotamia: Portrait of a Dead Civilization*. Revised edition, completed by Erica Reiner. Chicago: The University of Chicago Press.

Paradis, Michel, Hiroko Hagiwar, and Nancy Hildebrandt. 1985. *Neurolinguistic Aspects of the Japanese Writing System*. Tokyo: Academic Press, Inc.

Pillière, Linda, et al., eds. 2018. Standardising English: *Norms and Margins in the History of the English Language*. Cambridge: Cambridge University Press.

Ping, Chen. 1999. *Modern Chinese: History and Sociolinguistics*. Cambridge: Cambridge University Press.

Poibeau, Thierry, and Aline Villavicencio. 2017. *Language, Cognition, and Computational Models*. Cambridge: Cambridge University Press.

Pourciau, Sarah M. 2017. *The Writing of Spirit: Soul, System, and the Roots of Language Science*. New York:

Fordham University Press.

Rohlinger, Deana A. 2019. *New Media and Society*. New York: New York University Press.

Shen, Zhongwei. 2020. *A Phonological History of Chinese*. Cambridge: Cambridge University Press.

Silverman, Kenneth. 2003. *Lightning man: The Accursed Life of Samuel F. B. Morse.* New York: Alfred A. Knopf.

Singh, Simon. 1999. *The Code Book: The Science of Secrecy from Ancient Egypt to Quantum Cryptography*. New York: Anchor Books.

Snider, Keith L. 2018. *Tone Analysis for Field Linguists*. Dallas: SIL International.

Son, Suyoung. 2018. *Writing for Print: Publishing and the Making of Textual Authority in Late Imperial China*. Cambridge, MA: Harvard University Press.

Sproat, Richard. 2000. *A Computational Theory of Writing Systems*. AT&T Labs– Research. https://www.researchgate.net/publication/2533019_A_Computational_Theory_of_Writing_Systems.

———. 2023. *Symbols: An Evolutionary History from the Stone Age to the Future.* Berlin and New York: Springer.

Steele, Philippa M. 2013. *A Linguistic History of Ancient Cyprus: The Non-Greek Languages, and their Relations with Greek, c. 1600—300 BC*. Cambridge: Cambridge University Press.

Tam, Gina Anne. 2020. *Dialect and Nationalism in China, 1860—1960*. Cambridge: Cambridge University Press.

Tannen, Deborah, Heidi E. Hamilton, and Deborah Schiffrin, eds. *The Handbook of Discourse Analysis*. 2nd ed. Hoboken: Wiley Blackwell.

Thomas, Patrick, and Pamela Takayoshi. 2016. *Literacy in Practice: Writing in Private, Public, and Working Lives*. London and New York: Routledge.

Thurlow, Amy. 2019. *Social Media, Organizational Identity and Public Relations*. Routledge: London and New York.

Tsin, Tsuen-Hsuin. 1985. *Science and Civilisation in China Volume 5 Chemistry and Chemical Technology, Part I: Paper an Printing*. Cambridge: Cambridge University Press.

Tsu, Jing, and Benjamin A. Elman, eds. 2013. *Science and Technology in Modern China, 1880s—1940s*. Leiden and Boston: Brill.

Tsu, Jing. 2010. *Sound and Script in Chinese Diaspora*. Cambridge, MA: Harvard University Press.

Unger, J. Marshall. 1996. *Literacy and Script Reform in Occupation Japan: Reading between the Lines*. New York and Oxford: Oxford University Press.

Updegraff, Joe M. 1951. "The History and Development of the Typewriter." Master's thesis, The University of Southern California.

van Den Hout, Theo. 2020. *A History of Hittite Literacy: Writing and Reading in Late Bronze-Age Anatolia (1650—1200 BC)*. Cambridge: Cambridge University Press.

van Dijck, José. 2013. *The Culture of Connectivity: A Critical History of Social Media*. Oxford: Oxford University Press.

Watt, W. C., ed. 1994. *Writing Systems and Cognition: Perspectives from Psychology, Physiology, Linguistics, and Semiotics*. Dordrecht: Springer-Science+Business Media, B. V.

Wenzlhuemer, Roland. 2013. *Connecting the Nineteenth-Century World: The Telegraph and Globalization*. Cambridge: Cambridge University Press.

Wilson, Penelope. 2003. *Hieroglyphs: A Very Short Introduction*. Oxford: Oxford University Press.

Winston, Brian. [1998] 2003. *Media Technology and Society: A History from the Telegraph to the Internet*. New York: Routledge.

Yandell, Kay. 2019. *Telegraphies: Indigeneity, Identity, and Nation in America's Nineteenth-Century Virtual Realm*. Oxford: Oxford University Press.

Yeounsuk, Lee. 1996. *The Ideology of Kokugo: Nationalizing Language in Modern Japan*. Honolulu: University of Hawaii Press.

Yip, Moira. 2002. *Tone*. Cambridge: Cambridge University Press.

Yurou, Zhong. 2019. *Chinese Grammatology: Script Revolution and Chinese Literary Modernity, 1916—1958*. New York: Columbia University Press.

Zhou, Yongming. 2006. *Historicizing Online Politics*: *Telegraphy, the Internet, and Political Participation in China*. Redwood City: Stanford University Press.

B. A. 伊斯特林，1987，《文字的产生和发展》，左少兴译，北京：北京大学出版社。

冯时，2016，《中国古文字学概论》，北京：中国社会科学出版社。

谷衍奎编，2003，《汉字源流字典》，北京：华夏出版社。

高明，1996，《中国古文字学通论》，北京：北京大学出版社。

胡厚宣主编，1999，《甲骨文合集释文》，北京：中国社会科学出版社。

黄亚平、孟华，2001，《汉字符号学》，上海：上海古籍出版社。

姜继曾，2015，《简化字的由来》，成都：四川大学出版社。

刘志基，2015，《中国文字发展史·商周文字卷》，上海：华东师范大学出版社。

刘钊，2006，《古文字构形学》，福州：福建人民出版社。

李学勤主编，2012，《字源》，天津：天津古籍出版社。

裘锡圭，2013，《文字学概要》修订本，北京：商务印书馆。

苏培成编著，1992，《汉字简化字与繁体字对照字典》，北京：中信出版社。

唐兰，2005，《中国文字学》，上海：世纪出版集团·上海古籍出版社。

王云五、傅纬平主编，1937，《中国文字学史》，北京：商务印书馆。

新知识出版社编，1958，《1957年文字改革辩论选辑》，上海：新知识出版社。

亚瑟·布雷地利，2019，《导读德里达〈论文字学〉》，孔锐才译，重庆：重庆大学出版社。

杨树达，1988，《中国文字学概要·文字形义学》，上海：上海古籍出版社。

雅克·德里达，1999，《论文字学》，汪家堂译，上海：上海译文出版社。

中国学术名著提要·语言文字卷编委会编，1992，《中国学术名著提要·语言文字卷》，上海：复旦
　　大学出版社。

中国文字改革委员会拼音方案部编印，1955，《各地人士寄来汉语拼音文字方案汇编》第二册。

张书岩等编著，1997，《简化字溯源》，北京：语文出版社。

周克庸，2009，《汉字文字学》，贵阳：贵州人民出版社。

周有光，1961，《汉字改革概论》，北京：文字改革出版社。

Name Index

Subject Index

List of Figures